CLOSE READING

An Introduction to Literature

ELISABETH A. HOWE

Longman

Boston   Columbus   Indianapolis   New York   San Francisco   Upper Saddle River
Amsterdam   Cape Town   Dubai   London   Madrid   Milan   Munich   Paris   Montreal   Toronto
Delhi   Mexico City   São Paulo   Sydney   Hong Kong   Seoul   Singapore   Taipei   Tokyo

Senior Acquisitions Editor: Vivian Garcia
Executive Marketing Manager: Joyce Nilsen
Senior Supplements Editor: Donna Campion
Production Manager: Denise Phillip
Project Coordination, Text Design, and Electronic Page Makeup: GGS Higher Education
    Resources, A Division of PreMedia Global, Inc.
Senior Cover Design Manager/Cover Designer: Nancy Danahy
Cover Art: "Young Girl Reading," c.1776 (oil on canvas) by Jean-Honoré Fragonard.
    National Gallery of Art, Washington DC, USA/The Bridgeman Art Library
Senior Manufacturing Buyer: Roy Pickering

For permission to use copyrighted material, grateful acknowledgment is made to the copyright
holders on p. 296, which are hereby made part of this copyright page.

Library of Congress Cataloging-in-Publication Data

Howe, Elisabeth A.
  Close reading : an introduction to literature/Elisabeth A. Howe.
     p. cm.
  ISBN-13: 978-0-13-243656-4
  ISBN-10:   0-13-243656-6
1. Literature—Study and teaching.   I. Title.
  PN59.H68 2009
  807—dc22   2009009507

Longman
is an imprint of

www.pearsonhighered.com

ISBN-13: 978-0-13-243656-4
ISBN-10:   0-13-243656-6

Contents

2   Writing a Close Reading of a Poem   45

3   Close Readings of Poems   52

PART 2   PROSE   77

4   Introduction to Aspects of Prose Fiction   78

5   Writing a Close Reading of a Prose Passage   98

6   Close Readings of Prose Passages   104

PART 3   DRAMA   125

7   Introduction to Aspects of Drama   126

Appendix 3: Selected Short Stories   215

Appendix 4: Selected Drama   278

Appendix 5: Glossary of Literary Terms   287

Preface

A close reading aims to analyze in depth a short literary text—a poem, an extract from a prose work, or a passage from a play. Close reading, or explication, allows the student of literature to examine the language and structure of a text, as well as the ideas or feelings it expresses, and to investigate the intricate links between form and content. It can lead readers both to a greater appreciation of the text and to a greater awareness of the author's craft, and it helps them to see the specifically literary aspects of literature rather than reading solely for the ideas expressed. Close reading helps to sharpen critical reading skills and is a prerequisite for any form of literary analysis, since students should be capable of explicating texts themselves before moving on to assess different critical interpretations.

This book demonstrates the techniques required in order to analyze a literary text for a close reading. It is intended for Introduction to Literature classes, but could also be used in survey courses or courses dealing with a specific author, since the technique of close reading improves students' appreciation of any literary text.

The book is divided into three parts according to the three genres of poetry, prose and drama. It begins with poetry, partly because a poem can be read and analyzed in its entirety and partly because poems lend themselves especially well to close reading, since poets pay particular attention to all the expressive capabilities of language. However, if the reader or the instructor wishes to start with prose, for example, it would certainly be possible to begin with part 2, which is quite self-contained.

The first part of the section on poetry examines all the elements to be taken into account when analyzing a poem, such as vocabulary, figures of speech, sounds, rhythm, versification, and structure. For each of these features, the book offers first of all a discussion of its nature and importance, then a few examples, and finally several short exercises aimed at helping students with their own analysis of the elements of poetry. The exercises consist of short quotations illustrating the device in question, such as an interesting usage of certain words, a figure of speech, or a noteworthy example of rhythm or alliteration, followed by brief questions to the student. All the poems used in exercises and the majority of poems cited in this section are printed in appendix 2. Appendix 1 contains the International Phonetic Alphabet, essential for any discussion of the sounds of a poem.

The second part of the poetry section offers model explications, by the author, of various poems, and then several poems followed by questions aimed at helping students write close readings of their own. Individual instructors will no doubt choose to assign different poems from among those offered. Students could also write questions for each other on one or two other poems offered in appendix 2; and they should also be encouraged to write close readings on new poems, selected by the instructor or the student, without helpful questions.

The chapters on prose and drama proceed in the same way. The prose section examines the concepts of plot, characterization, narrative voice, setting, theme and style—again with examples and exercises. Next come model close readings of several prose texts, and finally passages followed by questions designed to guide students in their own work of close reading, to be assigned, again, according to the wishes of the professor or the students. Students might also be encouraged to write questions for each other on selected passages; and the final step is of course to assign passages without questions—either different excerpts from the short stories referred to in the course of this section (reprinted in appendix 3), or extracts from other prose works studied in class.

The important elements of a stage play—the actors' movements, gestures and facial expressions, the costumes, lighting and sets—are not always obvious when reading a play; if it is impossible to see the play at the theater, the reader should try to imagine such effects. This chapter examines these and other elements of drama, again giving examples. Once more, model close readings are followed by passages with questions, to be assigned at the instructor's discretion; the method can of course be applied to any play that is being studied by the class. Since complete plays are too long for the dimensions of this book, only the short play *Trifles* is reprinted in appendix 4; but the other plays used as exercises and models are readily available.

The aim of this book is to offer students guidelines in literary analysis, which they will then be able to apply to any text. Individual instructors will ask them to apply what they have learned here to other works. The poems, short stories and plays included in the appendices at the end of this book are mostly those used during the discussions of poetry, prose and drama, or in the exercises, model close readings or readings accompanied by questions. Instructors may wish to assign their students other parts of these works as new passages for close reading; there are also a few totally new poems. However, the book is not intended primarily as an anthology; it could be used in conjunction with a short anthology of literary texts, or with individual plays, short stories and poems.

ACKNOWLEDGMENTS

Much of the material in this book has been tried out on students in my classes at Assumption College. Thanks in particular to former students Sarah Mitchell, Susan Murphy and Richard Taylor for permission to reproduce essays written in my Introduction to Literature courses.

I would like to thank my colleague David Thoreen, of the English Department at Assumption College, for encouraging me to write the book.

My editor at Longman, Vivian Garcia, has provided invaluable help throughout the writing process. I am extremely grateful for her guidance in developing the project through successive drafts and for suggesting various modifications and additions. I also wish to thank the reviewers who read through an earlier manuscript version of the book and came up with many helpful suggestions for improvement. These reviewers are Joshua Dickson, SUNY-Jefferson Community College; Jacqueline Slater, The University of Memphis; Teresa Purvis, Lansing Community College; Rafeeq O. McGiveron, Lansing Community College; Carl Singleton, Fort Hays State University; Susan Stewart, Texas A&M; Glenn Hutchinson, UNC—Charlotte; Andrew Fleck, San Jose State University; Gary Montano, Tarrant County College; Kathryn N. Benzel, University of Nebraska—Kearney; and Bethany Blankenship, University of Montana Western.

Thanks are also due to my husband who has been living with this book for over four years now; his technical expertise and advice was much appreciated.

Introduction to Close Reading

A close reading analyzes poems or short passages of prose in depth. It is also called explication, a word from a Latin verb meaning "to unfold." Explication unfolds the text's meaning in relation to its formal and structural elements; it allows you the student—and indeed any reader—to examine the language and structure of a work as a function of its content, i.e., of the ideas, images or emotions it expresses. This process can lead to some exciting discoveries about the text; it will also encourage you to recognize the writer's craft and appreciate the way the text is put together as well as the ideas it contains. Any student of literature should be able to analyze (or explicate) a poem or a piece of prose or drama in this way before examining other critical interpretations of it. If you read other interpretations first, they will color your attitude to the text before you have even established your own view. It is better to work out your own assessment first.

A close reading or explication is written as an essay, with an introduction followed by a detailed analysis and then a conclusion. The introduction serves to situate the text in the context of the work from which it was taken, or of the author's works; it can also be used to point out certain general features of the passage or the poem as a whole. The main body of a close reading consists of a detailed analysis, line by line or sentence by sentence, of the text in question. The conclusion allows for some more general remarks, for example on the overall impression produced by the text, or a comparison with other texts that you know by the same author or by other authors.

Any literary text attempts to produce an effect on the reader, by creating for example a visual impression, a mood, or an emotion, or by illustrating some aspect of human nature or society. The aim of a close reading is to show how the different elements of a text combine to produce the desired impression. You will need to give consideration to various formal elements, such as use of particular vocabulary, specific sounds or rhythms, metaphors or other figures of speech—all of which can contribute to describing a scene or a person, underscoring an argument, or provoking an emotional reaction. The use of these formal devices is not simply decorative: in general they tend to reinforce or illustrate the sense of the text as expressed through the sheer meanings and connotations of words. A close reading explores the links between sense (or meaning), and the formal elements of a text, i.e., between what the text says and how it says it. Of course, not all texts contain examples of all devices: there are for example poems whose language is highly metaphorical and others containing no metaphors at all.

It is often useful, when trying to explicate a text, to put yourself in the place of the author, asking why he/she used a certain word instead of another or chose to repeat certain words or sounds. In any case, the aim of an explication is to discover *how* the text achieves its effects, and how it is structured, rather than simply to repeat *what* it says. If you find yourself paraphrasing the text, i.e., merely repeating, in different words, the meaning of the text, check yourself. If the text's meaning is obscure in places, for example because it employs rare or archaic vocabulary, then it might be necessary to explain its sense. Generally speaking, however, a close reading aims to analyze how a text achieves the effect it produces on the reader and not simply to point out its obvious meaning.

Many texts lend themselves to different interpretations by different readers: this is a sign of richness. But not all interpretations are necessarily valid: a close reading must be based on the text itself, and you must be able to cite words, phrases, or other elements from the text—e.g., rhythm, sound, structure—in order to back up your interpretation.

An explication can be attempted on a passage from any genre of literature: poetry, drama, or narrative prose. On the whole, however, the method works best with poetry, for at least two reasons: first because poems are usually shorter and can often be analyzed in their entirety rather than as an extract from a longer work; and second because poetry tends to express stylistic and linguistic effects in a more deliberate and concentrated fashion than prose. A poet chooses words for their sounds and rhythm as well as their meaning, and reflects at length on the use of imagery and figurative language; he or she will also pay attention to the overall form and structure of the poem. Thus the language of poetry tends to be very rich in stylistic devices and rewarding for close reading.

We will therefore begin with a section on poetry. Leaving aside for the moment the question of an introduction and conclusion, which will be dealt with in Chapter 2, we will first examine in turn the various elements involved in a close reading of a poem—vocabulary, figurative language, sound, rhythm, versification, and so on. When you come, eventually, to write a complete close reading, you will need to keep all these elements in mind as you analyze the poem line by line.

In the chapters that follow, words appearing in **bold** can be found in the Glossary of Literary Terms in appendix 5.

PART 1
POETRY

CHAPTER 1

Introduction to Aspects of Poetry

Poetry can be divided into two categories: narrative and lyric. Narrative poems, for example Keats's "The Eve of St. Agnes," tell stories, like a novel, and they tend to be long. Epics, such as Virgil's *Aeneid*, Homer's *Iliad*, or Milton's *Paradise Lost*, are narrative poems on a grand scale that recount the exploits of heroes and cover a vast canvas such as the fate of nations or of mankind as a whole. Another well-known type of narrative poem is the ballad, which tells a humbler story and was originally composed to be sung. Lyric poetry is a vast category that includes poems whose themes cover the whole gamut of human emotion and imagination. Though they can be of any length, lyrics tend to be shorter than narrative poems (and can be very brief indeed); they often have a musical quality (the word *lyric* comes from the Greek *lyre*, an instrument used to accompany the recital or singing of poems); and they tend to be more subjective than narrative poems, often expressing the feelings or thoughts of a speaker. The lyric is the predominant type of poetry in western literature.

Certain **formal characteristics** of poetry, such as rhyme or the division into lines, are encountered only in poems. Other features are simply more frequent in poetry than in prose, for example the use of figures of speech, or attention to rhythm and sound; poets use them frequently, to underscore the meaning of their lines. All these elements—repetition of sounds or of a particular rhythm, use of metaphors, symbols and other figures—tend to draw attention to the *language* of a poem: the reader is attracted not only to the poem's ideas but also to the way those ideas are expressed. Such elements enrich poetic language and make the study of poetry very rewarding: you will find, as you read poems closely, many layers of expression and of meaning. These multiple levels of expression can also lead to a certain ambiguity, since the significance of rhythms, sounds, metaphors, and symbols is not always immediately clear. Furthermore, they can often be interpreted differently by different readers. Different interpretations of poems are valid, as long as there is evidence within the poem to justify them. You should be careful, when discussing the meaning of a poem, to back up your interpretation with details taken from the poem.

Yet other elements of poetry belong as much to prose as to poetry—e.g., syntax (sentence structure) and choice of vocabulary—but in a poem they may function differently than in prose. In a traditional poem written with lines of regular length, the syntax of a phrase or sentence may or may not coincide with that of the verse line, producing different effects in each case. And while a prose writer usually tries to use as varied a vocabulary as possible, words are often repeated in poetry in order for example to emphasize the importance of certain words in the context of the poem, or perhaps to achieve an effect of monotony. Since poems are usually short compared to prose works, it will be more obvious to the reader if many words are chosen from one semantic field.

A famous twentieth-century French poet, Paul Valéry, compared the difference between prose and poetry to that between walking and dancing. The walker normally aims to reach a certain destination by the most direct route, as prose typically renders its meaning directly, whereas dancing progresses in a roundabout and repetitive manner. Poetry, too, involves repetition of various kinds, and like dancing it is based on rhythm and music.

The different elements of a poem—vocabulary, sounds, rhythm, figurative language— are not independent of one another but work *together* to achieve a certain effect in the poem or in a part of the poem. For example, a poem can convey an impression of calm by the use of appropriate words, but this choice of vocabulary will probably be reinforced by a smooth, flowing rhythm and by soft sounds rather than sharp, hard ones. Elsewhere, a more staccato rhythm and harder sounds might be employed to convey the impression of rapid movement. A close reading of a poem proceeds line by line in order to show how different poetic elements work together to produce the desired impression, and how such effects might vary as the poem develops.

First of all, however, the student needs to know what kind of effects to look for, and so we will begin by isolating the different elements of a poem, such as vocabulary, figurative language, rhythm, structure, and versification, on the understanding that eventually you will consider them all simultaneously, when analyzing a poem line by line.

One of the easiest elements to observe and analyze in a poem is its choice of words, and for this reason we will begin with a study of vocabulary.

VOCABULARY

The choice of vocabulary in a poem has an immediate effect on the reader. Different types of words will be used, for example, to create an atmosphere of mystery, from those selected to explain an idea, describe a natural scene, or celebrate a joyful event. The reader will be affected differently by vocabulary that is simple or highly literary, abstract or concrete, descriptive, **affective** (concerning the emotions), or **didactic** (aiming to teach or inform). When analyzing a poem's vocabulary, it is essential not only to observe the presence of certain types of words but also to suggest why they were chosen. If certain words are repeated, you should try to find the possible reasons for this repetition. You should consider, also, not only the **denotations** of words (their dictionary meaning), but also any **connotations** (wider associations) they may have for you or for others.

Let us take some examples.

In his well-known poem "I wandered lonely as a cloud," William Wordsworth clearly wishes to convey to the reader the feeling of joy brought to him by the sight of a "host" of daffodils. Accordingly, the words he chooses to describe the daffodils almost all relate to the idea of happiness. This is especially evident in the third stanza:

> The waves beside them danced; but they
> Outdid the sparkling waves in glee:
> A poet could not but be gay,

> In such a jocund company:
> I gazed—and gazed—but little thought
> What wealth the show to me had brought.

The concentration of positive words here ("danced," "sparkling," "glee," "gay," "jocund," "wealth") unmistakably illustrates the poet's happiness at the sight of the daffodils, both at the time and later, through memory. Words like "glee," "gay," and "jocund" are clearly affective—relating to emotion; "sparkling" is both descriptive, of waves in sunlight, and affective, since it contributes to the mood of happiness.

Sometimes, a poem may employ many words not just from one **semantic** field (area of meaning), as in the above example, but from two contrasting fields. An examination of the vocabulary can help to reveal the contrast. For example, in William Blake's enigmatic poem "The Sick Rose," the vocabulary can be divided between two areas of meaning, negative and positive:

> O rose, thou art sick.
> The invisible worm
> That flies in the night
> In the howling storm
>
> Has found out thy bed
> Of crimson joy,
> And his dark secret love
> Does thy life destroy.

This is a mysterious poem, in which the rose and the worm seem to represent symbols, perhaps of sexual love. We will discuss symbolism later, but, for now, an examination of the vocabulary alone can help to elucidate a basic contrast between a negative area of sickness, darkness, and destruction, and positive connotations relating to love and sexual pleasure. Apparently the rose (perhaps symbolizing a woman) is being defiled or desecrated by the "love" of the worm. Re-read the poem and consider into which category (negative or positive) you would assign each of the underlined words; you will probably find that there's an almost equal number in each category, illustrating the tension in the poem between light and dark, good and evil, pleasure and destruction.

Different poets may use vocabulary to emphasize different aspects of the same phenomenon. John Keats's "To Autumn" depicts fall as a season of plenty, especially in the first stanza. So many words here evoke ripeness and plenty; a few have been underlined; see how many more you can find and underline them too:

> Season of mists and mellow fruitfulness!
>   Close bosom-friend of the maturing sun;
> Conspiring with him how to load and bless
>   With fruit the vines that round the thatch-eves run;

> To bend with apples the mossed cottage-trees,
>   And fill all fruit with ripeness to the core;
>   To swell the gourd, and plump the hazel shells
> With a sweet kernel; to set budding more,
>   And still more, later flowers for the bees,
> Until they think warm days will never cease,
>   For summer has o'er-brimmed their clammy cells.

Nearly every line contains an expression depicting the idea of fullness. Also, all the words are very concrete: we not only infer an idea of plenty but also sense the warmth and lushness of the scene by visualizing the grapes and apples, gourds and nuts. Other elements of the poem, such as the sounds, back up the impression of "mellow fruitfulness," but even on the basis of the vocabulary alone, it is easy to see that the poet wishes to emphasize the image of autumn as the culmination, in nature, of the growing season: everything is ripe and round and soft and ready to be harvested. It is a season of warmth and sweetness.

Very different is the picture of fall in Shakespeare's sonnet "That time of year thou may'st in me behold." Feeling the approach of old age, he compares his own stage in life to the season of autumn, but rather than seeing autumn as a time of plenty he views it as a forerunner of winter and of death:

> That time of year thou may'st in me behold
> When yellow leaves, or none, or few, do hang
> Upon those boughs which shake against the cold,
> Bare ruined choirs, where late the sweet birds sang.

Instead of the lush images created by the vocabulary of the Keats poem, we find words suggesting bareness and destitution: "yellow leaves," "none," "few," "shake," "cold," "bare," "ruined."

When attempting to give a close reading of a poem, then, one of the first useful steps very often is to examine its vocabulary; an analysis of the types of words used can help to make sense of the poem, as in the examples above. Of course, other literary devices will contribute towards the overall effect (the alliteration of the /m/ and /n/ sounds in the first five lines of "To Autumn" certainly helps to convey an impression of fullness), and when analyzing a poem you will take all elements into account; but for the time being we are separating the different features of a poem in order to examine, one by one, the effects produced by each element—vocabulary, sounds, rhythm, figurative language, etc.—before putting everything together in a complete analysis.

A dictionary is often essential in order to write a close reading. Though you should always avoid **paraphrasing** the whole passage, it may, occasionally, be necessary to explain the meaning of individual words, for one reason or another. Poets—especially highly imaginative poets—occasionally invent words, which are called neologisms, and you should attempt to interpret the possible meaning of such words. The etymological meaning of a word (i.e., the meaning it originally had in another age or another language) may throw light on a poet's understanding of certain terms. A good dictionary will give etymological meanings. A poet from an earlier era, such as Shakespeare, may use words that have become archaic in modern English, in which case you should explain their meaning. At the other extreme, a contemporary author may produce slang expressions or vocabulary belonging to a certain dialect or geographical area that should also be elucidated in a close reading. Often, the explanation might be that the poet is trying to convey the voice of a certain kind of speaker. In addition, poets sometimes employ specialized or technical terms, as in Henry Reed's "Naming of Parts." Here are the first and final stanzas:

> Today we have naming of parts. Yesterday,
> We had daily cleaning. And tomorrow morning,
> We shall have what to do after firing. But today,
> Today we have naming of parts. Japonica
> Glistens like coral in all of the neighboring gardens,
>   And today we have naming of parts.
>
> . . . .
>
> They call it easing the Spring: it is perfectly easy
> If you have any strength in your thumb: like the bolt,
> And the breech, and the cocking-piece, and the point of balance,
> Which in our case we have not got; and the almond-blossom
> Silent in all of the gardens and the bees going backwards and forwards,
>   For today we have naming of parts.

The whole poem contains specialized vocabulary dealing with firearms, most of which is summarized in the final stanza ("the bolt . . . the breech . . . the cocking piece . . . the point of balance"). It is necessary to explain not what each word signifies exactly, but to point out that they are all technical words concerning firearms (whose presence was already suggested in the first stanza by the line: "And tomorrow morning, / We shall have what to do after firing"). This clarifies the situation of the speaker, who is apparently learning—along with his companions—how to fire a rifle, in some kind of military context. Next you may point out the essential contrast between the set of vocabulary relating to rifles and another set of words connected with nature and flowers (e.g., "Japonica" (a flowering shrub), "gardens," "almond-blossom," "bees"). Any valid interpretation of the poem has to take into account these two conflicting sets of vocabulary, the technical and the natural, the death-dealing and the life-giving.

Poets may employ a literary vocabulary, as in most of the poems quoted above, or deliberately choose a more familiar, conversational, or colloquial type of speech, either to appeal more readily to readers or to convey the tone of the poem's speaker, or for some other effect. Consider the following poem by Linda Pastan, published in 1988 and entitled "To a Daughter Leaving Home." You will find that every word of this poem might be used in everyday conversation (with the possible exception of "loping," which is nevertheless a common word). Some of these common, colloquial words have been underlined in the first few lines. As you read the poem, underline other words in the following lines that you consider to belong to "normal," everyday speech.

When I taught you
at eight to ride
a bicycle, loping along
beside you
as you wobbled away
on two round wheels,
my own mouth rounding
in surprise when you pulled
ahead down the curved
path of the park,
I kept waiting
for the thud
of your crash as I
sprinted to catch up,
while you grew
smaller, more breakable
with distance,
pumping, pumping
for your life, screaming
with laughter,
the hair flapping
behind you like a
handkerchief waving
goodbye.

The conversational style of this poem seems totally appropriate, since it is addressed to the poet's daughter, and because the situation it describes—teaching a child to ride a bike (though of course in the context of the poem this is also a metaphor for growing up and leaving home)—represents an everyday, family event. Certain words are repeated here: the roundness of the wheels is reflected in an amusing way in the rounding of the mother's mouth when she is surprised to see her daughter actually cycle away, "pumping, pumping"; here the repetition underlines the repetitive nature of the action of cycling, and also the effort involved. Again, the vocabulary of this poem is quite concrete and matter-of-fact ("bicycle," "wheels," "park," "thud," "crash," "hair," "handkerchief"), except for the final word, "goodbye," which is abstract and loaded with emotional impact, and refers back to the idea of "leaving home" in the poem's title.

As you study a poem's vocabulary, you should consider not only the obvious meaning, or **denotation**, of a word, but also any **connotations** the word may have for the reader. Poetry often plays with the multiple meanings of words. Some may be totally irrelevant and can be ruled out, but if two or three possible senses of a word seem valid, you should not feel obliged to *choose* between them. You should consider them all, because multiple significations enrich a poem; all may be implied. Enraptured with the magical power of words, poets often use them in original ways, playing imaginatively with all their possible meanings.

Poets often allude in their work to other works of literature or to historical or mythological events or characters. Such **allusions** suggest a comparison between the poem in which they appear and the work or event they refer to. They often shed light on some aspect or meaning of the poem at hand. Keats's "Ode to a Nightingale" contains many allusions. The first stanza, for example, mentions Lethe, the river of forgetfulness, according to Greek mythology, that ran through the Underworld and whose waters caused those who drank to forget their past. This allusion fits in with the references in this stanza to "hemlock" and "opiate"—other beverages that produce forgetfulness and numbness.

Exercises on Vocabulary

Read the following poems. What impression does each one produce on you and to what extent is the poem's vocabulary responsible for this impression? Use the questions to help you.

a)   Wild Nights—Wild Nights!
        Were I with thee
        Wild Nights should be
        Our luxury!

        Futile—the Winds—   5
        To a Heart in port—
        Done with the Compass—
        Done with the Chart!

        Rowing in Eden—
        Ah, the Sea!
        Might I but moor—Tonight—   10
        In thee!

                                                Emily Dickinson

1. What significance do you see in the repetition of certain words in this poem?
2. To what semantic field do most of the words in the last two stanzas belong? What reason can you find for this?
3. What allusion is made in the last stanza and what does it add to the poem's impact?

b)   It is a beauteous evening, calm and free,
        The holy time is quiet as a Nun
        Breathless with adoration; the broad sun

Is sinking down in its tranquillity;
The gentleness of heaven broods o'er the Sea:
Listen! the mighty Being is awake,   5
And doth with his eternal motion make
A sound like thunder—everlastingly.
Dear Child! dear Girl! that walkest with me here,
If thou appear untouched by solemn thought,
Thy nature is not therefore less divine: 10
Thou liest in Abraham's bosom all the year,
And worship'st at the Temple's inner shrine,
God being with thee when we know it not.

William Wordsworth

1. What kind of atmosphere is created in the first few lines? Which words contribute to the creation of that atmosphere?

2. What effect does the word "beauteous" have on you, as opposed to the more common *beautiful*?

3. What are the literal and metaphorical connotations of the word "Breathless" in line 3?

4. What is suggested by the verb "broods"?

5. What connection is there between the following words that appear in lines 1–11 of the poem—"holy," "Nun," "adoration," "heaven," "mighty Being," "eternal," "divine"? How does this semantic field (area of meaning) relate to the theme of the poem as a whole? What allusion in the last few lines also connects to this theme?

IMAGERY

The terms **imagery** and **image** refer simply to the concept of a picture in words, with or without the benefit of figurative language. Imagery provides a description of a scene, and this brings the scene closer to the reader, so that the latter feels more involved in the action of the poem. Several of the poems already quoted contain images; one can easily visualize Wordsworth's famous daffodils, for example:

Beside the lake, beneath the trees,
Fluttering and dancing in the breeze.

Wouldn't you agree that this image allows you to see the daffodils in your mind's eye much more forcibly than if the poet had simply said he had observed the wind blowing the daffodils? The reader can easily imagine, too, the daughter addressed in Linda Pastan's poem, who

. . .wobbled away
on two round wheels.

These lines not only present the reader with a clear picture, but also suggest, by the use of the word "wobbled," the mother's anxiety at her daughter's precariousness—both when she was learning to ride a bicycle and now that she is leaving home to launch into a life of her own.

A poet may use imagery to emphasize a certain aspect of a scene. Henry Reed's speaker in "Naming of Parts," describing

> . . .the almond-blossom
> Silent in all of the gardens and the bees going backwards and forwards,

stresses the useful industry of the natural world, represented by the bees, as compared with the potentially life-threatening activities of the soldiers. We saw in the section on vocabulary that Shakespeare, in "That time of year thou may'st in me behold," paints a sad picture of autumn,

> When yellow leaves, or none, or few, do hang
> Upon those boughs,

that immediately attunes the reader to the somber theme of the poem, whereas Keats's "To Autumn" uses vocabulary to create images of plenty. Obviously, there is a certain overlap between discussion of vocabulary and of imagery, since images are formed by words; indeed, sometimes the most appealing aspect of an image is the poet's imaginative use of words in creating it. Keats, for example, in "Ode to a Nightingale," evokes a glass of wine "With beaded bubbles winking at the brim," and describes a wild rose as "The murmurous haunt of flies on summer eves." Can you enjoy the use of words in these lines? Do they help you to visualize the glass of wine or the flowers?

Imagery can also serve to **structure** a poem, as in Shakespeare's "That time of year thou may'st in me behold," or in Byron's "She Walks in Beauty" where the whole poem revolves around the contrast between the images of "dark" and "bright" introduced in the first stanza.

Images do not necessarily involve comparison between two things, as in a metaphor or simile; they are simply pictures, and as such they often involve the sense of sight, but you will also find images that conjure up a taste or a scent, auditory images, and tactile images (concerning the sense of touch). In the following poem, "Meeting at Night" by Robert Browning, can you find images pertaining to the senses of sight, touch, smell and hearing? Mark the poem according to which senses you find illustrated.

> The gray sea and the long black land;
> And the yellow half-moon large and low;
> And the startled little waves that leap
> In fiery ringlets from their sleep,
> As I gain the cove with pushing prow,
> And quench its speed i' the slushy sand.

> Then a mile of warm sea-scented beach;
> Three fields to cross till a farm appears;
> A tap at the pane, the quick sharp scratch
> And blue spurt of a lighted match,
> And a voice less loud, through its joys and fears,
> Than the two hearts beating each to each!

FIGURATIVE LANGUAGE

Figurative language is used in prose but much more commonly in poetry; it implies a more imaginative use of language than normal, conventional usage. Figures include simile, metaphor and symbol; anaphora, oxymoron, antithesis and paradox; hyperbole and litotes; apostrophe and personification. Some **figures of speech**, also called **tropes**, involve substituting certain words for others or giving them a significance beyond their literal meaning; others, such as anaphora and antithesis, depend more on syntax, on the way sentences or lines are constructed. Figures of speech enrich poetic language—and we have seen that poetry tends, more than prose, to place value on language itself; it pays attention to the *way* things are expressed as much as to *what* is expressed. Figurative language often reinforces a thought, a mood, or an emotion, allowing the poet to express himself or herself in a more forceful, original, beautiful or moving way.

When analyzing a poem containing figurative language, you should not only point out the presence of a figure of speech, but also explain what it contributes to the poem. Rather than simply saying, "There is a metaphor in line 6," you should attempt to show, for example, how this metaphor reflects the speaker's mood; or how it is more beautiful, more original, or more striking, than a literal expression would have been. Alternatively, you may want to criticize the metaphor: not all metaphors are successful.

Simile and Metaphor

The best-known figures of speech are **simile** and **metaphor**. Both these figures compare two things, but a simile does so explicitly, by introducing a word such as "like" or "as," while a metaphor does so by directly substituting one word for another. We can see examples of both in the first stanza of Wordsworth's poem about daffodils:

> I wandered lonely as a cloud
> That floats on high o'er vales and hills,
> When all at once I saw a crowd,
> A host of golden daffodils;
> Beside the lake, beneath the trees,
> Fluttering and dancing in the breeze.

The speaker wanders "lonely as a cloud"; this simile compares him, all alone in nature, to a single cloud in a blue sky. What effect does the simile have? Does it emphasize his loneliness? Does it suggest his aimless wandering, as a cloud might appear to drift aimlessly across the sky? The cloud looks down on "vales and hills"—precisely the kind of area where the speaker is walking, which prepares the reader for the arrival of the daffodils in the next line. Here we find a metaphor: "a crowd / A host of golden daffodils," where the words "crowd" and "host" effectively suggest a vast number of flowers.

For both metaphors and similes, the words **tenor** and **vehicle** are used to denote the subject that is being compared (the tenor) and the item used as a means, or vehicle, of comparison. In the above examples "I" is the subject (tenor) being compared to a cloud, the vehicle. In lines 3–4, the words "crowd" and "host" form a vehicle to express the idea of a large number of daffodils (the tenor).

A very effective simile appears at the end of the poem we saw earlier, "To a Daughter Leaving Home":

> . . .the hair flapping
> behind you like a
> handkerchief waving
> goodbye.

Can you imagine long, straight hair "flapping" like a handkerchief? And handkerchiefs are often used to wave goodbye, so this simile returns us to the title and reminds us that the theme is not teaching a child to ride a bicycle, but the fact that the child has now grown up and is leaving home. The simile bridges the time-gap between the long-ago event, with the bicycle, and the present moment of imminent leave-taking, in a very effective way.

Original metaphors and similes that speak to the reader's imagination can contribute a great deal to our appreciation of a text. If a metaphor (or simile) is overused, however, it loses its force and becomes a convention, or even part of the everyday spoken language ("good as gold," "she's an angel").

Sometimes, a poem presents an **extended metaphor** or **extended simile**, i.e., a string of related comparisons that form the basis of the whole poem and combine to communicate its meaning. Examples are Shakespeare's "That time of year thou may'st in me behold" and Langston Hughes's "Harlem (A Dream Deferred)."

Apart from similes and metaphors, a vast number of other figures of speech are at the poet's disposal, some very common, others more rare. Many originated in the poetry of the Greeks and have names that come from Greek (like *metaphor*, from the Greek verb *metapherein*, "to transfer": in a metaphor, meaning is transferred from one word to another). The following list is not exhaustive, but contains the most-used figures of speech, in alphabetical order so that you will be able to refer to it more easily later. Remember that figures of speech are used not merely to "decorate" poems but to reinforce meaning in some way: try to determine what they contribute towards creating the mood, ideas, or emotions of the poem (or of a section of the poem).

Allegory

An allegorical poem contains a series of metaphors, all subordinate to a central idea, also expressed metaphorically, that governs the other metaphors. Allegory is often used to convey a moral message. An example is the long medieval French poem, *The Romance of the Rose*, in which the Rose represents the beloved lady (that is the central metaphor). The allegory illustrates courtly love: it narrates the progress of the poem's hero as he makes his way through a garden to arrive at the rose, i.e., gain the lady's love. On the way, he meets several figures (the subordinate metaphors) who help or hinder him: on the positive side, Beauty, Frankness, Courtesy, Youth, Welcome; and the negative figures of Hate, Envy, Age, Danger, Jealousy. These figures are personified abstractions; they speak and act like real people. This personification of abstract ideas, whose names begin with a capital letter, is a typical characteristic of allegory. A nineteenth-century example of allegory is "Up-Hill" by Christina Rossetti, which presents life and death in terms of a journey. More modern poets do not use allegory very frequently.

Anaphora

This device involves the repetition of the same syntactical structure at the beginning of several successive lines or stanzas. The repetitions produce a sense of expectation, as the reader wonders what will come after them, at the end. The suspense thus created allows the poet to emphasize an important idea, which follows on after the anaphora. An example can be found in Shelley's "Ode to the West Wind," whose first three stanzas, or paragraphs, contain the expression "O thou who . . ." or "Thou whose . . .," addressed to the wind and repeated several times, culminating in the exhortation "oh hear!"—also addressed to the wind—at the end of line 42. The poet is asking the wind to listen to his troubles, and the long introduction intensifies the solemnity of the injunction "oh hear!" Then, stanza or paragraph 4 begins with a new anaphora based on "If I were . . .": "If I were a dead leaf thou mightest bear; / If I were a swift cloud to fly with thee . . .," which continues through a few more lines and culminates in lines 51–54: ". . . I would ne'er have striven / As thus with thee in prayer in my sore need. / Oh, lift me as a wave, a leaf, a cloud! / I fall upon the thorns of life! I bleed!"

Antithesis

An antithesis emphasizes a contrast between two expressions or ideas by juxtaposing them, often giving them a similar syntactical structure in order to underline the contrast still further. The first stanza of Byron's "She Walks in Beauty" contrasts, through images concerning the stars, the concepts of "dark" and "bright":

> She walks in beauty, like the night
> Of cloudless climes and starry skies;
> And all that's best of dark and bright
> Meet in her aspect and her eyes.

Apostrophe

The poet addresses an absent person, a thing, or an abstraction, thus lending the person or thing a certain presence, in the context of the poem. In the case of an absent person (sometimes a person who has died), the speaker is often regretting his or her absence. In the case of things, apostrophe tends to personify them. Thus, in Blake's poem "The Sick Rose," the rose is personified as the poet "speaks" to it: "O rose, thou art sick." Apostrophes are often preceded, as here, by the interjection "O."

Hyberbole

Hyperbole represents a huge exaggeration. Wordsworth wants to create the impression of a vast number of daffodils, so he describes them as "Continuous as the stars that shine / And twinkle on the milky way," and claims to have seen "Ten thousand . . . at a glance." Similarly, the speaker of Robert Burns's "A Red, Red Rose" uses hyperbole to express his certainty that he will love his beloved forever:

> And I will luve thee still, my dear,
> Till a' the seas gang dry.

Here, the speaker no doubt means what he says, but hyperbole is often used to imply less by saying more: the more a speaker exaggerates his/her claim, the less it is likely to be taken at face value. This use of hyperbole is related to irony.

Irony

Irony is a complex phenomenon and probably more common in prose than in poetry. Briefly, it involves a discrepancy between what is said and what is meant, in the case of verbal irony; or between actual and expected outcomes, in the case of situational irony. In everyday life people make remarks such as "Fine weather we're having!" even though it is pouring with rain, when in fact they mean the opposite. This is a simple example of verbal irony. Saying the opposite of what one means tends to attract attention to the statement and make it more emphatic. Verbal irony often has an amusing effect, also. Characters in short stories, novels, and especially plays often speak to each other in an ironic tone; it is important for the reader to be aware of this irony, otherwise he or she may take at face value a remark that actually means the opposite of what the speaker intended.

Situational irony implies a difference between the actual situation and what it ought to be or what one might expect or hope for. In Henry Reed's poem "Naming of Parts," the situation is ironic: the speaker is aware of the beauty of nature all around him even as he dutifully takes part in his military training, learning the parts of a firearm. He is being taught to deliver death in the context of the renewal of life associated with spring. Situational irony can be called "cosmic irony" when it seems as though some cosmic force or fate is preventing humans from achieving the outcomes they expect or desire. Thus, at the end of Kate Chopin's "The Story of an Hour," the reader becomes aware of the ironic twist of fate that has caused Mrs. Mallard's death just when she thought she could be happy, as well as the irony of the doctor's diagnosis: that she has died of "joy that kills."

Irony should not be confused with sarcasm, which employs irony to hurt and belittle a person, saying the opposite of what is meant but with a scornful intent, for example if a teacher were to say to a student with difficulties: "Brilliant!"

Metaphor

See pages 13–14.

Metonymy

The figure of speech called metonymy involves the substitution of an attribute of a thing (or a person) to represent the thing itself. In Wordsworth's sonnet to Milton, for example (entitled "Milton! thou shouldst be living at this hour"), he uses the words "altar, sword, and pen" to refer to the Church, the military, and men of letters in contemporary England.

Oxymoron

An oxymoron is like an antithesis in that it juxtaposes apparently contradictory elements. An oxymoron is more concise, however, consisting often of just two words, frequently an adjective and a noun as in Romeo's series of oxymorons complaining about unrequited love (in Act 1, scene 1 of Shakespeare's play, before he meets Juliet): "O loving hate! . . . / O heavy lightness! serious vanity! . . . / Feather of lead, bright smoke, cold fire, sick health!"

Paradox

Paradox unites statements and ideas that seem contradictory or illogical but that are nevertheless revealed to possess a certain truth. Having proved in his sonnet "Death, be not proud" that death does not conquer us since we "wake eternally," John Donne concludes triumphantly with the apparently paradoxical statement "Death, thou shalt die." The final line of Shakespeare's sonnet "That time of year thou may'st in me behold" seems illogical ("To love that well which thou must leave ere long"), but makes sense in the context of the poem where the speaker has been warning his love that he is approaching old age and therefore death.

Personification

The poet speaks of an inanimate object or entity, often some aspect of nature, as if it were a person. Wordsworth personifies his daffodils when he describes them as "dancing" in the breeze, and later when he sees them "Tossing their heads in sprightly dance." Clearly, only humans can actually dance and toss their heads; these attributes make the daffodils seem more lively.

A completely different example is provided in Howard Nemerov's poem "The Vacuum":

> The house is so quiet now
> The vacuum cleaner sulks in the corner closet,
> Its bag limp as a stopped lung.

Only a person "sulks," but this vacuum cleaner is said to do so because its owner doesn't use it enough; the rest of the poem shows that he has become slovenly since the death of his "old woman." The vacuum represents her, because she used to use it so much, and her death is personified by the vacuum's bag, "limp as a stopped lung."

Simile

See pages 13–14.

Symbol

A symbol resembles a metaphor in that both compare two things by substituting one for the other. A symbol usually presents a concrete object that stands for an abstraction, as a set of scales symbolizes justice via the concept of evenhandedness. In a poem, the possible meaning of a symbol can be fairly easy or quite difficult to interpret, according to the hints and the context provided by the poet. "The Road Not Taken" by Robert Frost presents a symbol for which it is not difficult to find a satisfactory interpretation: it becomes obvious, as the poem unfolds, that the decision to choose a certain path in a wood symbolizes choices that must be made in life. The symbol is enhanced by the added question of how much the speaker's life has been influenced by his choosing not only one path rather than another, but specifically "the one less traveled by," meaning probably an unusual way of life, or a direction in life that few people choose.

Symbols add an imaginative dimension to the reading of poetry; the reader senses there is a hidden meaning and has to work out for himself or herself what it might consist of. But interpretations do not need to be definitive: symbols can often be understood in multiple ways, which can lead to different overall interpretations of the poem by different readers. This adds to the interest and richness of the poem.

Some poems present symbols that are really hard to interpret and seem to belong to the poet's private world. While not satisfying the reader with a ready meaning, they can fascinate by their suggestiveness. Reading "The Sick Rose" (quoted above in the section on vocabulary), one can visualize a real rose attacked by a pest that has eaten through the bud; yet the poem seems to be about more than this minor horticultural tragedy. Traditionally, roses have often been used in poetry to symbolize love or beauty, particularly feminine beauty. This rose is also personified ("thou art sick") as if to give it human qualities. Furthermore, the rose has a "bed/Of crimson joy," which suggests sexual love, and the word "love" is indeed mentioned in the following line, but it is not a positive, healthy feeling but a "dark secret love" that has made the rose sick. The reader gets the impression, without being totally sure, that the rose/woman is being defiled or destroyed by some malignant force or being, symbolized by the "worm" of line 2. Indeed, the worm, which is after all "invisible," might well be taken to represent an abstraction, an evil force or influence, since it belongs to the night, the storm, and the dark, and has the power of destruction. Then the "rose" would symbolize perhaps the "joy" of line 6. William Blake—like many later poets—frequently used symbols whose meanings were not obvious. But such symbols often possess a mysterious and intense quality whose power can prove more fascinating to the reader than ones that are more readily explained.

Colors are often given symbolic value, as in the expression "crimson joy" above. The color red can symbolize passion, as here, but also danger, blood, violence. Black is frequently used to suggest despondency, depression, and death; white evokes purity, and so on.

Synecdoche

This is a figure of speech in which a part of a person or thing stands for the whole, as a head of cattle can represent the whole beast, or a sail imply a boat.

Understatement

Understatement is the opposite of hyperbole. The use of understatement enables an author to imply more by saying less. We do this in everyday language by using expressions such as "Not bad!" to imply that something is in fact very good. Officially termed **litotes**, this form of understatement through negation of a negative word is one among many ways of understating. Some poems, for example, speak of tragic events in a restrained, matter-of-fact, or understated tone that often conveys more depth of emotion than a more exclamatory and overtly emotive style would do. Seamus Heaney's poem "Mid-Term Break" recounts events surrounding the death of a child, but the speaker never openly reveals his anguish or sense of tragedy at the death of his four-year-old brother, simply referring to the coffin, in a moving final line, as "A four foot box, a foot for every year." Like hyperbole, understatement is related to irony, in that it says something other than what it really means.

Exercises on Imagery and Figurative Language

For each of the following examples, say what figure or image it contains, how you interpret it, and whether it seems to you effective in evoking a certain scene, idea, picture or thought. Remember that all the poems quoted in these exercises are given in full in appendix 2.

a)   She walks in beauty, like the night
          Of cloudless climes and starry skies;
       And all that's best of dark and bright
          Meet in her aspect and her eyes
                                   "She walks in beauty" (1–4)
                                   George Gordon, Lord Byron

b)   Thou wast not born for death, immortal Bird!
                                   "Ode to a Nightingale" (61)
                                   John Keats

c)   And mid-May's eldest child,
       The coming musk-rose, full of dewy wine,
       The murmurous haunt of flies on summer eves.
                                   "Ode to a Nightingale" (48–50)
                                   John Keats

d)   Heard melodies are sweet, but those unheard
       Are sweeter.
                                   "Ode on a Grecian Urn" (11–12)
                                   John Keats

e)   This City now doth, like a garment, wear
       The beauty of the morning.
                                   "Composed upon Westminster Bridge" (4–5)
                                   William Wordsworth

f)   My vegetable love should grow
        Vaster than empires, and more slow;
        An hundred years should go to praise
        Thine eyes, and on thy forehead gaze;
        Two hundred to adore each breast,
        But thirty thousand to the rest.

"To His Coy Mistress" (11–16)
Andrew Marvell

g)   When I heard the learn'd astronomer,
        When the proofs, the figures, were ranged in columns before me,
        When I was shown the charts and diagrams, to add, divide, and
            measure them,
        When I sitting heard the astronomer where he lectured with much
            applause in the lecture-room,
        How soon unaccountable I became tired and sick. . . .

"When I heard the learn'd astronomer" (1–5)
Walt Whitman

h)   Consider also the poem **"Wild Nights—Wild Nights"** quoted above
        in the section on vocabulary, page 10.

Now read the following poem. Try to find examples of figurative language and explain what they add to the poem. Examine the use of vocabulary also. Use the questions to help you.

i)   That time of year thou may'st in me behold
        When yellow leaves, or none, or few, do hang
        Upon those boughs which shake against the cold,
        Bare ruined choirs, where late the sweet birds sang.
        In me thou see'st the twilight of such day   5
        As after sunset fadeth in the west;
        Which by and by black night doth take away,
        Death's second self, that seals up all in rest.
        In me thou see'st the glowing of such fire,
        That on the ashes of his youth doth lie,   10
        As the deathbed whereon it must expire,
        Consumed with that which it was nourished by.
        This thou perceiv'st, which makes thy love more strong,
        To love that well which thou must leave ere long.

Sonnet 73
William Shakespeare

1. What do you feel is the purpose of the repetitions in lines 1, 5, and 9 ("thou may'st in me behold," "In me thou see'st")?

2. What figure of speech is involved in lines 1–4, 5–8, and 9–12, and what does each of the three examples illustrate? Do they seem effective? Which one do you prefer?

3. Do you notice any subsidiary figures of speech in lines 3–4 and 7–8? (Note that the word "choir" can refer not only to a group that sings but also to the place where it sits in a church.)

SOUNDS

Unless you are a poet yourself you probably give little thought to the sounds of words as you write. Poets, however, very often choose words for their sound and rhythm as well as for their meaning. Poetry is intended to be read aloud. Before doing a close reading, therefore, you should read the poem aloud or listen to it being read; otherwise, the musical side of the poem—its sounds and rhythms—will be lost.

Poets often try to choose words whose sound reinforces, as far as possible, their meaning. When Keats, in "To Autumn," wants to give an impression of richness and heaviness, along with the idea of the buzzing of flies, he uses many words containing the sound /m/:

> And mid-May's eldest child,
> The coming musk-rose, full of dewy wine,
> The murmurous haunt of flies on summer eves.

The sound /m/ conveys perfectly the humming noise of flies, and Keats manages here to use it seven times in the space of three lines, with a couple of /n/ sounds for good measure, as well as the /z/ sound at the end of "flies" and "eves," which produce a similar impression. These choices are obviously deliberate; indeed, poets spend a great deal of time choosing words in order to take such effects into account. The repetition of certain sounds in one or more lines of poetry is known as **alliteration**.

The question of the appreciation of sounds is very subjective. A sound that appears soft to one person may seem harsh to another. The context, in terms of both sounds and meaning, can also affect the impression that a certain sound makes on us in a poem. Nevertheless, some reactions to auditory signals are fairly standard: certain sounds are generally considered more cheerful or sadder than others; certain sounds seem quicker or sharper, others softer. Imagine you are a poet writing a poem that describes the flow of a very wide river meandering slowly through the countryside: would you prefer, to evoke the movement of this river, words containing many /m/ and /l/ sounds, or words containing /t/, /d/, and /k/ sounds? If, on the other hand, you were writing not about a big, slow-moving river but about a mountain stream with rushing water, would you choose /m/ and /l/ sounds, or /s/ and /ʃ/ (sh)? And if you wanted to describe the lively hopping movements of a bird pecking grain on the ground, would you use words with /m/ and /l/ sounds, or /t/ and /k/? To produce an impression of heaviness, would you prefer /t/ and /k/? Or /g/, /p/, and /b/? On the whole, given these specific options, most people tend to choose the same way.

Repetition of vowels as opposed to consonants is often called **assonance**. The following lines from Tennyson's "Ulysses" provide a good example of assonance, with long vowel sounds that seem to imitate the lugubrious sound of the sea and suggest a certain solemnity:

> The long day wanes; the slow moon climbs; the deep
> Moans round with many voices.

International Phonetic Alphabet

It is very important to realize that alliteration and assonance imply repetition of sounds and not of letters. Sometimes these are identical, but occasionally letters appear without being pronounced (like the silent *b* in *doubt*), and therefore do not form part of an alliteration. Also, certain letters can be pronounced in two ways, like a *c*, which sounds like an /s/ before an *e* or an *i* (as in *ceiling* or *cite*), but like a /k/ before an *a*, an *o*, or a *u*, as in *candle* or *cup*. Similarly, a *g* can be pronounced as in *generate* (a soft g) or as in *gone* (a hard g). Vowels can also present discrepancies: the letter *e* in *get* is not pronounced like the *e* in *the* or the first *e* in *here*; furthermore, the letter *e* is often silent, as the second *e* of *here*. Therefore one cannot simply give the letters of the alphabet to denote sounds; the only way around this difficulty is to use the International Phonetic Alphabet (see appendix 1). Here, each symbol represents a unique sound; thus the /s/ symbol represents only the sound that can be written as either *s* or *c*, and /k/ represents the sound written as *k* or *c* (as in *cat*) or *qu* (as in *torque*) or *ch* (as in *anchor*).

An important sound effect can be created by **rhyme**, in poems with lines that rhyme. We will discuss the technical aspects of rhyme later, in the section on versification; for the moment we should note simply that rhyme, like **alliteration** (and **assonance**) in general, offers a repetition of sounds, placed at the end of the line—a privileged position making the effect even more noticeable.

Alliteration is not the same thing as **onomatopoeia**. Onomatopoeia directly imitates the sound of something, as the expression "tick-tock" imitates the sound of a clock, or the verb "buzz" imitates the sound of a bee. It is limited to rather few words in the language, whereas any consonant or vowel sound can be alliterated in order to convey a certain impression.

As with any aspect of a close reading, it is not sufficient to note the presence of alliteration; you should seek possible reasons for this choice of sounds. However, the reasons will not always be as clear as in the above examples. Although alliteration is often used to illustrate the sense of the line(s) where it appears, a poet might choose to repeat certain sounds simply to please the ear, to embellish the poem with a certain richness of sound. Another function of alliteration is to link words together, as in John Donne's "*D*eath, thou shalt *d*ie" at the end of "Death, be not proud . . ."; it can also serve to emphasize certain words, as does the sound /d/ in Keats's description of "the tiger-moth's deep-damasked wings," ("The Eve of St. Agnes," stanza 24) or the repeated /t/ and /f/ sounds in Tennyson's marvelous line describing the action of the dawn: "And beat the twilight into flakes of fire" ("Tithonus").

Exercises on Sounds

a)   Season of mists and mellow fruitfulness,
          Close bosom-friend of the maturing sun;
       Conspiring with him how to load and bless

With fruit the vines that round the thatch-eves run;
To bend with apples the mossed cottage-trees,
   And fill all fruit with ripeness to the core;   5
     To swell the gourd, and plump the hazel shells
With a sweet kernel; to set budding more,
   And still more, later flowers for the bees,
   Until they think warm days will never cease,
     For summer has o'er-brimmed their clammy cells.

"To Autumn"
John Keats

1. We examined this first stanza of Keats's "To Autumn" in the section on vocabulary, above. Now consider also the effect of the sounds in this stanza. Do you see examples of alliteration? What impression does this poem convey, and how do the sounds of this stanza reinforce that impression?

b)   Sundays too my father got up early
and put his clothes on in the blue-black cold,
then with cracked hands that ached
from labor in the weekday weather made
banked fires blaze. No one ever thanked him.   5

I'd wake and hear the cold splintering, breaking.
When the rooms were warm, he'd call,
and slowly I would rise and dress,
fearing the chronic angers of that house,

Speaking indifferently to him,   10
who had driven out the cold
and polished my good shoes as well.
What did I know, what did I know
of love's austere and lonely offices?

"Those Winter Sundays"
Robert Hayden

1. Identify examples of alliteration in the first stanza and comment on their effect.

2. Are the same sounds repeated in the rest of the poem? Is there any other alliteration in the last two stanzas?

RHYTHM

Rhythm concerns the movement or "beat" of the poetic line and is perhaps the most fundamental aspect of poetry. Many poems lack figures of speech or alliteration, for example, but all poems have rhythm. Rhythm can be understood in two senses: the rhythmic effects created by **meter**, which will be discussed in the section on versification, and, in a more general way, the effects that can be created in any type of poetry by the length of words and of lines, the presence or absence of punctuation, and **enjambment** (run-on lines).

On the whole, short words, short phrases, or an abundance of punctuation dividing the line into many short segments tend to create a rapid, jerky rhythm; whereas a slower, more flowing rhythm is produced by long words, long phrases or lines, and the absence of punctuation. Let us imagine again that you are a poet describing the slow-moving river we spoke of in the section on alliteration: will you choose a succession of short words and abundant punctuation to describe this river, or on the contrary long words and lines with little punctuation? And what kind of rhythm would you prefer in order to evoke a mountain stream?

Rhythm often varies in the course of a poem, as the mood or the scene described changes. Coleridge, describing in "Kubla Khan" the source of the "sacred river"— a spring bursting violently out of the ground—uses short, mostly monosyllabic, words (in the second of the following three lines) in order to create a jerky rhythm reinforcing the idea of the earth's breathless "pants" as it struggles to give birth to this "mighty fountain":

> And from this chasm, with ceaseless turmoil seething,
> As if this earth in fast thick pants were breathing,
> A mighty fountain momently was forced.

However, the rhythm slows down once the river starts flowing through the countryside:

> Five miles meandering with a mazy motion
> Through wood and dale the sacred river ran.

In both these examples, alliteration backs up the impression created by the rhythm and by the sense of the words: the noise of the water being forced out of the ground is suggested by the /s/ and /t/ sounds; in addition, the /k/ and /b/ or /p/ and /θ/ (*th*) sounds evoke the effort involved. In the first line of the other example, the repeated /m/ sound imitates the meandering flow of the river.

A rapid rhythm might simply create an impression of rapid physical movement, but can also be used to suggest nervousness or happiness, since these two mental states often translate into a heightened level of activity. Similarly, a slow rhythm might evoke a slow movement but also a sense of calm or heavy melancholy. The first two lines of Keats's "Ode on a Grecian Urn," with punctuation only at the end of the line and several words of two or three syllables, sets a tone of calm and slow, stately movement:

> Thou still unravished bride of quietness,
>   Thou foster child of silence and slow time. . . .

Notice, however, that by the end of the stanza the mood has become agitated, and the rhythm accelerates, with shorter phrases and words:

> What men or gods are these? What maidens loath?
> What mad pursuit? What struggle to escape?
> What pipes and timbrels? What wild ecstasy?

In "The Eve of St. Agnes," Keats uses a jerky, fast rhythm with short words and a lot of punctuation to convey the alarm of two secret lovers, woken by the rain on the window, who must run away before they are caught:

> 'Tis dark: quick pattereth the flaw-blown sleet:
> "This is no dream, my bride, my Madeline!"
> 'Tis dark: the icéd gusts still rave and beat:
> "No dream, alas! alas! and woe is mine!"

Along with the staccato rhythm, the alliteration of /t/ and /d/ contributes to the impression of anxiety and urgent movement. For poets often use several different poetic elements concurrently to create the same effect, namely that implied by the sense of the words.

A lilting or sing-song rhythm can create an impression of music or of dance; an extremely regular rhythm can be used to create a calm mood or a sense of monotony. Long pauses—usually marked by punctuation—can slow down the rhythm of a line, as can a succession of words that are difficult to pronounce.

Needless to say, rhythmic effects may change in the course of a poem, or even from one line to the next, in accordance with changes of tone, meaning, or feeling in different parts of the poem.

A device that can affect rhythm is **enjambment**. Enjambment is produced by a discrepancy between the verse line and the syntax: the meaning or syntactical structure of a line is not complete but spills over into the following line, thus creating a different rhythm. It is often used simply to create rhythmic variety, especially in long poems. Enjambment can also serve to produce an impression of length and slowness: since there is no marked pause between the lines, a smooth, flowing effect is achieved. The impact of a long, slow line can be doubled or tripled by juxtaposing two or three such lines with no punctuation or pause between them and with the sense continuing from one to the next, as in these lines from Tennyson's "Ulysses":

> Yet all experience is an arch wherethrough
> Gleams that untravell'd world whose margin fades
> For ever and for ever when I move.

The forward movement of the verse, from one line into the next, echoes the forward movement Ulysses describes, that keeps him constantly in motion in his quest for new experiences and scenery. The impression of length and slowness reinforces the idea of Ulysses's long journey.

Enjambment can also serve a somewhat different purpose. If the sense spills over from one line to the next, but after a word or two in the second line there is punctuation, especially a period, then that word or those words at the beginning of the second line are heavily emphasized: they are in a prominent place at the beginning of a line, the previous line has led up to them, and there is a pause after them. Thus the paradox in the following lines is made more obvious by the enjambment and by the pause after the first two words of the second line:

> Heard melodies are sweet, but those unheard
> Are sweeter; therefore, ye soft pipes, play on.

> **"Ode on a Grecian Urn"**
> John Keats

Enjambment used in this way creates variety in the poem's rhythm, but it also has a syntactic or semantic effect, since it stresses the meaning and impact of certain words by the use of punctuation and by exploiting their position in the verse line. We will therefore return to the question of enjambment in a discussion of meter and syntax in the section on versification.

Exercises on Rhythm

Consider the rhythm of the following lines and answer the questions. You might also find examples of alliteration, since sound and rhythm are often combined to produce the same impression.

> a)   The curfew tolls the knell of parting day,
> The lowing herd wind slowly o'er the lea,
> The plowman homeward plods his weary way,
> And leaves the world to darkness and to me.

> **"Elegy Written in a Country Churchyard"**
> Thomas Gray

1. How would you characterize the rhythm of this stanza and why was this type of rhythm chosen?

2. Do you see any examples of alliteration or assonance?

> b)   The shadow of the dome of pleasure
> Floated midway on the waves;
> Where was heard the mingled measure
> From the fountain and the caves.
> It was a miracle of rare device,
> A sunny pleasure dome with caves of ice!

> **"Kubla Kahn"**
> Samuel Taylor Coleridge

1. What effect does the rhythm of this stanza have on you? Does it seem appropriate to the content of these lines?

> c)   Season of mists and mellow fruitfulness!
>   Close bosom-friend of the maturing sun;
>   Conspiring with him how to load and bless
>   With fruit the vines that round the thatch-eves run.
>
> **"To Autumn"**
> John Keats

1. How would you describe the rhythm of these lines? Does it seem to match the poem's content?

Up to now we have been considering rhythm as a means to produce an individual effect. Poems in traditional verse also have a rhythm created by the verse itself. We now come to the questions of versification and meter.

VERSIFICATION

A quick comparison of, say, Wordsworth's poem about daffodils—or Keats's "To Autumn"—with Linda Pastan's "To a Daughter Leaving Home" or Walt Whitman's "When I heard the learn'd astronomer" at once reveals a distinct difference in the poems' **form**. The poems by Wordsworth and Keats are in metrical verse, with lines of the same length and a regular rhyme scheme. The more modern poems are in free verse, with lines of varying lengths, which may or may not rhyme. Many poets since the end of the nineteenth century have adopted free verse, which will be discussed later in this section. First, we should examine the characteristics of traditional verse.

The Verse Line

Prose does not have individual, distinct lines. It simply runs along to the edge of the page and then continues in the line below, with these breaks occurring arbitrarily depending on the width of the page and the size of the print. Poetry, however (even free verse), has distinct lines, which usually end well before the edge of the page and usually begin with a capital letter (though not always in modern verse). Lines of verse form a regular pattern and contribute to the poem's rhythm. Rhythm in this sense of repeated pattern is commonly referred to as **meter**.

Meter

It may be seen at a glance that the lines of "I wandered lonely as a cloud" are shorter than those of "To Autumn" ("Season of mists and mellow fruitfulness . . ."). A discussion of the length of a line of verse involves the question of **meter**. Line length and type in English verse are determined not by the sheer number of syllables but by their arrangement into units called **feet** and the consequent grouping of stressed (accented) and unstressed syllables. For this reason it is called accentual-syllabic verse.

All English words of more than one syllable require a stronger stress to be placed on one of the syllables than on the others. Thus the words *módern* and *númber*, for example, are stressed on the first syllable and no native speaker would pronounce them with a stress on the final syllable. The words *distínct* or *revéal*, however, have an unstressed syllable first and a stress on the second syllable. With three-syllable words there are three possibilities, as shown for example by *régular, howéver* or *unawáre*. Multi-syllable words will also have one stressed syllable (occasionally two, with extremely long words or compound words) and several unstressed, e.g., *discríminate, indivídual, unfórtunately*. Consider a few random English words of two syllables or more and work out where the stress falls—i.e., which syllable you pronounce with the most energy.

Poets writing in English—like Latin poets before them—take advantage of the language's stress patterns to create a metrical rhythm dependent on the arrangement of stressed and unstressed syllables within the verse line. A metrical foot (which can be marked by vertical lines) usually consists of either two or three syllables. Feet of two syllables include the **trochee** and the **iamb**. A **trochaic** foot has a stress on the first syllable and not on the second (/ u), as in the word *módern* or in the famous witches' chant from Shakespeare's *Macbeth*: "Dóuble, | dóuble | tóil and | tróuble;| / Fíre | búrn and | cáuldron | búbble." These two very regular trochaic lines have four feet each, and each foot contains a stressed syllable followed by an unstressed one. Much more common is the **iambic** foot—in fact, iambic rhythm is by far the most common in English poetry. It has an unstressed syllable followed by a stressed one (u /), as in the word *revéal* or for example in Byron's line: "She wálks| in béauty, líke| the níght." Note that the stressed and unstressed syllables that make up a foot may often divide a word in two, as with the word "beauty" in this line. Notice also that the verse line is pronounced no differently from the way you would say these words, "She walks in beauty, like the night" (or "Double, double, toil and trouble") in speech, should you so desire! Metrical verse merely uses a feature that already exists in the language—stressed and unstressed syllables—but arranges them into a pattern, called meter, which is usually maintained—with variations—throughout the poem, and creates a certain rhythm.

Determining the metrical rhythm of a poem (by establishing the pattern of stressed and unstressed syllables and the number of feet) is called **scanning**. The line "She walks in beauty, like the night" has four iambic feet and is therefore described as an iambic **tetrameter**, from the Greek word for *four*. A line of three feet would be termed a **trimeter**, and a line of five iambic feet, the most common of all in English poetry, an **iambic pentameter**, as in Shakespeare's "That tíme| of yéar| thou máy'st| in mé| behóld." Notice that words of one syllable may be stressed or not, generally according to the conventions of normal spoken usage; thus a noun like *year* will receive a stress rather than a preposition like *of*. The (inevitable) presence of monosyllabic words that may or may not be stressed allows for a great deal of play or "irregularity" within metrical patterns. Thus, Wordsworth's line "I wán|dered lóne|lly as| a clóud" is clearly an iambic tetrameter, yet you might hesitate to stress the word "as." You should say the line as you would normally speak it; the third foot would therefore contain two unstressed syllables (u u), the second syllable of "lonely" and the word "as." Such a foot, with two unstressed syllables, is called a **pyrrhic** foot. Similarly, in the Shakespeare line quoted above, one might wish to place a stress on the first word, "That": "Thát tíme| of yéar| thou máy'st| in mé| behóld." The first foot of this line, read in this way, would have two stresses (//), which would make it a **spondee** or **spondaic** foot. Poems are not composed completely in pyrrhic or spondaic feet, which are only used to provide variations on the iambic or trochaic foot. Variations of this kind arise in all good metrical verse: a too-insistent repetition of the same meter in every line would become boring to the reader/listener.

Feet of three syllables can be **anapests** or **dactyls**. A dactylic foot has a stressed syllable followed by two unstressed (/ u u), as in the words *innocent* or *élevate*. An anapestic foot displays the opposite pattern—two unstressed syllables followed by one stressed (u u /), as in the word *comprehénd* and as in these lines from Byron's poem "The Destruction of Sennacherib":

> The Asý|rian came dówn| like the wólf| on the fóld,
> And his có|horts were gléa|ming in púr|ple and góld;
> And the shéen| of their spéars| was like stárs| on the séa,
> When the blúe| wáve rolls níght|ly on déep| Galilée.

These lines are anapestic tetrameters—lines with four anapestic feet. The anapestic rhythm in this poem imitates the swift, rhythmic movement of the galloping horsemen racing into battle.

Each metrical unit is called a foot. The number of feet in a line determines its length, thus:

Metrical units

monometer (1 foot)
dimeter (2 feet)
trimeter (3 feet)
tetrameter (4 feet)
pentameter (5 feet)
hexameter (6 feet)
heptameter (7 feet)
octameter (8 feet)

Of these, pentameters, tetrameters and trimeters are by far the most common. As we have seen, the feet themselves can be categorized in the following way:

Feet

Iambic (an iamb): u /
Trochaic (a trochee): / u
Dactylic (a dactyl): / u u
Anapestic (an anapest): u u /
Spondaic (a spondee): / /
Pyrrhic: u u

Once a basic meter is established, most poems continue with the same stress pattern and number of feet throughout. For example, the lines of "I wandered lonely as a cloud" are all basically iambic tetrameters, with slight variations in the pattern of stresses; and those of "That time of year thou may'st in me behold" are all essentially iambic pentameters. Occasionally, a poet will create a pattern where one or two lines in a stanza have a different meter from the others, for example in Keats's "Ode to a Nightingale," where lines 1–7 are iambic pentameters, line 8 is an iambic trimeter, and lines 9-10 are again pentameters. Such changes in meter can simply provide variety; they can result in a lilting, musical rhythm, as in Coleridge's "Kubla Khan"; or they can serve to emphasize the line that stands out by being shorter or longer than the others, as in another poem by Keats, "La Belle Dame Sans Merci," in which the last line of each stanza is essentially an iambic dimeter, following three tetrameters:

> "O what can ail thee, knight-at-arms,
>   Alone and palely loitering?
> The sedge is withered from the lake,
>   And no birds sing."

Meter and Rhythm

Meter, then, sets a rhythmic pattern that pleases the ear of the reader. While patterns may be delightful, however, they can also become monotonous. Good poets always make variations within the basic meter, both to avoid monotony and to create the kinds of effect discussed in the section on rhythm, above; e.g., to suggest slowness or speed, lightness or heaviness, agitation, peace, melancholy, etc.

The eighteenth-century English poet Alexander Pope, in a section of his *Essay on Criticism*, a long poem on the art of writing poetry, illustrates the way rhythm and sounds can emphasize a meaning:

> When Ajax strives some rock's vast weight to throw,
> The line too labours, and the words move slow.

This poem is composed in iambic pentameters (cf. the line that introduces this passage: "The sóund| must séem| an écho| of| the sénse"), but in the lines quoted the rhythm is slowed by the extra stressed syllables ("róck's vást wéight"; "líne tóo lábours"; "wórds móve slów"), which helps to suggest the huge effort involved in throwing a heavy rock. Of course the alliteration helps, too, presenting harsh sounds that are difficult to pronounce ("Ajax strives," "rock's vast weight")—as usual, different devices combine to achieve a certain effect. In the following lines, Pope suggests an opposite kind of movement, a light, fleeting run:

> Not so, when swift Camilla scours the plain,
> Flies o'er th'unbending corn, and skims along the main.

Here, the fast-moving, light rhythm, created by the very regular stresses in the first line and extra unstressed syllables in the second, again provides "an echo to the sense," i.e., the impression of lightness and speed.

Another way to vary rhythm is to make pauses at different points in the lines. In the example from Pope, quoted above, strong pauses are marked by punctuation—after two syllables in the first line ("Not so,") and in the middle of the second. A strong pause in a line of verse is termed a **caesura**, and is marked, in scanning a poem, by a double vertical line, thus:

Not so, || when swift Camilla scours the plain,
Flies o'er th'unbending corn, || and skims along the main.

Not all lines contain pauses, and some contain more than one, usually a caesura (strong pause) and one or more lesser ones ("When yellow leaves, || or none, | or few, | do hang"). Some readers may make a pause in certain lines where others would not, especially when a pause is not marked by punctuation: the line "Season of mists and mellow fruitfulness" may be read as it stands, or with a pause after "mists": "Season of mists || and mellow fruitfulness."

Meter and Syntax

Generally speaking, syntax operates the same way in poetry as in prose, i.e., sentences have a subject and verb, and often an object, and perhaps also an adverbial clause, etc. As in prose, a preponderance of verbs will give an impression of activity and movement, whereas a succession of nouns accompanied by adjectives characterizes description. Poets tend, however, far more often than prose writers, to take liberties with syntax, because meter involves strict rules that the poet must combine with the requirements of syntax. The order of words in a poem—especially a traditional poem in rhymed verse—often does not coincide with the normal prose order. A poet may change word order for various reasons: to achieve a rhythmic effect, to emphasize a word by giving it a conspicuous position in a line, to place a rhyme-word at the end of a line, or because the order he adopts fits in better with the poem's meter. Thus Wordsworth in lines 2–3 of his sonnet "Composed Upon Westminster Bridge," writes:

Dull would he be of soul who could pass by
A sight so touching in its majesty

—whereas the normal word order would read: "He who could pass by a sight so touching in its majesty would be dull of soul." Wordsworth's version flows better rhythmically, provides a rhyme, and accentuates the word "Dull" by placing it at the beginning of both the sentence and the line. Similarly, Coleridge, in "Kubla Khan (lines 8–9)," inverts a verb ("blossomed") and its subject, giving:

And there were gardens bright with sinuous rills,
Where blossomed many an incense-bearing tree.

The normal word order (". . . where many an incense-bearing tree blossomed") would interrupt the iambic rhythm and cause a problem with the rhyme, whereas "tree" at the end of the line rhymes happily with "greenery" in line 11.

Such examples of altered syntax—sometimes requiring that the reader pay close attention—are innumerable in metrical verse, where the poet has to keep in mind the patterns of stressed and unstressed syllables, the number of feet, the rhythm, and the rhyme of his verse. An incompetent poet often alters word order in a clumsy, artificial fashion, but a good poet will succeed in skillfully adapting the syntax to his/her verse line so that the line still flows naturally, reconciling the requirements of both meter and syntax while avoiding clumsy or ridiculous inversions.

Punctuation, in poetry, functions as in prose to clarify syntax: phrases or clauses may be separated by commas; semi-colons create pauses within a sentence; colons announce what is to follow. Exclamation points and question marks have their normal effect. The presence of several exclamation marks in a poem or part of a poem usually indicates strong emotion, whether of surprise, happiness, anger, or despair. Expressing his yearning to escape the sufferings of life, the speaker of Shelley's "Ode to the West Wind" exclaims:

> Oh, lift me as a wave, a leaf, a cloud!
> I fall upon the thorns of life! I bleed!

Every stanza in the final part of this poem contains at least one exclamation point.

As we saw in the section above on rhythm, punctuation can affect a poem's rhythm. A total absence of punctuation can create a non-stop, flowing rhythm. It is easier to write a poem with no punctuation than a prose passage, since the breaks created by verse lines supply pauses and syntactic groupings that aid comprehension, whereas unpunctuated and uninterrupted prose would be very hard to follow.

The lines of a poem often form a complete syntactic unit, e.g., "Thou wast not born for death, immortal Bird!" in Keats's "Ode to a Nightingale." Sometimes, however, the sense of a line "spills over" into the following line and, as noted in the section on rhythm, this phenomenon is called **enjambment**. It affects a poem's rhythm, as we saw, but it can also have a syntactic or semantic function, i.e., it can affect our understanding of a phrase by accentuating certain words, as in the "Ode on a Grecian Urn":

> Heard melodies are sweet, but those unheard
> Are sweeter; therefore, ye soft pipes, play on.

The paradoxical thought in these lines is made more obvious by the enjambment and by the pause after the first two words of the second line.

Exercises on Meter

1. Establish the basic meter of the following poems or stanzas. (N.B. The complete poems are printed in appendix 2.) If you have trouble determining what the meter is—remember, there are always variations—try to find a line that does seem regular (e.g., lines 4–5 in the first example) and then check whether this appears to be the basic rhythm of all the lines.

2. Where do you perceive irregularities in the meter? What effect, if any, do these variations achieve? If the metrical rhythm is very regular, does that seem appropriate for the action in the poem?

3. Do any lines contain a caesura or shorter pause? Do such pauses create any special rhythmic or semantic effects?

4. Examine punctuation and discuss its role, if any, in each example.

5. Is the syntax straightforward (i.e., as it would appear in prose) or are there alterations to the normal word order? If so, do they help to accentuate any important word, provide a rhyme or improve the rhythm of the lines?

a)   Thou still unravished bride of quietness,
              Thou foster child of silence and slow time,
          Sylvan historian, who canst thus express
              A flowery tale more sweetly than our rhyme:
          What leaf-fringed legend haunts about thy shape   5
              Of deities or mortals, or of both,
                  In Tempe or the dales of Arcady?
          What men or gods are these? What maidens loath?
              What mad pursuit? What struggle to escape?
                  What pipes and timbrels? What wild ecstasy?
                                      "Ode on a Grecian Urn" (1–10)
                                                  John Keats

b)   Tyger! Tyger! burning bright
          In the forests of the night,
          What immortal hand or eye
          Could frame thy fearful symmetry?

          In what distant deeps or skies
          Burnt the fire of thine eyes?
          On what wings dare he aspire?
          What the hand, dare seize the fire?

                                              "The Tyger" (1–8)
                                                  William Blake

c)   She walks in beauty, like the night
              Of cloudless climes and starry skies;
          And all that's best of dark and bright
              Meet in her aspect and her eyes:
          Thus mellowed to that tender light
              Which heaven to gaudy day denies.

                                      "She Walks in Beauty" (1–6)
                                          George Gordon, Lord Byron

Rhyme

Another common characteristic of traditional versification is **rhyme**. That rhyme pleases the ear and aids in memorization is evident from the number of jingles, nursery rhymes, and songs in which it plays a part. In poetry, too, the sound-repetition inherent in rhyme has a pleasing effect; it can also serve the same function as alliteration of accentuating certain sounds in order to emphasize meaning or emotion; and it can be used to link words together to suggest affinity or, sometimes, opposition. A switch to new rhymes can indicate a movement to a new thought. Rhyme also has the function—like meter—of creating a pattern, thereby giving a certain coherence to the poem's form.

In scanning a poem, rhymes are indicated, very simply, by letters. If the first two lines of a poem rhyme, and then the next two, this is marked as: *aabb*. If, however, the first and third lines rhyme, and the second and fourth, we have a rhyme scheme *abab*. A line with which no other line rhymes would be marked: *x*.

Two lines of verse rhyme if their last words contain an accented vowel pronounced identically, preceded or, more often, followed by identical consonant sounds, e.g., *bird/heard, blow/low*. Notice that rhyme concerns pronunciation, not spelling; thus the words *bird* and *heard* form a perfect rhyme even though they are written differently. Conversely, you will occasionally encounter **eye-rhyme**: words whose sounds do not in fact rhyme but whose spelling indicates that one might expect them to, like the words *low* and *prow* in the first few lines of Browning's "Meeting at Night."

Rhymes are deemed **masculine** and **feminine**. Masculine rhyme falls on a final stressed syllable, while the less common feminine rhyme has a rhyming unstressed syllable following the rhyming stressed syllable, e.g., *shaking/breaking, flying/crying, rover/over*. These feminine rhymes all occur in John Masefield's poem "Sea Fever," which has a rhyme scheme *aabb* where all the a rhymes are masculine and the b rhymes feminine:

> I must go down to the seas again, to the lonely sea and the sky,
> And all I ask is a tall ship and a star to steer her by,
> And the wheel's kick and the wind's song and the white sail's shaking,
> And a grey mist on the sea's face and a grey dawn breaking.

So far, we have discussed only **end rhyme**, a characteristic feature of traditional verse. You may also encounter **internal rhyme**: rhymes occurring within a line, as in "Counting b<u>ells</u> kn<u>ell</u>ing classes to a close" (from Seamus Heaney's "Mid-Term Break"). Edgar Allan Poe's "The Raven" contains many internal rhymes, e.g.,

> Once upon a midnight dreary, while I pondered, weak and weary,
>
> . . . .
>
> While I nodded, gently napping, suddenly there came a tapping. . . .

Not all verse contains rhymes. **Blank verse**—unrhymed iambic pentameter—represents a cornerstone of the English poetic tradition, especially for long poems and verse drama. Shakespeare's plays are mostly composed in blank verse, as are Milton's epic, *Paradise Lost*, and Wordsworth's long poems such as "Lines Composed above Tintern Abbey." Blank verse has rhythm but not rhyme.

Many modern poets, beginning in the late nineteenth century and especially in the twentieth, take liberties with rhyme, either ignoring it completely, employing it occasionally but not regularly, or using **approximate rhymes**. These are rhymes that share similar but not identical vowel or consonant sounds, as in the second stanza of Edgar Allan Poe's poem "To Helen," where he rhymes "face" with "Greece": ". . . Thy hyacinth hair, thy classic face / Thy Naiad airs have brought me home / To the glory that was Greece / And the grandeur that was Rome." These lines also contain some approximate internal rhymes ("Thy hyacinth hair"/"Thy Naiad airs").

As you analyze a poem, consider the effects of the rhyme. Does it give the poem a musical quality? Does a change in rhyme mark a different turn of thought? Are words linked by rhyme also connected (or opposed) in meaning? (Given that, in a poem with traditional versification, all lines have to rhyme, such effects will prove exceptional rather than standard, but you should look out for them.) Certain words may be linked unexpectedly by rhyme; this can produce a comic or satiric effect, as when the speaker of T.S. Eliot's "Love Song of J. Alfred Prufrock" asks, "Should I, after tea and cakes and ices, / Have the strength to force the moment to its crisis?" The juxtaposition of "crisis" with a trivial word like "ices" devalues the notion of crisis.

Rhyme used only occasionally can have a startling effect, drawing attention to the rhymed words and therefore to the idea or emotion they convey. Thus, in Seamus Heaney's "Mid-Term Break," only the last two lines of the poem rhyme: "No gaudy scars, the bumper knocked him clear. / A four foot box, a foot for every year." The unexpected rhyme at the end of a poem without rhymes underscores the reader's sense of shock on learning that the speaker's dead brother was only four years old. Since these are the final lines of the poem, the rhyme also serves the purpose of concluding it. Indeed, rhyme often has the function of "rounding things off": Shakespeare, in his blank verse plays, frequently ends scenes with two rhymed lines, to mark their conclusion.

Stanzas

The lines of a poem are often, though not always, arranged in **stanzas**—groups of the same number of lines with the same meter and rhyme scheme, that are typographically set apart from each other. Thus Wordsworth's poem about daffodils is divided into four stanzas of six lines each, with a rhyme scheme *ababcc*. Robert Browning's "Meeting at Night" comprises two stanzas of six lines rhyming *abccba*; "Up-Hill" by Christina Rossetti has four stanzas of four lines rhyming *abab*; while William Blake's "The Tyger" comprises six stanzas of four lines rhyming *aabb*.

When explicating a poem, point out stanza formations and rhyme schemes and consider whether they affect the poem's impact. Often, the choice of verse patterns and stanza lengths will appear totally arbitrary, but sometimes you may find a connection between these aspects of a poem's form and its meaning. For example, **couplets** (lines rhyming *aabbcc*, etc.), since they form neat little pairs, are often used to sum up an argument, provide closure, or express pithy, epigrammatic statements. Satiric poets such as Alexander Pope tend to use couplets, as in his long satirical poem "The Rape of the Lock" or in his "Epigram Engraved on the Collar of a Dog Which I Gave to His Royal Highness":

> I am his Highness' dog at Kew;
> Pray tell me, sir, whose dog are you?

Long epic (or heroic) poems were often composed in couplets of iambic pentameters, whence the name **heroic couplet**.

A **tercet** is a three-line stanza, as in Tennyson's short poem "The Eagle." A specific type of tercet, **terza rima**, features a rhyme scheme where the second line of the first stanza provides rhymes for the first and third lines of the second stanza and so on (*aba*, *bcb*, *cdc*, etc.). Since this arrangement produces an odd number of lines and would therefore always leave one line without a rhyme, poems in terza rima usually have one or two extra lines at the end, rhyming with the middle line of the previous tercet, like Frost's "Acquainted with the night" and Shelley's "Ode to the West Wind."

The four-line stanza or **quatrain**, very common in English lyric poetry, usually has a rhyme scheme of *abab* or *abba*, though *aabb* is possible also. A six-line stanza is a **sestet**, as in "I wandered lonely as a cloud," and a stanza of eight lines is called an octave. Stanzas with an odd number of lines (other than tercets) are rare, but one example is Frost's "The Road Not Taken," which has stanzas of five lines, rhyming *abaab*.

Having adopted a certain type of stanza, the poet may include as many of them as he wishes in his poem. Certain forms, however, are **fixed** in a stricter way: their structure follows precise rules. In the **villanelle**, for example, five tercets are followed by a quatrain, and the rhymes are *aba* throughout (i.e., the same rhymes in each stanza, with an extra *a* in the quatrain, *abaa*). Furthermore, certain lines of the villanelle are repeated in their entirety: the first line of the poem becomes the last line of the second and fourth stanzas; the third line of the poem is repeated as the last line of the third and fifth stanzas; these two lines also form the last two lines of the poem. A good example of a villanelle is Dylan Thomas's "Do not go gentle into that good night."

You may not come across many examples of the villanelle; but one very popular **fixed form** is the **sonnet**, a poem of fourteen lines, usually in iambic pentameter. Because of its set form, the sonnet, like the villanelle, presents a challenge to the poet; but it appears that the effort to comply with certain rules can actually enhance the process of composition rather than hindering it. There are two types of sonnet. The **Petrarchan** (or **Italian**) sonnet, developed by the Italian poet Petrarch in the fourteenth century, splits the fourteen lines into an octave followed by a sestet (which in turn divide into two quatrains and two tercets), with a rhyme scheme *abbaabbacdecde* (allowing for some variations, especially in the sestet). Thus the rhymes in the sestet differ from those in the octave, and the transition (or "turn") often accompanies a shift in meaning: the octave tends to pose a problem or describe a situation and the sestet then offers a solution, a commentary or another view of the issue. The **Shakespearean** sonnet divides differently: into three quatrains and a couplet, usually with a rhyme scheme of *ababcdcdefefgg*. Each quatrain tends to develop a different aspect of the poem's theme, and the final couplet, with its neat rhyme, provides some form of resolution: a summary, a conclusion, or, sometimes, a mocking commentary.

Other named types of poem include the **ode** and the **elegy**, though they are characterized less by specific versification than by their subject matter. The ode is a fairly long, rather formal poem with stanzas of various lengths and meters, written in celebration of some event, person or thing; examples are Shelley's "Ode to the West Wind" and Keats's "Ode to a Nightingale and "Ode on a Grecian Urn." The elegy, as its name implies, is a lament for the dead, like Gray's "Elegy Written in a Country Churchyard."

Exercises on Rhyme and Stanza Forms

1. Establish the stanza forms and rhyme schemes of the following poems.

2. Do you find any link between these formal aspects of the poems and their content? Does rhyme help to structure the poem?

3. Are there any examples of internal rhyme? eye-rhyme?

a)
That time of year thou may'st in me behold
When yellow leaves, or none, or few, do hang
Upon those boughs which shake against the cold,
Bare ruined choirs where late the sweet birds sang.
In me thou see'st the twilight of such day   5
As after sunset fadeth in the west,
Which by-and-by black night doth take away,
Death's second self that seals up all in rest.
In me thou see'st the glowing of such fire
That on the ashes of his youth doth lie,   10
As the deathbed whereon it must expire,
Consumed with that which it was nourished by.
This thou perceiv'st, which makes thy love more strong,
To love that well which thou must leave ere long.

"That time of year thou may'st in be behold"
William Shakespeare

b)
He clasps the crag with crooked hands;
Close to the sun in lonely lands,
Ringed with the azure world, he stands.

The wrinkled sea beneath him crawls;
He watches from his mountain walls,
And like a thunderbolt he falls.

"The Eagle"
Alfred, Lord Tennyson

c)
She walks in beauty, like the night
    Of cloudless climes and starry skies;
And all that's best of dark and bright
    Meet in her aspect and her eyes:
Thus mellowed to that tender light   5
    Which heaven to gaudy day denies.

One shade the more, one ray the less,
    Had half impaired the nameless grace
Which waves in every raven tress,
    Or softly lightens o'er her face;   10
Where thoughts serenely sweet express
    How pure, how dear their dwelling place.

And on that cheek, and o'er that brow,
    So soft, so calm, yet eloquent,
The smiles that win, the tints that glow,   15
    But tell of days in goodness spent,
A mind at peace with all below,
    A heart whose love is innocent!

"She Walks in Beauty"
George Gordon, Lord Byron

Free Verse

Modern poets often refrain from using stanzas with a fixed number of lines—as they also often dispense with rhyme and meter. Such poetry, called **free verse** (from the French expression *vers libre*), arose in the second half of the nineteenth century (its first practitioner in English was Walt Whitman whose *Leaves of Grass* was published in 1855) and has become the most popular form of poetry, often called open form poetry. Indeed, poems written in English today are more often composed in free verse than in metrical verse. The expression "free verse" implies that this poetry is free—from rules of meter and rhyme. Nevertheless, it is poetry. It still has verse lines, but of varying lengths. The variations are not arbitrary (free verse is not simply prose printed like verse): usually the lines represent a whole entity—a self-contained phrase or a phrase that may be spoken in one breath. For free verse is more closely related than traditional rhyming verse to the patterns of oral speech. The rhythm of the lines tends to follow the rhythms of speech (rather than a metrical pattern). Although lines may be of any length, they usually remain within the limit of what may be spoken in one breath.

Lines of free verse are often grouped irregularly, into sections of different lengths, rather than into regular stanzas. The poet may take advantage of the variation in line lengths to emphasize certain lines—by concluding a section of long lines with a short one, for example. The first word of every line of free verse may be capitalized, as in Walt Whitman's "When I heard the learn'd astronomer," or—especially in more recent works such as Robert Hayden's "Those Winter Sundays"—capitals may appear only at the beginning of sentences, as in prose. The lines may or may not rhyme, or they may present approximate rhymes, or occasional rhyme. Alliteration and assonance are used as in metrical verse to mark connections between words or to highlight sounds that reflect meaning. And poets writing in free verse, like traditional poets, may use imagery and figures of speech. In particular they tend to favor anaphora (described above in the section on figurative language), which helps to link lines together at the beginning (as rhyme links them at the end) and can be used to build up to a climax.

We have already seen several examples of poems composed in free verse, such as Linda Pastan's "To a Daughter Leaving Home" whose lines are unrhymed and of irregular length, but varying only between two and six syllables; and Walt Whitman's "When I heard the learn'd astronomer," where some of the lines become so long that one stops counting syllables, though they can all be pronounced with one breath. Poems written in free verse retain a poetic quality that distinguishes them from prose: they use language in an imaginative and creative fashion and achieve their effects in a different way from prose. In Walt Whitman's poem "When I heard the learn'd astronomer," the use of anaphora ("When . . . When . . . When . . . When . . .") in the first four lines links them together, as they are also linked in meaning—all describing the act of listening to the astronomer's lecture and leading to the speaker's rejection of the situation in line 5. At this point the lines also become dramatically shorter—another indication of a change in direction. In the last line, where the speaker, rejecting the lecture-hall with its many occupants, wanders outside by himself and gazes "in perfect silence at the stars," the alliteration of /s/ in these words joins them together and implicitly contrasts this "silence" with the talk in the lecture theater. Again, alliteration of the sound /m/ is used effectively in the final line to suggest the pleasure afforded by the "mystical moist night air . . . ."

Another famous practitioner of free verse is T.S. Eliot. His "Love Song of J. Alfred Prufrock" has lines of varying length, arranged in groups of varying length. Many—though not all—lines have end rhyme, but they do not form a regular pattern; and frequently the very same word appears at the end of two adjacent lines, which traditionally was not considered a valid rhyme. Eliot's "Four Quartets" dispense with rhyme altogether.

Speaker, Voice, and Tone

Not all poems include a first-person speaker: ballads and narrative poems such as Tennyson's "The Lady of Shalott" or Keats's "The Eve of St. Agnes," are told objectively in the third person. A descriptive poem, though often fairly objective, like Tennyson's "The Eagle," may reveal the presence of a speaker (though no "I" is mentioned) through the choice of adjectives or the use of exclamation points and question marks. The multiple question marks in Blake's "The Tyger" seem to indicate the doubts and wonderment of a speaker; and the reader of Byron's "She Walks in Beauty" senses the narrator's attitude towards the woman described—even though no "I" is present in the poem—thanks to expressions like "tender light," "grace," "softly lightens," "thoughts serenely sweet," and so on.

Lyric poetry frequently is composed in the **first person**, however, with a speaker who may or may not represent the poet and with whom the reader can often identify. You cannot necessarily equate the "I" of the poem directly with the poet. S/he is the author, of course, but may modify his/her voice, use a purely conventional "I," or assume the voice of a fictitious or historical character. An extreme example of the latter option is the **dramatic monologue**, a type of poem in which the first-person speaker is identified, by name, by title, rank, profession, social status, or historical circumstance, and can thus be clearly distinguished from the poet. Such a character may or may not express the poet's own views, but the speaker of such a poem has an identity distinct from that of the poet. The title of a dramatic monologue often identifies the speaker at once, as in Browning's "Fra Lippo Lippi" or "Andrea del Sarto," Tennyson's "Ulysses" and "Tithonus," or T.S. Eliot's "The Love Song of J. Alfred Prufrock"; other details within the poem will help to place the speaker in society and fill out different aspects of his/her character and circumstances. Such a speaker cannot be confused with the author of the poem.

The Lyric "I" and the Poet's Persona

Even in poetry where the "I" of the poem is not identified in this way, you should refrain from assuming that the poet is the speaker of the text, referring rather to the narrator, to the "I" of the poem, or to the poet's **persona**. For in a poetic work, a poet adopts a persona, a voice that does not necessarily correspond to the everyday voice of the biographical poet. Wordsworth's voice as we hear it in his

(Continued)

poetry is not identical to that of his correspondence; nor does the persona he adopts in poems equate exactly to his biographical self as revealed for example in his sister Dorothy's diaries. Furthermore, a poet writing about an experience might choose to modify it for the purposes of his verse, altering circumstances to fit his needs. No doubt Wordsworth saw a "host" of daffodils, but he may have embellished certain aspects of the scene. When composing a poem, a poet may also modify his/her reactions to real events, exaggerating certain emotions or downplaying others.

The "I" of a **lyric poem** is thus a rather vague entity that may represent the poet's persona, but can also be seen as a universal "I" belonging to no one—and to everyone. This vagueness of the lyric "I" allows the reader to identify with the poem's speaker. The "I" who "wandered lonely as a cloud" can refer to Wordsworth, or to any reader of the poem reliving the experience of a glimpse of natural beauty. A reader may empathize with the speaker who exclaims "I fall upon the thorns of life! I bleed!" in Shelley's "Ode to the West Wind," or with Keats's persona complaining of "The weariness, the fever, and the fret / Here, where men sit and hear each other groan" in the "Ode to a Nightingale." You might easily relate to Robert Frost's narrator, in "The Road Not Taken," over the difficulty of deciding between two equally attractive choices—whether they be paths in a wood or in life; Linda Pastan's "To a Daughter Leaving Home" will resonate with any reader who has had the experience of bringing up a child who has subsequently grown up and left home—as, of course, with any reader who can sympathize with such a situation without having experienced it directly.

The presence of an "I" in a poem often leads to the introduction of a "you," whose identity may be as vague as that of the "I." In Matthew Arnold's "Dover Beach," the speaker invokes a "you" whom we know only as the beloved ("Ah, love, let us be true / To one another!") A poem can be composed solely in the second person; but the use of "you" immediately implies the presence of a speaker addressing the "you," so that the reader senses a speaker's voice. Such is the case in Blake's "The Sick Rose."

A poem may also include more than one voice. Christina Rossetti's "Up-Hill" presents a dialogue, with one speaker asking questions in a worried tone, and another answering with confidence:

> Does the road wind up-hill all the way?
>   Yes, to the very end.
> Will the day's journey take the whole long day?
>   From morn to night, my friend.

The question of **tone** in poetry simply concerns its emotional register, as when we talk of the "tone of voice" that a person uses in speech—sad, happy, angry, earnest, pleading, admiring, etc. Tone refers to the mood of the poem or to the tone of voice in which it might be delivered orally. In an oral context, tone is indicated by the inflections of the voice; on the printed page it is conveyed by the choice of vocabulary, by rhythm and sound, sometimes by the use of italics, exclamation marks, or other punctuation. Tone suggests the attitude of the speaker towards the subject of the poem, whether a character, an idea, a scene, an object, a place, etc. In Byron's "She Walks in Beauty," the speaker is clearly full of admiration for the woman described, in particular for the gentleness of both her physical appearance and her character:

> One shade the more, one ray the less,
>> Had half impaired the nameless grace
> Which waves in every raven tress,
>> Or softly lightens o'er her face;
> Where thoughts serenely sweet express
>> How pure, how dear their dwelling place.

The tone may change in the course of a poem, even several times in a long work, as the narrator's viewpoint develops or turns to different topics, or if there is more than one speaker, as in "Naming of Parts" (discussed above in the section on vocabulary, page 8). In this poem the two speakers are distinguished sharply by their respective tones: the sergeant business-like and down-to-earth, the narrator of the poem dreamy, and also expressing an **ironic** view of the sergeant. (For an explanation of **irony**, see the section on figurative language, page 16.)

Exercises on Speaker and Tone

1. Read Keats's "Ode on a Grecian Urn" (printed in appendix 2). Where and how do you detect the presence of a speaker?

2. Name a poem written in the first person where you feel that you personally can identify closely with the speaker.

3. Describe the tone of the following poems: "Acquainted with the Night" by Robert Frost, "To a Daughter Leaving Home" by Linda Pastan, "It is a beauteous evening" by William Wordsworth, "To His Coy Mistress" by Andrew Marvell (see appendix 2).

STRUCTURE

A good poem forms a whole entity with a definite **structure**. Many features of a poem combine to give it shape, including some of the elements we studied under "Versification," such as line-lengths, rhyme scheme, and the division into stanzas. One easy way to grasp the structure of a poem is to define its parts. Most poems can be divided into parts that reflect the development of its content—events, ideas, or emotions. Sometimes the parts correspond to formal features such as stanza-formation or rhyme scheme. For example, in "I wandered lonely as a cloud," the first stanza sets the scene, the second one emphasizes the sheer number of the daffodils, the third evokes their gaiety, in the eyes of the speaker, and the fourth concludes the poem, with a switch to the present tense, by suggesting how precious the memory of this experience has remained into the present.

The choice of **rhymes** (though often arbitrary) can play a structural role in a poem. We saw, for example, that in Petrarchan sonnets all the first eight lines share two rhymes, whereas the last six typically introduce a new "take" on the poem's theme, and with it, new rhymes. (This shift from the quatrains to the tercets is called a *turn*.) The rhyme scheme of a Shakespearean sonnet—*abab/cdcd/efef/gg*—often mirrors a similar division of thought in the poem's fourteen lines into groups of four/four/four/two. Shakespeare's "That time of year . . ." provides an excellent example.

In addition to these formal structures, poets organize poems in many less obvious ways, e.g.: by presenting parallel or opposite ideas in different sections of a poem; by progressing from the general to the particular, or vice versa; by posing and then answering a question; by syntactic divisions into phrases or sentences; by the progression of **images**; by the repetition of sounds, words, lines or phrases; and by giving a sense of conclusion at the end of the poem. In Shakespeare's "That time of year thou may'st in me behold," we see the imagery progress throughout the poem (though all the images relate to the central theme of the speaker's aging), moving from images of fall in the first four lines, to those of sunset in the next four, to the picture of a dying fire in the third quatrain, before concluding in the final two lines, addressed now in the second person to the beloved. The repetition of lines, grammatical structures, or words often helps to organize a poem, as in Robert Frost's "Acquainted with the night." The grammatical construction "I have" plus the past participle of a verb (e.g., "I have walked") repeats all through the first seven lines, but after line 7 (the middle of the poem) the construction does not appear again. This syntactic change is linked to the action of the poem: after line 7 the poem's "I" ceases to be as active as in the first half, where we read "I have walked . . . I have outwalked . . . looked . . . passed . . . dropped"; now, in the second half, the speaker stands still, listening.

Since a poem aims to be a whole, its ending should leave the reader with a feeling of completion, and poets have devised many ways of signaling closure other than simply reaching the end of the poem's material. The last line of "To a Daughter Leaving Home" brings the poem to an effective close with the word "goodbye" standing alone and reminding the reader of the title. Another way to mark the end is by repeating words, or a line, from the beginning of the poem. In "Acquainted with the night," the last line is the same as the first, "I have been one acquainted with the night," and it produces a sense of closure: the reader realizes at this point that the whole poem has been an illustration of that line. The line has a different impact at the end of the poem: the reader has learned of the speaker's unutterable sadness and loneliness and senses more strongly now than at the beginning all the negative implications of the word "night." Wordsworth's "I wandered lonely as a cloud" ends most appropriately with the important word "daffodils," and the impact of this concluding word is heightened by the alliteration of /d/ ("dances with the daffodils"). Furthermore, "daffodils" rhymes with "fills"—appropriately, since as we know the memory of the daffodils fills the speaker with joy. This rhyming couplet at the end of the poem also contributes to the sense of closure.

Other ways of concluding are for example to end with references to the close of day, sunset, or other phenomena that suggest finality. Surprise endings are also effective, as in Seamus Heaney's "Mid-Term Break." We have learned, in the poem, that there has been a death in the speaker's family, but only the last line reveals how young the dead brother was: "A four foot box, a foot for every year."

Structural devices of some kind are essential in **free verse**, given the absence (usually) of stanzas or a rhyme scheme. Long poems in free verse are often divided not into regular stanzas but into groups of lines resembling paragraphs in prose: verse paragraphs, you might say. T.S. Eliot's "The Love Song of J. Alfred Prufrock," for example, is split up in this way. Other ways of providing structure in free verse include varying the lengths of lines, syntactic divisions into sentences or phrases, and the repetition of words, images, phrases or grammatical forms. Consider Walt Whitman's "When I heard the learn'd astronomer":

> When I heard the learn'd astronomer,
> When the proofs, the figures, were ranged in columns before me,
> When I was shown the charts and diagrams, to add, divide, and
>   measure them,
> When I sitting heard the astronomer where he lectured with much
>   applause in the lecture-room,
> How soon unaccountable I became tired and sick, 5
> Till rising and gliding out I wander'd off by myself,
> In the mystical moist night-air, and from time to time,
> Look'd up in perfect silence at the stars.

You will have noticed that the repetition of phrases beginning "When" in the first four lines (which deal with the speaker's presence at a lecture featuring many "proofs," "figures," "charts and diagrams") contrasts with the total absence of such phrases in the last four, where the speaker, "tired and sick" of the lecture, has crept outside to enjoy the night air. Another formal indication of this thematic development is the contrast between the length of the first four lines and that of the last four. Thus, with the repetition of "When" (+verb) and the variation in line lengths, Whitman provides a structural framework that mirrors the development of ideas in the poem.

To summarize: the structural elements of a poem include certain aspects of versification (rhyme, line length, division into stanzas); syntactical devices (division into phrases or sentences); thematic parallels or oppositions; the progression of imagery; the repetition of sounds, words, lines, or grammatical forms; and devices that give a sense of closure.

Exercises on Structure

a)
> Death, be not proud, though some have callèd thee
> Mighty and dreadful, for thou art not so;
> For those whom thou think'st thou dost overthrow
> Die not, poor Death, nor yet canst thou kill me.
> From rest and sleep, which but thy pictures be, 5
> Much pleasure; then from thee much more must flow,
> And soonest our best men with thee do go,
> Rest of their bones, and soul's delivery.
> Thou art slave to fate, chance, kings, and desperate men,
> And dost with poison, war, and sickness dwell, 10

And poppy or charms can make us sleep as well
And better than thy stroke; why swell'st thou then?
One short sleep past, we wake eternally
And death shall be no more; Death, thou shalt die.

"Death, be not proud"
John Donne

1. Let us divide this poem into two parts, lines 1–8 and 9–14. How does the rhyme scheme support this division?
2. Do any syntactic elements (division into phrases or sentences) fit in with this division?
3. What thematic parallels or oppositions characterize the two parts?
4. What words, sounds or phrases are repeated? Do these repetitions help to structure the poem?
5. In Donne's day, the word "die" could rhyme with "eternally," as an eye-rhyme. What is the effect of this rhyming couplet at the end of the poem? Does the poem leave you with a sense of closure? Why (not)? Comment on the last phrase of the poem, "Death, thou shalt die."

CHAPTER 2

Writing a Close Reading of a Poem

PREPARING TO WRITE A CLOSE READING OF A POEM

Preparatory Reading

Do not attempt to write a close reading the day before the assignment is due! Allow yourself time to get acquainted with the poem. The more you read it, the more you will notice different aspects of it and pick out the effects of devices such as alliteration, rhythm and figurative language. Therefore, read the poem several times before beginning work. Reading aloud will help you hear rhythms and sounds. Make sure you understand the poem; if necessary, look words up in a dictionary. Remember what you read above (in the section on meter and syntax, pages 31–32) about word order in poems. Try **paraphrasing** the poem as if you were telling someone else what it's about. Consider the significance of the poem's title. Does the poem divide easily into parts?

Annotating the Poem

As you read, make notes in the margins or between the lines on any aspect of the poem that strikes you as interesting, remembering all the elements we have discussed—vocabulary, figurative language, sounds, rhythm, versification, tone, structure. These notes can take the form of highlighting, underlining, circling words or phrases, question marks, or marginal comments. Mark any stylistic features such as rhythmic patterns, images, repetitions of sounds or of words, and any structural devices or thematic parallels. Also, scan the poem if it is written in metrical verse and note the rhyme scheme. If necessary, make a photocopy of the poem rather than writing in your book. Alternatively, copy it out yourself: the action of writing out the poem will help draw your attention to details you might not notice when reading, such as punctuation or the way the poem is set out on the page and the relation of different parts of the poem to the overall structure. Use this copy to make notes on. You will be surprised how, each time you re-read the poem, you find more interesting points in it. The notes you make will form the basis of your close reading. The first poem of the model close readings below has been annotated in this way, as an example.

Audience

Consider the audience for whom you are writing. Generally speaking, you should assume that your reader knows the poem and has it available; you can therefore refer him/her to lines in the poem. No two explications are alike, however, so the person reading your work will no doubt have appreciated certain details of the poem differently from you. Present *your* reading of the poem, but without constantly saying "I feel this . . ." or "I think that . . . ." You are explicating the poem, pointing out its effects and the impression it makes on you, and of course your impression is somewhat subjective, but you don't need to keep pointing that out. (Notice that the present author, in the model readings offered below, did not find it necessary to use the first person at all.) You can simply say, "This beautiful metaphor introduces a note of optimism into the poem," rather than preceding the statement with "I feel that . . ." or "I think that . . .," unless you consider your impression to be substantially different from most readers', in which case you should explain why, and the use of "I" might then be appropriate. Beware, though, of reading things into a text: your interpretation must be *founded* on what is actually present in the poem, whether in the form of words or of sounds, rhythms, images, etc.

Quoting Titles

Use italics (or underlining) for the titles of works published independently, such as books and collections of poetry, e.g., *Leaves of Grass* by Walt Whitman. Use quotation marks for titles of individual poems (and also short stories or essays within a volume or collection), e.g., Byron's "She Walks in Beauty." Capitalize all letters in titles except those of short, unimportant words such as prepositions. Some poems do not have titles and are referred to by their first line, in which case you should capitalize only those words that have capitals in the first line, such as Whitman's "When I heard the learn'd astronomer."

Quoting From the Poem

When discussing a text, you will occasionally need to quote from it, briefly. (Avoid giving long quotes when you are working with a short piece, as you will be for a close reading.) Only use quotations to back up or illustrate the point you are making. There are a few simple rules for quoting texts in general and for poetry in particular. You should use quotation marks when quoting individual lines from a poem (unless the extract runs longer than four lines), and indicate the line number(s) in parentheses after your quotation. Mark the end of verse lines with a slash mark (/) with a space preceding and following it, thus: "She walks in beauty, like the night/Of cloudless climes and starry skies;/And all that's best of dark and bright/Meet in her aspect and her eyes" (1–4). Keep the punctuation exactly as in the original, except if you reach the end of your sentence. In Byron's poem a colon follows the word "eyes," but our sentence ended there and therefore a period was used. A quotation of more than four lines (which you probably will not need in a close reading) should start on a new line, indented one inch from your left-hand margin; quotation marks are not used. Then start a new line again to continue your own prose.

You may not change the wording of a quotation without signaling that you have done so. If you wish to omit some words, mark the omission with three spaced periods, thus: "Sundays too my father got up early/and put his clothes on in the blueblack cold,/ then with cracked hands that ached/... made/banked fires blaze." The syntax of the quote must fit in with the syntax of your sentence, so make sure that the verb tenses match and that singular subjects are not juxtaposed with plural verbs or vice versa. If there is a discrepancy, you have to find a way around it: either alter your sentence or edit the quote using square brackets ([ ]). For example, in the poem "Those Winter Sundays" just quoted, the speaker talks about his father polishing his shoes for him. He of course calls them "my ... shoes," but you should *not* write:

> The speaker says his father "polished my good shoes as well"

because if your subject is "the speaker," you need to say *his* shoes. You can write:

> The speaker says his father "polished [his] good shoes as well"

using square brackets to edit the word "my." Alternatively, you can displace the quotation marks and write:

> The speaker says his father polished his "good shoes."

Any of these alternatives is acceptable, but you may not alter words in a quotation without indicating that you have done so. Remember that you should use quotations selectively, as a way of reinforcing your interpretation of the poem, not as padding.

(For more information on integrating quotations, see part 4, "Moving Beyond Close Reading," pages 184–185.)

Paraphrasing

You may also **paraphrase** instead of quoting, thus:

> The speaker says his father polished his good shoes for him.

Paraphrasing simply means re-stating a phrase from a text in your own words, without quoting directly.

You should never resort to paraphrasing for its own sake, i.e., re-telling the poem's content: the person reading your work has read the poem and knows what it says. You should only paraphrase or quote lines in order to prove your point.

Clarity and Style

Write clearly. Do not try to incorporate learned-sounding words if you are not sure of their meaning. It is better to be simple, clear, and straightforward than convoluted and obscure. Re-read your own work. Reading it aloud may help you find problematic areas; if it doesn't make sense to you, it won't to another reader.

WRITING A CLOSE READING OF A POEM

Title

When you write an interpretive essay on a piece of literature, you need to find a title that reflects your argument in the essay (see part 4, "Moving Beyond Close Reading"). With a close reading, however, that is less necessary, since you are basically just explicating what the poem says and how it says it. Therefore, a title such as "A Close Reading of John Donne's 'Death, be not proud,'" or simply the poem's title, seems sufficient—though you could if you wished invent a more original title highlighting the poem's theme or salient features.

Introduction

Your detailed analysis should always be preceded by an introduction. The introduction serves to give information about the poem as a whole rather than comments on any individual line, word, or figure of speech. The introduction should, if possible, situate the poem in the poet's works and perhaps mention briefly the circumstances in which it was composed—but only if that has some relevance to the content of the poem. If the poem has a title, its significance can be discussed here or at the beginning of the detailed analysis. The introduction should also state the **theme** of the poem and describe its **tone**, say whether it can be divided into parts (this often aids in the interpretation of a poem) and mention its overall **versification**: meter and rhyme scheme, if any, and division into stanzas where appropriate. (All these features concern the poem as a whole: more detailed remarks concerning the effects of rhyme, sounds or rhythm in specific passages will be left for the body of the analysis.) An **epigraph** (a short quote from some other work placed at the head of the poem) forms part of the poem and should be commented on either in the introduction or at the beginning of the analysis. Epigraphs generally contain some thought that is relevant to the poem in hand and sheds some light on its meaning.

In order to situate the poem in the poet's works you need to know the title of the collection in which it appeared, and if possible the date of its publication. If you do not have this information—in an exam, for example—simply give the poem's title and the name of the poet, with an approximate date if possible. Again, if you know nothing of the circumstances of its composition, that is not essential, and indeed you should not weigh down your introduction with superfluous information. Avoid outlining the poet's complete biography; only mention any facts that directly concern the poem. For example, in a commentary on Wordsworth's poem about daffodils, you might mention in the introduction that Wordsworth often walked in the countryside and that he wrote about nature in many of his poems.

The **theme** of a poem can often be summarized in a sentence or two. In a purely descriptive poem, the theme might be that description itself, for its own sake, but more often the theme will consist of an idea or an emotion. Ask yourself what the poem is really *about*. Sometimes the theme is not what the poem talks about most of the time; thus in Linda Pastan's "To a Daughter Leaving Home," quoted in the section on vocabulary, page 8 (and in appendix 2), the whole poem describes teaching a young girl to ride a bicycle, but it is apparent, from the last two lines and the title, that the theme is more like: the pain of saying goodbye. The title is often crucial in establishing the theme, as in Pastan's poem; consider also Tennyson's "The Eagle," where the title is again vitally important, since the bird is not mentioned in the two stanzas of the poem.

Tone refers simply to the mood of the poem or to the tone of voice in which it would be delivered orally. The tone can be, for example, happy or sad, thoughtful or lively, serious or lighthearted, humorous, ironic, or deadpan. The tone of a poem can vary from one stanza or section to another; such changes should be indicated, along with the reason for them, either in the introduction or, if the changes are numerous, in the course of the analysis.

Finally (though these topics may be treated in any order), the introduction should describe the overall structure of the poem: its **versification** (number of stanzas, meter, rhyme scheme, etc.) or its free-verse characteristics, and its division into parts, where appropriate.

You may prefer to delay writing an introduction until you have completed the close reading, since certain aspects of the poem's theme or tone, for example, may become apparent only when you have analyzed the poem in detail.

Detailed Analysis

After the introduction, once you begin on the detailed analysis section of your close reading, you should proceed line by line, or perhaps stanza by stanza in a poem with very short lines. You should look simultaneously for any of the elements discussed above: interesting vocabulary, repeated words, effects of rhythm and sound; suggestions as to how any formal aspects of the poem such as meter, rhyme, or stanza-formation affect the poem or reinforce its sense; the impact of the imagery and of any figures of speech; the identity of the speaker and the way the tone of the poem is achieved; structural devices and whether they reinforce the poem's meaning—in other words, all the features we have examined above. These elements can be mentioned in any order, as you come across examples of them reading through the poem line by line. Try to keep all these aspects in mind (there is a summary below to which you can refer), but remember that not all poems will contain examples of every feature! Some poems contain no metaphors or other figures of speech (which might in itself be worth commenting on, since it suggests a desire to use very plain language), others might have no rhyme or alliterative effects. If certain effects are reproduced more than once, you can group them together; for example, if a word is repeated, you need to mention that fact only once, either at the first repetition or the second, whatever fits best into your essay. Remember that when you comment on any feature, e.g., the presence of a metaphor, you should always analyze what it contributes, in your view, to the poem. Does it embellish the poem or give it depth? Does it introduce, by association, some related idea or theme? Not all effects are successful: if you think a metaphor is weak or inappropriate in some way, for example, you should say so, but explain why.

Group your remarks into paragraphs. You may find that one paragraph per stanza works, or you may feel that certain remarks hang together but others belong in a separate paragraph, even though you are still dealing with the same stanza. Use the model close readings in the next section as a guide.

Beware of trying to devote one paragraph to metaphors, one to rhythm or alliteration, and so on. Remember that all the elements at any one point in a poem tend to combine to produce an effect related to the sense—and these effects will differ in different parts of a poem. You want to explain how, for example, rhythms and sounds in one place contribute to the overall impression created there. Elsewhere, rhythms and sounds will be put to different use, and you will comment on them when you come to them. Hence the need to proceed line by line. Try to avoid, however, beginning each sentence "In the next line . . ." or "In the next stanza . . . ." This would make your essay seem very mechanistic and boring to read.

Conclusion

When you have arrived in your analysis at the last lines of the poem and commented on those, don't stop there! You need to complete your close reading, like any essay, with a conclusion, which will leave behind the detailed analysis you have been doing and look at the poem in a more general way.

The conclusion should present a broad view of the poem. You can give your overall appreciation of it and say whether you think the poet achieved the aims he seems to have set himself. (You might find a poem successful, in this sense, even if it doesn't appeal to you personally.) Does the poem strike you as original, imaginative, amusing, profound, moving, richly descriptive? Using evidence from your own analysis of the poem, give your reasons for liking or disliking it. If you know other poems by the same poet, you could compare this poem to them, or comment on its significance in the author's work as a whole. You can also compare this poem to one by a different poet on a similar theme or with a similar mood. Or you can situate the poem in its historical and literary context, explaining whether it is typical of its times or seems to announce a future trend.

Revision

You should complete the first draft of your close reading with enough time left for revision and editing. When revising your work, look at its content and organization. You know what you mean to say in your paper, but will another reader be able to follow it? Are your arguments clear? Have you used quotations from the text to back up your points? Remembering that your task is to analyze and explicate the poem, make sure you have avoided paraphrasing, i.e., simply re-stating the poem's content in your own words. Check that your essay is suitably divided into paragraphs and that transitions are smooth and logical. Do not forget to include an introduction and a conclusion that stand apart from the line-by-line analysis.

In order to check the **style** of your work, it can be helpful to read it aloud; then if anything sounds awkward or unnatural, you will be more likely to notice it. If it sounds awkward to you, it certainly will to your reader, so make any necessary changes. Examine your choice of words: avoid colloquialisms, but do not try to use highly sophisticated vocabulary unless you are sure of being able to handle it accurately. Avoid wordiness for its own sake: make sure all your sentences add something to your essay. Try to incorporate some variety into the structure of your sentences. Finally, proofread your paper for errors of spelling, punctuation and grammar. Check that any quotations you have used match the syntax of your own sentences.

Avoiding Plagiarism

It goes without saying that your close reading should be your own work. It may be considered appropriate to discuss poems with your peers, or with a professor, before you begin writing; you might read your essay, before drawing up your final draft, to a person who could offer suggestions for improvement; but to allow anyone else to compose your paper for you would be a violation of academic integrity. Copying another writer's thoughts, whether from a book or the internet, without acknowledging the fact, constitutes an act of plagiarism. It is both dishonest and unfair to the original author. The internet provides

an easy resource for copying the work of others; but if your aim is to learn how to analyze texts yourself, then copying someone else's work is a waste of your time as well as
being dishonest. It can also lead to grave consequences: most schools have strict poli-
cies regarding plagiarism, which can lead to a failing grade or suspension.

If you are writing a research paper you will need to quote from secondary sources
and should always acknowledge them (see part 4, "Moving Beyond Close Reading,");
but for a close reading you should not need secondary sources at all. Your aim is to give
your appreciation of the poem, your "reading" of it.

Summary of Elements to Discuss in a Poem

I Introduction

a) situate poem in author's works, if possible, or define the era when it was written
b) overall **theme** (remember the title) and **tone**
c) **versification** (meter, line-length, rhyme scheme, free verse?) and **structure**
(stanzas, parts, refrain?)

II Detailed Analysis, Proceeding Through the Poem Line by Line

(These elements can be treated in any order, depending how they come up in
the poem. Several features may not be present at all.)

a) vocabulary (abstract, concrete, formal, colloquial, lyrical, dramatic?)
b) **imagery** (How does it develop throughout the poem? Keep in mind all the
senses, not just images based on sight.)
c) **figures of speech** (simile, metaphor, apostrophe, paradox, symbol, irony,
etc.) (Why are they used, in your view? What do they add to the poem?)
d) sounds (repetition, rhyme, alliteration, assonance)
e) **rhythm** (long, slow, fast, flowing, quick, jerky?)
f) any special effects of **versification** (metrical rhythm) or **enjambment**
g) syntax (word-order, imperatives, exclamations, questions, punctuation,
tenses)
h) rhetorical situation (speaker, addressee)
i) **tone** (emotional, matter-of-fact, didactic, sad, happy, remorseful, nostalgic?)
(You may need to go into more detail than in the introduction to your close
reading.)
j) structuring devices (vertical/horizontal, spiritual/physical, inner/outer,
light/dark; opening and closure of the poem)

III Conclusion

a) overall appreciation of poem and any relevant remarks of a general nature.
b) significance of poem, link with other works or with literary era, if possible or
relevant.

CHAPTER 3

Close Readings of Poems

In this section you will find, first of all, four examples of close readings, i.e., readings that are fairly complete, but which should be regarded as models rather than definitive versions. No reading is ever complete or perfect, since every reader interprets a poem in his or her own way, emphasizing different elements. After the models, you will find eight poems with questions designed to help you write close readings of your own. You will not be expected to write on all of these but should select as many as you feel are useful, or your professor assigns. You may eventually be asked to compose questions of your own, on a new poem, to offer to your fellow students. Finally, you will move on to writing a close reading of a new poem without questions to guide you.

The four model close readings offered here are of very different poems: a seventeenth-century sonnet by John Donne, a poem in free verse by Walt Whitman, and two twentieth-century poems by Seamus Heaney and Robert Hayden.

The text of "Death, be not proud" illustrates the kinds of notes and comments you might make in the margin or between the lines when first reading a poem, before expanding these notes into the first draft of your essay.

The final close reading, on Robert Hayden's "Those Winter Sundays," is followed by a commentary pointing out features of the reading you might want to keep in mind when tackling your own explication.

MODEL CLOSE READINGS

1. "Death be not proud" (1633)

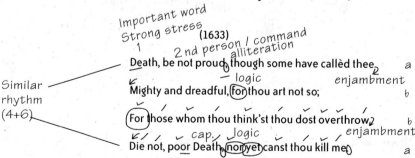

(4+6)   *(only)*
From rest and sleep, which but thy pictures be,   *a*   5
     logic
Much pleasure; then from thee much more must flow,   *b*

And soonest our best men with thee do go,   *b*
   death=rest
(4+6)   Rest of their bones, and soul's delivery.   *a* // *turn*

Thou art slave to fate, chance, kings, and desperate men,   *c*
     negative ...
concrete vocab.   And dost with poison, war, and sickness dwell,   *d*   10

More confident tone   And poppy or charms can make us sleep as well   *d*
     (pride)
And better than thy stroke; why swell'st thou then?   *c*

     alliteration
confident   One short sleep past, we wake eternally   *e* } *couplet*
     paradox   *(eye rhyme)*
And death shall be no more; Death, thou shalt die.   *e*
     1st word of poem, Same rhythm, same alliteration

John Donne (1572–1631)

One of the "Holy Sonnets" of John Donne, this poem was published posthumously, like most of his work, a few years after his death in 1631. Donne, ordained in the Church of England, often wrote on religious themes (though he is also famous for his love poetry); in "Death, be not proud," he proclaims with conviction his belief in a life after death and makes a logical argument of his case for the benefit of the reader. He addresses Death in a confident, even triumphant tone. Like most traditional sonnets, this one is composed in iambic pentameter. Structurally it is of the Petrarchan type, with two **quatrains** sharing rhymes, followed by a **sestet**, and with an overall rhyme scheme *abbaabbacddcee*. As suggested by this pattern of rhymes, the first two quatrains are closely connected in thought, as in most Petrarchan sonnets, while lines 9–14 introduce a slight change of tone and emphasis. The rhymes of the sestet have been arranged to end with a rhyming **couplet**, as in a Shakespearean sonnet, in order to provide a neat conclusion to the poem's argument.

The first words of the poem, "Death, be not proud," affect the reader very forcefully. "Death" is a striking word with which to open a poem, and it receives a stress that goes contrary to the basic iambic rhythm, thus emphasizing it even more. The word's importance is further reinforced by the alliteration of the sound /d/ at the beginning and end of this little phrase ("*D*eath, be not prou*d*"). The speaker addresses Death directly—as he will throughout the poem—with an apostrophe reinforced by a command ("be not proud"). The direct address to "Death" in the second person makes the speaker's argument seem more immediate and compelling. An echo of the alliteration of /d/ in the opening phrase continues in lines 1–2 ("callèd," "dreadful"), and the enjambment between lines 1 and 2 has the effect of emphasizing the important word "Mighty" at the beginning of the second line—again reinforced by a stress on the first syllable, as in line 1. A similar enjambment can be observed in lines 3–4, where the whole of line 3—now settled into iambic rhythm—builds up to the crucial statement "Die not." With this seemingly paradoxical statement ("For those whom thou think'st thou dost overthrow / Die not"), the speaker affirms his belief in the immortality of the soul; and he expects to know life after death himself: "nor yet canst thou kill me." Therefore he applies the adjective "poor" to "Death," who is, after all, powerless. The capitalization of the word "Death" makes death seem more like a person, reinforcing the apostrophe of the first line (and the whole poem). The four words of the phrase "Die not, poor Death" are again linked by an alliteration of /d/, recalling the first four words of the poem; these lines 1 and 4 are unified also by a very similar rhythm: four syllables followed by a comma and then the six remaining syllables. It is interesting to note the variety in the rhythm of the first quatrain: lines 1 and 4 have four syllables followed by six, whereas line 2 is divided into two equal halves, and line 3 is all of a piece, with no divisions. The rest of the poem also presents many rhythmic variations among its iambic pentameters, usually marked by punctuation.

To reinforce his persuasive strategy, Donne uses several logical connectors in these lines—conjunctions such as "for" meaning *because* (lines 2 and 3), "nor yet" (line 4), "then" meaning *therefore* (line 6)—that serve to structure his argument. The second quatrain expands on the argument of the opening lines, with a reasoning that again seems both paradoxical and logical. Since "rest" and "sleep," mere images of death (the word "but" in line 5 has the sense of "only"), give man pleasure, then death itself, a greater power, must lead to even greater pleasure ("then from thee much more must flow"). According to line 7, the best people die early and therefore experience sooner the release from toil ("Rest of their bones") and freedom from care ("soul's delivery") associated with life after death—a view which may seem paradoxical, but which accords with Christian doctrine concerning heavenly bliss. The punning use of the word "delivery" conjures up a vision of the soul being delivered into a new life like a baby into this life. Donne, and the other Metaphysical poets, frequently used puns and other plays on words.

Again the first and fourth lines of this quatrain are linked, as in the first quatrain: by the repetition of the word "rest" and by the division of the lines into four syllables followed by six, as in lines 1 and 4. Line 7, like line 3, has no pauses. Altogether, the rhythmic pattern of lines 5–8 closely resembles that of the first four lines. The syntax of lines 5–8 is very compressed: a verb such as "comes" has been omitted from lines 5–6 ("From rest and sleep . . . [comes] / Much pleasure"); and the whole of line 8 is in apposition to the word "thee" in line 7 (i.e. "thee" = Death = "Rest of their bones, and soul's delivery").

The "turn" from the octave to the sestet in a Petrarchan sonnet often accompanies a shift in meaning or emphasis. Here we see changes in vocabulary, rhythm, and tone. The vocabulary of lines 1–8 is singularly abstract, as befits a logical argument concerning life and death: "Death," "rest," "sleep," "pleasure," "soul," and "delivery" are all abstract nouns, accompanied by equally abstract adjectives such as "proud," "Mighty," and "dreadful." Lines 9–12, however, present more concrete words ("kings," "desperate men," "poison," "war," "poppy," "charms"), as the poet offers specific examples of Death's masters and of sleep-inducing agents. We also find a more staccato rhythm here, especially in line 9 with its many commas, and a more aggressive tone ("Thou art slave . . . " " . . . why swell'st thou then?"). The argument against Death is building up: it has no reason to be proud since it is "slave to fate, chance . . . " etc. In other words, Death can only strike when fate and chance or kings and "desperate men" conspire to create situations that cause men to die. The word "slave" here has a very negative connotation, as does Death's association with "poison, war, and sickness." Lines 10, 11, and 12 all begin with "And," giving the impression of an accumulation of arguments illustrating Death's powerlessness. Lines 11–12 argue that poppies (from which opium is made, that induces sleep) and charms (magic spells) can send us to sleep just as well as Death's "stroke"; so why should Death be proud? The phrase "why swell'st thou then?" recalls the expression "to swell with pride" and thus refers back neatly to the poem's opening line, "Death, be not proud."

Having proved, through the logical arguments of lines 1–12, that Death has no cause to be proud and is in fact powerless, Donne neatly summarizes his view of death in the last two lines of the sonnet, a rhyming couplet (in Donne's day, words ending in –ie, like "die" could rhyme—even if only for the eye—with words ending in –y like "eternally"). In accordance with Christian doctrine, the speaker maintains that after death "we wake eternally" at the Last Judgment. The alliteration of /s/ and the four monosyllabic words at the beginning of line 13 seem to emphasize the brevity of the "short sleep"; the phrase "we wake eternally" is bound together by the repetition of the /w/ and /i:/ sounds in "we," "wake," and "eternally." The tone of these last two lines is confident. The poem ends with a strikingly paradoxical statement, "Death, thou shalt die"; but the arguments of the preceding lines showing death's powerlessness, and the reference to eternal life and therefore the end of death in lines 13–14, make this paradox perfectly acceptable. The last four words mirror beautifully the opening of the poem, with the repetition of the address to "Death" followed by a comma, the identical rhythm ("Death, be not proud," "Death, thou shalt die"), and the same alliteration of the sound /d/. This phrase, "Death, thou shalt die," with its echo of the poem's beginning, provides a very satisfying ending to the poem, and a striking one that is likely to be preserved in the reader's memory.

This is a remarkably well-structured poem: each quatrain, and the final couplet, forms a single sentence; rhythmic parallels and identical rhymes link the first two quatrains together; and the poem's final words echo the opening phrase, with the same alliterative effect. Such an organized structure suits the poem's logical argument and didactic intent (the narrator no doubt seeks to convince others, as he himself is convinced, of the soul's immortality and therefore of the powerlessness of death). Given an underlying faith in the immortality of the soul, the arguments presented in this poem, though paradoxical at first glance, are convincing, and culminate in the triumphant affirmation of the last line: "Death, thou shalt die."

2. "When I heard the learn'd astronomer" (1865)

When I heard the learn'd astronomer,
When the proofs, the figures, were ranged in columns before me,
When I was shown the charts and diagrams, to add, divide, and
    measure them,
When I sitting heard the astronomer where he lectured with much
    applause in the lecture-room,
How soon unaccountable I became tired and sick,   5
Till rising and gliding out I wander'd off by myself,
In the mystical moist night-air, and from time to time,
Look'd up in perfect silence at the stars.

Walt Whitman (1819–1892)

Walt Whitman, a nineteenth-century American poet, was one of the first to write in free verse. The lines of "When I heard the learn'd astronomer" are clearly not subject to rules of meter: they are all of different lengths—with lines 3 and 4 being very long indeed—though all can be spoken with one breath, as is usual with lines of free verse. The theme of the poem concerns the narrator's preference for being alone in a natural setting as opposed to hearing a lecture about astronomy. The tone—like the vocabulary—is very matter-of-fact at the beginning but becomes more reflective at the end of the poem.

The first three lines of the poem present a sequence of words associated with a rather dry, abstract type of learning: "proofs," "figures," "columns," "charts," "diagrams." The "learn'd astronomer" offers this kind of material in his lecture, while inviting his audience to "add, divide, and measure." It is noticeable that the first four lines of the poem gradually increase in length, as if to illustrate the idea of a steady accumulation of facts and figures; or perhaps to suggest the increasing boredom of the poem's narrator as he feels the lecture will never come to an end. For although the astronomer's talk is well received ("with much applause") by the audience, the speaker of the poem becomes bored ("tired and sick" as he says in line 5) and leaves the room. The repetition of "lecture-room" after "lectured" in line 4 further stresses the negative connotations of the idea of lecturing.

Apart from their steady increase in length, another salient feature of the first four lines is the use of anaphora: lines 1, 3, and 4 all begin "When I . . . ." This figure has the effect of building up the reader's expectations; we are interested in knowing what will happen to the speaker next after this preamble. Also, this device serves to distinguish the first four lines of the poem from the next four. The whole poem forms one sentence, but it is clearly divided into two parts: the first half contains the repeated "When I . . . " construction, which disappears in the next lines; and the first four lines get progressively longer until line 4 is extremely long; whereas the last four are shorter and all much the same length. Other differences accompany the division into two parts: the verbs concerning the speaker in the first four lines are all passive: not "I listened to" which would be more active, but "I heard" (line 1), "I was shown" (line 3), and "I sitting heard" (line 4). The only active verb concerns the lecturer rather than the narrator: "he lectured" (line 4). In the second half the verbs concerning the narrator are active: "I became" (line 5) and especially "I wander'd off" (line 6) and "Look'd up" (line 8). Furthermore, in the first half he is with other people, indoors, and it is noisy ("much applause," line 4) whereas in the last four lines he is alone ("by myself," line 6), outside, and it is quiet ("silence," line 8).

Line 5 provides a transition explaining why the narrator felt the need to leave the lecture. The word "unaccountable" is grammatically puzzling: one would expect the adverb "unaccountably" ("For some reason that I don't understand"), and the reader tends to read that meaning into the word; yet in fact we have the adjective "unaccountable," which can only apply to the narrator (the "I" of line 5). Perhaps he wishes to suggest that whereas the astronomer counts and gives accounts, as illustrated in lines 1–3, the narrator himself is un-accountable, an entity that cannot be reduced to "proofs" and "figures." The present participles "rising" and, especially, "gliding" suggest the discreet, quiet way in which he makes his exit from the room. Alone now, he rejoices in the "mystical moist night-air": a more spiritual pleasure replaces the pleasure one might take in a lecture. The sense of enjoyment and of mystery is heightened by the strong alliteration of /m/ in this line. In the final line, the alliteration of /s/ links the words "silence" and "stars" in a way that suggests that silence belongs to the stars or to nature, as opposed to the noisiness associated with men in the first half of the poem. The lecturer talked about stars, to "much applause," but the narrator prefers to look at them. The word "perfect" accentuates the silence, but implies also that this moment of solitude, in nature, beneath the stars, constitutes for the narrator a moment of perfection.

One of the first poets to use free verse, Whitman became a master of the form, as this poem demonstrates. "When I heard the learn'd astronomer" is an extremely well-organized poem, despite the free-verse form. Its two halves are contrasted both formally and thematically in many ways. Moreover, by the subtle use of devices such as anaphora and alliteration, and by his choice of vocabulary, the poet manages to convince the reader that a mystical, solitary appreciation of nature is preferable to factual knowledge.

3. "Mid-Term Break" (1966)

I sat all morning in the college sick-bay
Counting bells knelling classes to a close.
At two-o'clock our neighbours drove me home.

In the porch I met my father crying—
He had always taken funerals in his stride—   5
And Big Jim Evans saying it was a hard blow.

The baby cooed and laughed and rocked the pram
When I came in, and I was embarrassed
By old men standing up to shake my hand

And tell me they were "sorry for my trouble,"   10
Whispers informed strangers I was the eldest,
Away at school, as my mother held my hand

In hers and coughed out angry tearless sighs.
At ten o'clock the ambulance arrived
With the corpse, stanched and bandaged by the nurses.   15

Next morning I went up into the room. Snowdrops
And candles soothed the bedside; I saw him
For the first time in six weeks. Paler now,

Wearing a poppy bruise on his left temple,
He lay in the four foot box as in his cot.   20
No gaudy scars, the bumper knocked him clear.

A four foot box, a foot for every year.

Seamus Heaney (b. 1939)

The author of "Mid-Term Break," Seamus Heaney, a well-known Irish poet, often writes about Ireland in his work, but this particular poem could take place in any country. It concerns the tragic death of the speaker's little brother while the speaker himself was away at school, and it is no doubt based on personal experience, since the poet's own brother died when he was young. The title, "Mid-Term Break," is bitterly ironic: a break from school is usually a joyful occasion, but here it represents a forced break—the speaker is going home for a funeral.

The poem's tone is interesting: the speaker merely records a description of events as they occur—his waiting, the homecoming, his parents' and neighbors' reactions, and finally a physical description of the dead child. He never mentions his own emotion. The style is simple and direct, not colloquial, but with a fairly everyday vocabulary and syntax.

The poem is written in tercets—seven groups of three lines, with one extra, separate line at the end. Unlike traditional terza rima, however, these lines do not rhyme, except for the last two lines. The basic meter is iambic pentameter, though there are many variations.

The first line suggests the tedium of waiting; the heavy stresses on the first four syllables emphasize the lengthiness of the time: "I sat all morning." Under the circumstances, he is not expected to attend classes and has been taken to the sick bay to wait. His sense of gloom and boredom is again apparent in line 2; all he can do is count the bells signaling the end of classes. The sounds in these two lines are heavy with repetitions of /b/ and /k/, which convey his heaviness of spirit, along with the assonance of /e/ in "bells" and "knelling." This last word at once suggests a funeral bell and the idea of an ending: not only are classes coming to a close, but a life. The mention of "two o'clock" in line 3 again implies that time has dragged for the boy. Nevertheless, at this point in the poem the reader does not yet know why.

The fact that the boy's father is crying in stanza 2, despite the fact that he had "always taken funerals in his stride," gives us a clue that a death has taken place. No doubt the boy has rarely, if ever, seen his father cry and it is a shock to him. Similarly, the name "Big Jim Evans" implies a "manly" attitude not normally given to sentiment. We see the speaker moving inwards from the porch, entering the house, meeting people, and noting various things, but in a somewhat haphazard way, as if he were too dazed to make sense of his surroundings. When he finally comes indoors he sees the baby, who apparently recognizes him, is pleased to see him, and of course does not understand what is going on: "The baby cooed and laughed and rocked the pram." This line is a regular iambic pentameter, one of few in the poem: lines 3, lines 13–14, and the last line are the only others. It is as if the pent-up emotion of this poem could not be contained in a regular meter. But the baby rocks the pram, unaware of this emotion. Given the situation, it is ironic that the speaker should be greeted in this joyful way.

Being a young boy, the speaker is embarrassed at being the center of attention when old men shake his hand and mutter that they are "sorry." Now that he has come in from the porch, through the throng of neighbors, whom he hears whispering as he goes past, the boy finally reaches his mother. Perhaps the idea of being "the eldest" gives him a feeling of responsibility towards her; at any rate, she "held his hand" both perhaps to comfort him and to give herself strength. The enjambment here from one stanza to the next, with "held my hand" at the end of line 12 and "In hers" at the beginning of the next line, seems to emphasize the closeness of the mother-son relationship. Of course the mother is suffering beyond endurance; unable even to cry, she "coughed out angry tearless sighs." This impression of dry anger is underscored by the progression of hard consonants: /d/, /t/, /g/, /t/, /s/.

Line 14 once again contains an allusion to time: "At ten o'clock the ambulance arrived" (another regular iambic pentameter); the speaker is stressing the inordinate length of this terrible day that began for him with his waiting all morning in the school sick bay. The first real mention of death comes in the following line, with its brutal reference to a "corpse," though the reader still does not know whose corpse this is.

In the next two stanzas the speaker is finally able to confront the "corpse" and concentrate on his own reaction to the tragedy. Nevertheless, there is no outpouring of grief: maintaining the restraint that has characterized the poem's understated tone up to now, the speaker continues to describe what he sees, but the reader senses the suppressed emotion behind the words. Alone with the dead boy in a bedroom, the first thing the speaker notices is that "Snowdrops / And candles soothed the bedside." The verb "soothed" (a personification) makes the reader see how the white flowers and the candles with their steady flames might indeed produce a peaceful, soothing effect. The whiteness of snowdrops and candles is a symbol of the purity of the dead child. He is literally white, too— "Paler now"—with the pallor of death, which makes the "poppy bruise" stand out even more vividly. (The dead boy is "Paler" than when his brother last saw him—six weeks ago because the older boy has been away at school; one can imagine how he was looking forward to seeing his brother again, alive, at the end of term or during a genuine "mid-term break.") Bruises are normally purple, but this one is more red (poppies are bright red), no doubt because it is so recent, or because the blood is still fresh in the wound. The contrast between the white snowdrops and red poppy is very striking. The word "Wearing" almost makes the "poppy bruise" seem, ironically, like a decoration. However, there are no "gaudy scars"—gashes or huge cuts—since "the bumper knocked him clear," a phrase that tells us how this child was killed, and helps to explain that the mother experienced anger as well as grief. Line 20 adds a note of pathos, "He lay in the four foot box as in his cot," telling us that the dead child was still young enough to sleep in a cot [crib].

This poignancy emerges even more from the final line, "A four foot box, a foot for every year." The dead brother was only four years old. The only one that does not form part of a tercet, this line is separated from all the others, so that it is very strongly emphasized. The alliteration of /f/ stresses the words and increases their impact, as does the rhyme ("clear/year") in the last two lines, since these are the only ones in the whole poem that rhyme. This rhyme helps to give a sense of conclusion to the poem, and all these devices contribute towards conveying the speaker's pity and sadness even though he uses not one emotional word in these last lines.

The controlled use of understatement is a characteristic and highly effective feature of this poem. Rather than exclaiming or using words associated with grief, the speaker concentrates on describing what happens and what he sees. Nevertheless, the reader senses his bewilderment and sorrow at the death of his little brother even more strongly than if he had expressed his emotions more directly. Our sense of the poignancy of this premature death culminates in the final line that establishes the child's age, not directly, but by comparing it to the length of the coffin. The impact of the poem is also enhanced by the poet's masterful control of sound and rhythm, imagery, and symbolism. Though this poem may be rooted in the poet's personal experience, its impact is universal as it evokes so effectively the grief and anguish resulting from the unnecessary death of a child.

4. "Those Winter Sundays" (1966)

> Sundays too my father got up early
> and put his clothes on in the blueblack cold,
> then with cracked hands that ached

from labor in the weekday weather made
banked fires blaze. No one ever thanked him.   5

I'd wake and hear the cold splintering, breaking.
When the rooms were warm, he'd call,
and slowly I would rise and dress,
fearing the chronic angers of that house,

Speaking indifferently to him,   10
who had driven out the cold
and polished my good shoes as well.
What did I know, what did I know
of love's austere and lonely offices?

Robert Hayden (1913–1980)

Robert Hayden, writing in the second half of the twentieth century, has composed "Those Winter Sundays" in free verse: the lines are of different (though similar) lengths, without metrical rhythm, and instead of beginning with a capital letter, the verse lines have capitals only at the beginning of a new sentence ("When the rooms were warm . . . ") or a new group of lines ("Speaking indifferently . . . "). However, this nod towards prosaic form (suitable no doubt for the prosaic actions depicted) is counterbalanced by the use of many poetic devices that accentuate the poem's main theme: the speaker's regret at never having appreciated his father's love. The tone of the poem is fairly matter-of-fact, mostly describing various actions, until the anguished question of the last two lines. Divided into three parts, the poem moves from enumerating the father's actions on past Sunday mornings in the first group of lines, to the speaker's actions as a child or adolescent in the second, while the third part describes the interaction (or lack of it) between them back at that time and the speaker's awareness now of the father's devotion and his own ingratitude.

The poem gives no definite indication as to whether the speaker is male or female, though the author is a man and could be writing about his own boyhood. The only other slight indication comes in line 12, which refers to the father polishing the speaker's shoes; since men's and boys' shoes tend to get polished more than women's, the reader might suppose the speaker is male. Recognizing that this evidence is not definitive, we will refer to the speaker as "he" only in order to avoid repetition of "he/she" and "his/her."

The word "Those" in the poem's title at once indicates that the speaker is referring to specific Sundays in the past, while the word "Winter" sets the tone for the cold evoked throughout the poem. According to the first line, his father got up early every day, even on Sundays ("Sundays too"); and the next lines explain why he got up early on Sundays in winter—to light the fires that would warm the house for everyone else. The idea of extreme cold is introduced by the striking expression "blueblack cold." Blue and black are cold colors, and make you think of hands being blue with cold, and the alliteration of the harsh sound /k/ at the end of one word and the beginning of the next, making them difficult to pronounce and echoing the /k/ in "clothes" earlier in the line, emphasizes the harshness of the weather. This alliteration continues in the following line ("cracked," "ached"), effectively evoking the idea of cold again, while the word "cracked" also echoes the sounds of "black" in "blueblack." One can feel the difficulty of dressing with fingers aching from the cold, and the next lines make explicit the pain in the father's hands, that "ached / from labor in the weekday weather." Apparently the father worked outdoors on weekdays, and so the skin on his hands is "cracked." The words "weekday" and "weather" are joined by the repetition of the /w/ sound, which might also remind the reader of the word "winter" in the title. Despite the pain in his hands, the father lit fires, or rather "made / banked fires blaze": in other words, he opened up a fire in a stove or furnace that had been damped down overnight. The vocabulary in this section, as in most of the poem, is very concrete and commonplace: words and phrases such as "got up early," "put his clothes on," "cracked hands," "labor," "cold," and, later, "polished . . . shoes" suggest an everyday environment.

The internal rhyme in line 5 between "banked" and "thanked" links these two words, but in a negative way: the father should have been thanked for making the fire blaze, but "No one ever thanked him." Apparently there were other family members apart from the speaker, but all equally ungrateful. The shortness of this sentence after the long preceding one gives it greater impact—appropriately since it provides the first clue as to the real theme of the poem.

The second stanza (or verse paragraph, since a "stanza" normally implies a group of lines with the same rhythm and rhyme scheme) contains four lines, as opposed to five in the first and third groups, which gives symmetry to the poem's form. Now the speaker turns to his own actions on these winter mornings—presumably when he was a child or a teenager—using the first person now rather than the third as in lines 1–5, so that the reader begins to realize that the poem's theme relates more to the son's feelings than to the father's actions. The verb forms "I'd wake," "he'd call," and "I would rise and dress" indicate the habitual nature of these actions. On waking—much later than his father—the speaker hears the cold "splintering, breaking"—an auditory image that perhaps represents the sounds of icicles cracking outside as the day warms up, or of some creaking noises within the house caused by the spreading warmth of the fire. The next line again contains alliteration of /w/ ("When," "were," "warm"), and this repetition of the initial sound of the word "warm" emphasizes the idea of warmth, so crucial in the poem. The vocabulary and imagery of the whole poem are divided between warmth and cold: here we have the "cold splintering, breaking"; the first group of lines mentions "blueblack cold" and the father's "cracked hands"; and in line 11 the "cold" is evoked again, though it has been "driven out" by the warmth of the "banked fires" of line 5 that are now blazing and making the rooms "warm" (line 7). The strong contrast between physical cold and warmth suggests also a metaphorical contrast, the cold representing the son's indifference and the warmth the father's affection.

The speaker rises and dresses "slowly," being reluctant to face "the chronic angers of that house"; apparently there are constant ("chronic") tensions between certain family members, though the poem doesn't specify whether it's between the parents (if there are two parents) or between the father and son, or other members of the household. The plural word "angers" seems to imply that more than one family member is involved. In line 10, the speaker notes that he spoke "indifferently" to his father on those mornings, but he clearly regrets that now, at the time of writing the poem, since he adds that his father had driven out the cold and polished his shoes "as well." The short, repeated exclamation of line 13 contrasts sharply with the preceding long sentence (lines 7–12) and effectively expresses the speaker's distress on realizing how unjustly he had behaved towards his father. The forceful repetition of "What did I know?" underscores his despair. The beautiful last line, with its subtle alliteration linking "love" and "lonely" and its echoing initial vowel sounds in "austere" and "offices," expresses the speaker's appreciation, now, for the kind of love that shows itself in actions ("offices"), expects no return ("austere and lonely"), and endures despite the lack of reciprocal affection—like the love of a father for his son. The vocabulary here—"love's austere and lonely offices"— after the concrete vocabulary dominating the rest of the poem, is abstract, as befits a reflection following on the description of a specific situation. These last two lines are framed as a question, but a rhetorical question expressing the speaker's real-ization that he understood nothing; he was too young at the time to understand the "lonely offices" of love, but he clearly does now and feels remorse; perhaps his father has since died so that he can no longer speak to him about it. The interrogative format of the last two lines makes the reader reflect on the issue raised.

With its fourteen lines, this poem resembles a sonnet, though a traditional sonnet not only has meter and a rhyme scheme, but also groups the lines differently, according to either the Petrarchan or the Shakespearean model. Hayden's poem does, neverthe-less, boast a definite structure, with its three groups of lines dealing first with the father's actions, then with the son's, and finally with the relation between them. Moreover, the last two lines, summing up the son's feelings in the form of a rhetorical question, resemble in their precision and pointedness the final two lines of many Shakespearean sonnets, which are often separated by rhyme from the rest of the poem, as these two lines are separated by forming a question and a complete sentence. Written in free verse, the poem is clearly not "free" structurally. Apart from its struc-tured form, it is bound together by the contrasting images of warmth and cold, which reflect the warm or cool feelings that the family members have for each other. These structural elements, together with the very effective use of alliteration and the haunting last two lines, make this a memorable poem.

Commentary on Model Close Reading #4

Notice how this close reading gives equal weight to the content of the poem (the speaker's recollections and emotions) and its form, i.e., all the poetic devices that are used to symbolize, illustrate, or reinforce these thoughts and feelings.

The introduction establishes the type of verse, points out the poem's main theme, and describes its tone. It divides the poem into three parts and explains the progression from one part to the next. Dividing a poem into parts, though not always necessary, can often help the reader to understand and analyze it.

The analysis moves through the poem more or less line by line, taking into account first of all the title (sometimes crucial in the elucidation of a poem's meaning). It exam-ines the devices in the first few lines that accentuate the notion of cold, such as colors ("blueblack") and harsh sounds. The everyday vocabulary is noted (and linked to the everyday activities described in the poem), and one possibly unclear expression ("banked fires") is explained. The analysis also points out how alliteration and internal rhyme can accentuate the impact of words and how a short sentence ("No one ever thanked him") among longer ones also tends to receive emphasis.

The significance of a change in point of view (from third to first person) is indi-cated, beginning in line 6. All the elements (vocabulary, sounds, imagery) of the strong contrast in the poem between warm and cold are noted, and the important connection is made between literary and figurative connotations of warm and cold, since the poem is about love, anger, and indifference, not just about warm fires in a cold house. It is often crucial to link a poem's imagery to its basic theme in this way.

Moving on to the last "stanza," the explication makes the connection between the speaker's past and his present, points out the effectiveness of a short repeated phrase ("What did I know"), and notes the various techniques that strengthen the impact of the poem's last line, not forgetting the effect of its final punctuation, a question mark. It is always advisable to pay particular attention to the last lines of poems: often the poet uses some device that gives a sense of closure, or provides a striking final image or, as here, leaves the reader pondering on a question.

In this close reading, the conclusion discusses the many aspects of this poem that provide structure. In a way, a poem in free verse requires structural and other poetic techniques even more than a poem in traditional verse, in order to establish its identity as a poem rather than a paragraph of prose.

TOWARDS CLOSE READING: POEMS ACCOMPANIED BY QUESTIONS

Using the foregoing models as examples and the questions as a guide, you can now write close readings of your own on whichever of the following poems you or your professor chooses. *Do not simply answer the questions,* but incorporate your answers into an essay (as in the models). Treat the questions as a general guide only, rather than simply answering them one by one. You do not need to deal with them strictly in order (though your reading should follow the poem line by line); if one or two questions seem incomprehensible to you, you can omit them; and of course you should not hesitate to add any independent observations of your own.

The poems are presented in chronological order.

1. "Sonnet #73: That time of year . . . " (1609)

That time of year thou may'st in me behold
When yellow leaves, or none, or few, do hang
Upon those boughs which shake against the cold,
Bare ruined choirs where late the sweet birds sang.
In me thou see'st the twilight of such day   5
As after sunset fadeth in the west,
Which by-and-by black night doth take away,
Death's second self that seals up all in rest.
In me thou see'st the glowing of such fire
That on the ashes of his youth doth lie,   10
As the deathbed whereon it must expire,
Consumed with that which it was nourished by.
This thou perceiv'st, which makes thy love more strong,
To love that well which thou must leave ere long.

William Shakespeare (1564–1616)

For the Introduction

(Consider the questions in any order.)

1. What kind of poem is this? (Count the lines.) Did Shakespeare write other poems of this type?

2. What is the theme of the poem?

3. Does the poem divide into parts? How?

4. What is the tone of the poem (emotional? matter-of-fact? persuasive?)

5. How would you describe the poem's style? How is its language different from that of our times?

6. Describe the meter and rhyme scheme of the poem.

For the Detailed Analysis

1. What "time of year" does the poet have in mind and how does he evoke this season?

2. What figure of speech operates in lines 1–3 and what does it suggest?

3. What atmosphere is evoked by the vocabulary of lines 1–4? What senses are involved in the imagery of these lines?

4. Comment on the rhythm of line 2 with its numerous commas.

5. Comment on the word "shake" in line 3.

6. What further figure of speech do you notice in lines 3–4? (Explain that "choir" can refer to a body of singers but also to the place where they sit in a church; "late" here means "lately" or "of late.")

7. Do you detect any alliteration in line 4? If so, what effect does it have?

8. What marks the change of topic in lines 5–8? How does this topic relate to the main theme of the poem?

9. What words from line 1 are repeated in line 5 and what effect does this repetition have? Who might "thou" be?

10. Who or what is "Death's second self" that "seals up all in rest" (lines 7–8)? What figure of speech is involved here and what effect does it have? How is death portrayed here? What is the speaker implying about himself?

11. Is there any alliteration in lines 7–8?

12. Do you detect any change in metrical rhythm in line 8 and what effect does it have?

13. What change of direction occurs in line 9 and how is it signaled?

14. What figure of speech appears in lines 9-12? Explain its meaning. [N.B. A fire "glows" when it has stopped burning fiercely; and when a fire goes out, that is because the fuel that "nourished" it has been used up ("consumed").]

15. What is the literal meaning of the word "expire"? Is that relevant here?

16. How does the figure of speech in these lines (9–12) compare to those of lines 1–4 and 5–9? What would be the equivalent of the "glowing . . . fire" in those lines?

17. How do the last two lines differ from the others in form and content?

18. What kinds of verbs go with the subject "thou" every time it appears?

19. Is the identity of the poem's addressee ("thou") now clear?

20. What is the speaker's advice to the poem's addressee in line 14? How does it relate to and summarize the rest of the poem?

21. What is the tone of the poem's concluding two lines?

22. Analyze the poem's overall structure. How many parts would you divide it into, and how are the parts marked? How do these parts fit in with the poem's rhyme scheme and punctuation?

For the Conclusion

1. What is your reaction to this poem? What are its strengths, in your view? Are there aspects of it that you dislike?

2. Does the poem seem effective in conveying its message?

3. How do the metaphors enrich the poem?

4. How does this Shakespearean sonnet compare to any others you may know?

2. "She Walks in Beauty" (1815)

She walks in beauty, like the night
    Of cloudless climes and starry skies;
And all that's best of dark and bright
    Meet in her aspect and her eyes:
Thus mellowed to that tender light   5
    Which heaven to gaudy day denies.

One shade the more, one ray the less,
    Had half impaired the nameless grace
Which waves in every raven tress,
    Or softly lightens o'er her face;   10
Where thoughts serenely sweet express
    How pure, how dear their dwelling place.

And on that cheek, and o'er that brow,
    So soft, so calm, yet eloquent,
The smiles that win, the tints that glow,   15
    But tell of days in goodness spent,
A mind at peace with all below,
    A heart whose love is innocent!

George Gordon, Lord Byron (1788–1824)

For the Introduction

1. Give the poet's name and the period when he was writing.

2. What is the poem's theme?

3. How would you describe the tone and vocabulary of the poem?

4. Describe the poem's form and versification.

For the Detailed Analysis

1. What is the effect of starting the poem with the word "She" with no indication of who "she" is?

2. How does the phrase "She walks in beauty" strike you (compared to saying, for example, "She is beautiful")?

3. What figure of speech is used in the first two lines and what kind of night does it evoke?

4. Comment on the alliteration in line 2.

5. What antithesis governs the whole of this first stanza? Is it effective in describing the woman?

6. What "tender light" is referred to in line 5? Comment on the use of the adjective "tender" here.

7. What would the normal (prose) word-order be in line 6? Why is day described as "gaudy"? (What is denied by heaven to "gaudy day"?)

8. Note that "Had" in line 8 equates to "Would have" (i.e., paraphrasing lines 7–8: "One shade more or one shade less would have almost impaired the nameless grace . . . "). What do these lines imply about the woman's beauty?

9. What color is implied by the word "raven" in line 9? How do lines 7–10 echo the imagery of the first stanza?

10. What effects are produced by the alliteration in lines 9–11?

11. What attributes of the woman are stressed by the vocabulary of this stanza?

12. Show how the emphasis in this stanza begins to move from the exterior to the interior.

13. Study the rhythm of these two stanzas. Does it seem to echo the thoughts expressed?

14. What words in lines 14–15 echo aspects of the woman evoked already in stanzas 1 and 2?

15. How does this stanza continue the movement from exterior to interior? How is the woman characterized?

16. What does the final exclamation add to the mood or tone of this stanza?

For the Conclusion

1. Show how the antithesis developed in the first stanza structures the whole poem.

2. What is the overall impression of the woman conveyed by the poem? What is the speaker's tone when describing her?

3. What is your opinion of the poem?

3. "Meeting at Night" (1845)

The gray sea and the long black land;
And the yellow half-moon large and low;
And the startled little waves that leap
In fiery ringlets from their sleep,

As I gain the cove with pushing prow,   5
And quench its speed i' the slushy sand.

Then a mile of warm sea-scented beach;
Three fields to cross till a farm appears;
A tap at the pane, the quick sharp scratch
And blue spurt of a lighted match,   10
And a voice less loud, through its joys and fears,
Than the two hearts beating each to each!

Robert Browning (1812–1889)

For the Introduction

1. What is the overall theme of "Meeting at Night"? (What does it describe?) It is divided into two stanzas; does this division reflect any difference in the content of the two parts?

2. What is the tone of the poem? (What feelings, if any, does the speaker express, and how?)

3. Describe the poem's versification.

For the Detailed Analysis

1. Consider the title and how it prepares us for the content of the poem.

2. How would you characterize the vocabulary of the first stanza? (abstract/concrete? literary/everyday? colorful/neutral? descriptive/emotional?)

3. What kind of picture does line 1 suggest? What contrast(s) do you see between this line and line 2? What do lines 3–4 add to the picture? How does the enjambment in lines 3–4 add to the impact of the lines?

4. Do you detect any alliteration in lines 1-4 and if so what is its effect?

5. What figure of speech appears in lines 3–4? Do you feel it adds to the impact of these lines?

6. Examine the syntax and punctuation of lines 1–4. What new element is introduced in line 5?

7. What is the effect of the alliteration in lines 5–6?

8. What senses are evoked by the imagery of the first stanza?

9. What word connects stanza 2 to stanza 1?

10. How does the first line of the second stanza contrast with the scene evoked in the first line of the first stanza?

11. Consider the syntax of the second stanza. Who crosses the beach and the "Three fields," and taps at the window-pane? What effect does the omission of a subject have in this stanza?

12. What is the effect of the alliteration in lines 9–10?

13. Noting the enjambment in lines 9–10, as in lines 3–4, examine the punctuation and rhythm of the second stanza as compared to the first.

14. What senses does the imagery of the second stanza evoke?

15. Whose voice do you imagine in line 11? Is the voice loud or soft, compared to the heartbeats?

16. How does the vocabulary of line 11 differ from the rest of the poem?

17. How do lines 11 and 12 contrast with the rest of the poem? What is your reaction to the image contained in line 12?

18. What is the significance of the exclamation point at the end of line 12?

19. Do lines 11–12 provide an effective conclusion to the poem? How do they relate to the poem's title?

For the Conclusion

1. What is your overall opinion of this poem? Did any aspect of the poem seem to you particularly original or striking?

2. This poem is by the famous Victorian poet Robert Browning. Have you read any other poems of his? Does this poem resemble them, or not?

4. "A noiseless patient spider" (1881)

> A noiseless patient spider,
> I mark'd where on a little promontory it stood isolated,
> Mark'd how to explore the vacant vast surrounding,
> It launch'd forth filament, filament, filament, out of itself,
> Ever unreeling them, ever tirelessly speeding them.   5
>
> And you O my soul where you stand,
> Surrounded, detached, in measureless oceans of space,
> Ceaselessly musing, venturing, throwing, seeking the spheres to connect
>   them,
> Till the bridge you will need be form'd, till the ductile anchor hold,
> Till the gossamer thread you fling catch somewhere, O my soul.   10

Walt Whitman (1819–1892)

For the Introduction

1. Give the poet's name and period, and describe the form of the poem.

2. Note the division of the poem into two parts; characterize the two parts and explain why you think it is thus divided.

3. What is the poem's theme?

For the Detailed Analysis

1. Comment on the adjectives "noiseless" and "patient" to describe the spider.

2. Comment on the syntax of lines 1-2. (The normal syntax would be "I mark'd [noticed] a noiseless, patient spider," but the poet has placed the object of the sentence first. How does this word-order affect the impact and the rhythm of the sentence?)

3. The spider is located on a promontory (a headland overlooking the sea). Why might the poet have chosen this location, in your view?

4. Do you feel that alliteration of the sound /p/ plays a role in lines 1–2?

5. [If you have trouble understanding lines 3–4, imagine a comma after the word "how" in line 3. Note also that a spider does throw out a single filament that attaches somewhere, prior to making the rest of the web.]

6. Do you detect alliteration in line 3? What effect does it have?

7. What aspect of the spider's surroundings does the poem emphasize?

8. What impression is created by the repetitions in lines 4–5?

9. The gap between lines 5 and 6 divides the poem into two halves. What distinguishes the two parts? Examine the sentence-structure in relation to these two parts.

10. What figure of speech is used in line 6 and what effect does it have?

11. How does the place where the speaker's soul "stands" (lines 6–7) compare with the place where the spider was located (lines 2–3)?

12. Do you detect alliteration in lines 6–8 and if so what effect does it have?

13. How does the soul's activity compare with that of the spider?

14. Comment on the use of so many present participles in lines 5 and 8. How does the soul's action resemble that of the spider?

15. Line 8 is the longest line of the poem. Do you see any particular reason for this?

16. What is the soul aiming to do, in lines 8–10?

17. In lines 9–10, what do you understand by "bridge" and "ductile anchor"? What is the relation between the spider in the first part and the soul in the second? What figure is involved here?

18. What is the effect of the repetition of "Till" in lines 9–10?

19. What effect do the last three words of the poem produce ("O my soul")? How does it compare with the first appearance of this phrase, in line 6?

For the Conclusion

1. What is overall theme of this poem, in your view, and how is it introduced? Do you find the poem effective?

2. Comment on the poem's overall structure. How "free" is this free verse? (N.B. Whitman was one of the first poets to write in *vers libres* or free verse.)

5. "We Wear the Mask" (1896)

We wear the mask that grins and lies,
It hides our cheeks and shades our eyes,—
This debt we pay to human guile;
With torn and bleeding hearts we smile,
And mouth with myriad subtleties.

Why should the world be over-wise,
In counting all our tears and sighs?

5

> Nay, let them only see us, while
> We wear the mask.
>
> We smile, but, O great Christ, our cries   10
> To thee from tortured souls arise.
> We sing, but oh the clay is vile
> Beneath our feet, and long the mile;
> But let the world dream otherwise,
> We wear the mask!   15

Paul Laurence Dunbar (1872–1906)

For the Introduction

1. Paul Dunbar was a black writer whose parents had been slaves. Does this information affect your reading of the poem? What is the theme of "We Wear the Mask," in your view?
2. What is the poem's tone? Does it alter in the course of the poem?
3. Describe the poem's form and versification.
4. Does the poem divide into parts and if so, how? Does it have a refrain?

For the Detailed Analysis

1. What does the first line add to the title? What is the effect of juxtaposing the two verbs "grins" and "lies"?
2. What does the "mask" represent? Why do "our cheeks" and "our eyes" need to be hidden?
3. What is the role of the dash at the end of line 2?
4. Whose "guile" is referred to in line 3?
5. Notice the repetition of "our" in line 2 and of "we" in lines 1, 3 and 4. Are these words repeated again in the poem? What is their significance or effect? To whom might "we" refer?
6. What note is introduced by line 4? How does this line relate to line 1?
7. In line 5, is "mouth" a noun or a verb? How does this line summarize the first stanza? Does "subtleties" rhyme with any other word?
8. Does the point of view change at all in the second stanza? What is the world's attitude towards "our tears and sighs"? What do the tears and sighs recall from the first stanza?
9. What is the effect of the word "Nay" in line 8, and what is meant by the phrase "let them only see us"? (Who are represented by "them" and "us" here? What is the significance of "only"?)
10. Note the repetition of the phrase "We wear the mask" in line 9. Is its effect here any different from in line 1?
11. Where has the phrase "we smile" already been used in the poem? Does it provide an internal rhyme here (l. 10)? Why do you think it is repeated here? How does it contrast with the rest of line 10?
12. How does the tone change in lines 10–11? What emotion is expressed here? Does the narrator seem to be looking beneath the "mask"? What figure of speech does the phrase "O great Christ" represent and what is its effect?

13. How does the expression "tortured souls" echo earlier expressions and how is it different?

14. Comment on the parallelism between "We sing" and "We smile"; what similar meaning underlies the similarity in form?

15. What is the impact of the word "oh" in line 12?

16. What are the implications of "the clay is vile/Beneath our feet" and "long the mile"?

17. How does line 14 recall an earlier statement? Does it also return to an earlier mood or tone?

18. Comment on the repetition of the phrase "We wear the mask" in the last line. How many times has it been repeated? Is its effect the same here as in previous lines? How does the addition of an exclamation point affect your reading of the line?

For the Conclusion

1. Show how the poem's rhymes help to bind it together.

2. If you did not know that the author of this poem was black, would you read it differently? Explain why or why not. Who would you take the "we" of the poem to represent?

6. "Acquainted with the Night" (1928)

I have been one acquainted with the night.
I have walked out in rain—and back in rain.
I have outwalked the furthest city light.

I have looked down the saddest city lane.
I have passed by the watchman on his beat   5
And dropped my eyes, unwilling to explain.

I have stood still and stopped the sound of feet
When far away an interrupted cry
Came over houses from another street,

But not to call me back or say good-by;   10
And further still at an unearthly height
One luminary clock against the sky

Proclaimed the time was neither wrong nor right.
I have been one acquainted with the night.

Robert Frost (1874–1963)

For the Introduction

1. How would you describe the tone of "Acquainted with the Night"? What are the connotations of the word "night" in the title?

2. Comment on the poem's form and rhyme scheme (if necessary, consult the paragraph on stanzas in the section on versification).

3. Can the poem be divided into parts and if so how do the parts differ?

For the Detailed Analysis

1. Notice the first word of the poem and its repetition in the next few lines. What is the effect of this insistence?

2. Does the word "night" appear to refer simply to a time of day?

3. The first line could read "I have been acquainted . . . " but in fact says "I have been one acquainted . . . ." What is the effect of the addition of the word "one"? Do you have any comment, also, on the word "acquainted"?

4. What is the relationship between the statement in this first line (a complete sentence) and the events described in the next three lines? How does the vocabulary of line 1 (abstract, concrete?) compare with that of lines 2–4? Could lines 2–4 be seen as illustrations of the opening statement made in line 1?

5. What is the effect of the phrase "and back in rain" following the dash, in line 2?

6. In line 3, what are the implications for the speaker of having outwalked "the furthest city light"? (What kind of area has the speaker reached?)

7. What kind of mood is created in lines 2–3? How is this confirmed in line 4? Is it really the lane that is "sad"?

8. What does line 6 add to our understanding of the speaker's mood?

9. What figure of speech is contained in the first five lines and what is its effect?

10. What changes occur in and after line 7? (Compare the sentence structure of lines 1–6 with that of the following lines.)

11. How does "I have stood still" in line 7 compare with "I have walked . . . outwalked . . . looked . . . passed by . . . dropped" in the previous lines? Does this change in line 7 herald a more general change in the action of the poem, and in its rhythm, in the following lines?

12. If the "sound of feet" stopped when the speaker stopped, what does that indicate? How does this fit in with the idea expressed in line 3?

13. What is achieved by the alliteration in line 7?

14. What does the "cry" of line 8 add to the mood? What are the implications of line 10?

15. What do you make of the "clock" in line 12?

16. What does line 13 convey about the speaker's mood?

17. What is the effect of the rhyming couplet at the end of the poem?

18. The final line repeats the first line of the poem. Does this line have the same effect the second time round, or is its impact different in some way? Does it give a sense of conclusion? Has the speaker's mood changed at the end of the poem?

For the Conclusion

1. Is the emotion of this poem conveyed directly, through emotive language, or indirectly through images? If certain images in the poem seem to you to convey feelings, what type of feeling do they express? Are the images effective?

2. Is everything clear in the poem or do certain elements seem mysterious? What is your reaction as a reader?

3. The form of this poem, with its recurring rhymes and repeated lines, could be described as tight and disciplined. How does that compare with its emotional content?

4. Have you read other poems by Robert Frost? How does this one compare to them?

7. "Naming of Parts" (1946)

Today we have naming of parts. Yesterday,
We had daily cleaning. And tomorrow morning,
We shall have what to do after firing. But today,
Today we have naming of parts. Japonica
Glistens like coral in all of the neighboring gardens,   5
      And today we have naming of parts.

This is the lower sling swivel. And this
Is the upper sling swivel, whose use you will see,
When you are given your slings. And this is the piling swivel,
Which in your case you have not got. The branches   10
Hold in the gardens their silent, eloquent gestures,
      Which in our case we have not got.

This is the safety-catch, which is always released
With an easy flick of the thumb. And please do not let me
See anyone using his finger. You can do it quite easy   15
If you have any strength in your thumb. The blossoms
Are fragile and motionless, never letting anyone see
      Any of them using their finger.

And this you can see is the bolt. The purpose of this
Is to open the breech, as you see. We can slide it   20
Rapidly backwards and forwards: we call this
Easing the spring. And rapidly backwards and forwards
The early bees are assaulting and fumbling the flowers:
      They call it easing the Spring.

They call it easing the Spring: it is perfectly easy   25
If you have any strength in your thumb: like the bolt,
And the breech, and the cocking-piece, and the point of balance,
Which in our case we have not got; and the almond-blossom
Silent in all of the gardens and the bees going backwards and
      forwards,
      For today we have naming of parts.   30

Henry Reed (1914–1986)

For the Introduction

1. What kind of situation does "Naming of Parts" seem to be describing?

2. Characterize the two voices that are heard in the poem. To whom do the voices seem to belong? What is the tone of each voice?

3. Describe the poem's form. Point out any repetitions of lines.

For the Detailed Analysis

1. Who speaks in the first lines, in your view? Who is represented by the word "we"?

2. Comment on the type of activities listed in lines 1–3.

3. What is the significance of the stress on what is done "Today," "Yesterday" and "tomorrow"?

4. Japonica (*chaenemoles*) is a bush or hedge with orange-red or pink flowers. See what else you can find out about it. Which speaker mentions this plant? What does it reveal about his attitude?

5. What figure of speech is employed in lines 4–5? Do you find it appropriate?

6. Line 6 repeats the first line. Does it sound the same, or does the line affect you differently now?

7. Comment on the vocabulary of lines 7–9 (and 13, 19–20, 25–27). What type of words are they? Who is uttering them? How do they relate to the title of the poem? How do they compare with the other speaker's vocabulary?

8. Is it significant that the speaker of lines 7–10 is demonstrating a "piling swivel" that his audience apparently doesn't have yet, and a "lower sling swivel" whose use they will not see until they get their "slings"? What does the *other* speaker's attitude appear to be to this situation? How does his repetition of the first speaker's words come across?

9. What kinds of things hold the second speaker's attention (lines 10–11)? Do you have any comment on the phrase "silent, eloquent gestures"?

10. What do lines 14–15 reveal about the first speaker's attitude towards his audience?

11. How do the descriptions of the blossoms, in lines 16–17, and the branches, in lines 10–11, contrast with the speakers' activities?

12. What is the tone of lines 17–18 ("never letting anyone see / Any of them using their finger")?

13. Comment on the uses of the word "spring" in lines 22 and 24. Show how this contrasting usage summarizes or encapsulates the attitudes of the two speakers.

14. Comment on the repetition of "backwards and forwards" and the verb "assaulting" in lines 22–23. Do you detect any alliteration here?

15. Who is speaking in the last stanza? What is the tone of this stanza? What purpose does it serve?

For the Conclusion

1. What kind of point do you think the poem tries to make by the contrast between the attitudes of the two speakers? Which speaker do you identify with more closely? Why?

2. Explain whether or not you like this poem and why.

8. "Harlem (A Dream Deferred)" (1951)

What happens to a dream deferred?
Does it dry up
Like a raisin in the sun?
Or fester like a sore—
And then run?   5
Does it stink like rotten meat?
Or crust and sugar over—
Like a syrupy sweet?

Maybe it just sags
Like a heavy load.   10
Or does it explode?

Langston Hughes (1902–1967)

For the Introduction

1. What do you know about the author, Langston Hughes, that might be relevant to this poem?

2. What "dream" might the poem refer to? (Consider the title.)

3. Describe the overall structure and form of the poem. (What kind of verse is this? Are there rhymes? How is the poem structured syntactically?)

For the Detailed Analysis

1. Note the positioning of the first line on the page compared to the other lines. How does the first line relate to the rest of the poem?

2. What does the slight alliteration in line 1 contribute, if anything?

3. What figure of speech is contained in lines 2–3? How can a dream deferred resemble a raisin? What are the implications of drying up, for a dream?

4. Do lines 2–3 provide an answer to the question in line 1?

5. Lines 4–5 present another question—or is it an answer? What are the implications of a dream that "fester[s] like a sore"?

6. Show how lines 6–8 present a similar form to lines 2–3. What elements are repeated?

7. What are the implications for the "dream deferred" if it starts to "stink like rotten meat"? What might happen to it if it were to "crust and sugar over"?

8. Do you detect any alliteration in lines 6–8? What effect does it have?

9. Are all these questions also answers? Are any of them optimistic?

10. What is the effect of the gap between lines 8 and 9?

11. Is the format of lines 9–10 the same as that of previous lines?

12. What might happen to the dream if it "sags / Like a heavy load"? What other images might the phrase "heavy load" conjure up, in the context of the poem?

13. How would you characterize the vocabulary of lines 2–10? How does it differ from that of line 1?

14. What is the significance of the gap between lines 10 and 11? And of the italics in line 11?

15. What is missing in this final question compared to the previous ones? Why this difference, in your view?

16. What are the implications of a dream that "explode[s]"?

17. Is the tone of line 11 different from that of previous lines?

18. Comment on the rhyme in lines 10–11. (Is its form the same as that of the other rhymes in the poem? What is its effect?)

For the Conclusion

1. Summarize the overall structure of the poem, taking into account syntactical presentation and repetitions of words and figures of speech. Since all the comparisons in the poem refer to one thing (the "dream deferred"), what kind of figure of speech organizes the whole poem?

2. How many "answers" are provided to the original question? Is any of the answers satisfactory? What are the implications of these answers as a response to the original question? Does the poem seem to present the final answer as the most likely? Is another answer possible?

3. What is the poem's overall impact? Do you find the poem effective?

COMPOSING QUESTIONS ON A POEM

A useful exercise now would be to attempt to write a series of questions like those above on a new poem, either one from appendix 2 or one assigned by your professor. Another student—or you yourself—will then use those questions as a basis for writing a close reading.

You will need to read the new poem several times, preferably over a period of at least a couple of days, in order to become familiar with it. Consider all aspects of the poem in great detail—its form, mood, ideas or emotions, rhythm, sounds, and structure. Use the "Summary of Elements to Discuss in a Poem" at the end of chapter 2 to help you focus on different aspects of the poem. Have another look at the questions offered on various poems in this chapter; divide your questions, as in those examples, into parts—introduction, detailed analysis, and conclusion. Make sure your questions would be clear to someone else. Do not ask questions that you could not answer yourself.

You will find that this process represents the major part of the work involved in doing a close reading. When you come to write a close reading on a totally new poem without helpful questions, you might do well to begin composing your explication by thinking up similar kinds of questions for yourself.

PART 2
PROSE

CHAPTER 4

Introduction to Aspects of Prose Fiction

Prose fiction represents a huge field within the domain of literature. Novels, short stories, memoirs, essays, and collections of letters are almost all written in prose. This was not always the case: much of the great fiction of classical and medieval literature was composed in verse, like Homer's *Odyssey* and Chaucer's *Canterbury Tales*. The modern novel in prose was not born until the seventeenth century and the short story even later.

Since close reading requires very detailed analysis, you will no doubt be asked to explicate an extract from a text, rather than a complete work. Explicating a passage in detail can, however, help you understand the work as a whole: elements of the style, ideas and narrative techniques of a specific paragraph should be related in a close reading to the complete work, and this process can bring greater insight into certain aspects of the work. In order to explicate a passage, you need to have read the entire story; for this reason the prose texts chosen to illustrate this section are all taken from short stories rather than novels or other longer prose works. Several stories are re-printed in appendix 3; you will need to read them in order to complete the exercises in this section. Once you have become familiar with procedures for explicating a prose text, you can also apply them to a passage from a longer work such as a novel.

Prose can be adapted to many stylistic and tonal registers, from the most colloquial style to highly formal, literary writing; from joke-telling to tragedy. It is used for description, narration, persuasion (in an essay, for example) and for **dialogue**, as well as for informational purposes in the vast domain of **didactic** texts (written to teach the reader something) such as textbooks, journal articles, newspapers, etc., which go beyond the scope of literature in the sense of creative writing with which we are concerned.

Some of the elements essential to the close reading of a poem will be required also in explicating a prose passage. **Figures of speech** (metaphors, similes, symbols, etc.) appear in prose works, too, though less frequently than in poetry where language is often used in a richer, more imaginative way. A study of word choice (vocabulary) will be relevant in prose as in poetry; but since prose does not have the short lines of verse, the effect of placing a specific word, or repeating a word, is less striking than in poetry. In fact, prose tends to avoid repetition of the same word more than once. As for **structure**, it may of course be a significant concept for an entire work in prose, but not necessarily for an extract chosen for a close reading. A poem should form a whole, which presumes a definite form or structure, but that would not apply to a single paragraph from a novel or short story.

Other features, however, specifically characterize prose fiction: when explicating a prose passage you will need to pay attention to concepts such as **plot**, **characterization**, **setting**, **point of view**, **style**, and **theme**. We will proceed to examine all these concepts, beginning with one that is very specific to fiction rather than poetry (except for narrative poems), namely: plot.

PLOT

Plot concerns the action of a story. It represents not simply a random sequence of events but a deliberate organization of events into a coherent shape. The events in a novel may often resemble those of real life, but in order to form a satisfying plot the author arranges them in a certain order and establishes logical links between them. It is difficult—though attempts have been made—to hold a reader's interest if he/she can find no causal connections between the main events. The author must organize the plot in a way that maintains readers' interest without letting them guess what will happen next. Do you like to be surprised when you read a story? Readers often like surprises—but only if they have been prepared by earlier details in the text; otherwise they appear totally arbitrary. Mrs. Mallard's death at the end of Kate Chopin's "The Story of an Hour" would seem hard to believe, if we had not been apprised in the very first line that she "was afflicted with a heart trouble." The presence of the cat in the wall at the climax of Edgar Allan Poe's "The Black Cat" has been prepared by the cat's disappearance a few days previously and by the description of the tomb in the wall built by the narrator.

The events constituting the plot are not necessarily presented in chronological order: often, the author starts with the "present"—the "now" of the narrative—in order to engage the reader, but later moves to a **flashback** into the past of one or more of the characters in order to reveal circumstances that have led up to the current situation or that explain a character's behavior. Faulkner begins "A Rose for Emily" at the time of Miss Emily's death but doesn't return to that moment in time until the last page of the story. All the intervening pages refer back to different points in Miss Emily's life in a series of flashbacks that gradually reveal more about her. Sometimes, certain details in a story seem to foretell, or foreshadow, subsequent events, a technique that is called **foreshadowing**.

Plots very often involve an element of **conflict**—either between two or more characters, between a character and the society he lives in, or within one character who is internally torn or divided. The resolution of the conflict signals the plot's dénouement.

Elements of Plot

A traditional plot comprises several parts: an **exposition** (or introduction) that introduces some of the characters, gives a few details about their circumstances, and indicates the setting—the place and era in which the action takes place. In a novel, this exposition may take up a page or several pages; in a short story it might consist only of a few lines or a couple of paragraphs. Following it comes the **development**, which almost always constitutes the main body of the story: from the initial situation events proliferate, with one incident leading to another, and the characters' personalities are gradually revealed. Again, in a novel this process can take up many chapters and involve complex interactions and extensive exploration of character. Finally, the development reaches a moment of **climax** or crisis, provoked by conflicting events or by the attitudes of different characters. It may be a moment when conflicts are resolved, or perhaps an event that reveals some telling aspect of a character's personality or situation. This turning point (another name for the climax of a narrative) can lead to a **dénouement** (from a French word that means "untying," as the knots of the plot are untied)—a conclusion or winding-down of the action, often very brief, that may suggest, for example, how characters have changed or the direction their lives might take in a hypothetical future after the end of the story.

The plots of novels and short stories may not conform exactly to the above outline. Often one of the parts is omitted, such as the exposition. Authors sometimes prefer to begin *in medias res*, i.e., plunging into the story without any kind of introduction (though they usually find ways of introducing background information, later on). Consider the first sentence of Updike's "A & P": "In walks these three girls in nothing but bathing suits." We don't know who is speaking or where he is (although the title gives us a clue). Wouldn't you say that this type of opening catches the reader's attention more effectively than if the narrator were to begin by explaining who he is, where he works, and when the incident took place? Or do you feel more comfortable when a story begins with an introduction that sets the scene?

A narrative may also end with the moment of crisis, without any dénouement or resolution. This creates a dramatic type of ending which can be very effective—though it must also conclude the action in a satisfying way, or reveal something significant about a character. Thus, at the end of "A Rose for Emily," the discovery by the townspeople of "a long strand of iron-gray hair" shocks them and the reader with the realization that Miss Emily has been in the habit of sleeping beside a corpse. This information simultaneously ties up the threads of the plot, adds another dimension to our knowledge of Miss Emily, and brings the story to a memorable close.

Even if a story does conclude with a dénouement, it may be ambiguous, open to different interpretations. At the end of Bobbie Ann Mason's "Shiloh" it is not clear whether Norma Jean, waving her arms near a steep drop by a river, is doing chest exercises, waving goodbye before committing suicide, or beckoning her husband to join her. It is up to the reader to decide which possibility fits in best with the substance of the preceding narrative. An author may choose to leave a character in a situation where he or she must make an important decision without revealing what that decision will be, preferring to let us decide in view of what we know about the characters and their circumstances. An ambiguous ending may be deemed more realistic (since we cannot know in real life what effect an incident in someone else's life will have on them); it also tends to provoke the reader and make him or her reflect more on the story's action. The lack of a definite sense of closure might seem frustrating at first for a reader, but texts that conclude ambiguously often remain longer in the memory, no doubt because we subconsciously strive mentally to furnish our own conclusion.

Short stories often end with a twist, an unexpected or ironic take on the narrative, as at the end of Kate Chopin's "The Story of an Hour." The climax here could be seen as the moment when Mrs. Mallard's husband, presumed dead, walks in the door. His wife has been reveling in the idea of the freedom his death represents for her, and when she sees him she dies of the shock. The last line of the story reads: "When the doctors came they said she had died of heart disease—of joy that kills." This provides a very effective and ironic conclusion: the doctors think she died because she was overjoyed to see her husband, but the reader, who has been privy to her thoughts on learning of his death, knows the emotion that killed her was more akin to despair.

In certain passages of a story, the narrator may show in detail what happens between two or more characters, perhaps with a description of their expressions and gestures or of their feelings, and with a dialogue that transcribes the actual words they speak to each other. This type of narrative presentation is called scene. Elsewhere, the narrative consists of summary: the narrator summarizes in a few sentences events that befall a character or several characters over a period of hours, days, weeks, or even years. Thus in Chekhov's "The Lady with the Dog" scene and summary alternate:

> She did not shed tears, but was so sad that she seemed ill, and her face was quivering.
>
> "I shall remember you . . . think of you," she said. "God be with you, be happy. Don't remember evil against me. We are parting forever—it must be so, for we ought never to have met. Well, God be with you. . . ."
>
> Here at the station was already a scent of autumn; it was a cold evening.
>
> "It's time for me to go north," thought Gurov as he left the platform. "High time! . . ."
>
> In another month, he fancied, the image of Anna Sergeyevna would be shrouded in a mist in his memory, and only from time to time would visit him in his dreams with a touching smile as others did. But more than a month passed, real winter had come, and everything was still clear in his memory as though he had parted with Anna Sergeyevna only the day before.

The characters' farewells at the station are presented as a scene, whereas the final paragraph provides a summary of a whole month. Novels and most short stories employ both methods of presentation. Readers find "scene" more lively and interesting, since they feel they are witnessing the action as it unfolds and hearing the characters' exact words. Summary, on the other hand, makes it possible to speed up the narrative and cover more ground.

When explicating a prose passage you should never recount the whole plot; always avoid plot summary for its own sake. Instead, mention only previous details of the plot that have bearing on the passage, or future events that are heralded by the passage in question. You should also place the extract in the context of the story, explaining whether it comes from the exposition, the development, or the conclusion; whether it forms part of a flashback or a chronological narration; and whether it constitutes scene or summary.

Exercises on Plot

1. Read the opening pages of "Araby" by James Joyce, "The Cask of Amontillado" by Edgar Allen Poe and/or "A & P" by John Updike, and "The Lady with the Dog" by Anton Chekhov. Do these short stories have an exposition or do they begin *in medias res*? If there is an exposition (introducing the characters and setting), where would you say it ends and the development of the action begins? What effect does it have on you as a reader if there is no exposition? How does the reader nevertheless manage to get to know the characters and situation in these stories? Do you prefer the beginnings with an exposition or without? Why?

2. Read "The Black Cat" by Edgar Allen Poe. Where would you place the climax of this story? Does it have a dénouement or resolution? If so what do we learn in it?

CHARACTERIZATION

Whereas the concept of plot concerns the action of a story, characterization refers to the depiction of the actors (or **protagonists**, as the main characters in a work of fiction are often called). There is a strong connection between plot and characterization: events may take a certain course precisely because of the character of one of the story's protagonists; and of course, conversely, a character's development may be influenced by events that occur in the plot.

Some characters are given a personality that never alters; others grow and their attitudes change, even sometimes in the course of a short story, but especially in a novel, which affords more scope for creating fully rounded characters who develop over time. Such characters are more interesting to the reader than **flat characters** possessing only one or two psychological dimensions, or **stereotypes**—stock characters illustrating just one human characteristic, such as the wicked stepmother, the nosy neighbor or the absent-minded professor.

Readers tend to expect fictional characters to conform to the characteristics of people they know in real life. You should not forget, however, that fiction is not life and that the characters—though usually resembling real people in many ways—are actually products of the author's imagination. The writer constructs the characters, as s/he does the plot, and chooses to give them a personality, or ideas, corresponding to the requirements of the plot.

A novelist often endows his or her characters with different functions within the work. Apart from possessing a psychological dimension, characters may represent a certain social type, or they may fulfill a philosophical function by defending or attacking ideas that the author sets out in the book. A single character may embody more than one of these functions: in the novels of Charles Dickens, for example, many characters, while remaining individuals in their own right, with their own psychological motivations, also typify a certain social milieu or class and exemplify various forms of social injustice.

Sometimes the reader is inclined to judge characters critically, sometimes to identify with them, or with one of them. The author can attempt to control our reactions by the way h/she presents the characters—introducing positive or negative comments from the narrator or other characters, involving them in certain kinds of action, revealing their inner thoughts, and so on.

Ways of Knowing a Character

When reading a work of fiction, you should consider not only what the characters are like but also *how* we know them, i.e., what means the author has adopted to acquaint us with them. For example, a narrator might provide a physical description of a character, which can often give the reader an idea of his or her personality. In James Joyce's "The Boarding House," for example, the narrator states that Mrs. Mooney is "a big imposing woman." The **narrator's** opinion about a protagonist might be offered: Mrs. Mooney, we are told, is "a determined woman." Or other characters in the story may express their opinions about a protagonist—though you should bear in mind that such judgments are subjective. No doubt the characters' own speech and actions will reveal their personalities. Readers tend to find it more satisfying to judge a protagonist's character from his deeds and words than by accepting a narrator's opinion. Finally, if the narrator is omniscient and therefore knows all there is to know about the characters (see the section below on **point of view**), s/he may also present certain characters' inner thoughts so that the reader knows them "from the inside." This technique distinguishes our knowledge of such fictional characters from our knowledge of real people: we know people's thoughts only if they reveal them to us themselves.

In a close reading of a passage from a short story or novel, you should consider how it adds to our knowledge of the characters' personalities: does it contain physical description, a character's speech or thoughts or actions, a judgment on the character made by the narrator or by other characters? Does it show the character developing or reinforce what we already know? Does it illustrate the psychological, social, or philosophical function of the character within the text as a whole?

Exercises on Characterization

1. What do we know about the characters in "The Boarding House" by James Joyce (or in another short story you have read)? By what means does the author acquaint us with them?

2. In "The Boarding House" and "The Lady with the Dog" by Anton Chekhov (or in another short story you have read), do the main characters' personalities change, or are their attitudes modified in the course of the story? How and why? Do any specific events in the plot shape the characters' development? Or is the plot determined by the characters' personalities?

3. Consider the characters of a short story you have read (e.g., "The Boarding House"). Are they interesting from a psychological, sociological, or philosophical perspective?

4. If you were writing a close reading on the following extract from "The Boarding House," what would you say as regards characterization?

Mr. Doran was very anxious indeed this Sunday morning. He had made two attempts to shave but his hand had been so unsteady that he had been obliged to desist. Three days' reddish beard fringed his jaws and every two or three minutes a mist gathered on his glasses so that he had to take them off and polish them with his pocket-handkerchief. The recollection of his confession of the night before was a cause of acute pain to him; the priest had drawn out every ridiculous detail of the affair and in the end had so magnified his sin that he was almost thankful at being afforded a loophole of reparation. The harm was done. What could he do now but marry her or run away?

POINT OF VIEW

The **point of view** of a literary text is determined by the identity of the **narrator** and the way he or she tells the story. (We will call the narrator "he" unless, as is often the case, the narrator of a specific story is clearly female.) A closely related term is **narrative voice**. The narrator's point of view—his attitude towards the plot and the characters—influences his telling of the story and therefore our response to it, so that our understanding of the characters and our reaction to events depend to a large extent on the way he presents them. Look for example at "The Storm" by Kate Chopin. The narrator telling this story dealing with a blatant case of marital infidelity does not suggest the characters should feel guilty ("They did not heed the crashing torrents, and the roar of the elements made her laugh as she lay in his arms") or that we should dislike them. The stress is on the joy their lovemaking brings to the protagonists. At the end, one of the families is shown happily eating dinner and the narrator concludes, in the final sentence, "So the storm passed and everyone was happy." A narrator with a more judgmental attitude might have cast a totally different slant on the story and ended with a moralistic conclusion. It is clear that, whatever our own personal views on adultery, the narrator of this story does not intend us to judge the case harshly.

Do not confuse the **narrator** of a story and the author. The latter, of course, chooses the narrator and his point of view, and to this extent is ultimately responsible for our reaction to the story. But the narrator is contained in the story, whereas the author is not. The narrator's point of view does not necessarily coincide with the author's. In "The Yellow Wallpaper" by Charlotte Perkins Gilman, the narrator is a woman who suffers from a mental illness and whose condition clearly deteriorates in the course of the story. The fact that Gilman herself had to undergo treatment for depression does not mean that she shared the actual experience of her narrator. The woman in this story may be considered a **persona** of the author, representing her, but she is not the author herself. The events of the story happen to her, not to Gilman.

Within the context of the story, then, the point of view belongs to the person telling it, i.e., the narrator. The same story told by a different narrator would be presented in an entirely different fashion, partly because his actual experiences would be different and partly because his attitude towards events and people would not be the same. Imagine "The Yellow Wallpaper" narrated by the husband!

First or Third Person Narration

Narratives are usually presented in either the **first** or the **third person**. (Second-person narration is possible and has been realized, but it seems more natural to tell a story with the pronoun "I" or "he/she" rather than "you.") In a first-person narrative, the narrator plays a part, whether major or minor, in the events he relates, using the pronoun "I" to speak of himself (or herself). The narrator of a third-person narrative, on the other hand, does not have a role in the story but tells it from the outside, using the third-person pronouns "he," "she," and "they" to designate the characters.

When an author begins writing a short story or novel he or she has to decide whether the narrator will use the first or the third person. The effect is not the same, so that the author has to choose the narrative voice that seems most suitable for creating the impression he wants to make on the reader. **First-person narrative** tends to make us sympathize more readily with the narrator, the person saying "I," for several reasons. First of all, a voice speaking in the first person appears more personal and closer to the reader. It allows us to identify quickly with the ideas and attitudes of the speaker and plunges us immediately into the speaker's situation. The reader can readily sympathize with a character speaking in the first person, and share in his or her emotions—for example when the narrator of James Joyce's "Araby" tells of his overwhelming infatuation with a girl with whom he barely dares to speak:

> Every morning I lay on the floor in the front parlour watching her door. . . . When she came out on the doorstep my heart leaped. I ran to the hall, seized my books and followed her. I kept her brown figure always in my eye and, when we came near the point at which our ways diverged, I quickened my pace and passed her. This happened morning after morning. I had never spoken to her, except for a few casual words, and yet her name was like a summons to all my foolish blood.

Since readers can identify easily with a voice speaking in the first person and may even feel tempted at times to substitute their own "I" for the narrator's, thus experiencing the latter's emotion more directly, authors tend to use first-person narration when they want the reader to share in a speaker's sensations. For example, Maupassant, in his short story "On the Water," uses the first person so that the reader will feel the narrator's fear all the more:

> The river was perfectly calm, but I was troubled by the extraordinary silence around me. All the creatures, frogs and toads, those nocturnal singers of the marshes, were silent. Suddenly a frog croaked close beside me, on my right. I shuddered.

First-person narration also allows us to get to know the speaker well, since he can tell us everything he feels and thinks directly, without the mediation of a different narrator. Therefore authors often tend to use first-person narration in a novel or story where the psychology of the protagonist is of paramount importance, such as Charlotte Perkins Gilman's "The Yellow Wallpaper," or when they want the reader to sympathize with the protagonist or enter into his reasons for acting in a certain way. A character writing in the first person will naturally be inclined, as we all are in life, to present his actions in the best light possible, make excuses for errors or immoral acts, or explain them away by insisting on his good intentions. For this reason, an author who wants us to sympathize with a character who is insane or has committed a crime, for example, might well choose to give the narrative voice to that character. In *The Outsider* by Albert Camus the reader tends to side with the narrator-protagonist, despite knowing that he has committed a murder for no real reason. We sympathize with the narrator of "The Yellow Wallpaper" and, while knowing she is on the verge of madness, are nevertheless ready to accept and agree with her conviction that many of her doctor-husband's prescriptions—absolute rest, no company, no writing—may actually be doing her more harm than good. Only first-person narration by the sick woman herself can successfully get that point of view across to the reader.

Sometimes a first-person narrator tells of events that happened to him long ago, for example when he was a child. This gives a dual perspective to the narrative: we see the child's thoughts and reactions to events, presented in the first person, and yet we may sense the presence of the older narrator, commenting on or judging the attitudes of his younger self. When the narrator of James Joyce's "Araby" describes, in the quotation given just above, how he used to follow a girl every morning but never dared speak to her, he comments that "her name was like a summons to all my foolish blood." The adjective "foolish" here represents a judgment from the older narrator telling the story, rather than from the young boy.

Narrators are not always reliable, especially first-person narrators. Sometimes we sense a discrepancy between what the narrator tells us and what we understand. "The Yellow Wallpaper" provides a good example: when the narrator declares, "I'm feeling so much better!" we know, from her remarks about "the woman behind the wallpaper" that in fact she's getting worse. When she exclaims, "How those children did tear about here! / This bedstead is fairly gnawed!" we realize that she is the one who has gnawed it. When reading a story with an **unreliable narrator**, you have to be on the lookout for such discrepancies between what the narrator says and the true situation. In a story like Edgar Allan Poe's "The Black Cat," for example, the narrator presents himself in a way that the reader might question. Huck in Mark Twain's *Huckleberry Finn* is also an unreliable narrator: he innocently believes what people tell him and accepts appearances at face value when the reader realizes that he should not, so that we constantly sense a discrepancy between the true nature of a situation and his perception and presentation of it.

A disadvantage of the first-person point of view is that it limits the scope of the narrative to the knowledge of one person. We may understand the narrator well, and perhaps identify closely with him, but we can see events and view other characters only through his eyes. Third-person narration allows us to know all the characters and witness the action from a less restricted viewpoint.

Third-person narrative can be presented by an **omniscient narrator**, i.e., one who, though not taking part in the action, knows everything about the events and the characters, even their inner thoughts and emotions. Unlike a real-life situation, where we can know other people's thoughts only if they communicate them, this type of narrator can get inside the heads and hearts of his characters and tell all. The narrator of James Joyce's "The Boarding House," for example, is omniscient: he presents the characters by all possible means—physical description, speech, actions, thoughts, and feelings. He successively enters the minds of each of the main characters in order to transcribe their thoughts. Thus we find out that although Polly has been flirting with a young man in the boarding house, her mother, Mrs. Mooney, "who was a shrewd judge . . . watched the pair and kept her own counsel," instead of intervening at once. We learn Mrs. Mooney's thoughts as she waits to speak to Mr. Doran about Polly: "It was seventeen minutes past eleven: she would have lots of time to have the matter out with Mr. Doran and then catch short twelve at Marlborough Street. She was sure she would win." We are informed of Mr. Doran's thoughts as he prepares for this interview: "The recollection of his confession of the night before was a cause of acute pain to him; the priest had drawn out every ridiculous detail of the affair and in the end had so magnified his sin that he was almost thankful at being afforded a loophole of reparation. The harm was done. What could he do now but marry her or run away?" We are also inside Polly's head at the end, while the interview takes place: "She waited on patiently, almost cheerfully, without alarm, her memories gradually giving place to hopes and visions of the future."

Although this narrator does not play a part in the story or comment on it directly in any way, we occasionally sense his presence through suggestions of irony. Apparently, for example, Mrs. Mooney "dealt with moral problems as a cleaver does with meat"! And the narrator says of her, as she awaits Mr. Doran, "She was sure she would win. To begin with she had all the weight of social opinion on her side: she was an outraged mother. She had allowed him to live beneath her roof, assuming that he was a man of honour, and he had simply abused her hospitality"; but we realize that the narrator intends us to question her status as an "outraged mother," since we know that Mrs. Mooney "watched the pair and kept her own counsel" long after the affair between the young people had become common knowledge. Far from being an "outraged mother," she has laid a trap for Mr. Doran in order to oblige him to marry Polly.

When reading prose fiction and in particular when explicating a prose text, always ask yourself why the author has chosen a certain point of view. The plot of "The Boarding House" centers on the trap set for Mr. Doran, and in order for us to realize that it is a trap we need to witness Mrs. Mooney's thoughts; and since Mr. Doran's reluctance to marry Polly is expressed only in his thoughts, we need to know them too. Hence the need for an omniscient third-person narrator.

The omniscient point of view is common in eighteenth and nineteenth century novels, but represents a fictional convention quite unlike the way we experience reality. Perhaps for this reason, another type of third-person narrative has become prevalent, involving only **limited omniscience**. With this point of view, the narrator reveals the inner thoughts and emotions of one character only, usually because that character is more interesting than the others: either he (or she) develops and changes more, or his/her personality is more complex. Alternatively, the narrator may concentrate on one specific character because we need to know that character's thoughts in order to understand the story. For example, in Kate Chopin's "The Story of an Hour," having learned of Mrs. Mallard's secret delight at the idea of her freedom, we realize that her death at the end is due to shock and despair at seeing her husband alive after all, rather than to joy, as her sister and the doctors believe. The narrator in "The Lady with the Dog," too, has limited omniscience: we follow Gurov, and witness his thoughts and emotions but not those of Anna Sergeyevna except insofar as we can guess them from her actions or speech. He develops and changes more than she does: from a womanizer who looks down on women and treats them very casually during his multiple affairs, he becomes, at the end, a man truly in love with a woman for whom he feels respect and tenderness.

Sometimes, an omniscient narrator plunges so deeply into a character's consciousness that he begins to incorporate the character's thoughts into the narrative with no transition. This is called the **stream of consciousness** technique. It acts like a combination of first- and third-person narrative, and its effect is to bring us closer into the character's mind. It can pervade the whole story or appear just occasionally. For example, towards the end of "The Lady with the Dog," when Gurov is waiting for Anna to stop crying, the narrator states: "He felt compassion for this life, still so warm and lovely, but probably already not far from beginning to fade and wither like his own. Why did she love him so much?" This question obviously represents a thought in Gurov's mind but it is presented as part of the third-person narrative. The most famous original practitioners of the stream of consciousness technique were James Joyce, Virginia Woolf, and William Faulkner. In *Mrs. Dalloway* by Virginia Woolf we often witness Clarissa Dalloway's—and other characters'—thoughts, incorporated into the third-person narrative in this way. The following passage concerns Ellie Henderson, invited to Clarissa's party:

It was an event to her, going to a party. It was quite a treat just to see the lovely clothes. Wasn't that Elizabeth, grown up, with her hair done in the fashionable way, in the pink dress? Yet she could not be more than seventeen. She was very, very handsome. But girls when they first came out didn't seem to wear white as they used.

Here, Ellie Henderson's actual thoughts ("Isn't that Elizabeth? She can't be more than seventeen," etc.), are given as reported speech, incorporated into the narrative. The narrator, in this novel and others by Woolf, floats in and out of the heads of different characters while maintaining third-person narration.

Finally, a third-person narrator can be objective (not omniscient), seeing things from the outside and giving characters' thoughts and emotions only if they express them in words or reveal them through physical expressions or gestures, just as in real life. Even an objective narrator, however, can guide us towards a certain response to a story. He chooses to relate certain events and not others, and his choice of words, e.g. descriptive adjectives such as "gloomy," "beautiful," "awe-inspiring," can affect our view of a scene. We have seen how the narrator of Kate Chopin's "The Storm," though presenting the characters' actions objectively, from the outside, nevertheless influences our interpretation of the story by stressing the joy of Alcée and Calixta and refraining from moral judgment.

Third-person narrators may ignore the reader's presence completely or address the reader directly. A first-person narrator might relate what has happened to him as if for himself, addressing no one in particular, or he might address the reader, or tell his story to a listener or a group of listeners. The narrator of Poe's "The Cask of Amontillado" tells his story to an auditor, apparently someone who knows him well: "You, who so well know the nature of my soul."

Exercises on Point of View

1. What novel or story do you know written in the first person? How does the first-person point of view affect your attitude towards the action or the characters?

2. How would you characterize the point of view in Nathaniel Hawthorne's "Young Goodman Brown" (appendix 3), and what reasons do you see for choosing it?

3. If you were explicating the following passage from "A Rose for Emily," what comments would you make about the point of view? The passage concerns Emily Grierson, the "Emily" of the title:

   That was when people had begun to feel really sorry for her. People in our town, remembering how old lady Wyatt, her great-aunt, had gone completely crazy at last, believed that the Griersons held themselves a little too high for what they really were. None of the young men were quite good enough for Miss Emily and such. . . . So when she got to be thirty and was still single, we were not pleased exactly, but vindicated.

SETTING

The **setting** of a novel or short story lends context to the events and characters. Though the importance of setting varies from work to work, it usually helps the reader to understand the characters and their situation. Characters are often, at least to some extent, the product of their environment, which includes physical location, historical era and social milieu. Harsh scenery might explain harshness in the characters; their attitudes may reflect the period when the story is set; and the kind of social environment in which characters evolve will help to determine their outlook and behavior. Thus, the background of the wild Yorkshire moors fits the passionate plot of Emily Bronte's *Wuthering Heights*; the events of Nathaniel Hawthorne's *The Scarlet Letter* are inextricably linked with the setting—Puritan New England; and the character and preoccupations of Jane Austen's protagonists reflect their social status and the social conventions of late eighteenth-century England.

Descriptions of setting can be **realistic** or **symbolic**, or sometimes both simultaneously. In the first two paragraphs of "A Rose for Emily" we read an account of the state of Miss Emily's house:

> It was a big, squarish frame house that had once been white, decorated with cupolas and spires and scrolled balconies in the heavily lightsome style of the seventies, set on what had once been our most select street. But garages and cotton gins had encroached and obliterated even the august names of that neighborhood; only Miss Emily's house was left, lifting its stubborn and coquettish decay above the cotton wagons and the gasoline pumps—an eyesore among eyesores.

This description is both realistic, with its mention of "gasoline pumps" or "garages and cotton gins," and symbolic. The strong emphasis on the idea of decline heralds the main theme of the story: not only Miss Emily herself but her whole family and the generation her family represented in the American South have suffered a decline since the Civil War, and a new age has been born. The decay of her house symbolizes the decline of her family's status and of its Old Southern values. The word "decay," mentioned in this passage, summarizes this idea and also foreshadows the discovery of the decayed body found at the end of the story.

Bear in mind that descriptions of setting, like the one above, are unlikely to be arbitrary. Do not be tempted to pass over descriptive details without considering their possible significance. In "The Story of an Hour," for example, Mrs. Mallard, alone in her room, having heard that her husband has died, sits by the window and sees

> in the open square before her house the tops of trees that were all aquiver with the new spring life. The delicious breath of rain was in the air. . . . The notes of a distant song which some one was singing reached her faintly, and countless sparrows were twittering in the eaves.

The positive connotations of "new spring life," "delicious breath of rain," "song," and "sparrows . . . twittering in the eaves" are not accidental but symbolize the optimistic feelings that Mrs. Mallard is about to experience now that she is free to live her life as she wishes: "There was something coming to her. . . . [S]he felt it, creeping out of the sky, reaching toward her through the sounds, the scents, the color that filled the air."

Sometimes, setting is used to provide an appropriate atmosphere, as for example in Hawthorne's "Young Goodman Brown" where the "diabolical" events take place in a dark forest, at midnight; or in Poe's "The Cask of Amontillado" where most of the action is set in a vault. A setting can also reflect a character's **mood**, or on the contrary provide a stark contrast to it.

Authors choose settings that are appropriate for the type of characters involved in a given story. If you are explicating a passage from a novel or short story, you should consider the impact that a specific setting might have on the characters and how their attitudes and behavior reflect elements of their physical, historical and social environment.

Exercises on Setting

1. Consider the three settings in "The Lady with the Dog" (Yalta, Moscow and the provincial town of S_____). What is their significance for the action of the story? How are the characters' attitudes and behavior influenced by the settings? How does the era in which the story is set affect the story?

2. What would you say about setting in a close reading of the following passage from Kate Chopin's "The Storm"?

   She went and stood at the window with a greatly disturbed look on her face. She wiped the frame that was clouded with moisture. It was stiflingly hot. Alcée got up and joined her at the window, looking over her shoulder. The rain was coming down in sheets obscuring the view of far-off cabins and enveloping the distant wood in a gray mist. The playing of the lightning was incessant. A bolt struck a tall chinaberry tree at the edge of the field. It filled all visible space with a blinding glare and the crash seemed to invade the very boards they stood upon.

3. What would you say about setting in a close reading of the following passage from Gilman's "The Yellow Wallpaper"?

   The most beautiful place! It is quite alone, standing well back from the road, quite three miles from the village. It makes me think of English places that you read about, for there are hedges and walls and gates that lock, and lots of separate little houses for the gardeners and people.

STYLE

Just as painters have a certain style that depends on their use of color and light, their brushwork, arrangement of subjects, and many other factors, so writers possess a style characterized by their choice of words, by their way of putting words together into sentences and paragraphs, their use of dialogue, figurative language and other elements. It is difficult to pinpoint the effects that make up an author's style; we will restrict ourselves to the most salient aspects of prose style. Generally speaking, the elements of prose writing that affect style are syntax (sentence-structure), punctuation, choice of words, and use of (or avoidance of) figurative language.

Prose is structured by syntax. Sentences may be long and complex with subordinate clauses introduced by relative pronouns ("who," "that," "which"), or by conjunctions like "because," "although," "when." Long sentences can also be held together in a looser way with paratactic syntax, i.e., a series of phrases linked simply by the conjunction "and." Or you may find shorter, more direct sentences. Such syntactic differences will depend to some extent on the nature of the work: a very literary or formal piece of writing will tend to have longer, more complex sentences than a passage of dialogue. But authors often alternate sentences of different lengths for the sake of variety, or to achieve specific effects: for example, a short sentence coming after a series of long ones will appear more dramatic and therefore attract attention. This effect can be magnified by placing the short sentence in a separate paragraph, as Faulkner does towards the end of "A Rose for Emily" with the shocking line "The man himself lay on the bed." This sentence forms a paragraph of its own and follows three much longer sentences.

Prose sentences are structured by punctuation (whereas in poetry, the verse lines, in addition to punctuation, structure the poem). Commas or semi-colons are used in order to create pauses in long sentences. Colons herald a statement illustrating an observation made in the first part of the sentence. Such divisions can affect the **rhythm** of a sentence: long, unpunctuated sentences can become heavy and slow to read; short phrases separated by many commas or semi-colons can create an impression of movement or agitation, as in this example from "The Lady with the Dog":

> She got up and went quickly to the door; he followed her, and both walked senselessly along passages, and up and down stairs, and figures in legal, scholastic, and civil service uniforms, all wearing badges, flitted before their eyes. They caught glimpses of ladies, of fur coats hanging on pegs; the draughts blew on them, bringing a smell of stale tobacco.

The short, staccato phrases here, divided up by multiple commas, create a hurried and agitated effect that is totally appropriate to the characters' circumstances at this point in the story. Though prose writers generally pay less attention than poets to rhythm, and though it can be hard to spot rhythmic effects when reading an entire novel, you should consider them when explicating a short passage of prose.

As in poetry, multiple question marks and exclamation points can create a dramatic or emotional effect in prose, for example in the following passage from Edgar Allen Poe's "The Black Cat": "The monster, in terror, had fled the premises for ever! I should behold it no more! My happiness was supreme!"

The choice of vocabulary and the juxtaposition of words contribute greatly to the style of a work. In any given passage you will probably find a certain number of neutral, "ordinary" words and other, more expressive ones. Try to characterize the vocabulary used: is it imaginative, pedestrian, concrete, abstract, literary, down-to-earth, colloquial, slang? Comment on and explain any specialized vocabulary—technical or foreign words or words belonging to a certain profession, social or geographical milieu, or historical era. For example, concerning Calixta's exclamation about the force of the rain, in Chopin's "The Storm"—"If this keeps up, *Dieu sait* if the levees goin' to stan' it!"— you would need to explain the significance of the "levees," the meaning of the French phrase *Dieu sait* and its implications for the setting of the story and Calixta's ethnic heritage, and comment on her accent indicated by the spelling of "goin'" and "stan.'" Of course, Calixta's vocabulary characterizes her way of speaking and is different from the narrator's style; you must distinguish between the style of the narration and that of the dialogue.

Certain stylistic effects concerning vocabulary (and syntax) depend to a large extent on the aim of the work or of a particular passage. A descriptive text often contains many adjectives and nouns, and verbs tend to be passive instead of active, since they aim to evoke a scene or an atmosphere rather than action. Here, for example, is a descriptive passage from Chekhov's "The Lady with the Dog":

> At Oreanda they sat on a seat not far from the church, looked down at the sea, and were silent. Yalta was hardly visible through the morning mist; white clouds stood motionless on the mountain-tops. The leaves did not stir on the trees, grasshoppers chirruped, and the monotonous hollow sound of the sea rising up from below, spoke of the peace, of the eternal sleep awaiting us.

Nouns and adjectives clearly predominate in this passage. Most of the verbs express passive attitudes ("were silent," "stood motionless"); the only verbs implying action are either negated ("did not stir") or used metaphorically ("spoke"), except for "chirruped"—but the chirruping of grasshoppers merely provides a background noise. Also, sentences in a descriptive passage, as here, often tend to be rather long, since they don't seek to create the impression of activity.

A narrative passage, on the contrary, will normally be characterized by the presence of many active verbs, since it relates characters' actions. Thus, a few lines later in the same story, we read:

> Then they met every day at twelve o'clock on the sea-front, lunched and dined together, went for walks, admired the sea. She complained that she slept badly, that her heart throbbed violently; asked the same questions, troubled now by jealousy and now by the fear that he did not respect her sufficiently. And often in the square or gardens, when there was no one near them, he suddenly drew her to him and kissed her passionately.

Verbs predominate in this passage, and they are all active ("met," "lunched," "dined," "went," "admired," "complained," etc.), suggesting energetic action and advancing the plot of the narrative.

A text aimed at persuasion, such as an essay, tends to use long sentences, divided into logical parts by colons and semi-colons. The vocabulary is usually quite literary with little use of colloquial words or colorful expressions (though exceptions could certainly be found). Logical conjunctions abound (e.g., "thus," "therefore," "so," "yet," "although," "if . . . then," "however," "nevertheless"), as well as words indicating emphasis such as "indeed," "certainly," "naturally," "obviously."

As for **dialogue**, it is of course heralded by quotation marks and, since dialogue represents a conversation, is often characterized by a more colloquial style than that of the surrounding narrative. Compare the following narrative and dialogue passages from Chopin's "The Storm":

> Bobinôt was the embodiment of serious solicitude as he strove to remove from his own person and his son's the signs of their tramp over heavy roads and through wet fields. . . . Then, prepared for the worst—the meeting with an over-scrupulous housewife, they entered cautiously at the back door. . . .
>
> "Oh, Bobinôt! You back! My! But I was uneasy. W'ere you been during the rain? An' Bibi? he ain't wet? he ain't hurt?" She had clasped Bibi and was kissing him effusively. . . .
>
> "I brought you some shrimps, Calixta," offered Bobinôt, hauling the can from his ample side pocket and laying it on the table.

Sometimes, however, especially in first-person narrative and especially in more modern texts, not only the dialogue but the whole story is told in a colloquial style, as in Updike's "A & P":

> She had on a kind of dirty-pink—beige maybe, I don't know—bathing suit with a little nubble all over it and, what got me, the straps were down. They were off her shoulders looped loose around the cool tops of her arms, and I guess as a result the suit had slipped a little on her, so all around the top of the cloth there was this shining rim.

Here, the casual, familiar diction ("beige maybe, I don't know," "what got me," "I guess") represents the voice of the narrator himself; he tells the whole story in this colloquial style. This creates the impression that he is speaking directly to us and makes us identify with him even more closely than if the first-person narration were conducted in a more formal style.

If certain words or images belonging to a specific context seem very prevalent in a story, or are repeated, you should take note of this fact and ask yourself why. In Joyce's "Araby," the preponderance of words with a religious connotation attracts attention: the former tenant of the narrator's house was a priest; the narrator uses the words "chalice," "prayers and praises," "adoration," and "harp" when thinking about the girl he loves; and, on finally reaching the almost empty "Araby" bazaar, he recognizes "a silence like that which pervades a church after a service." Ask yourself what this insistence on religious imagery signifies: not only the setting of the story in Catholic Ireland but also, probably, the nature of the boy's love, which to him is like a religion, possessing him utterly. He sees the girl as a kind of angel: "my body was like a harp and her words and gestures were like fingers running upon the wires." The repetition of religious imagery not only emphasizes his adoration of the girl but also acts as a unifying feature of the text.

In this same story the word "blind," repeated twice in the first paragraph, takes on special significance when juxtaposed with the expression of the narrator's disillusionment in the last paragraph: "Gazing up into the darkness I saw myself as a creature driven and derided by vanity; and my eyes burned with anguish and anger." We have also seen how the word "decay," mentioned in the second paragraph of "A Rose for Emily," becomes an important theme and is strongly evoked again in the final paragraph of the story.

Apart from recurring words and images, other stylistic features discussed above in the section on poetry also appear in certain prose works. Prose writers use **rhythmic effects** (see the paragraph on punctuation, page 92), **alliteration**, and especially **figurative language**, though less frequently than most poets. "Araby," a work dealing with love and enchantment (and subsequent disillusionment), provides many examples. The first paragraph contains a fine **personification**: "The other houses of the street, conscious of decent lives within them, gazed at one another with brown imperturbable faces"—humorously but accurately evoking the spectacle of well-maintained houses facing each other across the street. A few lines later we find an example of **alliteration** ("to the back doors of the dark dripping gardens where odours arose from the ashpits"), where the repetition of hard /d/ sounds echoes the harshness of the scene described. A **metaphor** effectively depicts rain falling on earth as "fine incessant needles of water playing in the sodden beds"; and the narrator illustrates love's power over him with a **simile**: "my body was like a harp and her words and gestures were like fingers running upon the wires."

Many works of fiction are written in a much plainer style with no figurative language. Such choices depend on the author's stylistic preferences and also, to a large extent, on the subject matter. "The Boarding House," also by James Joyce, dealing with a more prosaic subject than "Araby," is written in a plainer, more down-to-earth style. The first few sentences are characteristic:

> Mrs. Mooney was a butcher's daughter. She was a woman who was quite able to keep things to herself: a determined woman. She had married her father's foreman and opened a butcher's shop near Spring Gardens. But as soon as his father-in-law was dead Mr. Mooney began to go to the devil. He drank, plundered the till, ran headlong into debt.

One figure of speech that is very common in prose as well as poetry is the **symbol** (though by no means every novel or short story contains symbols just as many poems do not). A symbol (defined under "Figurative Language" in the section on poetry, page 18) is a concrete thing—a place or an object–that represents something abstract. Symbols provide a way of suggesting—rather than trying to state directly—the implications of a scene, event or state of mind that are perhaps difficult to define and go beyond the literal surface of things. Thus, the description of Miss Emily's decaying house at the beginning of "A Rose for Emily" can be interpreted as a symbol for something much larger: the decline of the whole pre-Civil War era with its assumptions and its values concerning class, gender and race.

Generally speaking, identifying the symbolic value of an object or a place broadens the story's significance for the reader, as in the above example, and gives him or her a more complete understanding of the work. We saw a symbolic setting in the images of spring in Chopin's "The Story of an Hour," which may be seen as a symbol of the fresh start in life that Mrs. Mallard looks forward to, believing herself to be alone now and free. Would you not agree, as a reader, that it feels more satisfying to view this scene, with its blue sky, sunshine, and birdsong, as a symbol of Mrs. Mallard's new freedom, than to consider these elements as purely accidental and arbitrary?

A particular object, or a setting, may take on symbolic significance because of its clear association with the theme of the story, as in the example of the decaying house in "A Rose for Emily"; or because of the amount of detail the narrator devotes to describing it, or its frequent recurrence in the story. The pink ribbons worn by Goodman Brown's wife in Hawthorne's "Young Goodman Brown," are mentioned several times and seem to have a significance beyond that of a simple decoration. They represent the wife, whose name is "Faith" and who stands for all that is good and pure in Goodman Brown's mind. In the same tale, Goodman Brown's companion on his night-walk in the forest carries a staff that "bore the likeness of a great black snake, so curiously wrought, that it might almost be seen to twist and wriggle itself like a living serpent." The vivid description of the snake-like appearance of this staff draws attention to its possible symbolic significance; and given the negative connotations of serpents, we may assume that the staff, and therefore its owner, is in some way associated with evil.

Another important aspect of the style, or tone, of certain works is **irony**. It was defined above, in the section on poetry (page 16), as "a discrepancy between what is said and what is meant, in the case of verbal irony; or between actual and expected outcomes in the case of situational irony." Irony occurs more frequently in prose than in poetry, but its use varies widely, with some authors avoiding it altogether and others using it frequently. Also, it may pervade a whole work, such as Jonathan Swift's essay "A Modest Proposal," or it may surface only at certain moments, in a character's situation, speech or behavior, or in a narrator's attitude towards a character. We feel the narrator's ironic assessment of Mrs. Mooney, for example, in Joyce's "The Boarding House," when he says of her, as she awaits Mr. Doran, "she had all the weight of social opinion on her side: she was an outraged mother." This statement is ironic because we know that Mrs. Mooney could have prevented the "outrage" but instead has deliberately maneuvered Mr. Doran into a position where he is obliged to offer to marry her daughter. She will be able to say, for the benefit of "social opinion," that she is an outraged mother, but there is an ironic discrepancy between this statement and the facts as the reader knows them.

An excellent example of situational irony occurs towards the end of Edgar Allan Poe's "The Black Cat" when the narrator, who has murdered his wife and bricked up her body in his cellar wall, needlessly raps on the wall with a cane, out of sheer bravado, as the police leave after fruitlessly searching his house. The noise causes the black cat, buried alive by accident with the wife, to howl from inside the wall, thus giving away the hiding place and exposing the narrator as a murderer.

Writers of short stories often like to end the story, like Poe in this example, with an ironic twist. The last line of Chopin's "The Story of an Hour" is ironic, in view of the reader's knowledge: "When the doctors came they said she had died of heart disease— of joy that kills." The great French short-story writer Guy de Maupassant often concludes his stories in this way, for example "The Necklace" and "The Jewelry."

It is always important, when analyzing a text, to keep in mind not only what it says but how it says it. A close reading sets out to show the connection between the two, to show, for example, how a certain setting or a certain point of view is appropriate for a particular story, or how various stylistic devices are used to reflect or reinforce ideas, attitudes, or emotions. Hence the need to study such features as syntax, punctuation, vocabulary, repetitions, symbolism, irony, and figurative language in the course of explicating a text.

Exercise on Style

Comment on the style of the following passage from "A & P" by John Updike:

> I go through the punches, 4, 9, GROC, TOT—it's more complicated than you think, and after you do it often enough, it begins to make a little song, that you hear words to, in my case "Hello (bing) there, you (gung) hap-py pee-pul (splat)!—the splat being the drawer flying out. I uncrease the bill, tenderly as you may imagine, it just having come from between the two smoothest scoops of vanilla I had ever known were there, and pass a half and a penny into her narrow pink palm, and nestle the herrings in a bag and twist its neck and hand it over.

THEME

Many prose works have an overall **theme** or central idea that does not equate to a summary of the events in the story. See if you can distinguish between the theme of a story (its "point") and its subject matter (what it's "about"), as well as its plot (the organization of events into a coherent whole). "A Rose for Emily" provides an excellent example of this distinction. The **plot** of the story begins at the moment of Miss Emily's death, then goes backwards in time to different periods of her life, before returning, at the end, to the "present," i.e., the time of her death. The subject of the story is Miss Emily's life, especially her love affair with Homer Barron and the extraordinary measures she took to keep him with her. But the **theme** goes beyond this: the symbolism of decay, along with various indications in the text about the changes coming over the town, point to a theme that could be summarized as: the transformation taking place in the South in the generations following the Civil War. The theme can usually be stated, as here, in one sentence. Identifying the theme tends to give a broader meaning to the work. It often takes the form of a generalization that applies not just to the characters in the work but to society, or a society, or human nature, in general.

Not all prose works have such a clearly identifiable theme as "A Rose for Emily" and indeed some stories may not boast a theme at all, if they are told simply for the sake of the story, as a "good yarn." Generally speaking, however, the theme is the motivation for the story, for the choice of events and for the presence of certain significant details. The implications of a work, and therefore its theme, are often open to interpretation, since different readers may find different aspects of the text significant. Thus the theme of Maupassant's "The Jewelry" might be summarized as: "appearances can be deceiving" (since M. Lantin's wife, while seeming so innocent and sincere, was apparently unfaithful to him for years). Alternatively (taking into account the final sentence of the story, which tells us that M. Lantin later remarried and was very unhappy with his second, virtuous, wife), the theme could be interpreted as: "faithfulness is not necessarily the best quality in a wife." Needless to say, you may disagree with the theme of a work, but you need to be able to formulate it according to suggestions contained in the text and should be able to give evidence supporting your interpretation.

Be prepared to explain whether and in what way the extract you are explicating relates to the overall theme of the work. This may be done either in your introduction, which concerns the passage as a whole, or in your conclusion.

Exercise on Theme

Read "Young Goodman Brown" by Nathaniel Hawthorne (or another short story of your choice). How would you define the theme of this story?

CHAPTER 5

Writing a Close Reading
of a Prose Passage

PREPARING TO WRITE A CLOSE READING OF A PROSE PASSAGE

Preparatory Work

Many of the suggestions made in the section "Preparing to Write a Close Reading of a Poem" (pages 45–47) will apply here also. Begin work on your explication well before it is due. Make sure you are very familiar with the complete work from which the passage is taken; if it is a short story, read it two or three times. (You cannot adequately explicate an extract unless you are well acquainted with the whole work because you need to relate it to the whole.) Then turn your attention to the extract to be explicated. Make sure you understand everything in it. Look up any words you're not sure of, or allusions (to other works, to mythology, the Bible, etc.). Consider the relevance of the title.

Making Notes

Make notes on any aspect of the text that strikes you immediately, such as the narrative voice, the type of writing (description? narration? dialogue?), the sentence structure and punctuation, and any stylistic features such as imagery, figurative language, repeated words or phrases. You might want to type the passage out, double-spaced, so that you can make notes directly onto the text more easily. Consider also at what point in the story's plot this extract appears and whether it reveals anything about any of the characters or the relationships between them.

For more suggestions on annotation, see part 4 "Moving Beyond Close Reading," chapter 10, page 169.

Audience

As with a poem, assume that you are writing for someone who knows the story and has it available to consult. Avoid over-use of the first person (see part 1, page 46, above).

Quoting from the Text

Remember that, although you are giving your own interpretation, it should be based on evidence in the passage or in the complete text. If necessary, include short quotations to back up or illustrate your points, using quotation marks. In the unlikely event that you need to quote a passage longer than four lines, start it on a new line, indented one inch from your left-hand margin, without quotation marks. Then start a new line again to continue your own writing. Keep any punctuation exactly as in the original, except if you reach the end of your sentence and therefore require a period. Mark omissions within quotations by three spaced periods, thus: "She had allowed him to live beneath her roof . . . and he had simply abused her hospitality." If the omission comes at the end of your sentence, use a period followed by three spaced periods: "She had allowed him to live beneath her roof, assuming that he was a man of honour. . . ." Remember that the syntax of your sentence must fit that of the quote. You cannot write:

> The narrator declares that "Her name sprang to my lips"

because you need a verb in the present tense to match "declares" and you need "his lips" to match your subject ("The narrator"). You would have to replace "sprang" and "my" by "[springs]" and "[his]"—using square brackets to point out the alterations to the original. This would be very clumsy, however, in such a short quotation. In a simple example like this, it is better to re-phrase your sentence. You could have the quotation stand on its own (not integrated into your sentence), preceded by a colon, and keep the original wording, thus:

> The speaker says: "Her name sprang to my lips."

You may also simply paraphrase the original:

> The speaker says that her name springs to his lips.

You should include page numbers in parentheses after quotations (except when quoting the actual passage you are explicating). This reference should appear after the quotation marks but before any punctuation, thus:

> The speaker says: "Her name sprang to my lips" (85).

For quotes within quotes, use single quotation marks, thus: "everyone called her simply 'the lady with the dog.'" With a page citation this would appear as: "everyone called her simply 'the lady with the dog'" (144).

Titles of short stories should be given in quotation marks, as for poems, but for titles of novels and collections of short stories (i.e., works published as independent volumes), use italics.

Only present quotations or paraphrase in order to back up your arguments. It can be very tempting, when writing on prose fiction, to re-tell the story in your own words. Remember that the person reading your work has read the story. Only mention events or details that corroborate or illustrate your point.

(For more information on using quotations, see part 4, "Moving Beyond Close Reading," pages 171 and 184–85.)

WRITING A CLOSE READING OF A PROSE PASSAGE

A close reading of a prose passage not only analyzes the text of the passage, sentence by sentence, considering both its content and its style, but also links the content and style of the passage to the complete work.

Title

When you write an interpretive essay on a piece of literature, you need to find a title that reflects your argument in the essay (see part 4, "Moving Beyond Close Reading", page 170). With a close reading, however, that is less necessary, since you are basically just explicating a passage from a longer work. Therefore, a title such as "Close Reading of a passage from Kate Chopin's 'Story of an Hour,'" seems sufficient—though you could if you wished invent a more original title highlighting the theme or salient features of the passage.

Introduction

The introduction to your close reading should situate the extract in the work from which it was taken and point out the overall characteristics of the passage. Name the title and author of the work and briefly explain in what context this passage appears. For a descriptive passage, explain where the scene takes place and its significance in the work. If certain characters are mentioned, identify them and explain their relationship and circumstances at this point in the story. Include only essential details relevant to the passage under discussion, without re-telling the whole story.

Also in the introduction you should identify the type of writing in the passage: explanation (in a didactic work), description, narration, persuasion, or dialogue. For a narrative passage, explain whether it consists of scene or summary; or there may be a combination of these elements. If the passage has an overall **tone**—humorous, mysterious, light-hearted, gloomy, dramatic, ironic, etc.—you should point this out and say whether it is typical of the work as a whole. If the extract seems to divide into parts or have some other kind of **structure**, point this out too. Unlike a poem, a passage taken from a longer prose work, being incomplete, may not have a particular structure; but sometimes a paragraph may be divided according to the progression of the argument (A + B therefore C), or the organization of a description ("above . . . below," "on the right . . . on the left," etc.).

Detailed Analysis

The introduction serves to give information about the whole passage. In the detailed analysis that represents the main body of your close reading, you should explicate the text phrase by phrase or sentence by sentence. As you proceed, keep in mind all the aspects of prose writing discussed above: plot, characterization, point of view, setting, style, and theme—but you may refer to them in any order, allowing the text to guide your remarks. Some passages will prompt you to comment more on characterization and setting but less on point of view or style, and vice versa. If there is nothing to say concerning a certain element, ignore it.

Thinking about **plot**, you will need to point out whether the passage is located in the exposition or if it forms part of the plot's development or dénouement. Does it represent a turning-point in the story? If part of the exposition, what details does it present which will later appear significant for the story or the characters? Does this passage move the plot forward and if so, how? Is it related to any element of **conflict** in the story? Are any specific ideas or emotions evoked in this passage and if so, how do they connect with the rest of the work or with the **theme** of the work? Whose is the **narrative** voice in the passage? How does the narrative **point of view** affect the narration both in this passage and in the work as a whole, and what is its effect on the reader? Regarding **characterization**, consider what the passage reveals about any of the characters. *How* does it increase our knowledge of them (through their appearance, words, or actions, or because the narrator or another character gives an opinion about them)? Does the knowledge of the characters we acquire in this extract fit in with what we already know about them? Will it be corroborated by what we learn about them later in the work? Does the passage enhance the psychological, social or philosophical function of any character(s)? Does it contribute details concerning the story's **setting**? Will the setting prove significant in the story? Does it help us understand the characters? Explain any **allusions** (to other works, to mythology, the Bible, etc.) and comment on their significance and appropriateness. Comment on the **style** of the passage, keeping in mind the following features (only some of which will be relevant): sentence structure and length, rhythm, punctuation, alliteration, vocabulary and imagery, figurative language including symbolism and irony. Are any words or expressions that appear in this passage repeated frequently elsewhere in the work and what is their significance, in your view? Is the style of the passage typical of the work as a whole? Is the style of the work suitable for its subject matter?

Conclusion

Do not forget to end your close reading with a conclusion. The conclusion of a close reading presents a more general view than the analysis. Consider the significance of the passage in the context of the complete work; how does it relate to the **theme** of the work? Is the work's title relevant to this extract? Is the **style** of the passage typical of the whole work? Does the passage provide a good illustration of the author's art? What is your overall evaluation of his or her art in this passage and in the complete work?

Revision

You should complete the first draft of your close reading with enough time left for revision and editing. Re-read your own work. Reading it aloud may help you find problematic areas; if it doesn't make sense to you, it won't to another reader. Check both the content and the organization of your work. Make sure your arguments are clear and that you have introduced suitable quotations from the text to back up your points, integrating them properly into your own sentences. Remembering that your task is to analyze and explicate the passage, make sure you have avoided paraphrasing, i.e., re-telling the story in your own words. Check that your essay is suitably divided into paragraphs and that transitions are smooth and logical. Do not forget to include an introduction and a conclusion that stand apart from the line-by-line analysis.

In order to check the **style** of your work, it can be helpful to read it aloud; then if anything sounds awkward or unnatural, you will be more likely to notice it. Examine your choice of words: avoid colloquialisms, but do not try to use highly sophisticated vocabulary unless you are sure of being able to handle it accurately. Avoid wordiness for its own sake: make sure all your sentences add something to your essay. Try to incorporate some variety into the structure of your sentences. Finally, proofread your paper for errors of spelling, punctuation, and grammar. Check that any quotations you have used match the syntax of your own sentences.

Avoiding Plagiarism

It goes without saying that your close reading should be your own work. To allow anyone else to compose your paper for you, or even parts of it, would be a violation of academic integrity. Copying another writer's thoughts, whether from a book or the Internet, without acknowledging the fact, constitutes an act of plagiarism. (Review the paragraphs on avoiding plagiarism in the section on poetry, pages 50–51.)

When writing a research paper you will need to quote from secondary sources and you should always acknowledge them (see part 4, "Moving Beyond Close Reading," pages 181–83); but for a close reading you are unlikely to need secondary sources.

Summary of Elements to Discuss in a Close Reading of a Prose Passage

I Introduction

a) Name the title and author of the work from which the passage is taken. Situate the passage in the context of the work (identify any characters mentioned in the passage and briefly explain their circumstances at this point in the narrative; explain the significance of **setting**, where appropriate).

b) Identify the type of writing (narrative, descriptive, etc.) and, where appropriate, its **tone**.

c) Analyze the **structure** of the passage, if appropriate.

II Detailed analysis, proceeding through the passage phrase by phrase, or sentence by sentence.

(These elements can be treated in any order, depending how they come up in the passage. Some features may have more significance than others, depending on the passage.)

a) At what point in the **plot** structure does this extract appear (exposition, development, dénouement)? Does the extract move the plot forward significantly?

b) Are any ideas or emotions evoked in this text that are significant for the work as a whole, or that relate to its **theme**? If there is an element of **conflict** in the work, does this text relate to it?

c) What is the **point of view** in the passage and how does it affect our attitude towards events or characters in the passage and in the work as a whole?

d) Does the extract reveal anything about the **setting** and how important is this setting to the story?

e) Does the passage contribute to our knowledge of the characters, and if so, how?

f) Comment on the **style** of the passage (effects achieved by syntax, punctuation, use of a certain type of vocabulary or imagery, repetitions, figurative language).

III Conclusion

(These are suggestions. Choose what seems most relevant to your passage. Add other comments of a general nature if you wish.)

a) Discuss the significance of the extract for the work as a whole, whether for the plot, the characterization, point of view, setting, style, or for a combination of these elements.

b) Relate the passage to the **theme** of the work.

c) Give your overall appreciation of the author's art in this passage and in the complete work.

CHAPTER 6

Close Readings of Prose Passages

In this section you will first find three model close readings. These are followed by seven prose passages accompanied by questions designed to help you write close readings of your own on whichever passages you or your professor choose. You may then be asked to compose questions of your own, on a new passage, to offer to your fellow students. Finally you will move on to writing an explication of a new passage without questions to guide you.

All the extracts are taken from short stories included in appendix 3; you should read the complete story before either reading a model explication or attempting to explicate one of the passages with questions.

The three model close readings are from Edgar Allan Poe's "The Black Cat," Anton Chekhov's "The Lady with the Dog," and Kate Chopin's "The Storm."

The text of the passage from "The Black Cat" illustrates the kinds of notes and comments you might make in the margins of a text on a first or second reading, before expanding these remarks into the first draft of your essay.

The final explication, on a passage from Kate Chopin's "The Storm," is followed by a commentary pointing out noteworthy features of the reading and of its approach to the text.

MODEL CLOSE READINGS

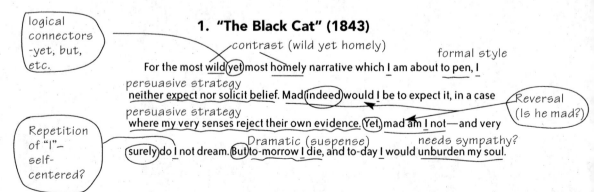

1. "The Black Cat" (1843)

logical connectors -yet, but, etc.

contrast (wild yet homely)

formal style

For the most wild yet most homely narrative which I am about to pen, I

persuasive strategy
neither expect nor solicit belief. Mad indeed would I be to expect it, in a case

Reversal (Is he mad?)

persuasive strategy
where my very senses reject their own evidence. Yet, mad am I not—and very

Repetition of "I"– self-centered?

Dramatic (suspense)

needs sympathy?

surely do I not dream. But to-morrow I die, and to-day I would unburden my soul.

1 2
My immediate purpose is to place before the world, plainly, succinctly, and
3 "homely"
without comment, a series of mere household events. In their consequences, these
1 2 "wild" 3 strong verbs.
events have terrified—have tortured—have destroyed me. Yet I will not attempt
1 "wild" 2
to expound them. To me, they have presented little but horror—to many they will
"homely" 1
seem less terrible than *baroques*. Hereafter, perhaps, some intellect may be found
"wild" "homely" 2
which will reduce my phantasm to the commonplace—some intellect more
unreliable?
calm,more logical, and far less excitable than my own, which will perceive, in the
"wild" "homely"
circumstances I detail with awe, nothing more than an ordinary succession of very
natural causes and effects.

1, 2, 3- balance (sane? reliable)

1, 2- balance (sane?

Edgar Allan Poe (1809–1849)

The first paragraph of Edgar Allan Poe's "The Black Cat" introduces the narrator who claims to have undergone an experience that defies belief, of which he plans to give a totally factual and unadorned account. The passage presents neither description nor narration (a narrative is announced but not begun); instead, its aim is persuasion: the narrator wishes to persuade the reader in advance of the veracity of his fantastic tale. This introductory paragraph also attempts to create suspense by hinting at a dreadful story without giving any details yet as to its nature.

The first sentence immediately sets up a contrast, between "wild" and "homely," that will recur throughout the paragraph. On the one hand, the narrator's story will be "homely" or down-to-earth, ordinary (a few sentences later he refers to "household events"), but on the other hand it will be "wild," telling of experiences that have "terrified" and "tortured" him. He claims in this first sentence that he does not expect the reader to believe his tale—but this is part of his persuasive strategy; of course he wants the reader to believe his story is true. He is saying, in effect: "Believe me or not, but this really happened." The strategy continues in the next sentence, where he suggests he would be "mad" (crazy) to expect the reader to believe him "in a case where [his] very senses reject their own evidence." In other words, he himself has trouble giving credence to his own story, yet the "evidence" of his own eyes and ears proves that it happened. Again, this statement aims to persuade the reader that the story is true, and the following sentence backs up the claim by insisting that the narrator is totally sane ("mad am I not"). However, the very denial of madness at once alerts the reader to the possibility that the narrator may, in fact, be mad, whereas the thought might not have entered our heads if he had not broached the subject. Thus the author, Poe, cleverly manipulates our opinion of the narrator, planting a doubt in our minds concerning his sanity both thanks to and in spite of the latter's own words.

The persuasive intent of the passage emerges also from the use of conjunctions and adverbs such as "yet" (three times), "but," "indeed," and "surely"—logical connectors that reveal both the careful construction of the paragraph and its aim of influencing the reader's opinion. The formal style of the piece is typical of the era when it was written (the first half of the nineteenth century), giving us such expressions as "the . . . narrative which I am about to pen" and "I would unburden my soul" (for "I wish to unburden . . ."), and inversions like "Mad indeed would I be . . ." and "mad am I not." Moreover, the style is very elegant and carefully crafted, with well-balanced phrases and sentences, such as the opposition between "Mad indeed would I be . . ." and "Yet, mad am I not" in the second and third sentences.

The fourth sentence of the paragraph contains a shocking statement: "But to-morrow I die," which at once arouses the reader's interest. This declaration adds to the feeling of suspense already created by the hint that the narrator may be mad (though he denies it) and by the suggestion that his story will be incredible and "wild." The whole paragraph continues to build on this suspense. At this point, then, we understand that the narrator is writing his story the day before his death, but as yet we have no idea how or why he is to die.

This opening paragraph of the story forcefully establishes the first-person point of view at once, with seven repetitions of the pronoun "I" in the first four sentences. The focus on "I" may give the impression that the narrator is somewhat self-centered, which the ensuing narrative certainly corroborates; as usual, however, first-person narration tends to make the reader sympathize with the narrator, especially one who announces: "to-morrow I die, and to-day I would unburden my soul." We feel ready to lend an ear to such an unfortunate man. More importantly for this particular story, the first-person point of view guarantees, theoretically, the veracity of the narrative. If we were to read this story in a third-person version, our immediate reaction might be to dismiss it as utter nonsense. But the first person narrator vouches for its authenticity, with the "evidence" of his senses. He continues to insist on the validity of his narrative in the following sentence, promising to render "plainly, succinctly, and without comment" a true account of his experiences.

Again, here, we find the contrast between the "wild" and "homely" aspects of his story: first he claims it represents merely "a series of . . . household events," but then we learn that these events have "terrified," "tortured," and "destroyed" him. These increasingly strong verbs culminating in "destroyed" might smack of hyperbole if we did not know that he is soon to die, presumably because of the "events" in question. The verbs neatly balance in their threefold insistence the three adverbial phrases of the previous sentence, "plainly, succinctly, and without comment." The narrator's style maintains its elegant equilibrium, however "terrified" he may have been by events. He adds that he will not attempt to "expound" the events, i.e., explain them in detail, implying that readers may draw their own conclusions.

The final sentences elaborate further on the contrast between the "wild" and "homely" nature of his story. Though he views the events it relates with "horror," other people might see them as merely "*baroques,*" i.e., bizarre or grotesque (the word is in italics because it was still considered a foreign word); what to him is a "phantasm" (an illusion or perhaps a supernatural experience) might seem to others "commonplace"; and what he relates with "awe" others might perceive as "nothing more than an ordinary succession of very natural causes and effects." These last two sentences presenting the two contrasting views are again remarkable for their balance, which underscores that contrast: the first sentence opposes "To me . . ." and "to many . . .," while the second predicts "some intellect . . . which will reduce . . ." and "some intellect . . . which will perceive. . . ." Apart from the artistic merit inherent in such a balanced and elegant style, these structures suggest a lucidity that backs up the narrator's claim to be totally sane.

Readers generally tend to believe narrators, since the latter provide the authority for the truth of the story; but narrators are sometimes unreliable, either because they attempt deliberately to fool the reader or because they themselves are blind to some aspect of their own situation. This opening paragraph, with its hint of the narrator's possible madness, its reference to his "excitable" intellect, and its suggestion of an unbelievable story to come, should alert the reader to the possibility that its narrator might not be totally reliable. On the other hand, the controlled, lucid, balanced, and elegant style seems to argue in favor of his powers of judgment, so that the reader is not sure what to think and is eager to read the story itself.

This first paragraph of the story builds up suspense by implying that the tale to follow is incredible (but true), terrifying and awe-inspiring according to the narrator—though to some it may appear "homely" and "commonplace." We are also curious about the fact that the narrator is to die the following day, and interested in the "phantasm"—a supernatural apparition or at least one that deceives the senses. By the end of the paragraph the reader is very anxious to hear what kind of story this might be. It is a suitably suspenseful introduction to a tale of the supernatural.

2. "The Lady with the Dog" (1899)
trans. Constance Garnett

At Oreanda they sat on a seat not far from the church, looked down at the sea, and were silent. Yalta was hardly visible through the morning mist; white clouds stood motionless on the mountain-tops. The leaves did not stir on the trees, grasshoppers chirruped, and the monotonous hollow sound of the sea rising up from below, spoke of the peace, of the eternal sleep awaiting us. So it must have sounded when there was no Yalta, no Oreanda here; so it sounds now, and it will sound as indifferently and monotonously when we are all no more. And in this constancy, in this complete indifference to the life and death of each of us, there lies hid, perhaps, a pledge of our eternal salvation, of the unceasing movement of life upon earth, of unceasing progress towards perfection. Sitting beside a young woman who in the dawn seemed so lovely, soothed and spellbound in these magical surroundings—the sea, mountains, clouds, the open sky—Gurov thought how in reality everything is beautiful in this world when one reflects: everything except what we think or do ourselves when we forget our human dignity and the higher aims of our existence.

Anton Chekhov (1860–1904)

The action in the first part of "The Lady with the Dog" takes place in Yalta, a holiday resort on the Black Sea where Gurov and Anna Sergeyevna have met. They are both married but are on holiday in Yalta without their spouses. After knowing each other for a week and spending a lot of time together they have become lovers, in the evening prior to this passage. Later, when Anna had recovered from her feelings of guilt, they took a cab out of town to Oreanda and now, in this extract, we see them looking out over the sea in the early hours of the morning. It is basically a descriptive passage but the sight of the magnificent view leads both the narrator and Gurov to reflect on abstract, spiritual issues: beauty, perfection, human mortality. A corresponding movement within the passage from concrete to abstract accompanies this change of focus. The tone is hopeful, even optimistic. The text can be divided into three parts: first the description, in the first three sentences, then some thoughts that apparently originate in the mind of the narrator, in the fourth and fifth sentences; and finally Gurov's own thoughts in the long last sentence.

Yalta itself is portrayed as a busy resort, a place where people meet, as Anna and Gurov have met; but Oreanda, some way out of town, provides a more peaceful setting and a magnificent view. Even its name has a pleasant, harmonious sound. Arriving at Oreanda, Gurov and Anna sit down "not far from the church," and this is not by chance: after their lovemaking, Anna, overcome with remorse, has invoked religion, talking of sin and forgiveness. The proximity of the church, as well as the infinite expanse of the sea, contributes no doubt to the quasi-religious musings of the narrator and Gurov.

The first sentence, with its progressively shorter phrases, acts as an introduction to the description that follows. It is the only sentence in the passage denoting actions and contains the only active verbs, "sat" and "looked down." Already the third verb of the sentence, "were silent," introduces the kind of verbs denoting passive states that are typical of descriptions and that predominate in the rest of the passage: "was visible," "stood," "will sound," "lies hid," "seemed," "did not stir" (an active verb negated). The one active verb later in the passage concerns the grasshoppers, but their chirruping only forms part of the background noise for the characters. It is a noise characteristic of warm climates, reminding us of the southern setting of the story. Like most descriptions, the passage contains many adjectives and nouns: "morning mist," "white clouds," "motionless," "mountain-tops," "leaves," "trees." The description is of a beautiful scene, with the vast sea in the distance, the "morning mist" and "white clouds . . . on the mountain-tops"; its dominant mood is calm: the clouds "stood motionless," the leaves "did not stir" and the sound of the sea "spoke of . . . peace."

The concrete nouns of the description in this first section give way, in the middle of the third sentence, to a much more abstract vocabulary. As the narrative turns from the view itself to the meditation inspired by the view, we encounter abstract nouns such as "peace," "eternal sleep," "indifference," "life," "death," "eternal salvation," "movement," "progress," "perfection." The view of the sea, stretching out to infinity, often leads, in literature and in life, to thoughts of eternity and of human mortality, as here. Indeed, despite the beauty of the scene, the "monotonous hollow sound" of the sea introduces an ominous note, for the "peace" it speaks of represents that of "the eternal sleep awaiting us"—the peace of death.

The use of "us" in this sentence is curious, introducing the first person into a third-person narrative. Up to now the narrator has displayed "limited omniscience": he describes the appearance, speech, and gestures of both characters, but concentrates on Gurov and gives only Gurov's thoughts. We have learnt about his family, his unfaithfulness to his wife, his attitude towards women, whom he calls "the lower race"; we know that when he noticed Anna at Yalta he thought to himself: "If she is here alone without a husband or friends, it wouldn't be amiss to make her acquaintance." But we have not heard the narrator's own voice before this moment (except through ironic comments such as "yet [Gurov] could not get on for two days together without 'the lower race'"), nor will we hear it subsequently. It is as if the narrator, peering over Gurov's shoulder at the view from Oreanda, feels moved to voice his own thoughts on contemplating the vast expanse of the ocean. The story of Gurov and Anna takes second place for a moment to a meditation on human transience versus the permanence of nature, and nature's indifference to man: the sea sounded this way before Yalta and Oreanda existed and will continue to sound, "indifferently," when "we are all no more." Again, the narrator uses the first person pronoun, including himself in the narrative. This sentence has a distinct structure, using the same verb first in the past tense, then in the present, then in the future: "So it must have sounded . . . so it sounds now and it will sound . . . ."

The inclusion of the narrator, through the use of the pronoun "us" and the possessive adjective "our," continues in the next sentence, beginning "And in this constancy . . . ." The thought in this sentence is somewhat obscure: the "constancy" or permanence of nature and its indifference to human life supposedly represent a hidden "pledge" of "our eternal salvation" (i.e., if nature continues then we must also?) and of human "progress towards perfection." The notion that human life is constantly improving from one generation to another was widespread in the nineteenth century, which saw huge material progress, and is often voiced by various characters in Chekhov's plays, for example Trofimov in *The Cherry Orchard*. The idea is emphasized here by the repetition of "unceasing." The syntax of this sentence is well balanced: with two phrases beginning "in . . .," "in . . ." answered by three phrases beginning "of . . .," "of . . .," "of . . . ."

Altogether this passage contains six sentences, which become progressively longer as meditation replaces narration. The last two, beginning "And in this constancy . . ." and "Sitting beside a young woman . . .," take up more than half the paragraph between them. Generally speaking, narrative sentences often tend to be shorter, evoking successive actions, whereas descriptive and meditative passages like this one give rise to longer sentences.

The final sentence of the passage brings us back to Gurov and to the "limited omniscient" point of view that operates in the rest of the story: we know Gurov's thoughts but not Anna's—no doubt because his point of view is more interesting since he is the one who changes in the course of the narrative. The narrator's reflections that we have just heard, given in the first person plural, about "our eternal salvation" and "unceasing progress towards perfection" were apparently shared by Gurov and were perhaps intended to represent his thoughts, since we now find him musing on similar topics, such as "the higher aims of our existence" and the fact that "everything is beautiful in this world." His ideas are inspired by his appreciation of the beauty around him ("these magical surroundings") and by Anna ("who in the dawn seemed so lovely"). The alliteration of /s/ in the first half of the sentence ("Sitting," "beside," "seemed," "so," "soothed," "spellbound," "surroundings," "sea") has a peaceful, soothing effect. The second half of the sentence, however, introduces a more serious note, and a thought that Gurov may be entertaining for the first time: everything is beautiful in the world, "except what we think or do ourselves when we forget our human dignity and the higher aims of our existence." From the description we have received of Gurov's life up to now it does not seem as though he has given much thought in the past to "the higher aims of our existence." Married to a woman he does not love, he has been unfaithful to her with countless women; he scorns women in general, calling them "the lower race," but gets bored in the company of men. His multiple affairs with women have been superficial and have always turned into "a regular problem of extreme intricacy, and in the long run . . . [become] unbearable." Totally absorbed in himself and his own pleasure, he has never devoted himself either to a cause or to another person. He has enjoyed a social life in Moscow ("restaurants, clubs, dinner-parties, anniversary celebrations . . . entertaining distinguished lawyers and artists . . . playing cards . . .") that would leave little time for reflection on "the higher aims of our existence." Perhaps this moment with Anna Sergeyevna at Oreanda represents his first realization that there might be more to life than the social whirl. Certainly he begins to change after his affair with Anna in Yalta: we see him dissatisfied with his superficial life in Moscow, continually thinking of Anna when he had expected to forget her and eventually seeking her out and resuming their relationship.

The main interest of this story lies in the development of Gurov's character; indeed its theme could be summarized thus: even a superficial middle-aged womanizer can fall in love and be transformed by the experience. This moment at Oreanda seems to mark the first step in this development. The previous evening, when Anna expressed remorse for having made love with him, he was impatient and bored, irritated by her tears. But by the end of the story, when Anna weeps, he wants to "say something affectionate," feels "compassion" for her, and realizes that "only now when his head was grey he had fallen properly, really in love—for the first time in his life."

This passage provides a moment of pause in the action of the story but suggests an important step in the development of Gurov's character from a purely selfish man to someone capable of fully loving another human being, feeling deep emotion and appreciating the spiritual values of human life. The theme of the story seems to be that such a transformation is always possible, even at an advanced age. The passage also presents an interesting movement from the third to the first person and back again, and it illustrates some of Chekhov's favorite ideas about progress and the perfectibility of life on earth. These thoughts are inspired by the beauty of the setting, the view from Oreanda over the vast ocean that gives rise to thoughts of infinity, eternal life, and spiritual values.

3. "The Storm" (c. 1899)

They did not heed the crashing torrents, and the roar of the elements made her laugh as she lay in his arms. She was a revelation in that dim, mysterious chamber; as white as the couch she lay upon. Her firm, elastic flesh that was knowing for the first time its birthright, was like a creamy lily that the sun invites to contribute its breath and perfume to the undying life of the world.   5

The generous abundance of her passion, without guile or trickery, was like a white flame which penetrated and found response in depths of his own sensuous nature that had never yet been reached.

When he touched her breasts they gave themselves up in quivering ecstasy, inviting his lips. Her mouth was a fountain of delight. And when he possessed   10
her, they seemed to swoon together at the very borderland of life's mystery.

He stayed cushioned upon her, breathless, dazed, enervated, with his heart beating like a hammer upon her. With one hand she clasped his head, her lips lightly touching his forehead. The other hand stroked with a soothing rhythm his muscular shoulders.   15

The growl of the thunder was distant and passing away.

Kate Chopin (1851–1904)

This passage represents the climax of the plot of Kate Chopin's "The Storm." The two main characters, present though not named in this extract, are Calixta and Alcée. The setting is in the South, where violent summer storms are common. (Judging by the French names and the reference at one point to the levees, the action probably takes place in or near New Orleans.) Alcée, caught by the storm, has taken shelter at Calixta's house at a moment when she is alone there; her husband and son have gone to the store. Alcée and Calixta have not been together alone since her marriage five years previously, but they were strongly attracted to each other before that, and share a memory of a day when they kissed passionately. Now, remembering that day, they fall into each other's arms. The language of this extract is mostly descriptive, evoking passionate abandonment.

The references to "crashing torrents" and "roaring elements" indicate the violence of the storm, which clearly serves as a symbol of the characters' violent passion as well as providing the story's title. This first sentence sets the tone of the passage, which is one of joy and delight. Calixta laughs as she lies in Alcée's arms; both these people are married, but they feel no sense of guilt as they abandon themselves to their passion. The omniscient third-person narrator of the story clearly does not condemn the characters for their actions. The stress in this extract is on their joy, and the question of infidelity is not even mentioned. The next sentence suggests that Calixta is "as white as the couch she lay upon"; the previous paragraph also referred to her white throat and breasts; and the third sentence of this passage calls her a "creamy lily." White is a color associated with purity and its repetition here helps to convey an impression of innocence rather than guilt.

The bedroom, that "dim, mysterious chamber," has already been described, when Alcée first came into the house, as "dim and mysterious" with its "white monumental bed." The description of the "firm, elastic flesh" of Calixta's young body is conveyed in a simile: "like a creamy lily that the sun invites to contribute its breath and perfume to the undying life of the world." This beautiful sentence implies that, just as the warmth of the sun brings out the perfume of a lily, so the essence of Calixta's sensuous nature is revealed in this act of love with Alcée. The passion shared by the two lovers, suppressed in the past, now involves them both in a sensuous experience such as neither of them has ever known before, despite being married: Calixta's body is "knowing for the first time its birthright," and Alcée feels a response in the "depths of his own sensuous nature that had never yet been reached."

The narrator's indulgent attitude towards the lovers appears in the positive phrases used to describe Calixta's passion, with its "generous abundance" and lack of "guile or trickery"; and again the image of a "white flame" suggests purification rather than debasement. The verb "penetrated" has an overt sexual connotation here. The next paragraph, too, is totally positive, with its mention of "quivering ecstasy" and the jubilant metaphor "Her mouth was a fountain of delight." The following sentence hints at an almost spiritual ecstasy achieved by this physical embrace as they "swoon together at the very borderland of life's mystery." The narrator sees their love not as a tawdry affair but as something that opens up the protagonists' souls to "life's mystery."

In the next sentence "cushioned" suggests Calixta's ample form. The succession of short phrases separated by commas ("breathless, dazed, enervated") seems to imitate Alcée's breathlessness, whereas the final sentence of the paragraph, even and unpunctuated, conveys a sense of calm, as Calixta strokes his shoulders "with a soothing rhythm." Calixta's gestures, as she kisses Alcée on the forehead and strokes him, suggest tenderness. Their lovemaking is now over and the final sentence of the passage draws a symbolic parallel with the storm: "The growl of the thunder was distant and passing away."

This passage is clearly crucial for the story, representing the climax of the action and stressing the joyousness of this unexpected moment of passion during a brief storm. The dénouement following this extract consists in a description of their contented parting, of the happy meal Calixta shares with her husband and son on their return, and of Alcée's "loving" letter to his wife; and it culminates with the final sentence of the story: "So the storm passed and everyone was happy." This sentence again highlights both the symbolic link between the storm and the moment of passion and the narrator's forgiving attitude towards the lovers. This story provides a good example of how a narrator, without giving an overt opinion on the events and characters in a story, can nevertheless influence the reader's reaction to them.

Commentary on Model Close Reading #3

Notice how the above reading moves steadily through the passage, commenting on everything that seems worthy of attention and using many of the concepts we have been studying, such as narrative voice, setting, figurative language, and symbolism. Notice also the constant effort to connect *what* is being said to *how* it is expressed— through use of significant words, symbols, figurative language, and rhythmic variations. A close reading should always try to make this link between content (ideas, emotions, sensory impressions) and form or language.

The introduction provides enough information about Alcée and Calixta's past without going into unnecessary detail, for example about their marriages or about the circumstances of their current meeting. The details given are those that are relevant to this passage. The introduction also establishes the setting and relates it to the storm.

The reading moves next into a detailed analysis of the extract, beginning with the first sentence. Notice how, here and elsewhere, quotations are given from the passage, but only very short ones, e.g. "crashing torrents," "roaring elements," and later, "as white as the couch she lay upon," "creamy lily," etc. In a close reading you rarely need to quote more than a few words at a time.

Since the storm gives the story its title, it seems important to consider its possible symbolic significance, which is not difficult to find in this tale of violent passion. Having established this connection via the phrases "crashing torrents" and "roaring elements," the close reading then deals with another important question brought up in the first sentence by Calixta's laughter, namely the moral attitude of the third-person narrator towards the events described. This leads to consideration of another symbolic reference appearing in the next two sentences, that of whiteness and purity.

Notice that the writer of this close reading, when pointing out figures of speech, never simply states "There is a simile in line 4," which tells the reader nothing, but points out the significance of the similes "like a creamy lily," "like a white flame," or the metaphor "Her mouth was a fountain of delight," and explains what they contribute to the text. The impact of every significant word or phrase is also noted, such as "generous," "without guile or trickery," "penetrated," "quivering ecstasy," "life's mystery," "cushioned."

The issue of rhythm and punctuation is not forgotten, but brought up only where it appears relevant, i.e., in reference to the short phrases imitating breathlessness ("breathless, dazed, enervated") that contrast with the calmer, even rhythm of the next two sentences.

The conclusion summarizes the essential themes of the passage—the link between storm and passion, the joyful nature of Calixta's and Alcée's love-making unclouded by feelings of guilt, and the importance for the reader of the narrator's attitude towards their encounter.

Notice in particular how this reading stays close to the passage throughout, examining every important detail in the passage but ignoring aspects of the story that are not referred to here. For instance, the fact that Calixta and Alcée are both married is mentioned, since that is relevant to the moral stance of the narrator, but no information is given about Calixta's husband and son or Alcée's wife. Events occurring in the story after this passage are referred to only in the conclusion, and again only insofar as they are relevant to themes brought up in this passage, namely the symbolism of the storm and the attitude of the narrator towards Calixta's passionate encounter with Alcée.

TOWARDS CLOSE READING: PROSE PASSAGES ACCOMPANIED BY QUESTIONS

Using the foregoing models as examples and the questions following each passage as a guide, you can now write close readings of your own on whichever of the following passages you choose or your professor assigns. *Do not simply answer the questions*, but incorporate your answers into an essay (as in the models). Treat the questions as a general guide only, rather than simply answering them one by one. You do not need to deal with them strictly in order (though your reading should move through the passage sentence by sentence); if one or two questions seem incomprehensible to you, you can omit them; and of course you should not hesitate to add any independent observations of your own. After this practice, you should be able to write a close reading of a prose passage without questions to guide you.

The texts are presented in chronological order.

1. "Young Goodman Brown" (1835)

But something fluttered lightly down through the air, and caught on the branch of a tree. The young man seized it, and beheld a pink ribbon.

"My Faith is gone!" cried he, after one stupefied moment. "There is no good on earth; and sin is but a name. Come, devil! for to thee is this world given."

And maddened with despair, so that he laughed loud and long, did Goodman   5
Brown grasp his staff and set forth again, at such a rate, that he seemed to fly along the forest-path, rather than to walk or run. The road grew wilder and drearier, and more faintly traced, and vanished at length, leaving him in the heart of the dark wilderness, still rushing onward, with the instinct that guides mortal man to evil. The whole forest was peopled with frightful sounds; the creaking   10
of the trees, the howling of wild beasts, and the yell of Indians; while, sometimes, the wind tolled like a distant church-bell, and sometimes gave a broad roar around the traveler, as if all Nature were laughing him to scorn. But he was himself the chief horror of the scene, and shrank not from its other horrors.

Nathaniel Hawthorne (1804–1864)

For the Introduction

1. Name the author and title of the story. Explain Goodman Brown's situation at this point in the story. (Where is he, where has he come from, what has he just seen?)

2. How would you characterize the type(s) of writing in this passage (description, narration, dialogue)?

3. What is the tone of the passage?

4. How would you analyze the structure of the passage? (Can it be divided into parts?)

For the Detailed Analysis

1. What is the significance of the "pink ribbon" that flutters down into a tree? Why does Goodman Brown exclaim on seeing it "My Faith is gone"? Who is Faith? What are the connotations of the name? Why does Goodman Brown conclude, "There is no good on earth"? What are the implications of the exclamation "Come, devil! for to thee is this world given"?

2. Comment on the use of words and expressions such as "beheld," "cried he," "thee," and "did Goodman Brown grasp his staff. . . ."

3. What are the connotations of the title "Goodman"?

4. What is the cause of Brown's "despair" and why does he now proceed at such a fast rate?

5. How would you characterize the vocabulary of the second and third sentences of the final paragraph?

6. Is the description here realistic or symbolic? What is the significance of the story's setting?

7. Explain the significance of the phrase "with the instinct that guides mortal man to evil."

8. Why is Nature said to be laughing Goodman Brown to scorn, and in what sense is he "the chief horror of the scene"?

9. Does the passage contribute to our understanding of the social, psychological, or philosophical dimension of the main character, Goodman Brown?

10. Explain the reference to "Indians"; how does it relate to the story's setting?

11. Comment on the syntax of the sentence beginning "The whole forest. . . ."

12. At what point in the plot does this passage appear? Does the passage move the plot forward significantly?

13. What is the point of view in the passage, and in the story as a whole?

13. Does the passage contribute to our understanding of the social, psychological, or philosophical dimension of the main character, Goodman Brown?

For the Conclusion

1. Is the style of this passage typical of the work as a whole?

2. What would you say is the theme of the story? How does this passage relate to the theme?

3. What is your overall appreciation of this passage and of the complete work?

2. "The Story of an Hour" (1894)

She arose at length and opened the door to her sister's importunities. There was
a feverish triumph in her eyes, and she carried herself unwittingly like a goddess
of Victory. She clasped her sister's waist, and together they descended the stairs.
Richards stood waiting for them at the bottom.

 Some one was opening the front door with a latchkey. It was Brently Mallard   5
who entered, a little travel-stained, composedly carrying his grip-sack and
umbrella. He had been far from the scene of accident, and did not even know
there had been one. He stood amazed at Josephine's piercing cry; at Richards's
quick motion to screen him from the view of his wife.

 But Richards was too late.   10

 When the doctors came they said she had died of heart disease—of joy that kills.

Kate Chopin (1851–1904)

For the Introduction

1. Name the title and author of the work. Where in the work do these paragraphs
   appear?

2. Explain who the characters are: the initial "She," Richards, Brently Mallard.

3. Explain the circumstances that have brought the characters together.

4. Identify the type(s) of writing in this passage (narrative, description, dialogue).

5. Can the passage be divided into parts and if so, how?

For the Detailed Analysis

1. How would you characterize the style of the first two sentences? (Consider the
   vocabulary and figurative language.) Is it typical of the passage and of the work as
   a whole?

2. What form have the sister's "importunities" taken?

3. Why does Mrs. Mallard have a look of "feverish triumph" in her eyes? What do we
   know about her reaction to the news of her husband's death? Relate this to the
   point of view chosen for this story.

4. What do you think of the comparison of Mrs. Mallard to "a goddess of Victory"?

5. Show how the passage interweaves description and narration. How well can you
   picture the scene?

6. What is the effect of the first two sentences of the second paragraph in the passage?

7. How do you react to the husband's name, Brently Mallard? What kind of picture of
   him is evoked by the few details given: "a little travel-stained, composedly carrying
   his grip-sack and umbrella"?

8. Do we learn much about the personality of the characters in this passage? In the
   story as a whole? Is it important for us to know them well? Why (not)?

9. Why do Richards and Josephine react as they do when Brently Mallard enters?

10. What is the effect of the short sentence "But Richards was too late," placed in a paragraph of its own?

11. Relate the final sentence to the first sentence of the story.

12. Explain the irony of the final sentence.

13. What moment would you identify as the climax of this story? Does it have a dénouement?

For the Conclusion

1. What would you say is the theme of this work and how does this passage relate to it?

2. What is your opinion of the story's ending?

3. "The Lady with the Dog" (1899)
trans. Constance Garnett

"Don't remember evil against me. We are parting forever—it must be so, for we ought never to have met. Well, God be with you."

The train moved off rapidly, its lights soon vanished from sight, and a minute later there was no sound of it, as though everything had conspired together to end as quickly as possible that sweet delirium, that madness. Left alone on the   5
platform, and gazing into the dark distance, Gurov listened to the chirrup of the grasshoppers and the hum of the telegraph wires, feeling as though he had only just waked up. And he thought, musing, that there had been another episode or adventure in his life, and it, too, was at an end, and nothing was left of it but a memory. . . . He was moved, sad, and conscious of a slight remorse. This young   10
woman whom he would never meet again had not been happy with him; he was genuinely warm and affectionate with her, but yet in his manner, his tone, and his caresses there had been a shade of light irony, the coarse condescension of a happy man who was, besides, almost twice her age. All the time she had called him kind, exceptional, lofty; obviously he had seemed to her different from what   15
he really was, so he had unintentionally deceived her. . . .

Here at the station was already a scent of autumn; it was a cold evening.

"It's time for me to head north," thought Gurov as he left the platform. "High time!"

Anton Chekhov (1860–1904)

For the Introduction

1. Name the title and author of the story. At what point in the action of the story does this extract appear? Whose are the opening words and in what circumstances? Where are the characters? Why?

2. What type(s) of writing does this extract display (narration, description, dialogue)? Does it have a particular tone?

3. Can the passage be divided into parts and if so, how?

For the Detailed Analysis

1. At what point in the plot structure does this episode take place? Is there a certain irony in Anna's words "We are parting forever" for the reader who has read the whole story?

2. How do Anna's words at the beginning of this passage relate to her attitude throughout her affair with Gurov? How do her words relate to the conflict in the characters' lives? Contrast the syntax of the first three sentences (Anna's speech) to that of the rest of the passage.

3. How do the syntax and punctuation of the first sentence in the long paragraph relate to what it describes? What explicit symbolic association is made in this sentence regarding the train's speedy disappearance?

4. What is being characterized as a "sweet delirium" and "madness"? Who is making this comparison? What is the point of view in the passage? Is it the same in the rest of the work? Why do you think the author chose to use this point of view?

5. Do you think there is a deliberate contrast between the image of Gurov "gazing into the dark distance" and his feeling that "he had only just waked up"? What is the significance of the latter phrase here? Are there other moments in the story where Gurov appears to "wake up"?

6. Have we already heard "grasshoppers" in the story? How do they relate to the setting of this part of the story? Has the setting played a significant role in the story so far?

7. Contrast the verbs and the type of vocabulary of these first two sentences with those of the rest of the passage beginning "And he thought, musing. . . ."

8. How does Gurov see his affair with Anna at this point? Relate his thoughts here to what we know about other affairs he has had.

9. What significance do the four spaced periods appear to have (after "memory")?

10. What emotions does Gurov experience at this point? Can they be linked to Gurov's future development and to the overall theme of the work?

11. Anna called Gurov "kind, exceptional, lofty" whereas Gurov thinks he did not deserve these epithets. What does Gurov's thought in this sentence reveal concerning his own opinion of himself? What, in Anna's experience of life, might make her inclined to exaggerate Gurov's positive qualities?

12. What is the significance of the four spaced periods at the end of the paragraph?

13. How do we learn that autumn is approaching? What other senses were evoked in the passage? What might be the significance of the reference to autumn, in the context of the story? And in the context of Gurov's life?

14. What does the final sentence announce regarding Gurov's movements, the progress of the plot and the different settings in the story?

For the Conclusion

1. Is this passage significant for the development of Gurov's character? Can it be related to the theme of the work? (What is its theme?)

2. What is your overall assessment of Gurov and of the story?

4. "Araby" (1914)

When the short days of winter came dusk fell before we had well eaten our
dinners. When we met in the street the houses had grown sombre. The space of
the sky above us was the colour of ever-changing violet and towards it the lamps
of the street lifted their feeble lanterns. The cold air stung us and we played till
our bodies glowed. Our shouts echoed in the silent street. The career of our play   5
brought us through the dark muddy lanes behind the houses where we ran the
gantlet of the rough tribes from the cottages, to the back doors of the dark
dripping gardens where odours arose from the ashpits, to the dark odorous
stables where a coachman smoothed and combed the horse or shook music
from the buckled harness. When we returned to the street light from the kitchen   10
windows had filled the areas. If my uncle was seen turning the corner we hid in
the shadow until we had seen him safely housed. Or if Mangan's sister came out
on the doorstep to call her brother in to his tea we watched her from our shadow
peer up and down the street. We waited to see whether she would remain or
go in and, if she remained, we left our shadow and walked up to Mangan's steps   15
resignedly. She was waiting for us, her figure defined by the light from the half-
opened door. Her brother always teased her before he obeyed and I stood by
the railings looking at her. Her dress swung as she moved her body and the soft
rope of her hair tossed from side to side.

James Joyce (1882–1941)

For the Introduction

1. Name the author and title of the work. At what point in the work does the extract
   appear and what do we know at this point about the narrator of the story?

2. What type of writing do we find in this passage (description, narration, dialogue)?
   How would you characterize its tone?

3. Is any kind of structure or progression discernible in the passage?

For the Detailed Analysis

1. At what point in the plot does the passage appear (exposition, development,
   dénouement)?

2. What is the point of view in the story? How is it modified in this particular
   passage? Consider the narrator's age as he writes the story as opposed to when he
   experienced the narrated events.

3. (N.B. In Ireland at that time—early 20th century—people ate "dinner" in the middle of the day and "tea" in the late afternoon or early evening.) What information
   concerning the setting emerges from the first four sentences? Notice the colors
   and other details described.

4. What figure of speech is contained in the sentence beginning "The space of
   sky . . ." and what if anything does it add to the description of the scene? Do you
   detect any alliteration in this sentence?

5. What senses are evoked in the first half of the passage (from the beginning to " . . .
   the buckled harness")?

6. In the sentence beginning "The career of our play . . .":

   a) What does the reference to "rough tribes from the cottages" imply about the narrator and his friends?
   b) Is any alliteration present here and if so what effect does it have on the reader?
   c) Comment on the phrase "shook music from the buckled harness."
   d) Does this sentence add anything to our impression of the story's setting?
   e) Notice the repetition of the word "dark." Can it be linked to other words in the preceding sentences? To other words in the following sentences of the passage? Or to the word "blind" in the first sentence of the work?

7. What temporal progression is indicated by the sentence beginning "When we returned to the street . . . "? (Note that the word "areas" here refers to a small paved or asphalted yard at the back or side of a house.)

8. Why do the boys hide from the narrator's uncle and Mangan's sister?

9. Note again the contrasts between light and dark. Where is Mangan's sister placed? Is this significant?

10. What is the narrator's attitude as Mangan teases his sister?

11. How would you characterize the narrator's description of Mangan's sister in the last sentence? Does it reveal anything of his feelings towards her?

12. Does the passage move the plot forward at all?

13. What does it tell us about the main character (the narrator)? Does it contribute to our knowledge of the social, psychological, or philosophical dimension of the characters and their lives?

For the Conclusion

1. How significant is this passage in the context of the complete work? Can you relate this extract to the overall theme of the work? (Consider it in relation to the first and last lines of the work as well as to the story itself.)

2. Does this passage succeed in bringing alive the scene it describes, in your view? Give your overall appreciation of the author's art in this passage and in the complete work.

5. "A Rose for Emily" (1931)

Already we knew that there was one room in that region above stairs which no one had seen in forty years, and which would have to be forced. They waited until Miss Emily was decently in the ground before they opened it.

   The violence of breaking down the door seemed to fill this room with pervading dust. A thin, acrid pall as of the tomb seemed to lie everywhere upon this room decked and furnished as for a bridal: upon the valance curtains of faded rose color, upon the rose-shaded lights, upon the dressing table, upon the delicate array of crystal and the man's toilet things backed with tarnished silver, silver so tarnished that the monogram was obscured. Among them lay a collar and tie, as if they had just been removed, which, lifted, left upon the surface a pale crescent in the dust. Upon a chair hung the suit, carefully folded; beneath it the two mute shoes and the discarded socks.

The man himself lay in the bed.

William Faulkner (1897–1962)

For the Introduction

1. Name the title and the author, and briefly explain the situation at this point in the story (whose house are we in and who is Miss Emily? Who is the man on the bed?).

2. What type of writing dominates in this passage (description, narrative, dialogue)? How would you characterize the style of the passage?

3. Does this extract have a structure of any kind (can it be divided into parts)?

For the Detailed Analysis

1. At what point in the plot does this extract take place (development, crisis, dénouement)?

2. What happened in the story "forty years" ago?

3. What is the point of view in the passage? Does it affect our attitude towards the events related? Who are "they" in the second sentence? What does this sentence imply about people's attitude towards Miss Emily?

4. Note that the beginning of the second paragraph mentions "violence." Has there been violence earlier in the story? Why does the door have to be broken down? What is the effect of the violence?

5. The first sentence of paragraph 2 refers to "dust." Has dust already been mentioned in the story? What other references to dust appear in this paragraph? Why such insistence? What other words in the following sentences of this paragraph indicate that nothing in this room has been touched for a long time?

6. What do you think of the reference to a "tomb" in the second sentence of paragraph 2, and of its rhyme with "room"?

7. What new note does the idea of a "bridal" chamber introduce?

8. Comment on the repetitions in the second half of the second sentence. (What figure of speech is involved here and what is its effect?)

9. Do you have any comment on the repetition of the color "rose" here? Do you think there is any connection between this color and the title of the story "A Rose for Emily"?

10. Why were there a "man's toilet things" (i.e., comb, brushes, mirror) in the room? What was the monogram on them?

11. Do these items reveal anything about Miss Emily's social status?

12. What do you think of the detail in the next sentence (the "pale crescent in the dust" left by the collar)?

13. Consider the effect of the adjective "mute" applied to shoes.

14. What does the expression "carefully folded" indicate? Why had Miss Emily kept all these items of men's clothing?

15. What is the impact of the last sentence, standing in a paragraph of its own? Who is the man? Why is his body there?

For the Conclusion

1. What is your overall assessment of the style of this passage?

2. Does the passage add anything to our knowledge of the social, psychological, or philosophical dimension of the main character, Miss Emily?

3. Can you relate the passage to the story's theme?

6. "A & P" (1961)

All this while, the customers had been showing up with their carts but, you know, sheep, seeing a scene, they had all bunched up on Stokesie, who shook open a paper bag as gently as peeling a peach, not wanting to miss a word. I could feel in the silence everybody getting nervous, most of all Lengel, who asks me, "Sammy, have you rung up this purchase?"   5

I thought and said "No" but it wasn't about that I was thinking. I go through the punches, 4, 9, GROC, TOT—it's more complicated than you think, and after you do it often enough, it begins to make a little song, that you hear words to, in my case "Hello (*bing*) there, you (*gung*) hap-py *pee*-pul (*splat*)!"—the *splat* being the drawer flying out. I uncrease the bill, tenderly as you may imagine, it just having   10
come from between the two smoothest scoops of vanilla I had ever known were there, and pass a half and a penny into her narrow pink palm, and nestle the herrings in a bag and twist its neck and hand it over, all the time thinking.

John Updike (1932–2009)

For the Introduction

1. Name the title and author of the story.

2. Identify the characters mentioned in the passage—Stokesie, Sammy, Lengel.

3. Where are the characters, and what is the situation at this point in the story?

4. Identify the type(s) of writing in this passage (narrative, description, dialogue).

For the Detailed Analysis

1. What is the point of view in this story? What is the significance of the point of view in this passage and in the story as a whole?

2. Relate the point of view to the style of the passage. Comment on the expression "you know" and the reference to "sheep" in the first sentence.

3. What kind of "scene" is Sammy referring to in the first sentence?

4. Comment on the expression "as gently as peeling a peach."

5. Explain the significance of "4, 9, GROC, TOT."

6. Comment on the use of "you" in the second sentence of the second paragraph and the syntax and punctuation of this sentence. Comment on the verb tenses in this sentence and in the whole passage.

7. Comment on the style of the final sentence, specifically the adverb "tenderly," the reference to the "two smoothest scoops of vanilla," the adjective "narrow," the verb "nestle," and the expression "twist its neck." How would you characterize Sammy's writing style?

8. The second paragraph begins and ends with references to Sammy "thinking." What is he thinking about?

9. Does this passage add anything to our knowledge of the psychological, social, or philosophical dimension of Sammy's character?

10. At what point in the plot does this passage occur?

For the Conclusion

1. Does the use of the first person in this story help you identify with the narrator?

2. What is your overall response to this passage and to the work as a whole?

7. "A Pair of Tickets" (1989)

And now I see her again, two of her, waving, and in one hand there is a photo, the Polaroid I sent them. As soon as I get beyond the gate, we run toward each other, all three of us embracing, all hesitations and expectations forgotten.

"Mama, Mama," we all murmur, as if she is among us.

My sisters look at me, proudly. "*Meimei jandale*," says one sister proudly to   5
the other. "Little Sister has grown up." I look at their faces again and I see no trace of my mother in them. Yet they still look familiar. And now I also see what part of me is Chinese. It is so obvious. It is my family. It is in our blood. After all these years, it can finally be let go.

My sisters and I stand, arms around each other, laughing and wiping the tears   10
from each other's eyes. The flash of the Polaroid goes off and my father hands me the snapshot. My sisters and I watch quietly together, eager to see what develops.

The gray-green surface changes to the bright colors of our three images, sharpening and deepening at once. And although we don't speak, I know we all see it: Together we look like our mother. Her same eyes, her same mouth, open in surprise to see, at last, her long-cherished wish.

Amy Tan (b. 1952)

For the Introduction

1. Name the author and title of the story, and mention anything relevant you know about the author.

2. Where are the characters mentioned in this passage, and why? (Explain briefly.)

3. At what point in the story does this extract appear?

4. Can the passage be divided into parts?

For the Detailed Analysis

1. Identify the "I" of the first line. Is the first-person point of view important for this story? (What have we learned of the narrator's thoughts and feelings?)

2. Who is the "her" of the first sentence and in what sense does the narrator "see her again"? Does she play a central role in the story? Explain how there are "two of her."

3. Why did the narrator send them a photo? What role do photos play earlier in the story?

4. Explain the "gate" referred to in the second sentence.

5. What kind of "hesitations and expectations" are now "forgotten" and why?

6. Why do the sisters exclaim "Mama" if the mother is not present? (What does this reveal about the mother's role or significance?)

7. Notice the repetition of "proudly" in the third paragraph. Is it important to the narrator that her sisters should regard her with pride?

8. Have we already come across the expressions *meimei* and *jandale* in the story? Are they significant words? Relate *meimei* to the narrator's name.

9. Comment on the repetition of the word "sisters" here.

10. How do you reconcile the fact that the narrator sees no trace of her mother in her sisters' faces with her perception that "they still look familiar"?

11. Why does the narrator say, "And now I also see what part of me is Chinese"? (Relate this statement to the mother's words at the beginning of the story.) What has the narrator's attitude been in the past towards her Chinese heritage?

12. Comment on the length and syntax of the next three sentences. Relate the words "It is in our blood" and "it can . . . be let go" to the mother's words at the beginning of the story. Does the repetition of these exact words provide structure to the text?

13. What is the significance of the gap before the next paragraph?

14. Why does the narrator repeat the phrase "My sisters and I" at the beginning of the next two sentences?

15. Why do you think the sisters are laughing and crying at the same time? Have we already seen simultaneous laughter and tears?

16. The father takes a Polaroid picture and hands it to his daughter, who watches it develop with her sisters. Does this scene remind you of an earlier one in the story? What has changed?

17. Comment on the "bright colors" of the images that appear in the photo. What was the connotation of bright colors (especially pink and yellow) for the narrator? Has her perception changed?

18. What is the role of the photograph here and how does it relate to earlier ones? (Link it to the theme of the narrator's identity.)

19. What else might be said to be "sharpening and deepening" in addition to the photographic image?

20. Is it significant that the narrator knows they "all see it" even though they "don't speak"?

21. What is the effect of the photo? How is it important to the narrator's cultural identity that she and her sisters "look like [their] mother"? What was her attitude towards her mother in the past? Has it changed?

22. Explain the significance of the phrase "long-cherished wish" in the context of the story.

For the Conclusion

1. What would you say are the main themes of this story?

2. How do the Polaroid photos mentioned in this extract and the rest of the story reconcile past and present?

3. How does the narrator develop in the course of the story? Can she be seen as a bridge between East and West? Does the narrator appear to have changed at the end of the story?

4. What is your overall appreciation of this story?

COMPOSING QUESTIONS ON A PROSE EXTRACT

A useful exercise now would be to attempt to write a series of questions like those above on a new passage, either from one of the stories reprinted in appendix 3 or one assigned by your professor. Another student—or you yourself—will then use those questions as a basis for writing a close reading.

You will need to read the complete story and re-read the relevant passage several times in order to become familiar with it. Consider all aspects of the passage in great detail—how characters, a scene, or ideas and feelings are presented, any conflicts to which it refers, use of irony or symbolism, the type of language used, and how the extract relates to the plot and theme of the story as a whole. Use the "Summary of Elements to Discuss in a Prose Passage" in the previous chapter to help you focus on different aspects of the passage. Have another look at the questions offered on various extracts above; divide your questions, as in those examples, into parts—introduction, detailed analysis, and conclusion. Make sure your questions would be clear to someone else. Do not ask questions that you could not answer yourself.

You will find that this process represents the major part of the work involved in doing a close reading. When you come to write a close reading on a totally new prose passage without helpful questions, you might want to begin composing your explication by thinking up similar kinds of questions for yourself.

PART 3
DRAMA

CHAPTER 7

Introduction to Aspects of Drama

Most plays are not written to be read but to be performed before an audience in a theater. You should therefore never lose sight of a play's theatrical aspects. In the theater it is not only the words that count but also the movements and gestures of the actors, the scenery, costumes, and lighting. To fully appreciate a play one needs to see it performed, but of course this is not always possible. And reading a play does have certain advantages: it allows you to appreciate the language at leisure, which can be rewarding, especially with the plays of Shakespeare and other playwrights who incorporate poetic language into the dialogue; and it allows you to look back at earlier scenes, which is impossible at the theater. But scenes from a play can be acted out in class: even this activity will help to make you more aware of the many theatrical aspects of a play that add another dimension to the text. When explicating an extract from a dramatic text you will need to use your imagination to visualize actions and gestures that might accompany the words, an actor's facial expression and tone of voice, the possible reaction of his interlocutor (the person to whom he is speaking) and, in some cases, the characters' costumes and the décor and lighting used in the scene.

Many of the comments in this section can be applied also to film. Movies enact dramas between characters just as plays do, and like plays can by analyzed in terms of their **dialogue, characterization, plot, theme, and setting**. As in theater, film actors interpret their roles, providing appropriate gestures, expressions, and tone of voice, under the supervision of a director—though of course films are usually made only once, whereas plays are re-enacted night after night and are constantly re-played with different actors and directors. In this section we will be discussing theater in particular, but without losing sight of film where appropriate.

On reflection, the conventions of theater are rather curious: the audience listens to actors—real people pretending to be fictional characters—who talk among themselves, apparently spontaneously but in fact reciting a text they have learned by heart, and who, most of the time, completely ignore the presence of the audience watching them. For the length of the performance, then, the audience is required to "suspend disbelief," in other words to forget the actors are playing a part and accept them as the characters whose roles they play. The term **suspension of disbelief** implies a willingness to believe; in other words, the audience members become so immersed in the fictional world of the play that they almost believe it is real. Convention dictates that the actors play out their parts as if between four walls, as if they were not seen and heard by the audience on the other side of that transparent "fourth wall." Sometimes, playwrights deliberately challenge this convention, instructing an actor to address certain lines of his or her part directly to the audience. This device reminds the spectators that they should not "suspend disbelief," allowing themselves to be carried away by the fictional action of the play as if it were real; instead they should retain their critical faculties, reflect on the play's action and apply it to their own lives. They should remember, for example, that the kinds of horrors or injustices they are watching on stage can occur also in real life. It is a favorite device of playwrights who attack social injustice, such as Bertolt Brecht. As well as speaking directly to the audience, characters may talk about theater and acting, which again reminds the audience they are at a play. Shakespeare does this in the famous soliloquy beginning "All the world's a stage" from *As You Like It* (Act 2, scene 7) and in Macbeth's observation: "Life's but a walking shadow, a poor player/That struts and frets his hour upon the stage,/And then is heard no more" (*Macbeth*, Act 5, scene 5)— a comment that applies to humans in general as well as to Macbeth in his situation. There are several good examples in Beckett's *Waiting for Godot*, for instance when Pozzo makes a long, dramatic speech about the sunset, then turns to Vladimir and Estragon asking, "How did you find me?" as if he were an actor who had just delivered a **monologue** or **soliloquy**. Such allusions seem to suggest that the characters in the play are merely acting out roles, as we all do in life.

For the members of the audience, the concrete presence of the actors on the stage creates a much more direct and lively kind of communication than in a work of prose fiction. The actors' voices, facial expressions, and gestures express a great deal with an immediacy that cannot be achieved by the written word, and therefore the audience experiences the characters' emotions more directly and more strongly. The physical presence of the actors makes the drama more intense, more exciting, and more real. Also, if you have been to a play at the theater, would you not agree that the presence of other audience members contributes to the theatrical experience? There is often a sense of community, of shared emotion or shared laughter that unites the audience for the duration of the play.

The great Greek philosopher Aristotle urged mimesis in the theater—the idea that the action of a play should imitate life, presenting the kinds of emotions, situations, and experiences that human beings face in real life. Plays are often judged according to their degree of verisimilitude, and audiences appreciate complex characters displaying typical human characteristics, attitudes, and reactions. The opposite point of view is also valid, however: the theater is not life, so what would be the point of creating plays that merely repeat what we know from our own lives? Why go to the theater to see a re-run of Life? Answers may be found to this question, e.g., a theatrical performance can help us gain perspective on our own situation and see how other people might react faced with similar problems to the ones we encounter in life. Nevertheless the view that theater should not merely resemble life is valid, and tends to lead to a different type of theater, more radical and experimental than one governed by mimesis.

Drama is often subdivided into two broad categories, tragedy and comedy—though these both shade off into other subgenres, including **tragicomedy**, which unites elements of both, and **melodrama**, a type of play that is neither tragic nor comic but highly (or overly) dramatic, with swashbuckling characters and a fast-moving, complicated plot.

A **tragedy** is a play that depicts the downfall and often the death of a hero. The Greek philosopher Aristotle's definition of tragedy, in his *Poetics*, has influenced playwrights for centuries. The tragic hero, in this classical view of tragedy, is a noble person (often of royal blood) who, whether unwittingly as in the case of Oedipus, or in the name of a strongly held belief or principle as in the case of Antigone, commits a deed that, although heroic, is forbidden according to the laws of men or of religion. The tragic error committed by the hero—sometimes due to a **"tragic flaw"** (such as pride) in his character—leads to his downfall. Usually, at some point towards the end of the play, the hero comes to a realization of the grave error he has committed and is overcome with grief. While representing humanity in general, tragic heroes appear to exist on a higher plane than most mortals, and the emotions they experience, especially their anguish and suffering, seem more intense than those of ordinary men. Their fate inspires pity and fear in the audience—pity for their fate and fear of sharing it—and leads to a sense of emotional release called **catharsis** at the climax of the play, which usually ends with the death, or some fatal affliction, of the hero. More modern tragedies adapt certain aspects of the classical pattern; for example, the hero may possess the nobility of character associated with a tragic hero, without being of noble blood. Shakespeare's tragedies are very different in many ways from Greek tragedy, which stipulated—in order to heighten the intensity of the drama—that the action should all take place in one location and within the space of twenty-four hours. Shakespeare's tragedies, on the contrary, often cover a period of weeks or months, as in *Hamlet*, and move from one place to another—from the exterior of the castle at Elsinore, to various rooms inside, to Polonius's house, to a "plain" somewhere in Denmark, to a churchyard, and back to a hall in the castle. Also, again in order to heighten the tragic intensity, Greek tragedies were serious in mood throughout, with none of the comic elements that provide moments of relief in Shakespeare's tragedies.

Unlike tragedies, comedies end happily. The protagonists are more likely to be ordinary people than heroic or noble figures. There are many different types of comedy, though they all share the aim of amusing the audience—which does not preclude instructing them at the same time. In **satires**, for example, the playwright amuses the audience by ridiculing characters that epitomize a human vice such as jealousy or avarice or a fault prevalent in contemporary society such as snobbery, hypocrisy, cruelty, or unfairness to women or other minorities. Such plays have a serious side: the playwright aims to correct the ills of society while making an audience laugh. The aim of romantic comedies such as *A Midsummer Night's Dream*, on the other hand, is basically to entertain.

Satires depend largely on comedy of character: the character displaying the targeted failing or vice is funny, or ridiculous, because of his personal characteristics, attitudes, way of expressing himself, mannerisms, etc. Other sources of comedy are: situation, language, and **farce**. A situation can be funny in itself, for example if one character (A) hides, and two other characters (B and C) discuss him or her, not realizing s/he is in hiding. The audience, however, knows that A can hear everything they say, and this situation can give rise to laughter, depending on what B and C say to each other. An example of just such a situation occurs in Molière's play *Tartuffe* when Tartuffe attempts to seduce Orgon's wife while Orgon himself is hidden under a table. Such situations, relying for their humor on the fact that the audience knows more than at least one of the characters, are examples of **dramatic irony**.

Comedy of language, as the name implies, means that the characters' language is funny in some way. Either they make witty remarks or jokes, which provoke laughter in the audience, or their speech habits are somehow amusing, like Mrs. Malaprop's inappropriate use of words in Sheridan's *The Rivals* (which has given rise to the term "malapropism"). **Farce** depends on a cruder kind of humor, on repetitions, highly unlikely situations and, most of all, slapstick. Characters throwing pillows, hitting each other, bumping into things or falling down provide the least subtle type of comedy but one which, properly handled and not overdone, delights audiences. Even great playwrights like Shakespeare and Molière use farce, among other comic devices, in their comedies.

A **tragicomedy** is a play that makes the audience laugh and cry simultaneously, such as many of Chekhov's plays. In *The Cherry Orchard* (which he subtitled "A Comedy"), we feel sympathy for the plight of the family of Mme. Ranevskaya, forced to sell the house where they grew up, with its beautiful orchard for which they feel such nostalgic affection; but at the same time we have to laugh at their incompetence, their inability to focus on seeking a solution to the problem— as well as at the many amusing traits of several of the characters, and at their language. Beckett's *Waiting for Godot* (subtitled "tragicomedy") enacts an essentially tragic view of human life; but the play contains many examples of situational and linguistic comedy, as well as farcical moments like the opening scene where Estragon is struggling to remove his boots, or the scene in Act 2 where Estragon and Vladimir keep passing each other the three hats.

There are also realist dramas—plays that are neither tragedies, comedies, nor tragicomedies but simply dramatic enactments of human dilemmas, based on everyday life, with realistic characters and settings. Arthur Miller and Henrik Ibsen wrote realist dramas. The **Theater of the Absurd**, which arose around the middle of the twentieth century, though often retaining some realistic features, also exploits elements of the absurd to point out the meaninglessness and absurdity of human existence. The plays of Ionesco and Beckett fall into this category. The second half of the twentieth and the beginning of the twenty-first centuries have seen experimental theater of all kinds flourish, from plays with no scenery or props to ones that involve highly inventive and imaginative stagecraft. Conventional notions of characterization and plot are often abandoned also: in plays such as Ionesco's *The Bald Soprano* or Beckett's *Waiting for Godot* there is no plot to speak of (though both plays do suggest *themes*), and the characters are devoid of personality.

In order to explain how actors should move at certain moments, or react to specific situations, or to indicate what tone of voice they should adopt at a given point in the play, playwrights sometimes have recourse to **stage directions**. You will have seen such notes, generally in parentheses and in italics, accompanying the text. At the beginning of a play, or of a scene, they may give some indications as to the scenery or props required; and during the course of the play, stage directions often guide the actor by suggesting how s/he should look at another character, what kind of gesture s/he should make, or what tone s/he should use at that point in the play. However, actors themselves also adopt gestures and expressions that they deem suitable for the character they are playing; and ultimately it is the stage director who is responsible for such choices and for the staging and performance of the play in general. He directs the actors' movements and gestures in accordance with his interpretation of their roles and of the play as a whole. Hundreds of different versions of a play like Shakespeare's *Hamlet*—both on stage and on film—emphasize different aspects of the plot and different interpretations of the relationships between the characters, e.g., between Hamlet and his mother, Hamlet and Ophelia, or Hamlet and his father. When explicating an extract from a play you should, of course, take any stage directions into account, but also put yourself in the position of the director and imagine how you would organize and stage the scene.

One of the greatest differences between a work of prose fiction and a play is the absence, in plays, of a narrator analyzing characters or giving an opinion on events. There is no narrative voice or "point of view" in the theater. Aside from a few stage directions in the printed text of some plays, we learn everything through the characters' **dialogue**, without the mediation of a narrator. Let us therefore begin our study of the elements of drama by a consideration of dialogue.

DIALOGUE

Since the text (or script) of a play consists entirely of dialogue, the latter must serve not only to reveal the personalities of the characters but also to fulfill the functions of narrative in a prose work, i.e., to advance the plot and provide details about the setting, the period, and the circumstances of the characters.

At the beginning of a play in the theater, various actors appear on the stage. We may already have some idea of the period and the location of the action from the sets and costumes—though more details will probably emerge from the dialogue—but we do not know who the characters are, what their relationship is to each other, or why they are together. We learn all this from the dialogue; yet it must be revealed in a natural way through the characters' speech. They cannot explain too much too quickly, for the sake of the audience; this would produce a very artificial dialogue, since characters do not need to explain to each other what they already know. One of the challenges before a playwright, then, is to create a dialogue that remains natural for the characters while informing the audience. Thus, in the first page of dialogue of Susan Glaspell's play *Trifles*, we quickly learn a great deal about both the basic situation that has brought the characters to the Wrights' farmhouse, and about the relations between them, yet the characters speak to each other perfectly naturally:

(*The women have come in slowly and stand close together near the door.*)

COUNTY ATTORNEY (*rubbing his hands*): This feels good. Come up to the fire, ladies.

MRS. PETERS (*after taking a step forward*): I'm not—cold.

SHERIFF (*unbuttoning his overcoat and stepping away from the stove as if to mark the beginning of official business*): Now, Mr. Hale, before we move things about, you explain to Mr. Henderson just what you saw when you came here yesterday morning.

COUNTY ATTORNEY: By the way, has anything been moved? Are things just as you left them yesterday?

SHERIFF (*looking about*): It's just the same. When it dropped below zero last night, I thought I'd better send Frank out this morning to make a fire for us—no use getting pneumonia with a big case on; but I told him not to touch anything except the stove—and you know Frank.

COUNTY ATTORNEY: Somebody should have been left here yesterday.

SHERIFF: Oh—yesterday. When I had to send Frank to Morris Center for that man who went crazy—I want you to know I had my hands full yesterday. I knew you could get back from Omaha by today, and as long as I went over everything here myself—

COUNTY ATTORNEY: Well, Mr. Hale, tell just what happened when you came here yesterday morning.

HALE: Harry and I had started to town with a load of potatoes. We came along the road from my place; and as I got here, I said, "I'm going to see if I can't get John Wright to go in with me on a party telephone." I spoke to Wright about it once before, and he put me off, saying folks talked too much anyway, and all he asked was peace and quiet—I guess you know about how much he talked himself; but I thought maybe if I went to the house and talked about it before his wife, though I said to Harry that I didn't know as what his wife wanted made much difference to John—

This opening dialogue shows us that the County Attorney (Mr. Henderson) is in charge, because it is he who wants to know that nothing has been moved, complains that: "Somebody should have been left here yesterday," and instructs Mr. Hale to tell his story. No doubt the actor's manner and bearing would help to convey this impression. Also, the basic division between the men and the women, so important in the rest of the play, is signaled at once, both in actions and in the dialogue. The men enter first and do all the talking, initially; and the characters stand in two separate groups, the men by the stove and the women "close together near the door." This separation is emphasized in the dialogue, when Mrs. Peters, who is most certainly cold, given the temperature outside, nevertheless hesitates to approach the stove and stays with the other lady, insisting: "I'm not—cold." The emphasis on nothing having been touched alerts us to the likelihood that a crime has been committed, though we don't know its nature yet. And Mr. Hale's speech gives us some important information about Mr. Wright, without actually appearing to dwell on his character traits: it emerges from Hale's story firstly that Mr. Wright didn't like a lot of talking and didn't talk much himself, and secondly that he didn't have much respect for his wife's wishes about anything. Both these facts will become significant later, but they are introduced here quite casually, as asides in a conversation: "I guess you know about how much he talked himself"; and "though I said to Harry that I didn't know as what his wife wanted made much difference to John." At the same time, the dialogue is totally natural; the characters speak to each other and for each other, not just for the audience. The Sheriff refers to an incident in "Morris Center" that kept him busy the previous day. They talk about Harry and about Frank, whom we don't know and will never meet, but they all know them and are aware that Frank has a reputation for carrying out orders to the letter: "I told him not to touch anything except the stove—and you know Frank." Also, Mr. Hale's report on his arrival at the farm the previous morning is given in a natural, conversational style, with references to potatoes and the possibility of a shared ("party") telephone line as well as his remarks concerning Mr. Wright's character that help us to start building a mental picture of him.

In a theatrical dialogue, then, the characters speak for two audiences simultaneously— their interlocutor(s) on the one hand and the spectators on the other. The dialogue must be both natural and informative. If characters begin telling each other things that they can be expected to know already, for the sake of the audience, the illusion of a realistic conversation collapses and the dialogue becomes artificial. Ionesco exploits this artificiality—to comic effect—at the beginning of *The Bald Soprano* (a play belonging to the type of drama known as the **Theater of the Absurd**): Mrs. Smith, talking to her husband (who merely grunts in reply to her observations) tells him what they have both eaten for dinner—soup, fish, mashed potatoes, and salad, and that they have eaten well because, she says, "we live near London and our name is Smith"—facts of which he must be aware already! She also points out to him later that their younger daughter's name is Peggy. Here the dialogue is patently—and deliberately—absurd.

In more conventional plays, authors find a way to allow such factual information to emerge more naturally from the dialogue. Here is another example, from the beginning of Chekhov's *The Cherry Orchard*: Lopakhin announces that the train has arrived and—no doubt stretching and yawning as he speaks—reprimands himself for having fallen asleep: "I came here specially to meet them at the station and then I overslept." So we know some people are arriving, though not who. Lopakhin then goes on, in a speech addressed half to himself and half to the servant Dunyasha who is with him, to muse about Lyubov Andreyevna. We learn that she has lived abroad for five years, as he wonders what she will be like now. This thought leads him to recollect an incident when she looked after him when he was a boy and his peasant-father had struck him. From the few sentences devoted to this memory we realize that it is surely Lyubov Andreyevna who will arrive on the train, that she is the lady of the house, that Lopakhin admires her greatly, that he himself has risen above his peasant origins and become a rich man but still feels like a peasant at heart: "See, I was reading a book and didn't understand a thing. I fell asleep reading it." His little speech is motivated by the fact that he is waiting, with nothing to do but reminisce, and of course by Lyubov Andreyevna's imminent arrival. Even his falling asleep and missing the train is linked to his remarks about being a peasant and therefore finding it hard to concentrate on a book. Thus the dialogue at the beginning of this play manages both to sound realistic and to tell us a lot about the basic situation in a short space.

As well as sounding natural, dialogue must be very clear, so that spectators can grasp the essential details of the situation. The reader of a novel, forgetting or missing some incident or explanation, can look back and re-read the appropriate passage. Since this is impossible in the theater, all essential information must either be given very clearly or repeated. In fact, playwrights often arrange to have characters repeat, in a totally natural way and perhaps with different wording, something they have already said in the course of the dialogue.

The kind of language used varies enormously from play to play. A playwright wishing to give the impression of a realistic dialogue between characters addressing each other with apparent spontaneity, using conversational language, has to avoid literary turns of phrase and vocabulary in favor of the language of speech, with its relatively simple syntax and short or incomplete sentences. Have you noticed how often people hesitate, interrupt themselves, and repeat themselves, in the course of a conversation? A really natural-sounding dialogue will therefore include colloquial expressions, hesitations, repetitions, and pauses. Notice the hesitations and pauses, for example, in the following passage from *Trifles*:

> MRS. HALE: She liked the bird. She was going to bury it in that pretty box.
>
> MRS. PETERS (*in a whisper*): When I was a girl—my kitten—there was a boy took a hatchet, and before my eyes—and before I could get there— (*Covers her face an instant*) If they hadn't held me back, I would have— (*Catches herself, looks upstairs, where steps are heard, falters weakly.*)—hurt him.
>
> MRS. HALE (*with a slow look around her.*): I wonder how it would seem never to have had any children around. (*Pause.*) No, Wright wouldn't like the bird— a thing that sang. She used to sing. He killed that, too.

It is worth commenting on such aspects of dialogue, when writing a close reading of a dramatic passage.

However, the dialogue of plays doesn't always imitate the language of speech. In ancient Greek tragedy and many neo-classical tragedies, conversational language is out of the question, since these plays were composed in verse and aimed for linguistic qualities matching the nobility and elegance of the main characters and the seriousness of the plots. Shakespeare uses elegant poetic discourse for the noble characters in many of his plays, both comedies and tragedies, but more everyday language for more rustic characters, servants, etc. Thus Horatio, in *Hamlet*, notes that dawn is breaking in poetic terms:

> But look, the morn in russet mantle clad,
> Walks o'er the dew of yon high eastern hill,

whereas the gravediggers speak in conversational style—albeit the style of the early seventeenth century—and in prose: "Will you ha' the truth on't? If this had not been a gentlewoman she should have been buried out o' Christian burial." Similarly in a comedy such as *A Midsummer Night's Dream*, the main characters— fairies and lovers—express themselves in blank verse while Bottom and his friends speak in plain prose. A character's language may also change according to his situation and his interlocutors.

Twentieth and twenty-first century plays display a great deal of linguistic variety: there are poetic dramas such as the plays of T.S. Eliot; plays where the characters for the most part use the language of intelligent conversation; and others that imitate the colloquial language of everyday life. Sometimes, characters have their own personal vocabulary, accent or way of speaking, which helps define their social class, level of education, or personality. Often servants and guards, for example, speak a different language from their masters. Such differences should be pointed out, in a close reading.

When analyzing a passage of dialogue, it is also important to remember that the words of the person speaking will have an impact on the interlocutor and might produce not only a verbal response but perhaps also certain gestures or facial expressions. Try to imagine what these movements or expressions might be, both on the part of the speaker and of the interlocutor. Tone of voice and gestures can convey a wide range of emotions—humor, anger, surprise, affection, irony, etc. Consider how you would instruct the actors to react during this speech if you were the director. Occasionally, gestures and tones of voice are suggested in stage directions but most often it is up to the individual actor or the stage director to decide.

You should also reflect on the speaker's motivation. The dialogue of a play doesn't always express exactly what the characters think; they hide the truth, tell lies, or say one thing to one interlocutor and something else to another. Since the spectators see and hear everything, they often know better than some of the characters when a speaker is telling the truth, which puts the spectators in a better position to understand the situation fully. This can give rise to the phenomenon called **dramatic irony**—where the spectator knows more than certain characters about what exactly is going on. Examples abound, especially in comedies. In Shakespeare's *Much Ado About Nothing*, our delight in the love-match between Benedick and Beatrice depends on our knowledge of the negative comments the two have made about each other earlier, to other characters, while each of them remains unaware of the other's criticism.

In the case of comedies, you should also consider whether the language of the passage is comic, and if so, in what way. Do they make witty remarks or jokes, or are their speech habits somehow amusing?

Apart from the basic dialogue of a play, you may encounter monologues, soliloquies, and asides. A **monologue** is a long uninterrupted speech by one character. A speech is called a **soliloquy** when the character speaks alone on the stage, meaning that the character gives voice to his or her thoughts. This valuable device allows us to learn the character's true thoughts and feelings, which he or she might not reveal in dialogue with other characters. Soliloquies also represent an opportunity to deliver a well-structured, thoughtful speech, complete with figures of speech and other ornaments, so that they often become famous, like Hamlet's "To be, or not to be" meditation on suicide. **Asides** are shorter phrases that again represent a speaker's thoughts and are not addressed to an interlocutor on stage but are "overheard" by the audience; or they may be addressed to one interlocutor but not to other characters on the stage. In Act 2, scene 3 of *Much Ado About Nothing*, for example, many asides occur, spoken both by Benedick to himself as he overhears the other characters' conversation from his hiding place, and by the other characters to each other as they secretly observe him.

Exercises on Dialogue

Remember that to complete these and other exercises, you will need to have read the relevant plays.

Characterize the dialogue of one of the following extracts. Consider whether it appears natural, informs the audience, and whether it sounds literary or colloquial.

Does the language contain any symbolism or "hidden meanings"? Are there examples of dramatic irony? How does the manner of speaking reflect the characters' motivations or private thoughts? What gestures or expressions might accompany the words or reflect the reaction of an interlocutor to the words spoken? (Mark or underline significant words or phrases in the passage and then write out your conclusions.)

1.   COUNTY ATTORNEY: What—was she doing?
     HALE: She was rockin' back and forth. She had her apron in her hand and was kind
          of—pleating it.
     COUNTY ATTORNEY: And how did she—look?
     HALE: Well, she looked queer.
     COUNTY ATTORNEY: How do you mean—queer?
     HALE: Well, as if she didn't know what she was going to do next.

                                                          Susan Glaspell, *Trifles*

2.   RANK: But I'm quite forgetting what I came for. Helmer, give me a cigar, one of the
          dark Havanas.
     HELMER: With the greatest pleasure. (*Holds out his case*)
     RANK: Thanks. (*Takes one and cuts off the tip*)
     NORA : (*striking a match*) Let me give you a light.
     RANK: Thank you. (*She holds the match for him; he lights the cigar.*) And now
          good-bye.
     HELMER: Good-bye, good-bye, old friend.
     NORA: Sleep well, Doctor.
     RANK: Thanks for that wish.
     NORA: Wish me the same.
     RANK: You? All right, if you like—Sleep well. And thanks for the light.

                                                     Ibsen, *A Doll House*, Act 3

3.   MME. RANEVSKAYA: (*looking out of the window into the orchard*): Oh, my childhood, my
          innocent childhood. I used to sleep in this nursery—I used to look out into the
          orchard, happiness waked with me every morning, the orchard was just the
          same then . . . nothing has changed. (*Laughs with joy*) All, all white! Oh, my
          orchard! After the dark, rainy autumn and the cold winter, you are young again,
          and full of happiness, the heavenly angels have not left you . . . If I could free
          my chest and my shoulders from this rock that weighs on me, if I could only
          forget the past!

                                                Chekhov, *The Cherry Orchard*, Act 1

CHARACTERIZATION

Since there is no narrator, in a play, to explain the characters' thoughts and motives, the audience relies largely on the dialogue for information about them. Sets and costumes can reveal something of a character's social status and personality traits, but basically we get to know characters through what we see them doing and saying, and through what other characters say about them. Some characters seem oblivious to their own character traits—especially their shortcomings—so that we often feel we know them better than they know themselves. Also, they do not always tell the truth, and may say one thing to one interlocutor and something different to another. Hamlet pretends to be mad and only reveals to certain characters—and therefore to the audience—that this is a pretense. But the audience hears and sees everything and is thus able to understand the whole situation, often better than some of the characters, giving rise to **dramatic irony**.

In a realistic play that in many ways imitates life, characters usually resemble real people. Audiences tend to appreciate characters with recognizable human traits whose emotions, reactions, and motivations derive from common human experience. Spectators may even at times "forget" they are in the theater and react to the action on stage as if it were real, identifying with characters, weeping or rejoicing with them in a **"suspension of disbelief"** (discussed above, pages 126–27). In more experimental plays, characters often appear artificial or strange but may be seen to symbolize certain aspects of life or of a social milieu, like the characters in Ionesco's plays or the two tramps in Beckett's *Waiting for Godot*.

Dramatic characters are often described as "flat" or "rounded." A rounded character has the depth and complexity of a human being, and may develop or change in the course of the play. The personality of flat characters—usually the minor characters in a play—is not explored in depth. Stock characters or **stereotypes** are one-dimensional: they exemplify only one human characteristic and are always portrayed in all situations as, for example, haughty or jealous or naïve. They are most commonly found in comedies, where the playwright often aims to make fun of a particular human trait or failing.

Before actors even begin to rehearse a play they study the characters whose roles they are interpreting in great depth, ultimately becoming so familiar with them that they feel they know them from the inside. Actors not only learn the lines for a given character but identify with him or her, which enables them always to speak the lines in an appropriate **tone**, and to accompany the words with suitable facial expressions and gestures. Sometimes, stage directions indicate the tone, expression, or gesture that an actor should adopt in a given situation; for example, at the beginning of *A Doll House*, when Nora's husband offers her money, the stage directions say:

> NORA (*turning quickly*): Money!

Her quick turn, along with the exclamation, indicates her enthusiasm for the proffered banknotes. A page or so later, Helmer's attitude towards his wife is signaled by his admonitory gesture:

> HELMER (*shaking an admonitory finger*): Surely my sweet tooth hasn't been running
> riot in town today, has she?

Similarly, in Susan Glaspell's *Trifles*, many stage directions indicate gestures or expressions the actors should adopt, for example when Mrs. Hale and Mrs. Peters find the strangled bird and "*Their eyes meet. A look of growing comprehension, of horror*" passes over their faces; subsequently the County Attorney walks in "*as one turning from serious things to little pleasantries*" and when he asks "Is there a cat?" Mrs. Hale "*glances in a quick covert way*" at Mrs. Peters, because the two ladies have already discussed the fact that there was no cat but want to give the men the impression there was. But such stage directions cover only certain moments, and are frequent only in relatively modern plays. Generally speaking, the actor must decide for himself what gestures, expressions, and tone of voice to use in order to convey his sense of the character's personality and illustrate the character's reactions to events or words. Of course, different actors will interpret a character in different ways and they must stick to a coherent interpretation of the role. A good actor will succeed in convincing the audience that the character would in fact behave in exactly that way, speak in just that tone, and use the kind of body language the actor has adopted.

Be prepared to explain, when writing a close reading of a dramatic passage, what it reveals about the personality and motivation of the character(s) speaking, and what it suggests about other characters. In addition, you should show how the speakers' motivations and reactions affect the progress of the plot. Consider also the kinds of gestures or facial expressions the speakers might employ in performance, given their characterization, in the section of dialogue you are analyzing, as well as the tone of voice you think they would adopt. In the case of comedy, consider whether the character speaking is comic and in what way.

Exercises on Characterization

How do the following extracts reflect what you know about the characters speaking? Do they reveal anything new about the personality of the characters? What gestures or expressions might the characters make that reflect their personality? Would they adopt any particular tone of voice? Are they "flat" or "rounded" characters?

1. (The *MAID ushers in MRS. LINDE, who is in traveling dress, and shuts the door.*)
    MRS. LINDE (*in a dejected and timid voice*): How do you do, Nora?
    NORA (*doubtfully*): How do you do—
    MRS. LINDE: You don't recognize me, I suppose.
    NORA: No, I don't know—yes, to be sure, I seem to—(*suddenly*) Yes! Christine! Is it really you?
    MRS. LINDE: Yes, it is I.
    NORA: Christine! To think of my not recognising you! And yet how could I—(in a gentle voice) How you have altered, Christine!
    MRS. LINDE: Yes, I have indeed. In nine, ten long years—
    NORA: Is it so long since we met? I suppose it is. The last eight years have been a happy time for me, I can tell you. And so now you have come into the town, and have taken this long journey in winter—that was plucky of you.
    MRS. LINDE: I arrived by steamer this morning.
    NORA: To have some fun at Christmas-time, of course. How delightful! We will have such fun together!

    Ibsen, *A Doll House*, Act 1

2. MRS. PETERS: The law has got to punish crime, Mrs. Hale.
    MRS. HALE (*not as if answering that*): I wish you'd seen Minnie Foster when she wore a white dress with blue ribbons and stood up there in the choir and sang. (*A look around the room*) Oh, I wish I'd come over here once in a while! That was a crime! That was a crime! Who's going to punish that?

MRS. Peters (*looking upstairs*): We mustn't—take on.

MRS. HALE: I might have known she needed help! I know how things can be—for women, I tell you, it's queer, Mrs. Peters. We live close together and we live far apart. We all go through the same things—it's all just a different kind of the same thing. (*Brushes her eyes, noticing the bottle of fruit, reaches out for it.*) If I was you, I wouldn't tell her her fruit was gone.

Tell her it ain't. Tell her it's all right. Take this in to prove it to her. She—she may never know whether it was broke or not.

Glaspell, *Trifles*

PLOT

The plot of a play—or a film—usually depends at least to some extent on the characters' personalities. Their interactions with one another move the plot along. As in a novel, a dramatic plot represents the playwright's molding of events into a coherent and satisfying whole, and the progress of events is often dictated by the characters' actions and reactions, by their decisions and by their attitudes towards one another. In Ibsen's *A Doll House*, for example, Nora refrains from telling her husband about the debt she has contracted to pay for his medical care when he was gravely ill, because he is so adamant about the iniquity of borrowing money. Consequently she has to pay back the debt in secret and he therefore sees her as a spendthrift. This situation affects his attitude towards her, and eventually hers towards him, and thus influences the development of the plot. It also gives power to the money-lender who knows Nora's secret, and this also affects the way events unfold.

In general, therefore, the characters' psychology largely determines the development of the plot. Events that occur out of the blue to set things right tend to disappoint the audience, at least in relatively serious plays, as being too arbitrary. In a comedy, such events (called **deus ex machina** because it's as if a god came down in a machine to organize human lives) are more acceptable.

The plot of a play often involves an element of **conflict**. Frequently this takes the form of conflict between two or more characters concerning issues such as love, power, money, moral codes, human rights, war and peace, etc. Alternatively, conflict might arise between a character or group of characters and the society in which they live (as for example in Molière's *The Misanthrope*), or between the past values of a social group and present ones (as in Chekhov's *The Cherry Orchard*). The conflict may also exist largely in the mind, or the heart, of a single character as he or she struggles to decide on a course of action, deal with his or her feelings, or come to terms with an event. And in many plays, especially such complex ones as Shakespeare's *Hamlet*, all these forms of conflict may be found simultaneously. Hamlet is at odds with many of the other main characters, with court society as a whole since Claudius became king, and with himself.

Dramatic tension is an important aspect of a play. We wonder how the characters will resolve the various conflicts they face. Often the tension builds up, creating a feeling of suspense that is temporarily resolved but then leads to a new situation involving new tensions. Hamlet wants to avenge his father's death but is not sure whether to trust the ghost until the play within the play confirms his suspicions about his uncle; when he finds his uncle alone the tension mounts: we feel sure he will kill him. But Hamlet decides not to because his uncle is at prayer. There follows a very tense and dramatic scene with his mother (his relationship with her represents another source of tension in the play), during which Hamlet kills Polonius by mistake—another dramatic moment. Then he is sent away to England; but the tension mounts again when we see him return and he witnesses Ophelia's burial and attacks Laertes. Our knowledge of the king's suggestion of poisoning Laertes's sword contributes to the tension of the terrible final scene of the play.

Surprise is another common element of drama. Like conflict, surprises are "dramatic" in the commonly accepted sense of the word. They keep the audience guessing and wondering what will happen next.

Elements of Plot

A plot normally comprises several parts: first an **exposition** that enables the audience to learn the characters' identity and their circumstances; then the longest section of the play, the **development**, in which the action progresses and the situation becomes more complex, leading to some kind of crisis or **climax**. This pattern is often illustrated by a triangle, with the apex representing the climax of the action half-way through the play. This can happen, but very often the climax is nearer the end, and a play may include, in any case, more than one critical moment. For Hamlet—trying to decide whether he should kill his uncle at the bidding of his father's ghost—a climactic moment of sorts occurs when he learns for sure that his uncle killed his father, thanks to the play within the play. Another crisis comes when he fails to kill Claudius at prayer, and yet another when he kills Polonius by mistake. All these events occur in Act 3. But if *Hamlet* is a play about a man seeking to avenge his father's murder, then an important climax must be the moment when he finally kills the murderer, his uncle, which occurs in the last scene of the play. The **dénouement** (or "untying") of a plot represents the action towards the end of the play when the crisis is past, the tensions resolved and the threads of the plot untangle, so that we see how things will turn out and what the future may hold for the main characters.

Plays are usually divided into acts and scenes (though Greek plays are divided into scenes, with choral interludes). Shakespeare's works are in five acts, but it is common also to have fewer than five: Ibsen's *A Doll House* has three acts, Chekhov's *The Cherry Orchard* has four, *Waiting for Godot* has two; and there are many one-act plays, such as Glaspell's *Trifles*. Scenes usually change when extra characters appear on stage, or leave it, or of course when the location alters.

Exercise on Plot

Consider the plot of a play you have read. Where would you say the exposition ended and the development began? What do you consider to be the climax of the play? What kinds of conflict does the play enact and between whom?

If you have not yet read a play, describe the plot of a favorite movie. Could it be said to have the equivalent of an "exposition"? Can you identify its climax, i.e. the culminating moment after which the action winds down? Does the plot develop in a straight line or does it include flashbacks? What kinds of conflict does the movie enact and between whom?

THEME

Like prose works, most good plays and movies have an overall **theme** or central idea that does not equate to a summary of the events. Generally speaking, the theme is the motivation for the author's choice of certain kinds of character and events and for the presence of certain significant details. The implications of a play or film, and therefore its theme, are often open to interpretation, since different readers may find different aspects meaningful. One theme of *A Doll House* is the emancipation of women. The idea of male condescension towards women underlies both this play and *Trifles*. *Hamlet* has many themes, for example indecision, vengeance, appearance versus reality, the mother-son relationship. Since different themes within one play will strike different readers more or less forcefully, there is often room for much discussion concerning "what the play is really about"—just as after a movie you and your friends may interpret its theme or "meaning" differently. But you must have evidence from the play—or the movie—to back up your interpretation of its theme(s); you can't just vaguely say that it seems to be about "jealousy" or "forgiveness," for example; you must offer solid reasons to substantiate your impressions.

When explicating a passage from a play you should explain in what way the extract relates to the overall theme of the work. This may be done either in your introduction, which concerns the passage as a whole, or in your conclusion.

Exercises on Theme

If you have read one of the following plays, relate the content of one of the passages below to the theme(s) of the respective play. Alternatively, discuss the theme(s) of a different play you have read or of a movie you have seen. Remember that such a discussion should not simply tell what the film or play is "about," i.e., its action or story-line. Try to work out what the "point" of the drama is or what basic idea(s) it illustrates, e.g. love (what aspects of love?), courage, loyalty, faithfulness, memory, nostalgia, hypocrisy, treachery, forgiveness, and so on.

1.   QUEEN: Good Hamlet, cast thy nighted colour off,
             And let thine eye look like a friend on Denmark.
             Do not for ever with thy vailed lids
             Seek for thy noble father in the dust;
             Thou know'st 'tis common; all that live must die
             Passing through nature to eternity.

      HAMLET: Ay, madam, it is common.
      QUEEN: If it be,
             Why seems it so particular with thee?

HAMLET: Seems, madam! Nay, it is; I know not 'seems.'
'Tis not alone my inky cloak, good mother,
Nor customary suits of solemn black,
Nor windy suspiration of forc'd breath,
No, nor the fruitful river in the eye,
Nor the dejected haviour of the visage,
Together with all forms, modes, shows of grief,
That can denote me truly; these indeed seem,
For they are actions that a man might play:
But I have that within which passeth show;
These but the trappings and the suits of woe.

Shakespeare, Hamlet, Act 1, sc. 1

2. MRS. PETERS (*to the other woman*): Oh, her fruit; it did freeze. (*To the County Attorney.*) She worried about that when it turned so cold. She said the fire'd go out and her jars would break.
SHERIFF: Well, can you beat the women! Held for murder and worryin' about her preserves.
COUNTY ATTORNEY: I guess before we're through she may have something more serious than preserves to worry about.
HALE: Well, women are used to worrying over trifles.
(*The two women move a little closer together.*)

Glaspell, Trifles

3. LOPAKHIN: Your estate is only fifteen miles from the town; the railway runs close by it; and if the cherry orchard and the land along the river bank were cut up into lots and these leased for summer cottages, you would have an income of at least 25,000 rubles a year out of it.
GAYEV: Excuse me . . . What nonsense!
MME. RANEVSKAYA: I don't quite understand you, Yermolay Alexeyevich.
LOPAKHIN: You will get an annual rent of at least ten rubles per acre, and if you advertise at once, I'll give you any guarantee you like that you won't have a square foot of ground left by autumn, all the lots will be snapped up. In short, congratulations, you're saved. The location is splendid—by that deep river. . . . Only, of course the ground must be cleared . . . all the old buildings, for instance, must be torn down, and this house, too, which is useless, and of course, the old cherry orchard must be cut down.
MME. RANEVSKAYA: Cut down? My dear, forgive me, but you don't know what you're talking about. If there's one thing that's interesting—indeed, remarkable—in the whole province, it's precisely our cherry orchard.

Chekhov, The Cherry Orchard, Act 1

Setting

The action of any play or movie takes place in a certain location and sometimes the **setting** plays an important role in the unfolding of the plot: characters may act in a certain way precisely because of their environment. Obviously the possibilities in film are enormous compared to theater, where only so many scene changes can be tolerated. However, setting can help us understand the characters of a play and explain their behavior. Stage sets often indicate the characters' lifestyle, whether they are rich or poor, upper-class or bohemian, etc. For example, the stage directions at the beginning of *A Doll House* specify: "A comfortable room, tastefully but not expensively furnished." The audience knows therefore as soon as the curtain rises that the family is quite well-off but not extremely rich or ostentatious. On the other hand, the décor of the two tramps in *Waiting for Godot* represents simply "A country road. A tree"—a minimalist setting that seems appropriate for their minimalist existence.

Sets can also suggest the historical period of the action; if a play is set in medieval times, say, or in sixteenth century Italy or eighteenth century England, the set designer will choose a suitable background, and furniture, draperies, etc. appropriate for the period, following the instructions contained in the play's stage directions. These instructions can be very elaborate as in *A Doll House*, where Ibsen specifies a piano, a porcelain stove with a fire burning, armchairs, a round table and a rocking chair, engravings on the walls, shelves with china ornaments, a bookcase with bound books, carpeting. Alternatively, stage directions may give very few details concerning the setting, in which case the stage director and set designer must expand on them to create a setting in accordance with their knowledge of the play's action, location, period, and characters. Shakespeare gives very little detail about setting. *Hamlet* mostly takes place at the royal castle in Elsinore, with the location moving from the battlements to various rooms and halls in the castle, to a room in Polonius's house and to the graveyard where Ophelia is buried; but no detail is given about any of these locations.

Some plays, like Shakespeare's and many modern plays, involve frequent scene changes according to the needs of the action. Nowadays, complicated set changes can be accomplished with remarkable speed thanks to revolving stages and other mechanical devices, so that frequent changes of scene are possible. For the Greeks this was not the case: they performed plays in the open air without a curtain, and all the action unfolded in one place. This had to be a neutral location, where all the characters in the play could legitimately appear: usually it would be a hall in a palace, or the front of a palace, since most of the characters, at least in the tragedies, were of royal blood.

Some modern playwrights prefer a **symbolic** setting to a **realistic** one. For the set of *Waiting for Godot*, the tree need not even resemble a real tree; it could be a stylized tree representing "nature" just as the two tramps no doubt represent humanity in general and the road perhaps symbolizes a direction to take—or not to take. Some plays have simply the bare stage as a setting, which might in itself symbolize barrenness, or might be intended to allow the audience to imagine a set for themselves. Even a realistic setting may include symbolic details: one of the first things we see as the curtain rises on *The Cherry Orchard* is the cherry trees in full bloom in the orchard that plays such a crucial role in the play's action. In Chekhov's *The Seagull*, the dead bird seems to symbolize Nina, the young protagonist who will suffer and be cast aside. In *Trifles*, too, the dead canary clearly symbolizes Mrs. Wright, who "used to sing real pretty herself."

When analyzing part of a dramatic text, comment on the setting if this seems relevant to the passage. Try to imagine the set you would create if you were the set designer, whether you would make it realistic or symbolic; and consider its significance for the action of the play and the behavior of the characters.

Costumes, Props, Lighting, Sound Effects

Like the stage set, costumes can indicate the period when the action of the play (or film) takes place. In *The Cherry Orchard* the women might wear long dresses or skirts, the servants the appropriate attire for peasants or servants in Russia at the time. Shakespeare's plays are often performed in Elizabethan costume with the men in doublet and hose and the women in long gowns. If the action is set in Italy—as so many of his plays are—then Italian period costumes might also be used. His plays and others are often presented in modern dress, too, which implies that the characters and action of the play don't belong exclusively to the era in question but also to our own age, or indeed to all ages.

Costume can play a crucial role in a play, as for example when female characters dress as men—which happens rather often in Shakespeare's plays—or servants and their masters change places and exchange clothes, as in Marivaux's *The Game of Love and Chance*. Costumes can tell us something of a character's social status and even about a character's personality: a flirtatious woman will wear a different costume from a more prim or serious female character. Costumes may also take on a symbolic value, like Hamlet's black clothes (he talks of his "inky cloak") or Nora's clothes in *A Doll House*. In Act 1 she comes home wearing regular street clothes; towards the end of Act 2 she wraps herself in a colorful shawl and dances a wild tarantella, with her hair falling around her shoulders; both the dance and the shawl seem to reflect her conflicting emotions and her desperation. In Act 3 the contrast between Nora and her husband is illustrated by their dress: Nora wears a bright Italian costume but he is in evening dress, reflecting the stiffness of his character. Later, towards the end of the play, she changes back into her normal clothes: the play-acting is over, the doll-wife is leaving to live her own life and become herself.

Some props in a play simply serve to help establish a setting; others (like the handkerchief in Othello, or the birdcage and dead bird in *Trifles*), are crucial for the development of the plot; and some take on symbolic value, like Yorick's skull in *Hamlet*.

Lighting can serve to dramatize certain moments, such as a storm, or indicate the time of day—dawn, sunset, nightfall, etc. *Hamlet* opens in the dark, at midnight, but by the end of the first scene the lighting must change to signify the coming of dawn, as Horatio remarks: "But, look, the morn in russet mantle clad, / Walks o'er the dew of yon high eastern hill." *The Cherry Orchard* begins at dawn; Dunyasha comes on stage holding a candle, but soon puts it out because it's getting light; the lighting should get steadily brighter throughout the first part of Act 1. At certain moments in the course of a play, spotlights may be used to draw attention to a particular character.

Sound effects are important in some plays. Drums in a Shakespeare play may announce an advancing army, trumpets the arrival of a king. There is a moment in Act 3 of *The Cherry Orchard* when all the characters are sitting outside, deep in thought, when they hear a strange distant sound, like the snapping of a string, that gradually dies away. We never learn what causes the sound, but it suits the melancholy atmosphere of the moment. It comes again at the end of the play, emphasizing the sadness of leaving and of parting. Also at the end, when all the characters (except Firs) have left the stage, the audience hears the sound of an ax cutting down the cherry trees, which symbolizes many themes of the play: the destruction of beauty, the end of an era and of a certain social group, and the advent of a new age.

CHAPTER 8

Writing a Close Reading of a Dramatic Passage

PREPARING TO WRITE A CLOSE READING OF A DRAMATIC PASSAGE

Review the section on "Preparing to Write a Close Reading of a Prose Passage" (pages 98–99) for comments on such issues as leaving yourself plenty of time, familiarizing yourself with the work from which the passage is taken, looking up allusions or words you don't know, annotating the passage, avoiding over-use of the first person, and managing quotations: the same advice applies to explicating a passage from a play. As with prose fiction, refrain from re-telling the plot of the whole play; instead, concentrate on the passage and what, in your view, it reveals about the play and the characters. If you want to give a quotation from a play in verse, you can use the act, scene, and line numbers: 3, ii, 67 would refer to Act 3, scene 2, line 67. Arabic numerals may also be used, thus: 3, 2, 67. For plays in prose, just use act and scene numbers; or your professor may prefer you to use page numbers for greater accuracy.

WRITING A CLOSE READING OF A DRAMATIC PASSAGE

A close reading of a dramatic passage not only analyzes the text of the passage, sentence by sentence, but also links the content and style of the passage to the complete work; for example, it points out what the passage reveals about the speaker and relates that to the speaker's behavior in the rest of the play. You should keep in mind not only the words on the page but how you think they might be interpreted in performance, imagining the actors' gestures, expressions, and tone of voice.

Introduction

The introduction to your close reading should name the title and author of the play, situate the passage in the play, explain who the speaker of the passage is and to whom he or she is talking and (briefly) in what circumstances. You should say whether the passage is part of a dialogue, a monologue, or a soliloquy, whether it is in prose or in verse, and characterize the overall tone of the passage (comic, tragic, ironic, etc.).

Detailed Analysis

The introduction serves to give general information about the whole passage. In the detailed analysis that represents the main body of your close reading, you should explicate the passage phrase by phrase or sentence by sentence. As you proceed, keep in mind all the aspects of drama discussed above: dialogue, language, characterization, gestures and expressions, tone of voice, plot, setting, costumes, lighting, and sound effects where appropriate. Refer to these elements as they come up in the passage. Of course some texts will prompt you to concentrate more on characterization, some on language or gestures, others on setting, and so on, depending on the nature of the extract. If there is nothing to say on a certain element, ignore it.

Regarding **dialogue**, you will need to think how naturally it manages to convey information to the audience; whether the characters on stage mean everything they say; whether the passage contains examples of **dramatic irony**; the speaker's tone of voice and what gestures or facial expressions—whether indicated by stage directions or not—might accompany the dialogue in the case of both the speaker and his or her interlocutor(s). You should also examine the language of the passage: does it resemble spoken language and if so how? Or is the language more literary and if so, what literary qualities does it have? Explain any difficult words or allusions. Is the language a source of comedy? As always, comment on any features of **style** such as sentence-length, punctuation, vocabulary, and use of figurative language, symbols, irony etc. (See the section on style in part II, on prose, pages 91–96.) If the play is in verse, what poetic qualities does it have? (See part I, on poetry, above.) Are any words appearing in this passage repeated often elsewhere in the work and if so, what is their significance, in your view? Is the style of the passage typical of the work as a whole? Is the speaker's language idiosyncratic in any way, i.e. does he or she have a characteristic way of speaking?

Thinking about **characterization**, consider what the passage reveals about the speaker or about any other character. If the character has obvious shortcomings, is he or she aware of them? Does the knowledge we acquire in this extract fit in with what we already know about the character(s)? Will it be corroborated by what we learn later in the play? Are the characters in this extract "flat" or "rounded"? Does the speaker adopt any gestures or facial expressions that seem to reveal his or her personality? How do you visualize the characters on the stage? Do they provoke laughter? Does the personality of the character(s) in this extract affect the progress of the plot and if so, how?

At what point in the **plot** does this extract appear? Does the passage refer to any element of **conflict** in the play and if so, of what kind? Does it contain an element of dramatic tension or surprise? In a comedy, does the passage enact a comic situation? How do the events or information contained in this passage affect the plot?

Does the **setting** play a role in this passage? How do you visualize it? Might it reflect the period when the action takes place? Is it symbolic or realistic? What does it reveal about the characters?

Is there any indication about what costume the speaker is wearing? If not, how do you imagine he or she would be dressed and why?

Does the scene from which this passage is taken involve any special lighting or sound effects?

Conclusion

Do not forget to end your close reading with a conclusion. The conclusion of a close reading presents a more general view than the analysis. Consider the significance of the passage in the context of the complete work: how does it relate to the **theme** of the play? Is the style of the passage typical of the whole work? In the case of comedy, what types of comedy are contained in the passage? Does the passage provide a good illustration of the author's art? What is your overall evaluation of his or her art in this passage and in the complete work?

Revision

You should complete the first draft of your close reading with enough time left for revision and editing. Re-read your own work. Reading it aloud may help you find problematic areas; if it doesn't make sense to you, it won't to another reader. Check both the content and the organization of your work. Make sure your arguments are clear and that where necessary you have introduced suitable quotations from the text to back up your points, and have integrated them properly into your own sentences (see page 47). Remembering that your task is to analyze and explicate the passage, make sure you have avoided paraphrasing, i.e., re-telling the plot in your own words. Check that your essay is suitably divided into paragraphs and that transitions are smooth and logical. Do not forget to include an introduction and a conclusion that stand apart from the line-by-line analysis.

In order to check the **style** of your work, it can be helpful to read it aloud; then if anything sounds awkward or unnatural, you will be more likely to notice it. Examine your choice of words: avoid colloquialisms, but do not try to use highly sophisticated vocabulary unless you are sure of being able to handle it accurately. Avoid wordiness for its own sake: make sure all your sentences add something to your essay. Try to incorporate some variety into the structure of your sentences. Finally, proofread your paper for errors of spelling, punctuation, and grammar.

Avoiding Plagiarism

It goes without saying that your close reading should be your own work. To allow anyone else to compose your paper for you, or even parts of it, would be a violation of academic integrity. Copying another writer's thoughts, whether from a book or the Internet, without acknowledging the fact, constitutes an act of plagiarism. If you are writing a research paper and quote from secondary sources, you should always acknowledge them (see part 4, "Moving Beyond Close Reading,"); but for a close reading you should not need secondary sources at all.

Summary of Elements to Discuss in a Dramatic Passage

I Introduction

a) Name the title and author of the work from which the passage is taken, situate the passage in the play, explain who the speaker of the passage is and to whom he or she is talking and (briefly) in what circumstances. Is the passage part of a dialogue, a monologue, or a soliloquy? In prose or in verse? What is the overall tone of the passage (comic, tragic, ironic, etc.)? Does it divide into parts?

II Detailed analysis, proceeding through the passage phrase by phrase, or sentence by sentence.

(These elements can be treated in any order, as they come up in the passage. Some features may have more significance than others, depending on the passage.)

a) Does the **dialogue** convey information to the audience naturally? Do the characters on stage mean everything they say? Does the passage contain examples of **dramatic irony**? What gestures or facial expressions would accompany the dialogue? Does the language of the passage resemble spoken language and if so how? Is the language a source of comedy? Is the play in verse or in prose? Comment on any features of **style** such as sentence-length, punctuation, vocabulary, repetitions, use of figurative language, symbols, irony etc. Does the speaker have a characteristic style?

b) Does the passage contribute to our knowledge of the characters, and if so, how? Are the characters in this extract "flat" or "rounded"? Does the character adopt any gestures or facial expressions that seem to reveal his or her personality? Does the character provoke laughter? Does the personality of the character(s) in this extract affect the progress of the plot and if so, how?

c) At what point in the **plot** does this extract appear? Does the passage refer to any element of **conflict** in the play and if so, of what kind? Does it create dramatic tension or contain any element of surprise or any comedy of situation?

d) Does the **setting** play a role in this passage? How do you visualize it? What does it reveal about the characters?

e) Do costumes, lighting or sound effects play a significant role in this passage?

III Conclusion

(These are suggestions. Choose what seems most relevant to your passage. Add other comments of a general nature if you wish.)

a) Discuss the significance of the passage for the work as a whole, whether for the plot, the characterization, language, setting, staging, or for a combination of these elements.

b) Relate the passage to the **theme** of the play.

c) In the case of comedy, what types of comedy are contained in the passage?

d) Give your overall appreciation of the author's art in this passage and in the complete work.

CHAPTER 9

Close Readings of Dramatic Passages

In this section you will find first of all two model close readings of extracts from plays, followed by five dramatic passages accompanied by questions designed to help you write close readings of your own. You will not be expected to write on all of these but should select as many as you feel are useful or your professor assigns. You may eventually be asked to compose questions of your own, on a new extract, to offer to your fellow students. Finally you will move on to write a close reading of a new dramatic passage without questions to guide you.

For reasons of space, only one short play, *Trifles*, is reprinted in appendix 4. The other plays referred to in this section (Shakespeare's *Othello* and *Hamlet*, Ibsen's *A Doll House*, and Chekhov's *The Cherry Orchard*) are readily available, however, whether on-line or in published form. You should read the complete play before either reading a model close reading or attempting to explicate one of the passages with questions.

The model close readings are from Ibsen's *A Doll House* and Susan Glaspell's *Trifles*. The text of the passage from *A Doll House* illustrates the kinds of notes and comments you might make in the margins of a text on a first or second reading, before expanding these remarks into the first draft of your essay.

The second model close reading, from Susan Glaspell's *Trifles*, is followed by a commentary pointing out noteworthy features of the reading and of its approach to the text.

MODEL CLOSE READINGS

1. *A Doll House* (1879)

HELMER. [*calls out from his room*] Is that my little lark twittering out there?

separate
Possessive
Playful but condescending

NORA. [*busy opening some of the parcels*] Yes, it is!

likes shopping. Christmas
consents to his condescending attitude

HELMER. Is my little squirrel bustling about?

playful but condescending

NORA. Yes!

HELMER. When did (my) squirrel come home?   5

he mustn't notice!

NORA. Just now. [*puts the bag of macaroons into her pocket and wipes her mouth.*]

his name   money!

Come in here, Torvald, and see what I have bought.

Busy/Important/Male   (can't resist)

HELMER. Don't disturb me. [*A little later, he opens the door and looks into the room,*

still busy   money   *teasing tone,*

pen in hand.] Bought, did you say? All these things? Has (my) little   *but critical*

money theme. She wastes it

spendthrift been wasting money again?   10

NORA. Yes, but, Torvald, this year we really can let ourselves go a little. This is the first

setting

Christmas that we have not needed to economise.

His constant refrain

HELMER. Still, you know, we can't spend money recklessly.

wheedling tone

NORA. Yes, Torvald, we may be a wee bit more reckless now, mayn't we? Just a tiny wee bit!

vague   but happy

You are going to have a big salary and earn lots and lots of money.   15

setting

HELMER. Yes, after the New Year; but then it will be a whole quarter before the   *cautious*

salary is due.

scornful

NORA. Pooh! we can borrow till then.

shocked! 1ˢᵗ use of her name   playful, but . . .

HELMER. Nora! [*goes up to her and takes her playfully by the ear.*] The same little

condescending

featherhead! Suppose, now, that I borrowed fifty pounds to-day, and you   20

spent it all in the Christmas week, and then on New Year's Eve a slate fell   *practical*

on my head and killed me, and—

won't listen to practical / unpleasant matters

NORA. [*putting her hands over his mouth*] Oh! don't say such horrid things.

HELMER. Still, suppose that happened—what then?

NORA. If that were to happen, I don't suppose I should care whether I owed   25

money or not.   *Attached to him.*

HELMER. Yes, but what about the people who had lent it?

inconsiderate?

NORA. They? Who would bother about them? I should not know who they were.

Condescending towards women in general   he's said this before

HELMER. That is like a woman! But seriously, Nora, you know what I think about that.

rigid maxim   flowery

No debt, no borrowing. There can be no freedom or beauty about a home   30

unbending? pompous?   flowery

life that depends on borrowing and debt. We two have kept bravely on the

rigid mentality

straight road so far, and we will go on the same way for the short time longer

that there need be any struggle.

    deliberately?   weary tone

NORA. [*moving towards the stove*] As you please, Torvald.

submits to her attraction   conciliatory (but condescending)

    HELMER. [*following her*] Come, come, my little skylark must not droop her wings.   35

                                          money

What is this! Is my little squirrel out of temper? [*taking out his purse.*]

Nora, what do you think I have got here?

               enthusiasm   money theme

    NORA. [*turning around quickly*] Money!

Henrik Ibsen (1828–1906)

A Doll House, Act 1

Ibsen's *A Doll House* is considered a realist play, i.e., one whose characters are ordinary peo-ple (as opposed to nobility, for example), speaking in prose and involved in situations such as might arise in real life. Also, the sets of a realist play evoke a specific place—often, as here, a room in a house. The stage directions at the beginning of the play specify a room "furnished comfortably and tastefully, but not extravagantly." The question of extrava-gance comes up frequently in this initial dialogue between Torvald Helmer and his wife Nora. Apart from a very brief exchange between Nora and a porter who has delivered a Christmas tree and to whom she has given an extremely generous tip, these lines represent the play's opening dialogue.

Nora has just come in from the street, carrying several parcels. She has checked by lis-tening at her husband's study door that he is at home, but has not called out to him, either because she doesn't like to disturb him or because she is more interested in open-ing the parcels. These packages represent one of the many props in the play, such as the piano, the Christmas tree, the bag of macaroons—many of which have a symbolic value as well as being part of the realistic décor. Helmer hears her opening the parcels and calls from inside his room; he doesn't address her by name or ask "Is that you?" but instead uses the expressions "my little lark" and "my little squirrel." These nicknames imply a cer-tain condescension on his part, and the associated verbs, "twittering" and "bustling about," also indicate Helmer's condescending attitude towards Nora's activities. The rep-etition of the possessive pronoun "my," which continues throughout the dialogue, sug-gests Helmer's possessive attitude towards his wife. Already, then, in the first few lines of the play, we have the impression of a man who seems to consider his wife his property and views her as charming but frivolous; a few lines later he calls her a "featherhead."

Apart from Helmer's little phrases involving squirrels and birds, and some of his rather pompous longer speeches, the language of the passage, and of the play as a whole, is realistic and natural, for example when Helmer sticks his head round the door saying "Bought, did you say?" or when he insists: "Still, suppose that happened—what then?"

The stage directions make it easy for a reader to visualize the opening scene, with Helmer calling out from the study and Nora absorbed in opening her parcels, hum-ming happily to herself and eating macaroons. It is significant that when she invites Helmer to come out she hides the macaroons; we will learn later that he doesn't approve of her eating sweets. This detail suggests the severity that we will find to be characteristic of Helmer, and it seems more appropriate for a child-parent relationship than for a husband and wife. Significant, too, is the fact that Helmer's immediate response to her invitation is "Don't disturb me" (he, the responsible husband, being engaged in important pursuits), but when her words sink in he emerges from the study saying, "Bought, did you say?" (with a word order that stresses the word "Bought"), and calling his wife "my little spendthrift." It is easy to imagine his figure standing in the doorway, "*pen in hand,*" with a rather anxious expression on his face. He accuses her— albeit in a playful, teasing tone—of "wasting money again." These lines introduce the main theme of this passage, one that remains crucial throughout the play: that of spending money recklessly. Helmer considers his wife's spending extravagant, and she is continually trying to justify herself and to wheedle more money out of him. He has recently accepted a post as manager of a bank, and Nora thinks he will now earn "lots and lots of money" and points out that it's the first Christmas when they haven't needed to economize; but he insists that doesn't mean they can "spend money recklessly." They conduct this exchange in a light-hearted, bantering tone, emphasized by Helmer's gesture of taking Nora by the ear. The reader of this passage can imagine that the actress playing Nora would speak in a bright and hopeful tone ("we may be a wee bit more reckless now, mayn't we? Just a tiny wee bit!") and adopt a pouting expression. Helmer's voice conveys affection, as well as condescension, as he asks "Has my little spendthrift been wasting money again?" and calls her "The same little featherhead!"

Nevertheless, their words indicate a serious underlying difference in their attitudes, which is brought out more strongly in the next part of the dialogue. Apparently, Helmer will not receive his augmented salary for three months; Nora dismisses this inconvenient fact with a derisory exclamation, "Pooh!" and suggests they could borrow money for that length of time, but Helmer finds this idea totally unacceptable and is shocked into exclaiming reproachfully "Nora!"—using her real name for the first time instead of an expression like "my little lark." Thus the audience learns her name, and Nora uses his several times in the course of the dialogue.

When Helmer talks about what would happen if he were to die on New Year's Eve, Nora, predictably, won't even listen, covering his mouth with her hand and declaring that if she were to lose him nothing else would matter anyway, including the debt owed to the people they borrowed from. "That is like a woman!" retorts Helmer, in a remark suggesting that his condescending attitude embraces all women, not Nora alone. He speaks seriously in the following lines about the need to avoid debt and their own success so far in this regard. No doubt he is right, but there is a suggestion of rigidity in his phrase "No debt, no borrowing," and his references to "the straight road" and "struggle." He is attached to principles, whereas Nora is attached to people, in particular to her family including Helmer himself. The language in his little speech about debt reveals a tendency on his part towards flowery phrases ("There can be no freedom or beauty about a home life that depends on borrowing and debt. We two have kept bravely on the straight road so far . . ."), indicating a certain pomposity or at least an inclination to take himself very seriously, as indeed we will find he does throughout the play.

His speech leaves Nora discouraged or bored; one can imagine the polite but uninterested expression on her face as she listens to him, matching her response: "As you please, Torvald." Interestingly enough, as she moves toward the stove he follows her, as if attracted in spite of himself, while adding another conciliatory but condescending remark: "Come, come, my little skylark must not droop her wings." No doubt her move to the stove was deliberate on her part, encouraging him to follow and thereby showing her power over him. This manipulative behavior works, because he then offers her money, which she accepts with alacrity; her enthusiasm is conveyed by her gesture (*"turning around quickly"*) and by her exclamation: "Money!" One gets the impression that this kind of scene is probably repeated fairly often in the Helmer household.

It seems significant that Nora does not protest about Helmer's nicknames for her; in fact when he asks, "Is that my little lark twittering out there?" she replies, "Yes, it is." She appears to accept his dominance in their relationship and his infantilizing treatment of her. In fact, she responds in a child-like tone, as if adopting the role he assigns her. But perhaps in this too she is manipulating her husband—appearing to go along with his playful teasing in order to achieve her ends. *A Doll House* was written in the nineteenth century, when it was difficult for a woman to defy her husband openly. Nevertheless, by the end of the play we will see Nora learn to stand up to Helmer. We will discover also that her reason for requesting money was a valid one. She has never discussed it with Helmer because he treats her like a child; their marriage has been based on playful mockery rather than on genuine communication and respect.

In a very few lines, this opening passage has introduced us to some of the basic themes of the play: the conflict over money that divides Helmer and Nora; and his condescending and possessive attitude towards her, with all that such an attitude implied in the nineteenth century about a wife's subservience to her husband. Nora is a "rounded" character who will develop and change; in this passage she still acts like a dutiful wife, whatever she may be thinking, but at the end of the play she will go off on her own to live her own life without depending on either a father or a husband as she has always done. The passage also outlines already the contrast between the characters of the husband and the wife: he has strong principles and appears cold and unbending, whereas she is more emotional and light-hearted. The divisive theme of money and the opposition between the two main characters will propel the plot of the play to its inevitable end.

2. *Trifles* (1920)

MRS. HALE: You didn't know—her?

MRS. PETERS: Not till they brought her yesterday.

MRS. HALE: She—come to think of it, she was kind of like a bird herself—real sweet
 and pretty, but kind of timid and—fluttery. How—she—did—change.
 (*Silence; then as if struck by a happy thought and relieved to get back to everyday*   5
 things.) Tell you what, Mrs. Peters, why don't you take the quilt in with you?
 It might take up her mind.

MRS. PETERS: Why, I think that's a real nice idea, Mrs. Hale. There couldn't possibly be
 any objection to it, could there? Now, just what would I take? I wonder if her
 patches are in here—and her things. (*They look in the sewing basket.*)   10

MRS. HALE: Here's some red. I expect this has got sewing things in it. (*Brings out a fancy
 box.*) What a pretty box. Looks like something somebody would give you. Maybe
 her scissors are in here. (*Opens box. Suddenly puts her hand to her nose.*) Why—
 (*Mrs. Peters bend nearer, then turns her face away.*) There's something wrapped up
 in this piece of silk.   15

MRS. PETERS: Why, this isn't her scissors.

MRS. HALE (*lifting the silk*): Oh, Mrs. Peters—it's— (*Mrs. Peters bend closer.*)

MRS. PETERS: It's the bird.

MRS. HALE (*jumping up*):But, Mrs. Peters—look at it. Its neck! Look at its neck! It's all—
other side *to*.   20

MRS. PETERS: Somebody—wrung—its neck.

(*Their eyes meet. A look of growing comprehension, of horror. Steps are heard outside. Mrs. Hale slips
box under quilt pieces, and sinks into her chair. Enter Sheriff and County Attorney.
Mrs. Peters rises.*)

COUNTY ATTORNEY (*as one turning from serious thing to little pleasantries*):   25
Well, ladies, have you decided whether she was going to quilt it or knot it?

MRS. PETERS: We think she was going to—knot it.

Susan Glaspell (1876–1948)

Susan Glaspell's one-act play, *Trifles*, concerns the murder of Mr. Wright, who has
been found strangled in bed with a rope around his neck. Mrs. Wright, the only suspect,
has been arrested. Now, the following day, the County Attorney, the Sheriff (Mr. Peters),
and Mr. Hale, a neighboring farmer who discovered the body, have come to the house to
investigate. It is a farmhouse and the whole play takes place in the kitchen, "*a gloomy
kitchen,*" according to the stage directions. Accompanying the men are Mrs. Hale and the
Sheriff's wife, Mrs. Peters, who has permission to take a few clothes and other articles to
deliver to Mrs. Wright in prison. The men are convinced that Mrs. Wright committed the
crime but are searching for evidence of a motive. The two ladies talk in the kitchen while
the men explore upstairs, and this passage represents part of that dialogue plus a short
exchange with the men when they return. It takes place more than half way through the
short play. The ladies have already discovered various items of interest in the kitchen,
including part of a quilt that Mrs. Wright was making and an empty birdcage with a broken door, which will prove to be one of several important props in the play. Just before
this passage they have been speculating about what happened to the bird.

Mrs. Hale is a local woman, the wife of a neighbor, and has known Mrs. Wright
for a long time. In the opening question of this passage she seems reluctant to name
Mrs. Wright, asking instead, "You didn't know—her?" with the dash marking her hesitation
to name a suspected murderer. On hearing that Mrs. Peters did not know her neighbor,
Mrs. Hale starts to talk about her, but immediately interrupts herself (another dash marks
this interruption) as she is struck by the idea of a resemblance between Mrs. Wright and a
bird. She has already told Mrs. Peters that before her marriage Mrs. Wright used to sing in
the town choir; now she states that Mrs. Wright was "real sweet and pretty, but kind of timid
and—fluttery." But again, that was in the past, long ago, for Mrs. Hale adds, emphatically,
"How—she—did—change." Here the dashes (perhaps translated into pauses in speech)
mark the emphasis she places on these words as she contemplates the possible effect
on Mrs. Wright of living with her husband. Since we know Mrs. Hale considers the late
Mr. Wright a hard, cold man, we may assume she blames him for the change in his
wife. A pause ("*Silence*") follows her remark as its implications become apparent both
to Mrs. Peters and to the audience. The rest of the stage directions here indicate
Mrs. Hale's change of tone from the seriousness of that statement to the "*happy thought*"
that strikes her next, namely the suggestion that Mrs. Peters might take Mrs. Wright's quilt
work to her in jail—a kind thought that reveals her concern for Mrs. Wright. Her tone

must also convey at this point that she is *"relieved to get back to everyday things"*: she was uncomfortable with the feeling of sadness produced by her realization of how much Mrs. Wright has changed over the years.

Mrs. Hale's language here—like that of all the characters in the play—is very natural and colloquial. In the sentence: "She—come to think of it, she was kind of like a bird herself—real sweet and pretty, but kind of timid and—fluttery," the dashes marking hesitations or interruptions and the expression "kind of" are typical of spoken language, as is the phrasing of Mrs. Peters' response: "Why, I think that's a real nice idea, Mrs. Hale."

Mrs. Peters agrees that it would be a good idea to take the quilt to Mrs. Wright, but her next sentence reminds us that she is the Sheriff's wife and careful always to follow the rules: "There couldn't possibly be any objection to it, could there?" The play does set up a distinction between the two women: in general Mrs. Hale is more inclined to defend Mrs. Wright, and feels sorry for her, whereas Mrs. Peters insists that "the law is the law" and objects when Mrs. Hale re-sews part of the quilt that had been badly stitched, saying nervously, "I don't think we ought to touch things."

Mrs. Peters wonders what exactly she should take to Mrs. Wright and both women start to look in the sewing basket—one of the many props mentioned in the play's stage directions. We can imagine them, wearing their coats in this cold kitchen, their heads bent together over the sewing basket. In it they find a fancy gift box ("Looks like something somebody would give you"), and open it in search of scissors. The stage directions give us the first clue that something strange is in the box, as Mrs. Hale *"puts her hand to her nose"* in a gesture of revulsion. Mrs. Peters turns her face away at the smell and we can imagine her expression too as she registers the unpleasant odor. The reference to a "piece of silk" goes along with the "pretty box": both would be used to wrap up something precious. The suspense mounts as Mrs. Peters exclaims, "Why, this isn't her scissors" and Mrs. Hale, lifting the silk, cries (with dashes indicating her hesitation): "Oh, Mrs. Peters—it's—"; then we see Mrs. Peters bending closer, remarking "It's the bird," and Mrs. Hale jumping up in astonishment as she notices how the bird has died. The repetitions and exclamation points suggest that she shouts rather than says, "But, Mrs. Peters—look at it! Its neck! Look at its neck! It's all—other side *to*." This is a climactic moment in the play because of the similarity between the way the bird died and the way Mr. Wright died. Mrs. Peters, less excitable than Mrs. Hale, underscores the significance of their find by her deliberate, emphatically spaced out observation: "Somebody—wrung—its—neck." The implications of this fact, in a household where the husband has recently been found strangled with a noose around his neck, dawns on them both simultaneously, as the stage directions make clear. The *"look of growing comprehension, of horror"* on their faces indicates that they are beginning to make the connection between the death of the bird and the death of the man, and to realize that they have discovered the motive that eludes their husbands. Just at this moment we hear the men's approaching footsteps; the audience is in suspense wondering if the ladies will inform the men of their discovery, but instead, Mrs. Hale hides the box containing the bird—indicating a sense of solidarity with Mrs. Wright. Another similarly suspenseful moment will come at the end of the play when Mrs. Hale succeeds in hiding the box in her pocket just as the men re-enter the room.

At this point, Mrs. Peters rises—perhaps simply to distance herself from the bird, perhaps with the intention of telling the men about it; the actress playing the role should make that clear. In any case, she does not tell, maybe because the men's patronizing attitude towards the women comes out so strongly in the County Attorney's tone of someone *"turning from serious things to little pleasantries."* His question refers to methods of quilting, which have already been mentioned in the play. Now, after the discovery of the dead bird, Mrs. Peters' reply is highly significant: "We think she was going to—knot it" (again, a dash indicates a meaningful pause). The symbolism of the knot, the strangled bird and the noose that killed Mr. Wright is lost on the men but clear to the audience, which makes this an example of dramatic irony. Interestingly enough, the Attorney doesn't bother to ask why the ladies have decided in favor of knotting over quilting—he is simply making pleasant conversation about what he considers a womanly "trifle." Significant too is the fact that Mrs. Peters says nothing about the bird, apparently going along with Mrs. Hale's decision to hide it, even though it would have provided the men with the evidence of a motive they have been seeking. In this play, it is the women who solve the question of a motive for the murder, but they hide the evidence in order to protect another woman who they feel has been unjustly treated.

This passage is important for the development of the plot since it reveals Mrs. Wright's possible motive for killing her husband, but also because it shows the other women protecting her, by hiding the bird. Susan Glaspell later re-wrote this play as a short story with the title "A Jury of Her Peers." In this extract we see the beginning of that "jury's" findings. Mrs. Hale says more than once that Mr. Wright was a cold, hard man, and senses that he oppressed his wife who, after her marriage to him, lost her youthful gaiety, stopped singing, and led a cheerless, lonely life. She realizes how attached Mrs. Wright must have been to the one thing that brought her any happiness—the canary that Mr. Wright strangled. She clearly feels a strong allegiance to the wife against the husband and succeeds in winning over Mrs. Peters to the same view, even though they both realize that Mrs. Wright did kill her husband. The play was written at the beginning of the twentieth century, at a time when the husband's role in a marriage was dominant. Its basic theme concerns the emancipation of women: it suggests that women should have the right to lead their own lives and not be totally subservient to their husbands' will, as Mrs. Wright was. It also implies that women are quite as able or intelligent as men: the men in the play have a very condescending attitude towards the women who, they say, concern themselves with "trifles"; in fact, however, it is the women who discover the motive for the crime, for which the men search in vain. Altogether, despite being so short, the play illustrates some important ideas, differentiates sufficiently between the characters for us to feel we know their personalities, and develops an interesting plot.

Commentary on Model Close Reading #2

This explication incorporates many of the features of drama discussed above to analyze the passage and link it to the play as a whole. It examines the nature of the dialogue, the speakers' language, tone and gestures, what the passage reveals about the characters and how it furthers the plot, the use of dramatic irony, and how the passage relates to the overall themes of the play.

The introduction names the play and its author, situates the passage in the play, mentions the setting, and explains the characters' circumstances. It is always necessary when dealing with an extract from a longer work to give some background information. Notice, however, that such information is kept to a minimum: only details that have a direct bearing on this passage are mentioned, such as the relationship of the characters to each other, the manner of Mr. Wright's death, and the items that the ladies have already found (the quilt and the birdcage). The question of tone, which might sometimes be dealt with in an introduction, is left to the detailed analysis, since there are so many variations in tone in this passage.

The analysis pays attention not only to what the characters say but also to their manner of speaking, as revealed by the punctuation and the stage directions. It considers the implications beneath the words, for example when Mrs. Hale declares emphatically "How—she—did—change," leading us to think about Mrs. Wright's life with her husband. It analyzes the possible significance of pauses in the women's speech. It aims to dig beneath the surface, to show the psychological implications of the characters' speech and tone, for instance when Mrs. Hale moves from the serious statement "How—she—did—change" to the "happy thought" of taking Mrs. Wright's quilt to her in jail, or when a series of exclamation points indicates that a character is upset and probably shouting. The significance of the contrast in tone between the Attorney's flippant, condescending question at the end and Mrs. Peters' highly serious reply is also analyzed.

Differences between the characters are indicated—not only the obvious ones between the men and the women, but also the more subtle differences between the two women, as reflected in Mrs. Peters' question: "There couldn't possibly be any objection to it, could there?"

Notice that when the analysis points out that the language of the passage is fairly colloquial, it backs up that statement with examples from the text—the expression "kind of" and the use of dashes to indicate hesitation.

The gestures that characters make are indicated, with an explanation of their psychological implications, as when Mrs. Hale jumps up in horrified astonishment when she realizes how the bird has died, or when she hides the box containing the bird—an action that reveals her decision to support Mrs. Wright rather than help the sheriff.

The symbolism of the "knot" (in the quilting and in the rope that killed Mr. Wright) is explained, along with the dramatic irony inherent in Mrs. Peters' final remark in this passage and the implications of her silence about their discovery of the bird. This leads into a discussion, in the conclusion, of the passage's relation to the central theme of the play, namely women's rights and women's capabilities.

TOWARDS CLOSE READING: DRAMATIC PASSAGES ACCOMPANIED BY QUESTIONS

Using the foregoing models as examples and the questions following each passage as a guide, you can now write close readings of your own on whichever of the following passages you choose or your professor assigns. *Do not simply answer the questions*, but incorporate your answers into an essay (as in the models). Treat the questions as a general guide only, rather than simply answering them one by one. You do not need to deal with them strictly in order (though your reading should move through the passage sentence by sentence); if one or two questions seem incomprehensible to you, you can omit them; and of course you should not hesitate to add any independent observations of your own. After this practice you should be able to write a close reading on dramatic passages without questions to guide you.

The texts are presented in chronological order. They are from Shakespeare's *Hamlet* and *Othello*, Ibsen's *A Doll House*, Chekhov's *The Cherry Orchard*, and Susan Glaspell's *Trifles*.

1. *Hamlet* (c. 1600)

(Enter Polonius)

HAMLET: God bless you, sir!

POLONIUS: My lord, the queen would speak with you, and presently.

HAMLET: Do you see yonder cloud that's almost in shape of a camel?

POLONIUS: By the mass, and 'tis like a camel, indeed.

HAMLET: Methinks it is like a weasel.   5

POLONIUS: It is backed like a weasel.

HAMLET: Or like a whale?

POLONIUS: Very like a whale.

HAMLET: Then I will come to my mother by and by. (*Aside*) They fool me to the
   top of my bent. (*Aloud*) I will come by and by.   10

POLONIUS: I will say so. (*Exit*)

HAMLET: By and by is easily said. Leave me, friends. (*Exeunt all but* HAMLET)
   'Tis now the very witching time of night,
   When churchyards yawn and hell itself breathes out
   Contagion to this world; now could I drink hot blood,   15
   And do such bitter business as the day
   Would quake to look on. Soft! now to my mother,
   O heart! lose not thy nature; let not ever
   The soul of Nero enter this firm bosom;
   Let me be cruel, not unnatural;   20
   I will speak daggers to her, but use none;
   My tongue and soul in this be hypocrites;
   How in my words soever she be shent,
   To give them seals never, my soul, consent! [*Exit*]

William Shakespeare (1564–1616)
Hamlet, Act 3, sc. 2

For the Introduction

1. Situate the passage in the play.
2. How would you divide this extract into parts? What kinds of speech does it contain? Is the speech in prose or in verse? What is the tone of the language in each part?
3. Who are the speakers? Is anyone else present on stage?
4. What important event has occurred earlier in the same scene? What effect has this had on Hamlet?
5. What is Hamlet's attitude towards Polonius in this scene?

For the Detailed Analysis

1. What is Hamlet doing when Polonius arrives? In what tone does Hamlet greet Polonius? What is his attitude towards him elsewhere in the play?

2. What is Polonius's message to Hamlet? (Find the meaning of "presently" in Shakespeare's day.) Is this the first such message he has received? What effect does this message seem to have on Hamlet?

3. What tone does he adopt with Polonius? Is Polonius aware of it?

4. Is there any resemblance between a camel, a weasel and a whale? What is Hamlet's point in asserting that the cloud looks like these various animals? (Think about Polonius's answers.) Could there even be more than one reason why Hamlet initiates this little dialogue? (Think about the role he is playing at court.)

5. What gestures or facial expressions might accompany this dialogue between Hamlet and Polonius?

6. How prompt is Hamlet in obeying his mother's summons? Why do you think he needs to repeat twice that he will come "by and by"?

7. What is the point of the aside, "They fool me to the top of my bent" (meaning "to my utmost capacity," "to the utmost").

8. Do you feel there is any mental reservation behind Polonius's parting remark, "I will say so"? What expression or gesture might accompany his words?

9. Is there some humor in Hamlet's rejoinder?

10. Who leaves when Hamlet says "Leave me, friends"?

11. How does the mood change at this point and what else changes?

12. What would you say was the "witching time of night"? What happens when churchyards "yawn"?

13. What kind of vocabulary does Hamlet employ now?

14. Why does Hamlet feel he could "drink hot blood"? Is he often in such a mood? What kind of "bitter business" does he contemplate?

15. What figure of speech is contained in the lines "such bitter business as the day / Would quake to look on"? Does it add anything to the idea expressed?

16. Does Hamlet seem reluctant now to go and see his mother?

17. What figure of speech is represented by the expression "O heart!"? What "nature" does he refer to? Why does he allude to Nero? (What was Nero's relationship with his mother?) Does this allusion seem apt to you? (What does Hamlet mean by not wanting to resemble Nero? Why would he be tempted to?) Why is he planning to be "cruel" with his mother?

18. What do you think of the line "I will speak daggers to her, but use none"? If he speaks "daggers" to his mother, how will his tongue and his soul be "hypocrites" (i.e. contradict each other)? What form of the verb is "be" here?

19. If you look up the word "shent" in the penultimate line, you will find it is the past participle of an obsolete verb "to shend," meaning "to hurt," "disgrace," or "destroy." "How" and "soever" were normally written as one word, "howsoever"; "however" in modern English. So: "However hurt she may be by my words."

20. How do you understand the last two lines? Bear in mind that a "seal" authenticates a document ("words"). Does this advice that Hamlet gives to himself remind you of some advice the ghost gave to him?

21. What does this whole speech reveal about Hamlet's attitude towards his mother? What else have we seen of his attitude towards her in the play so far?

For the Conclusion

1. Is there some humor involved in this passage? Does humor occur at other moments in this tragedy?
2. What does this passage contribute to our understanding of Hamlet?
3. Does it add to the dramatic tension of the play?

2. *Othello* (c. 1604)

IAGO: My noble lord—

OTHELLO: What dost thou say, Iago?

IAGO: Did Michael Cassio, when you woo'd my lady
   Know of your love?

OTH: He did, from first to last. Why dost thou ask?

IAGO: But for a satisfaction of my thought;   5
   No further harm.

OTH: Why of thy thought, Iago?

IAGO: I did not think he had been acquainted with her.

OTH: O, yes, and went between us very oft.

IAGO: Indeed!

OTH: Indeed! Ay, indeed! Discern'st thou aught in that?   10
   Is he not honest?

IAGO: Honest, my lord?

OTH: Honest! Ay, honest.

IAGO: My lord, for aught I know.

OTH: What dost thou think?

IAGO: Think, my lord!

OTH: Think, my lord!
   By heaven, he echoes me,
   As if there were some monster in his thought   15
   Too hideous to be shown. Thou dost mean something.
   I heard thee say but now, thou lik'dst not that,
   When Cassio left my wife; what didst not like?
   And when I told thee he was of my counsel
   In my whole course of wooing, thou criedst, 'Indeed!'   20
   And didst contract and purse thy brow together,
   As if thou then hadst shut up in thy brain
   Some horrible conceit. If thou dost love me,
   Show me thy thought.

IAGO: My lord, you know I love you,   25

William Shakespeare (1564–1616)
Othello, Act 3, sc. 3

For the Introduction

1. Who is Othello? Why does the play bear his name as the title?
2. What is the relationship between Iago and Othello?

3. What are Iago's feelings towards Othello, as revealed earlier in the play?
4. Situate this scene in the play. Where does it take place?
5. What kind of speech is contained in this passage? Is it in verse or in prose?
6. Can the passage be divided into parts?

For the Detailed Analysis

1. How do you visualize the setting of this scene?
2. Who has just left the stage at this point in scene 3? Why does Othello appear not to have heard Iago in line 1 of this passage?
3. How does Iago feel towards Michael Cassio? (See Act 1, scene 1). Why does he bring up Cassio's name at this point? Why does he ask this question about Cassio's knowledge of Othello's love for Desdemona ("my lady")? (See Iago's soliloquies at the end of Act 1 and at the end of scene 1 of Act 2.)
4. Why does Othello call Iago "thou" while Iago calls Othello "you"?
5. Show how Iago is toying with Othello in lines 2-5 of the passage.
6. How does Othello's answer in line 8 play into Iago's hands?
7. What is the significance of Iago's "Indeed!" in line 9? What would the tone of this exclamation be, in your view?
8. In what tone would Othello pronounce "Indeed!" each time in line 10? What does he mean when he asks if Iago discerns anything ("aught") in that, and by the question "Is he not honest?"
9. Is Cassio "honest," in fact? (Is he faithful to Othello?) Who knows this?
10. What does Iago achieve by echoing "Honest, my lord?" instead of answering the question?
11. What might be the intonations used in the four repetitions of "honest" in line 11? What gesture or expression might accompany the words?
12. What is the irony of this quadruple repetition in view of Iago's own position?
13. Explain the underlying ambiguity of Iago's final answer "for aught I know" (i.e., "as far as I know"), which prompts Othello to ask, "What dost thou think?"
14. Point out the parallelism between lines 13 and 11. What does Iago gain here by merely repeating Othello's words?
15. In what tone does Othello say, "Think, my lord!"? What expression or gesture might the actor employ here?
16. To whom does Othello appear to address lines 14-16?
17. What figure of speech is contained in these lines? What kind of "monster" might he have in mind here?
18. Explain what Othello is referring to in lines 17-18. (See lines 35-40 of Act 3, scene 3, especially line 39.) What suspicion has Iago created by saying "I like not that"?
19. Why does Othello again bring up Iago's exclamation "Indeed!" from line 9 of the passage? What kind of thoughts might have led him to "contract and purse [his] brow together"?
20. What does the word "conceit" mean in line 23? Relate the "horrible conceit" to the "monster in his thought / Too hideous to be shown" of lines 15-16.
21. What thought is Othello asking Iago to reveal (line 24)? Does Iago really have such a thought?
22. Iago responds not to the injunction to reveal his thought, but to the phrase "If thou dost love me," to which he answers, "My lord, you know I love you."

Comment on this line in view of what we know about Iago, remembering that in Act 1, scene 1, he declares, "I am not what I am." What term is used to describe the discrepancy here between our understanding of Iago's words and Othello's?

For the Conclusion

1. What does the passage reveal about Iago's character? And about Othello?
2. How does this passage further the plot of the play?
3. How is it related to the main themes of the play?

3. *A Doll House* (1879)

HELMER: My dear, I have often seen it in the course of my life as a lawyer. Almost everyone who has gone to the bad early in life has had a deceitful mother.

NORA: Why do you only say—mother?

HELMER: It seems most commonly to be the mother's influence, though naturally a bad father's would have the same result. Every lawyer is familiar with the fact.   5 This Krogstad, now, has been persistently poisoning his own children with lies and dissimulation; that is why I say he has lost all moral character. (*holds out his hands to her*) That is why my sweet little Nora must promise me not to plead his cause. Give me your hand on it. Come, come, what is this? Give me your hand. There now, that's settled. I assure you it would be quite   10 impossible for me to work with him; I literally feel physically ill when I am in the company of such people.

NORA: (*takes her hand out of his and goes to the opposite side of the Christmas Tree*) How hot it is in here; and I have such a lot to do.

HELMER: (*getting up and putting his papers in order*) Yes, and I must try and read   15 through some of these before dinner; and I must think about your costume, too. And it is just possible I may have something ready in gold paper to hang up on the Tree. (*Puts his hand on her head.*) My precious little singing-bird!

(*He goes into his room and shuts the door after him.*)

NOR:. (after a pause, whispers) No, no—it isn't true. It's impossible; it must be impossible.   20

(*The NURSE opens the door on the left.*)

NURSE: The little ones are begging so hard to be allowed to come in to mamma.

NORA: No, no, no! Don't let them come in to me! You stay with them, Anne.

NURSE: Very well, ma'am.

(*Shuts the door.*)   25

NORA: (*pale with terror*) Deprave my little children? Poison my home? (*a short pause. Then she tosses her head.*) It's not true. It can't possibly be true.

Henrik Ibsen (1828–1906)
A Doll House, Act 1

For the Introduction

1. Name the author and title of the work and explain where the passage was taken from in the play.
2. When was the play written? Is this relevant to the issues it raises?

3. Identify Helmer and Nora. Explain (briefly) their circumstances at this point in the play. Who is the person they talk about (Krogstad) and what do we know about him?

For the Detailed Analysis

1. How do you visualize the setting at this point in the play?
2. What is Helmer's tone like in his opening sentences (up to "moral character")?
3. Is his profession as a lawyer a significant element of his characterization?
4. What does he mean by "goes to the bad"? Why is he talking about lies and dissimulation? What offence has Krogstad committed?
5. What is the significance of Nora's question "Why do you only say—mother?" and of the dash here? In what tone of voice does she ask this question?
6. Do you necessarily agree with Helmer's assertion that Krogstad has been "poisoning" his own children and has lost all moral character? What might this assessment reveal about Helmer's own character? How does his language strike you?
7. Is there an element of dramatic irony present at this point in the text?
8. Note the gesture in the stage directions. What change of tone might accompany the gesture?
9. How does Helmer refer to his wife? Is this ironic?
10. Why would Nora wish to plead Krogstad's cause? What gestures, suggested in the text, indicate her reluctance to give the promise Helmer asks for?
11. Why would Helmer be working with Krogstad? What do you think about his statement about being "physically ill" in the company of "such people"?
12. Why do you think Nora moves to the other side of the tree? Why does she feel hot suddenly, and why does she state at this point that she has a lot to do (what is the effect of her words)?
13. How do you visualize Helmer's manner as he gathers his papers together? Does his tone change again at this point? What is he planning to hang on the tree in gold paper?
14. What do his final gesture and words convey? Characterize Helmer's manner of speaking to his wife.
15. What is the tone of Nora's speech right after her husband leaves? What is "impossible"? Note the difference between "It's impossible" and "It must be impossible."
16. Why is Nora so vehement about not wanting her children to come in, and how is this vehemence expressed?
17. What is the significance of Nora's last words in the scene? How does she look? Why does she think she may deprave her children or poison her home? What does she conclude?
18. Does this passage increase the dramatic tension in the play?
19. Does the language of the passage seem natural?
20. How does the passage affect the plot of the play?

For the Conclusion

1. In what way(s) does the passage illustrate the basic theme of the play?
2. Does the passage add anything to the conflict between Nora and Helmer?
3. What do we learn about the two main characters from this extract? Do they appear to be "flat" or "rounded" characters?

4. *The Cherry Orchard* (1903-04)

TROFIMOV: Varya is afraid we'll suddenly fall in love with each other and has been
        following us around for days. She's so narrow-minded she can't understand
        that we are above love. To avoid all the petty and illusory things that prevent
        us from being free and happy, that is the aim and meaning of our life. Forward!
        We are moving irresistibly towards that bright star burning in the distance!   5
        Forward! Don't fall behind, friends!

ANYA: (*clapping her hands*) How well you speak! (*Pause*) It's wonderful here today.

TROFIMOV: Yes, the weather is amazing.

ANYA: What have you done to me, Petya, why don't I love the cherry orchard as I used
        to? I used to love it so tenderly, I thought there was no place on earth   10
        better than our orchard.

TROFIMOV: All Russia is our orchard. Our land is great and beautiful and there are
        many wonderful places in it. (*Pause*) Think of it, Anya, your grandfather,
        great-grandfather and all your ancestors were serf-owners, they owned living
        souls; don't you feel human beings looking at you from every tree, every leaf,   15
        every trunk in the orchard? Don't you hear voices . . . ? Oh, it's terrifying, your
        orchard is a terrible place; when you walk through it in the evening or at night
        the old bark on the trees gleams faintly and the old cherry-trees seem to be
        dreaming of things that happened a hundred or two hundred years ago and
        seem oppressed by dreadful visions. What is there to say? We are at least two   20
        hundred years behind, we have absolutely nothing yet, no definite attitude
        towards the past, we just philosophize, complain that we're bored, or drink
        vodka. It's so clear: in order to begin living in the present we must first redeem
        our past, finish with it; but that can only be done through suffering and
        through extraordinary, unceasing labor. Understand that, Anya.   25

ANYA: The house we live in has long ceased to be our house and I will go away, I give you
        my word.

TROFIMOV: If you have the housekeeping keys, throw them into the well and go. Be free
        as the wind.

ANYA: (*Ecstatically*) How well you said that!   30

                                          Anton Chekhov (1860–1904)
                                     The Cherry Orchard, Act 2

For the Introduction

1. Name the title and author of the work and situate the passage in the play.
2. Who are the characters speaking and how do they relate to the play's main
   characters?
3. What are the circumstances of this dialogue? What is the setting?

For the Detailed Analysis

1. Who is Varya? What is Trofimov's attitude towards her? Why would she not want
   Trofimov and Anya to fall in love? Do you think they *are* in love?
2. What is Trofimov's attitude towards love? What do you think of this?
3. What kind of vocabulary does Trofimov use?

4. What is his tone like in this speech? What gestures might the actor use?
5. Does Trofimov suggest *how* to move "Forward"? What friends is he addressing?
6. What effect do his words have on Anya? How do you visualize her gesture and her expression? What do you think she does during the pause indicated in the stage directions?
7. Why do you think she connects her loss of feeling for the orchard with Trofimov? Do other characters in the play love the orchard "tenderly"?
8. Trofimov declares, "All Russia is our orchard." What figure of speech does this statement represent and what does he mean by it?
9. What is his view of the orchard and how does he express it? How does it contrast with that of Mme. Ranevskaya or Gaev?
10. What does he find "terrifying"? What "dreadful visions" does he refer to?
11. What kind of language does he use to describe the orchard at night? What figure of speech does he use?
12. When Trofimov says "we," who is he referring to? Who is two hundred years behind what?
13. "[W]e just philosophize, complain that we're bored, or drink vodka": does this statement apply to any group of people in the play? If so, who?
14. How does he propose to remedy the situation?
15. How is his language different from that of the other characters in the play, and why? (Consider his vocabulary, the length of his sentences, and his use of figurative language.)
16. Trofimov talks of "unceasing labor." Does he work himself?
17. What is his attitude towards Anya?
18. In what sense has the house ceased to be their own, as Anya says?
19. What do you think of Trofimov's final advice?
20. What is Anya's reaction to it? How do you visualize her facial expression?

For the Conclusion

1. What do we learn from this passage about these two characters? Will they be together again in the play?
2. Does this passage move the plot forward?
3. How does this passage relate to the play's theme(s)?

5. *Trifles* (1920)

MRS. HALE: She liked the bird. She was going to bury it in that pretty box.

MRS. PETERS (*in a whisper*): When I was a girl—my kitten—there was a boy took a hatchet, and before my eyes—and before I could get there—(*Covers her face an instant.*) If they hadn't held me back, I would have—(*Catches herself, looks upstairs, where steps are heard, falters weakly.*)—hurt him.   5

MRS. HALE (*with a slow look around her*): I wonder how it would seem never to have had any children around. (*Pause.*) No, Wright wouldn't like the bird—a thing that sang. She used to sing. He killed that, too.

MRS. PETERS (*moving uneasily*): We don't know who killed the bird.

MRS. HALE: I knew John Wright.   10

MRS. PETERS: It was an awful thing was done in this house that night, Mrs. Hale. Killing a
    man while he slept, slipping a rope around his neck that choked the life out of him.

MRS. HALE: His neck, choked the life out of him.

(*Her hand goes out and rests on the birdcage.*)

MRS. PETERS (*with a rising voice*): We don't know who killed him. We don't *know*.   15

MRS. HALE (*her own feeling not interrupted*): If there'd been years and years of nothing,
    then a bird to sing to you, it would be awful—still, after the bird was still.

MRS. PETERS (*something within her speaking*): I know what stillness is. When we home-
    steaded in Dakota, and my first baby died—after he was two years old, and
    me with no other then—   20

MRS. HALE (*moving*): How soon do you suppose they'll be through, looking for the evidence?

MRS. PETERS: I know what stillness is. (*Pulling herself back.*) The law has got to punish
    crime, Mrs. Hale.

Susan Glaspell (1876–1948)

For the Introduction

1. Name the title and author of the play.
2. Who are Mrs. Hale and Mrs. Peters? Where are the other characters?
3. What is the situation at this point in the play?

For the Detailed Analysis

1. What bird is Mrs. Hale referring to and how did it die? And what is the "pretty box"?
2. In what tone does Mrs. Hale speak this first sentence?
3. Why does Mrs. Peters speak "*in a whisper*"?
4. What is the effect of the punctuation in her first sentence?
5. What is the effect of her gesture (covering her face)?
6. What is conveyed by the dash and the gesture between "I would have . . ." and
   "hurt him"? Why does Mrs. Peters look upstairs? Relate her little story to the plot
   of the play. Is it significant that Mrs. Peters (not Mrs. Hale) tells this story?
7. Why does Mrs. Hale look slowly around? What is the significance of her remark
   about the absence of children? Of the pause?
8. Why does she think Mr. Wright would not have liked the bird?
9. Who used to sing? What does Mrs. Hale mean by saying "He killed that, too"?
   Where are her remarks leading (what is the logic behind them)?
10. Why does Mrs. Peters move "*uneasily*" and say they don't know who killed the bird,
    and what is the implication of Mrs. Hale's rejoinder, "I knew John Wright"?
11. Why does Mrs. Peters, speaking directly to Mrs. Hale, remind her that "an awful
    thing was done in this house. . . . Killing a man while he slept, slipping a rope
    around his neck that choked the life out of him"?
12. Why does Mrs. Hale echo her ("His neck. Choked the life out of him"), and what
    is the significance of her gesture as she says this? Is the birdcage an important
    prop in the play?
13. Why does Mrs. Peters' voice rise as she says, "We don't know who killed him.
    We don't *know*"? Why the repetition and the emphasis on "*know*"? Why does
    Mrs. Peters say this? What gesture or expression might accompany her words?

14. In what tone do you imagine Mrs. Hale saying the next sentence? What is the significance of the dash before the word "still"?

15. How does this speech of Mrs. Hale's affect Mrs. Peters? Why do the stage directions specify "*something within her speaking*"? How would an actress convey that impression? Is Mrs. Peters' reminiscence about her dead child significant at this point?

16. How does the stage direction here ("*moving*") indicate a change of atmosphere? What is ironic about Mrs. Hale's question? Relate it to the theme of the play.

17. What is the significance of Mrs. Peters' repeating "I know what stillness is"? And of her final statement, "The law has got to punish crime, Mrs. Hale"? In what sense is she "*Pulling herself back*" as she says this?

18. Does the language of this whole passage strike you as natural? Does it resemble the language of the rest of the play?

For the Conclusion

1. Show how the passage differentiates between the two women. Would you say they are "flat" or "rounded" characters?

2. How does the passage add to the dramatic tension of the play? Is it important for the play's outcome?

3. What is your overall assessment of the playwright's art, in this passage and in the play as a whole?

COMPOSING QUESTIONS ON A DRAMATIC PASSAGE

A useful exercise now would be to attempt to write a series of questions like those above on a new passage, either from the play in appendix 4 or one assigned by your professor. Another student—or you yourself—will then use those questions as a basis for writing a close reading.

You will need to read the complete play and to re-read the specific passage several times, in order to become familiar with it. Consider all aspects of the passage in great detail—the characters' circumstances, what the passage reveals about the speaker, what gestures might accompany the text, the type of language used, any conflict or dramatic tension, and so on. Use the "Summary of Elements to Discuss in a Dramatic Passage" in the previous chapter to help you focus on different aspects of the text. Have another look at the questions offered on various dramatic passages in this chapter; divide your questions, as in those examples, into parts—introduction, detailed analysis, and conclusion. Make sure your questions would be clear to someone else. Do not ask questions that you could not answer yourself.

You will find that this process represents the major part of the work involved in doing a close reading. When you come to write a close reading on a totally new dramatic passage, without helpful questions, you might do well to begin composing your explication by thinking up similar kinds of questions for yourself.

PART 4

MOVING BEYOND CLOSE READING: OTHER TYPES OF WRITING ABOUT LITERATURE

Close reading is the basis of literary analysis. It allows you, through close study of a poem or a passage from a longer work, to get to grips with many fundamental aspects of the text and really understand how it functions. It gives the reader an insight into the structure, style, and themes of the work, which represents the first step in literary study. However, you will probably be required also to assess whole short stories, novels, plays, or long poems, rather than analyze extracts. You will want to study literary works in a wider context, relating them to social, psychological, or historical issues, or to aesthetic movements; you may choose to read several works by one author and discuss what they have in common, or to compare one author with another.

CHAPTER 10

Short Essays

TYPES OF ESSAY

For these more general essays you will often be able to use the concepts you studied as a preparation for close reading. In writing about a prose work, you might choose or be asked to consider the significance in a given story of elements such as setting, point of view, or plot structure. Considering for example "A Pair of Tickets" by Amy Tan, you could write an essay on the importance of setting and show how, in effect, the whole story is structured around the West/East settings, San Francisco and Guangzhou (Canton), which frame the West-meets-East theme that constitutes the story's plot. The play *Trifles* would also be a good candidate for an essay on the importance of setting. In this work that takes place in a cold farmhouse kitchen, the accent on the coldness of the setting clearly ties in with the character of the murdered man, and the props contained in the kitchen—from the burst jam jars and the dirty roller towel to the quilting, the birdcage and the dead bird—all form part of the evidence proving Mrs. Wright's guilt. The analysis of a character's development or a comparison between different characters can also provide interesting essay topics. Think about Nora in Ibsen's *A Doll House*: how does she change in the course of the play and what events or conversations contribute towards the development of her character?

You may choose an essay topic relating the theme of a literary work to a general question such as, for *Trifles*, the relations between the sexes or the nature of justice. The men in the play have a very condescending attitude towards the women, and yet it is the latter who solve the mystery of Mrs. Wright's motive. And they conceal this information from the men, i.e., from the law, which clearly requires the reader to consider the nature of justice in such a case. Comparing two works or authors can prove a very fruitful way of understanding both of them better, since the one tends to illuminate the other (assuming they share certain features that can serve as a basis for comparison). Differences will also emerge and provide further insight into both texts. You could, for example, analyze the similarities and differences between the heroes of James Joyce's *Araby* and John Updike's *A & P*, both of whom undertake a "crusade" for a girl. A comparison of the treatment of the same theme in two different poems will reveal much about the poetic style and technique of them both, as well as about the subject matter.

PREPARATORY WORK

When you first start reading a text, before you even think about writing your essay, you should annotate the text. If you know your essay topic before you begin reading, you can focus your notes on aspects of the text that seem relevant to that topic; if not, your annotations and comments will help you later to identify a suitable topic yourself or provide information about an assigned topic. You can make your annotations in the margins of your text or, if you don't wish to do that, in a special notebook. Longer comments will probably overflow the margins anyway, so that you should plan on using a notebook or note cards.

As you read, make notes on anything that strikes you as being of interest, whether it concerns the characters (their attitudes, the way they are presented) the point of view (how it affects our reading of the story), the plot structure (conflicts, surprises, flashbacks, foreshadowing), the setting, the theme, symbolism, irony, etc. Also note elements of style such as repetition, sentence structure, figurative language, and, in the case of poems especially, rhythm and sounds. In other words, take note of the same literary elements that we saw in discussing the close reading of poetry, prose, and drama, except that of course you cannot go into such detail with a complete work as with a short passage. The same kinds of features, however, may provide material for a more general essay also.

In addition, consider such wider aspects of the text as its portrayal of society. Is the text critical of any social group? Does the characters' behavior reflect their social background? Note also any elements of conflict, whether between characters or within one character or between a certain character and his social environment. Mark passages that relate to these questions. Write comments, for example, about the feeling that a poem produces in you, or the atmosphere a particular passage creates, or about the motivations of characters as they act and speak. How do they talk to each other? Are they telling the truth? What are the relationships between them like? Think about the main character: does s/he achieve his/her goals? How? If not, why not? Also, what impression do these characters make on you? Consider the positive and negative aspects of their attitudes and behavior (characters in good fiction are rarely all black or all white). How do economic conditions affect their lives? What aspects of their cultural background or heritage are revealed in the work? You might want to bring to bear information from other courses you have taken, such as psychology (to analyze a troubled character) or history (to throw light on a historical novel or play), or theology, politics, etc.

If you write notes in this way as you read, beginning your essay will come as less of a shock. If you have to choose your own topic, look at the comments and annotations you have made during the process of reading (and re-reading) and select items that might produce an interesting angle from which to view the text and ultimately provide material for an essay. Ask yourself questions about the text: your answers could form the basis of an essay topic. Once you have a topic, you can work your notes up into rough paragraphs relating to that topic and make additions based on re-reading and further reflection. Make a short outline of the essay you plan to write; this outline can and probably will be modified later but will serve as an initial guide in writing a first draft of your essay and will help to keep you focused on your topic.

Before beginning to write, consider your audience. Literary scholars writing articles for publication in journals or books will use a different style and assume more literary knowledge on the part of their readers than you are expected to do. You should view your audience as someone who has read the text and knows it fairly well. Therefore you don't need to summarize its plot or explain the relations between the characters; only present details that are relevant to your topic or argument. However, the person reading your essay is interested in knowing your opinion of the text or your interpretation of some aspect of it. People's perceptions of literature vary because literary texts are rich and can give rise to multiple interpretations. Your readers' understanding of the work may be different from yours—though an interpretation is valid only if details from the text can be cited to support it. In order to convince readers of the validity of your interpretation, you need to present your argument and persuade them of its credibility by supporting your ideas with evidence from the text.

WRITING THE ESSAY

When writing an essay that, unlike a close reading, aims to discuss a whole work or argue a topic concerning one or more works, you need to find a title. Your title should both attract attention and inform the reader of your topic. A title like "The Importance of Setting in Amy Tan's 'A Pair of Tickets'" is informative but not particularly attractive; you might prefer something like: "West Meets East: The Settings in Amy Tan's 'A Pair of Tickets'" (or simply: "West Meets East in Amy Tan's 'A Pair of Tickets'"; in your introduction you could then make clear your focus on the importance of setting). For an essay on the question of legal justice in *Trifles* you could use a title such as: "*Trifles:* The Nature of Justice." Never use simply the title of the work discussed, but try to indicate the angle from which you are approaching it. This "angle" constitutes your thesis, or the argument you are planning to make concerning some aspect of the work. A good essay doesn't simply describe elements of a work but makes an argument and presents evidence from the text to back it up. In the case of "A Pair of Tickets," for example, rather than merely pointing out the two main settings of the story, you might set out to prove the significance, for the main character, of their final merging.

Both the title and the introduction might actually be the parts you write last, since you might not know the exact scope of your essay until you have finished writing it. Be that as it may, your introduction should name the author and title of the work(s) on which you are writing and clearly state your topic and how you plan to address it. When naming authors, both male and female, use the whole name on the first occasion and just the surname subsequently. When citing titles, use italics for the titles of whole published works, such as plays and novels (e.g., Henrik Ibsen's play *A Doll House*), but double quotation marks for titles of poems and short stories (e.g., John Keats's poem "To Autumn," Amy Tan's "A Pair of Tickets"). (Poems and short stories are published in collections; the title of the collection would be in italics).

Include biographical or historical information about the author only if it relates to your topic, and if so, explain what the connection is. The importance of a good introduction cannot be overstated: the reader will not want to continue if he doesn't understand what subject you are planning to discuss. If you are writing for a class, your professor needs to know your topic from the outset, otherwise she cannot tell if what you are saying is relevant or not.

As you write, keep your topic constantly in mind. Do not introduce extraneous material, no matter how interesting. Keep relating the points you are making to your subject. Even if the connection is clear in your head, it might not be to the reader, so it's a good idea to point out the links explicitly; it will help to keep both you and the reader focused on the topic under discussion.

Use evidence from the text to reinforce the points you make. You can either paraphrase material, i.e., re-tell it in your own words, or use direct quotations. Quotations have the advantage of giving the reader the flavor of the original text, as well as helping to prove your point. When paraphrasing, be careful to limit yourself to the information required to back up your argument; don't be carried away into telling more of the story than you need: plot summary for its own sake is always irrelevant. Reproduce quotations exactly as they were in the original, including punctuation. Any changes you make should be marked by placing the altered material in square brackets, but this practice should be employed sparingly.

Make sure you integrate quotations properly into the syntax of your own sentence: the pronouns you use, for example, must match those in the text, and the same need for accuracy applies to verb forms, singular and plural, which must correspond, and to tenses: if you are writing in the present tense you cannot use a quote in the past tense as an integral part of your sentence. It would be better to paraphrase the information.

You should use quotations to back up your claims but not too many. In a short essay of two to three pages, a few words or a sentence or two in quotation marks will suffice. Reserve the use of longer, indented quotations for longer essays. (For more information on procedures with quotes and on quoting titles, see below, in the section on research essays, pages 184–85.)

In your essay you will have several points to make illustrating your topic or supporting your argument. Try to arrange them in some logical way, for example by following the order in which they occur in the text, or by dealing with small points first and leading up to your major argument or most forceful point: it is better to work up to a climax than to start with a bang and then trail off. Each point you make should have a paragraph devoted to it, and only one major fact or claim should be included in each paragraph. The first sentence (**topic sentence**) of each paragraph makes clear what aspect of the question you are about to address and the rest of the paragraph elaborates on it.

Finally, you should complete your essay with a conclusion. Do not simply repeat the goals you set yourself in your introduction. Try to say something that genuinely concludes or summarizes your argument or exposition while also opening up the scope of the question or indicating a new perspective. You might suggest for example that the conclusions you have reached in examining this one work have validity for other works or for life in general. If you've been discussing the importance of setting in "A Pair of Tickets," say, you could conclude by pointing out first that the settings form an integral part of the plot and of the main character's life and second that the Chinese setting of the story provides the American reader with an opportunity to glimpse some of the values and attitudes of a different culture. If you have written on the relations between the sexes in *Trifles*, you might speculate in your conclusion about what progress has been made in attitudes towards women since the date the play was written.

When writing about literary works it is customary, easier, and more natural to use the present tense. Of course this does not mean you will never use the past tense, to indicate past actions in the characters' lives, but you should stick to the present as the basic tense of your commentary (e.g., "The king is [basic tense] unhappy because he has lost [in the past] his former power"). Beware however of switching from the present to the past tense for no reason.

Try to avoid referring to yourself directly in the first person. Just state facts as you see them, rather than prefacing them with "I feel" or "I think that." Use the first person only if you want to stress that your opinion is very different in some way from other people's views of a work, e.g., "Most readers see the main protagonist of *A & P* as a hero, but I disagree strongly." Even here you don't really need the "I." You could say, "Although most readers consider the protagonist of *A & P* a hero, there are strong reasons to question that view."

REVISION

After writing a first draft, set it aside for a day or two. If peer review forms part of your class, you will get input from a classmate before moving on to a second draft. Otherwise, you might ask someone else to read it for you and ask them if your argument seems convincing and if you have provided enough evidence; ask also if your writing seems clear and to the point. In the absence of other readers you will have to determine these things for yourself, but a break of a day or two is useful in giving you a fresh perspective on your own writing. Take your draft and check for the following:

- Does each paragraph begin with a topic sentence and illustrate a distinct point?
- Are the transitions between paragraphs smooth?
- Have you used evidence from the text to back up your claims?
- Are quotations appropriately integrated into your text?
- Have you provided an introduction that outlines the direction you take in the essay? Does your conclusion summarize your argument without slavishly repeating statements from your introduction? Does it offer some wider view or a new perspective on the question?
- Are your sentences of an appropriate length and of varied construction?
- Does your essay consist of analysis rather than mere summary?

Adjust your writing in accordance with the answers to these questions, and proofread it for grammatical or spelling errors. If you have time, you may return to the essay again later for further revision or addition of new material that has occurred to you. Most writers revise their work several times, so you shouldn't feel that this is an unusual process or that you are taking an unduly long time over it.

SAMPLE SHORT ESSAYS

The following essays were written by students in an Introduction to Literature course. Three such essays appear: the first addresses the effect of voice in a poem, the second discusses the setting of a short story, and the third deals with the question of conflict in a play.

Sample Short Essay on a Poem ("Naming of Parts")

For the first short essay the assignment was to discuss the effect of voice (speaker, tone, diction) in a poem; the student chose "Naming of Parts" by Henry Reed.

Richard Taylor

Professor Howe

LTC 140

18 March 2009

Life and Death in "Naming of Parts": A Juxtaposition of Voices

Henry Reed's "Naming of Parts" achieves a powerful effect through its use of two differ-ent voices. The poem contains five stanzas of six lines; in the first four lines (or three and a half, to be exact) of every stanza except the last one, we hear the voice of a speaker who appears to be a sergeant drilling his men in the use of weapons. In the final two and a half lines, however, another voice is heard—that of the poem's narrator, who has a very different voice from that of the sergeant. This narrator speaks in the first person plural ("we") because he is part of a group of soldiers listening to the sergeant. The final stanza presents only this voice, recapitulating the sergeant's instructions, but in an ironic tone that emphasizes his radi-cally different view of the world.

The sergeant begins by summarizing for his men the activities of the day: "Today we have naming of parts. Yesterday, / We had daily cleaning. And tomorrow morning, / We shall have what to do after firing." His style corresponds to his businesslike attitude: the sentences are short, clear, and factual, and the vocabulary ("parts," "daily cleaning," "firing") refers to the matter at hand—firing a gun. The contrast, when the soldier's voice takes over, is very striking: "Japonica / Glistens like coral in all of the neighboring gardens." Here the vocabulary concerns plants rather than guns, the sentence is longer, and it contains a simile, "Japonica / Glistens like coral." The flowers of the japonica shrub are shiny (so that "Glistens" is an appropriate verb) and the color of coral. Significantly, this narrator, instead of paying attention to the sergeant, allows his attention to wander to the "neighboring gardens"; evidently he is more interested in flowers than in guns.

The last line of this first stanza, and of all the stanzas, is shorter than the others. In general, the impact of a short line among longer ones is stronger. This line appears simply to repeat one of the sergeant's statements, "And today we have naming of parts," and yet the reader senses that the soldier's way of saying the line differs from the sergeant's. The latter barks out his instructions, whereas the soldier, making a mental contrast between the process of "naming parts" and the sight of the japonica glistening in the gardens, speaks the line "And today we have naming of parts" with an ironic twist. Being a shorter line it receives an emphasis that accentuates the soldier's irony as he echoes the sergeant's words. Soldiers have to look at weapons, not gardens.

This ironic contrast becomes more explicit in the next stanza. The sergeant's voice drones on, talking about "sling swivels" and "piling swivels" and incidentally hinting at a certain lack of organization in the army: the soldiers are unable to use sling swivels since they have not yet received their slings; they also do not possess piling swivels ("And this is the piling swivel, / Which in your case you have not got"). The soldier-narrator's voice returns towards the end of the fourth line, once more describing a natural scene: "The branches / Hold in the gardens their silent, eloquent gestures, / Which in our case we have not got." The "silent, eloquent gestures" of the branches contrast here, by implication, with the noisy mechanical gestures of the parade ground. Indeed, the soldier neatly parodies the sergeant's phrase: silent, eloquent gestures are precisely what "in our case we have not got." Again, the brevity of this last line emphasizes its ironic impact, suggesting implicitly that the young soldier's values are superior to those of the sergeant.

The army is bound by rules; according to the sergeant, the safety-catch "is always released / With an easy flick of the thumb," and "please," he adds, "do not let me / See anyone using his finger." Again the soldier dreamily turns his attention away from rules towards the "blossoms," noting that they are "fragile and motionless" and again parodying the sergeant as he imagines the flowers "never letting anyone see / Any of them using their finger."

In the fourth stanza the sergeant continues his factual description of mechanical objects, using short sentences such as "And this you can see is the bolt." Demonstrating the action of the bolt, which can slide "Rapidly backwards and forwards," he adds: "we call this / Easing the spring," which prompts the soldier-narrator to indulge in a play on words as he draws a parallel between the action of the bolt and the activities of bees in spring: "And rapidly backwards and forwards / The early bees are assaulting and fumbling the flowers: / They call it easing the Spring." This last line, shorter than the others in the stanza, emphasizes once again the ironic discrepancy between the sergeant's message and the narrator's version: the former refers to a spring in the mechanism of a death-dealing weapon, whereas the soldier means the season of spring, with all its connotations of re-birth. His language is also much more imaginative than the sergeant's, evoking a delightful picture of the bees "assaulting and fumbling the flowers."

The sergeant is concerned with nomenclature ("Naming of Parts"); all through the poem his vocabulary is limited to the enumeration of the mechanical parts of a gun—the sling swivel, the safety-catch, the bolt, the breech, etc. The narrator's words, on the other hand, evoke nature and nature's renewal: "Japonica," "gardens," "branches," "blossoms," "bees," "flowers," "Spring." In the final stanza, however, the two voices merge: the soldier repeats the sergeant's words in his own voice, clearly mocking the insistence on mechanical parts and also implying a contrast between the parts of a gun—an instrument of death— and images of spring: the bees, "going backwards and forwards" in their business of pollination, represent the renewal of life associated with spring.

Thus the poem, through the juxtaposition of two voices, provides an ironic commentary on the theme of war. The thing which "in our case we have not got" is ultimately a "point of balance": instead of paying attention to the beauties of nature and the miracle of nature's annual re-birth, mankind is intent on violence and self-destruction. Henry Reed succeeds in conveying this message simply by juxtaposing the two voices of the poem and letting the reader draw his own conclusions.

Commentary on the Essay

Clearly an essay rather than a line-by-line close reading of the poem, this paper focuses firmly on the question of voice in "Naming of Parts." Other aspects of the poem, such as structure, rhythm, or versification, would be relevant in a close reading, but not to the topic assigned for this essay.

The title chosen by the student at once arouses the reader's curiosity, but the student leaves the reader in suspense regarding the theme of life and death, only gradually revealing the implications of the contrast between the world views of the sergeant and the narrator. This adds to the essay's interest.

The introduction identifies the two voices, describes how they merge in the final stanza and mentions the note of irony that will characterize the whole poem. It also analyzes the structure of the poem insofar as that is relevant to the question of voice.

The essay is well organized, following the poem stanza by stanza, but not in an overly mechanical way; the student avoids, for example, the temptation to begin every paragraph "In the next stanza . . . ," which would be boring for the reader.

The student analyzes each speaker's vocabulary, sentence-length, and use (or not) of imaginative language or figures of speech, not for their own sake but in order to show the differences between the voices and the differing world views that they imply. In this context, he also pays attention to the impact of the shorter lines at the end of each stanza, which lend emphasis to the soldier's words and to his ironic viewpoint. He points out the numerous parallels and repetitions, which again often suggest an ironic stance. At the end of the essay the full impact of the difference between the two speakers is revealed, namely that one supports the claims of nature and of life while the other remains unimaginatively fixated on the mechanism of a gun, unaware of the irony involved in examining death-dealing weaponry in the midst of such beautiful, spring-like surroundings. The conclusion appropriately expands the impact of the poem by suggesting that the sergeant's view represents that of mankind in general.

The essay is well written with varied vocabulary and syntactical constructions. Punctuation is adequate and the style clear and concise. The paragraphs are coherent, each one focusing on one idea and introduced by a topic sentence. Quotations have been used effectively, but are limited to short words and phrases, which is suitable for an essay of this length.

Sample Short Essay on a Short Story ("A Pair of Tickets")

For the second sample student essay, the assignment was to write three to four pages on the impact of setting (or point of view) in a short story (or in two stories).

Sarah Mitchell

Professor Howe

LTC 140

20 February 2009

Mitchell 1

"A Pair of Tickets": Setting and the Sense of Identity

In many literary works the setting can have a dramatic impact on the characters and the direction that the plot takes. From the basic elements of time and place an entire story can take shape. In Amy Tan's "A Pair of Tickets" there are actually two settings: San Francisco and Guangzhou, China. Together they serve to lead the reader to a clearer understanding of the story's main character by providing insight into the way time and place have affected her.

The protagonist of "A Pair of Tickets," Jing-Mei Woo, has long denied her Chinese heritage as a result of growing up in the United States. She comments ironically: "all my

Caucasian friends agreed: I was about as Chinese as they were" (168). She further distances herself from any Chinese relation through her lamentations about what she classifies as her mother's "Chinese behaviors," which include picking her teeth in public and haggling with store owners over prices (169). It is her upbringing in the initial setting, San Francisco, which leads Jing-Mei to feel the way she does. Because she knows only the westernized American culture into which she was born, she finds no guilt in laughing at her mother for "being colorblind to the fact that lemon yellow and pale pink are not good combinations for winter clothes" (169). Her place in modern America allows Jing-Mei to see herself as very Californian, because she has direct knowledge of no other culture. As a result, the only way she can see her mother is through those same impatient, American-tainted eyes.

However, when Jing-Mei travels to another setting it is almost as though her very character undergoes a complete transformation. As the train in which she is riding crosses over the country's border Jing-Mei can almost feel herself "becoming Chinese" (168). She enters an entirely different cultural realm than the one she grew up in, highlighted initially through the aunt who greets her, "an old woman in a yellow knit beret . . . holding up a pink plastic bag" (173). The ethnic differences are further evidenced on her cab ride through the city. Jing-Mei is astonished at the landscape she drives by, "row after row of apartments, each floor cluttered with laundry hanging out to dry on the balcony" (174). Almost before she is through marveling at the living conditions in China, she witnesses the working environment there, as shown by men and women "working without safety straps or helmets" (174). Yet no sooner has Jing-Mei been exposed to this lifestyle than she is whisked away by the taxi and deposited into the world of upper-class Chinese, or tourists: she and her father arrive at a "magnificent" hotel complete with uniformed bellhops, color televisions, and fully-stocked mini-bars. As she sits in her hotel room with family she has never met before, dining on cheeseburgers, French fries, and apple pie, Jing-Mei can barely relate this world to the "Communist China" she has read about (175). Again her thoughts are influenced by the time and place in which she was born: because Jing-Mei has never experienced real Chinese life first-hand, her previous opinions could be derived only from second-hand information. For many reason, physically coming to China transforms not only her thoughts but her as a person as well.

Through Jing-Mei's father's words the setting digresses into yet another era, pre-World War II China. It is ironic that it is here, in this very modern and Western-inspired hotel, that Jing-Mei first begins to feel the roots of her heritage. As her father describes the horrific hardships her mother endured while attempting to escape from the invading Japanese, including abandoning her twin infants rather than watch them perish alongside her, Jing-Mei begins to realize "how much [she] had never known about her" (181). In many ways, Jing-Mei also begins to understand here how much she doesn't know about herself as well, including the past history of her family.

When she finally comes face to face with her long-lost half-sisters at the airport, Jing-Mei at last grasps, as she says, "what part of me is Chinese. ... It is my family." (182). This setting, an airport, usually serves only as an intermediate point between two different locations but in this story it actually connects two different lifestyles. In this pivotal moment, Jing-Mei's Americanized past merges with her undeniable Chinese heritage, and the setting highlights not only the distance but the connection between the two.

The author of "A Pair of Tickets" also uses the element of setting to give the reader a glimpse of another way of life. Though setting may be one of the most noticeable elements in a short story, its significance for the plot and the attitudes of the characters is often overlooked. Yet if, as the editors of *The Norton Introduction to Literature* suggest, "one of the functions of literature is to help us understand others and the way they see the world," then setting is indeed an essential element(159). It provides an opportunity for us to step outside of our own ethnic backgrounds and gain, however briefly, a transcultural viewpoint on the world.

Work Cited

Tan, Amy. "A Pair of Tickets." *The Norton Introduction to Literature.* Ed. Jerome Beaty, et al. 8ᵗʰed. New York: Norton, 2002. 168–82. Print.

Commentary on the Essay

The student who wrote this essay has thought about the way the two settings of the story have affected the development of the main character's personality and her sense of identity. She has therefore chosen a title reflecting the link between setting and identity, rather than simply the title of the story itself or a bland title such as "Setting in 'A Pair of Tickets.'" She has chosen details from the text that prove her points convincingly, such as Jing-Mei's Californian friends' assertion that she was "as Chinese as they were" and her youthful resentment of her mother's "Chinese behaviors." She has incorporated quotations (all appropriately short) showing Jing-Mei's awakening of interest in the culture of China and her gradual identification with her own Chinese family, beginning with her growing understanding of her dead mother. In particular, she makes the connection between the main character's self-knowledge and her knowledge of China and the Chinese.

The essay remains focused on the question of setting and its relation to the main character's sense of identity. All the points made and the quotations cited are relevant to this topic. The introduction begins by asserting the importance of setting in general, then announces that the essay will examine the role it plays in "A Pair of Tickets" and links the notion of setting in this story to that of identity (". . . the setting serves to lead the reader to a clearer understanding of the story's main character"), which will be the focus of the essay. Each paragraph begins with a topic sentence, and each paragraph covers one main point: in the second paragraph, Jing-Mei's denial of her Chinese heritage; in the third, her exposure to and more accepting attitude towards Chinese culture; in the fourth, the awakening of a stronger sense of kinship with her own mother; and in the fifth, her sense of belonging to a Chinese family and the use of the airport setting to symbolize the meeting of West and East that takes place both literally and within Jing-Mei. Finally, the conclusion offers a slightly new perspective on the question with the suggestion that setting allows the reader a view of another way of life.

The style of the essay is clear, sentences are of varying length and construction, and the essay contains no spelling or grammatical errors. The references in parentheses are to pages in the anthology used for the course, which was the only text quoted. They are correctly placed after the quotation marks but before sentence punctuation. Finally, documentation is given in an appropriate format.

Sample Short Essay on a Play ("Trifles")

The assignment for the third student essay given here was to outline the major conflict(s) in the play *Trifles* by Susan Glaspell. Here is the text of the essay, followed by a commentary.

Susan Murphy   Murphy 1

Professor Howe

LTC 140

15 April 2009

The War of the Sexes in *Trifles*

Conflict is an essential element in most drama, and *Trifles* by Susan Glaspell illustrates several different areas of conflict—in the relationship between the spouses in the Wright marriage and—most importantly—in the relationship between the sexes in general. The male characters clearly consider the women's ideas and pursuits inferior to their own, and yet the play proves them wrong. The final moments of the play also introduce a further problematic issue concerning verdicts of guilt and innocence.

From the very first moments of the play, before the dialogue begins, the men take the lead. They come on stage first and make straight for the stove, whereas the women enter "slowly" and "stand close together near the door"—affirming their solidarity and their separation from the men. Even when invited to approach the fire, Mrs. Peters, the sheriff's wife, after taking a step forward, changes her mind and stays with Mrs. Hale.

The men are investigating a murder, and they become very businesslike: the sheriff steps away from the stove "as if to mark the beginning of official business," and the County Attorney wants to know if anything has been touched since the day of the murder, and asks if anything has been found that would indicate a motive, only to be told by the sheriff that there's "Nothing here but kitchen things." This dismissive phrase implies both that nothing of interest could possibly be found in a kitchen and that it is beneath their dignity to look around a kitchen, the domain of women. Mr. Hale, too, on hearing about Mrs. Wright's concern for her jam, remarks condescendingly that "women are used to worrying over trifles," at which the two women "move a little closer together."

Trifles being the title of the play, it is obvious that in fact they are worth "worrying over." First, the women find a quilt that Mrs. Wright had begun making, and they wonder "if she was going to quilt it or just knot it." The men, returning at that moment from their investigation of the bedroom, catch this remark and make fun of it, totally oblivious to the symbolism of the idea of knotting in view of the fact that Mr. Wright died with a noose round his neck.

Mrs. Hale resents the County Attorney's scorn but accepts their subservient position as women: "I don't know as there's anything so strange, our takin' up our time with little things while we're waiting for them to get the evidence." This does not prevent her from altering the badly stitched portion of Mrs. Wright's quilt, though Mrs. Peters protests nervously, but ineffectually: "I don't think we ought to touch things." There is a distinction made between the two ladies, Mrs. Hale being more enterprising and forthright, Mrs. Peters (who is married to the sheriff) more ready to defer to the men's viewpoint: "the law is the law," she says. Ultimately, this difference in viewpoint does not amount to a conflict, since the women end up sticking together in defense of Mrs. Wright.

In the course of their conversation, however, they uncover many conflicts within the Wright household. Mrs. Hale remembers that, before her marriage, Mrs. Wright "used to wear pretty clothes and be lively" and sang in the choir, but that she changed after her marriage to Mr. Wright, whom she describes as "a hard man. . . . Like a raw wind that gets to the bone." Mrs. Wright used to be "sweet and pretty, but kind of timid and—fluttery." The implication is that in this marriage to a "hard" husband, Mrs. Wright lost her sweetness and liveliness. "How—she—did—change," exclaims Mrs. Hale wonderingly—the dashes here indicating slow and thoughtful speech. She and Mrs. Peters piece together the final conflict between Mr. and Mrs. Wright after finding a birdcage with a broken door, and also the strangled bird: "No, Wright wouldn't like the bird—a thing that sang. She used to sing. He killed that, too," she declares, and adds a moment later: "If there'd been years and years of nothing, then a bird to sing to you, it would be awful—still, after the bird was still." The dead bird is strong evidence of the conflict between Mr. and Mrs. Wright and also evidence that could constitute, for a jury, a motive for killing Mr. Wright with a noose.

The conflict between the men and the women in the play continues as the latter decide whether to reveal the evidence they have found or hide it. The County Attorney again speaks condescendingly to the women ("as one turning from serious things to little pleasantries") when he asks, "Well, ladies have you decided whether she was going to quilt it or knot it?" Later the men are heard searching for a clue as to the murderer's reason for choosing "this strange way of doing it," and the women's eyes meet as they consider whether or not to reveal the existence of the dead bird, which would provide exactly the clue the men seek regarding the choice of murder instrument. At the last minute the women hide the bird, in order to protect Mrs. Wright, just as the County Attorney enters the kitchen asking facetiously, "Well, Henry, at least we've found out that she was not going to quilt it. She was going to—what is it you call it, ladies?" Mrs. Hale replies, her hand covering the bird hidden in her pocket, "We call it—knot it, Mr. Henderson." Thus the men in the play act as if the women are inferior, yet it is the women who find the evidence and solve the murder, in the kitchen, while the men blunder around looking at the barn and the windows.

The conflict between the men and the women in Trifles illustrates an even more fundamental conflict, between verdicts of guilt and innocence. Clearly, Mrs. Wright murdered her husband; yet the two women in the play find her innocent. With their sensitivity to the plight of a lonely woman with no children or family, married to a hard man who barely spoke to anyone and who strangled her one joy in life, her pet canary, they feel that Mr. Wright shared a measure of guilt and decide to protect Mrs. Wright.

Susan Glaspell wrote Trifles at the beginning of the twentieth century, when husbands had all the power and authority in a marriage. The conflict between Mr. and Mrs. Wright shows the kind of situation this could lead to and illustrates one of the play's main themes, namely that guilt and innocence are relative terms and that victims are sometimes as guilty as their murderers. At the same time, the conflict between the men and the women in the play enables us to see that the reasoning and observational powers of women are by no means inferior to those of men. *Trifles* is a very short play, but it enacts conflicts that are as weighty and important today as in the author's own time.

Commentary on the Essay

In this essay the student considers first of all what types of conflict are enacted in *Trifles* and suggests, appropriately enough, two areas of conflict: between the partners in the Wright couple, and between the men and the women in general. She suggests at the end of the introduction that the women are proved superior, but without revealing yet how this comes about, and hints at a further area of conflict centered on notions of guilt and innocence, but again without giving away the details. This is an effective introduction since it makes the reader want to know more.

The student avoids plot summary, always a temptation when discussing a novel or play; instead she gives only the basic information necessary concerning the murder and the manner in which the dead man was killed. She concentrates on highlighting the remarks and gestures that reveal the men's attitudes towards the women and the women's reactions. She doesn't forget to consider stage directions—the elements that one would *see*, at a performance. She notes for example the implications of the different stances of the men and the women at the beginning of the play, and of the men's often flippant, facetious tone as they address the women, which reveals their attitude towards them. Plenty of quotations are provided to illustrate the student's points, but only short sentences or phrases, as is appropriate in an essay of this length.

The essay gradually reveals how the women solve the murder, proving themselves superior to the men who look down on them; and the final paragraphs appropriately connect the women's decision to hide their evidence with the wider issue of guilt and innocence, which provides a satisfying conclusion.

WRITING AIDS

For help with your own writing style, consult *The Elements of Style*, a well-known guide by William Strunk, Jr.

For conventions concerning the layout of text in papers, use the latest edition of *The MLA Handbook for Writers of Research Papers*. Published by the MLA (Modern Language Association), the *MLA Handbook* provides detailed information on all aspects of the mechanics of writing, including how to incorporate quotations and provide footnotes. (It stipulates for example that research papers should be double-spaced; the student essays given above were originally typed double-spaced, though printed with single spacing here.) The *Handbook* is published in paperback and is an essential tool for anyone writing essays or, especially, research papers, whether for an English class or for publication.

An excellent online resource for help with writing is Purdue University's Online Writing Lab (OWL): www.owl.english.purdue.edu/owl. An online site where you can practice elements of writing is provided by Prentice-Hall at http://wps.prenhall.com/ipractice/.

CHAPTER 11

Research Papers

A research paper may deal with similar topics to the ones mentioned above, but in addition to giving your own view of the topic backed up by evidence from the primary text, you will be expected to include material from secondary sources. (The primary text is the piece of literature you are studying; secondary texts are works by critics and scholars about that piece of literature.) You will need to follow the same steps outlined above to familiarize yourself with the work and select an appropriate topic, but you will also need to research some secondary texts.

SEARCHING FOR SECONDARY TEXTS

A search in the catalogue of a college or university library, or a public library, with the work of literature as subject (rather than title) will produce a list of the library's holdings of secondary sources on that work. Alternatively, use an author's name in the "subject" line to retrieve titles of books about the author and his works. You may search the catalogues of other university libraries, if your library's holdings are inadequate for your topic, and borrow books from those other libraries through Inter-Library Loan (ILL). It usually takes only a few days for books to be sent through ILL—but you will need to allow some extra time.

To find appropriate secondary sources you may need to consult a bibliography. Any serious critical study obtained from your library (especially one published by a university press) will conclude with a Bibliography indicating major works on your author or primary text. On a larger scale, you can consult huge bibliographies such as *American Literary Scholarship* or the *MLA International Bibliography of Books and Articles in the Modern Languages and Literatures* (including English and American literature), which lists books (and articles in academic journals) published in a given year. The *General Periodicals Index* gives references to general and scholarly periodicals. Many university libraries now offer these and other database indexes on line.

Other guides include the "Oxford Companions," e.g., *The Oxford Companion to English Literature*, *The Oxford Companion to American Literature*, etc., and encyclopedias such as *Merriam-Webster's Encyclopedia of Literature*. There are bibliographies that specialize in individual genres—poetry, prose, and drama—and others that deal in the literatures of different countries. A useful introduction to research methods in literature is Nancy L. Baker's *A Research Guide for Undergraduate Students: English and American Literature.*

If you are studying a famous work by a much-studied author, the amount of material available in sources such as the *MLA International Bibliography* can be overwhelming. Limit yourself to recent works (since they will probably refer to or incorporate material from earlier studies) or ones that seem particularly relevant to your topic. If you have trouble locating secondary sources or finding your way around a database, ask your reference librarian for guidance. Librarians are experienced in doing searches and documenting sources and will probably be able to find what you need very quickly. Next time, you will manage better on your own. Don't spend too much time searching for secondary sources: remember that your goal is to read some articles or chapters from relevant books that provide different perspectives on your topic—not to establish an exhaustive bibliography on it.

Literary authors themselves sometimes write books or essays on poetics or on the art of fiction-writing, for example, which can be fruitful sources of material for your essay.

You should be aware that literary criticism takes many forms. Beginning in the twentieth century, several divergent critical approaches to literature were developed in accordance with certain theoretical or philosophical views and disciplines. In chapter 12 you will find a brief overview of the major approaches—Historical and Biographical Criticism, Formalism or New Criticism, Marxist Criticism, Structuralism, Archetypal and Psychoanalytic Criticism, Deconstruction, Feminist and Gender Criticism, and Reader-Response Criticism.

TAKING NOTES FROM SECONDARY SOURCES

When you have found some secondary sources relevant to your topic you need to read them and make notes. This too can be a time-consuming process: beware of taking too many notes. Your aim is not to re-write the book but to select from it short passages and brief quotations that you think will be useful for your paper, and to *reference the source and the page number.* This is crucial; if you forget to note where the passage appeared, you may waste a good deal of time later searching for it. There are many ways to approach note-taking—you can use a notebook or a pad of paper or write directly onto a computer or, probably best of all, use index cards. Then you can use one card per idea or quotation, classify them into groups and sub-groups, and change the order in which you arrange them as your thoughts about the content and organization of your essay develop. Put the name of the source and the page number at the top of each card. When you use the secondary author's own words, as distinct from your paraphrasing of his ideas, be sure to enclose them in quotations marks. Later, when composing your essay, you will want to include some quotations, and it will be convenient to have them already marked. Otherwise you will have to waste time returning to the secondary source to find the exact quotation.

AVOIDING PLAGIARISM

When you quote a secondary source or paraphrase material from it, *you must acknowledge the source.* It's acceptable to use other people's ideas—that is why you are looking at secondary texts—but only if you give recognition to the authors of those ideas. Even if you take information from the Internet, you should acknowledge the source. (But material from the Internet should be treated with caution anyway, when writing a research essay. Since anybody can post assessments of literary works on the Internet without necessarily knowing enough about the subject to avoid inaccurate or biased interpretations, many of them are not worth reading and certainly not worth quoting.) Using other people's thoughts without recognition constitutes plagiarism, which you should avoid at all costs. Not only is plagiarism dishonest but, if you plagiarize someone else's work instead of producing your own, you are wasting your time, since presumably your goal is to learn how to write a good research paper yourself—one that recognizes other people's interpretations and comments but subordinates them to your overall design.

INCORPORATING SECONDARY SOURCES INTO YOUR PAPER

The aim of a research paper is not to let your secondary sources tell the whole story but to incorporate them into an essay whose overall content and direction is governed by you. You are writing on a certain topic, making an argument, persuading your reader of some truth about the primary text, and providing evidence both in the form of quotations from that text and contributions from secondary texts. You can quote (or paraphrase) secondary material to reinforce your own claims or to argue against; or you can present opposing interpretations from two or more different sources and discuss their relative merits, keeping the primary text always in focus. Readers of your paper should not feel that you are simply surveying other scholars' opinions, but that you are using them in order to guide your readers to a conclusion.

ORGANIZING YOUR PAPER

Once you have gathered enough material—or enough to make a start on your paper—you should begin organizing it into a coherent shape. If you have used index cards, arrange them in an appropriate order. Put aside any that appear irrelevant, but don't discard them in case you change your mind later. Make an outline of the essay you plan to write: simply list the points you want to make and note any accompanying references to secondary texts. You will add an introduction and conclusion in due course. Then start writing. Don't worry about whether everything follows on logically, for now; you can rearrange your paragraphs later if necessary. Just try to write as much as possible on each point in your outline. Avoid wordiness, however: don't repeat yourself or use more words than you need to express your thought. Above all, stick to the point, i.e., *your* point. The secondary sources you employ probably make all kinds of interesting observations about the primary text; include only those that contribute to your topic. Define any key terms, such as specialized literary terms used in your secondary texts. Don't just quote those texts, but explain why you are using them, i.e., their connection with your argument.

Otherwise, for the drafting, re-writing, and revision of a research paper, follow the guidelines set out in chapter 10 (pages 168–72) for other interpretive essays: find an appropriate title, write an informative introduction, arrange your material in a logical order, illustrate your points with quotations, and compose a conclusion that both summarizes your argument and presents the wider implications of the topic. The introduction and conclusion may need to be more substantive than for a shorter essay because of the need to relate your research to your paper topic.

INTEGRATING QUOTATIONS

1. Always introduce quotations by identifying the speaker. Make clear to your reader why you are including this quotation.

2. Short quotations of less than four lines can be integrated into your own sentence, longer ones will be indented and stand apart (see below #8).

3. Short quotations have to fit into the syntax of your own sentence: the pronouns you use, for example, must match those in the text. In other words, you cannot write:

Gurov thought that it was "time for me to go north."

Instead you can either paraphrase the sentence:

Gurov thought that it was time for him to go north

or simply quote Gurov's thoughts without attempting to integrate them into your sentence, introducing them, as here, with a comma:

Gurov thought, "It's time for me to go north."

The same need for accuracy applies to verb forms, singular and plural, which must match, and to tenses: if you are writing in the present tense you cannot use a quote in the past tense as an integral part of your sentence. It would be incorrect to write:

When Gurov arriv**es** suddenly at the theater, Anna "glanc**ed** at him and turn**ed** pale."

It would be better to paraphrase the information.

4. Indicate any changes or omissions you make.
   Alterations or additions should be marked by placing the altered or added material in square brackets, thus:

Gurov thought that it was "time for [him] to go north"

but this practice becomes fussy and should be employed sparingly.
   Indicate omissions by three spaced periods, thus:

"[T]his practice . . . should be employed sparingly."

If your sentence ends with an omission, use a period in the normal way and follow it by three spaced periods.

5. Place commas and periods inside quotation marks:

Gurov thought, "It's time for me to go north."

However, if the quotation is followed by parentheses, you should close the quotation first, follow it by the material in parentheses, and place the comma or period after that.

Gurov thought, "It's time for me to go north" (97).

Other punctuation, such as a colon, semi-colon, or dash, comes after the quotation marks; question and exclamation marks go inside if they belong to the quotation but outside if they are part of your sentence.

6. If you have a quotation inside a quotation, use single quotation marks for the second one:

"Gurov thought, 'It's time for me to go north.'"

7. For verse quotations integrated into your own sentence, use a slash mark (/) preceded and followed by a space, to indicate the move from one line to the next, as in this quotation from Browning's "Meeting at Night": "The gray sea and the long black land; /And the yellow half-moon large and low." Keep the original punctuation (including all capitals) except where you reach the end of your sentence and require a period.

8. For longer quotations (usually more than four lines), introduce them by a sentence of yours ending in a colon, then indent the quotation ten spaces (one inch) from the left margin, without using quotation marks, thus:

After Gurov's sudden arrival at the theater, the narrator says:

She glanced at him and turned pale, then glanced again with horror, unable to believe her eyes, and tightly gripped her fan and the lorgnette in her hands, evidently struggling with herself not to faint.

9. When quoting titles, use italics for works published independently, such as novels, plays, or collections of poetry, e.g., *Leaves of Grass* by Walt Whitman. Use quotation marks for titles of individual poems, short stories, or essays within a volume or collection, e.g., Byron's "She Walks in Beauty" or "The Black Cat" by Edgar Allan Poe. Capitalize all letters in titles except those of short, unimportant words such as prepositions. Some poems do not have titles and are referred to by their first line, in which case you should capitalize only those words that have capitals in the first line, such as Whitman's "When I heard the learn'd astronomer."

For more information about quotations and many other points regarding the mechanics of writing, see *The MLA Handbook for Writers of Research Papers*. Alternatively you may consult Purdue University's Online Writing Lab (OWL): owl.english.purdue.edu/owl, or practice elements of writing at Prentice-Hall's iPractice site: http://wps.prenhall.com/ipractice/.

DOCUMENTATION

When writing a short essay it might be sufficient simply to indicate pages in parentheses after each quotation, if they are all from one work; but when you are quoting several sources you will need to document them more fully, both as a means of acknowledging them and as a way to give the reader the information necessary to consult them. The commonest way to do this (and the one recommended in *The MLA Handbook for Writers of Research Papers)* is to provide a list of works cited at the end of your paper, beginning on a separate sheet. The list of works cited should include only works from which you have quoted or paraphrased material. (A bibliography would also include works you merely consulted.) For the presentation of Web-based materials in a Works Cited list, see the *MLA Handbook*. Books or articles in the list should be presented in the following way:

Books

1. The author's name: last name first, then first name and middle initial or name, followed by a period.
2. The book's title, in italics, followed by a period.
3. The city where the book was published, followed by a colon; the name of the publisher, followed by a comma; the year of publication, followed by a period. (This information can be found on the page after the title page in most books.)
4. The medium of publication (Print).

Articles

1. The author's name, as above.
2. The title of the article, enclosed in quotation marks, with a period before the closing quotes.
3. The title of the journal or periodical, in italics, followed by the volume number and issue number in arabic numerals and the year of publication in parentheses, all followed by a colon, the inclusive range of page numbers, and a period.
4. The medium of publication (Print).

List the works alphabetically by the author's last name. Begin at the left margin, but indent all subsequent lines in an entry, so that the authors' last names stand out and are easy to see. Here are two examples, first for a book and then for an article:

Booth, Wayne C. *The Rhetoric of Fiction*. Chicago: University of Chicago Press, 1961. Print.

Christ, Carol T. "Self-Concealment and Self-Expression in Eliot's and Pound's Dramatic Monologues." *Victorian Poetry*, 22.2 (1984): 217–26. Print.

REFERRING TO WORKS CITED IN THE COURSE OF YOUR PAPER

This procedure is fairly simple. When you have quoted or paraphrased from someone else's work in the body of your essay, indicate where the material came from in a parenthetical reference at the end of your sentence. Give only the author's last name and the appropriate page(s); if your readers wish to consult the document, they can find the reference in your list of works cited and read the relevant book or article for themselves. Here is an example:

> It is true that Stephen's interior monologue in *A Portrait of the Artist as a Young Man*, unlike speech in a dramatic scene, does not "lead us to suspect that the thoughts have been in any way aimed at an effect" (Booth 163).

If you actually mention the author's name in the course of the sentence quoting the passage, you do not need to repeat it in parentheses: just give the page number(s). If you have cited more than one work by the same author, give the title (or an abbreviated form of it) between the author's name and the page number (Booth, *Rhetoric of Fiction*, 163).

You can find many more details about the art of documentation, including footnotes and endnotes if you should need to use them, in *The MLA Handbook for Writers of Research Papers*. Again, you may also wish to consult Purdue University's Online Writing Lab (OWL): owl.english.purdue.edu/owl, or practice elements of writing at Prentice-Hall's iPractice site: http://wps.prenhall.com/ipractice/.

CHAPTER 12

Brief Introduction to Literary Criticism

Literature has been studied and assessed ("criticism" implies an assessment, not necessarily negative) at least since the time of the Greeks, but the twentieth century saw a proliferation of literary theories. Several divergent critical approaches to literature were developed in the twentieth century in accordance with certain theoretical and philosophical viewpoints. Different types of criticism can illuminate different aspects of a work—but they are also limited to a certain way of viewing it. Most readers, therefore, would not wish to adhere solely to one type of criticism—while recognizing that the insights each one can provide may be unique. The following list is not exhaustive, and the descriptions of each kind of criticism are deliberately very brief.

You can find out more about literary theory in many publications, such as Jonathan Culler's *Literary Theory: A very Short Introduction* (1999) or Steven Lynn's *Texts and Contexts* (2000), written for beginners in the field of literary theory. Other good choices are *A Reader's Guide to Contemporary Literary Theory* (1997) by Raman Selden and Peter Widdowson, and K. M. Newton's *Interpreting the Text: A Critical Introduction to the Theory and Practice of Literary Interpretation* (1990). Also, for each type of criticism you can find works that explain its goals and characteristics.

After each short discussion of different kinds of literary criticism you will find a few questions of the type one might ask when viewing a text from the standpoint of that kind of criticism. The questions refer mostly to three of the texts that appear in appendix 3—William Faulkner's "A Rose for Emily," Nathaniel Hawthorne's "Young Goodman Brown" and James Joyce's "Araby." Some of these questions may require a certain amount of research on your part.

HISTORICAL CRITICISM

Until the beginning of the twentieth century, critics writing about literature based their commentaries on a historical and biographical study of the text. **Historical criticism** places the text in its historical and cultural context and views it as a reflection of the attitudes and values of people (including the author) living at that time. Thus, a historical study of Shakespeare's *The Merchant of Venice* would include research into contemporary attitudes towards Jews in order to explain the portrayal of Shylock. Similarly, for *Othello*, a historical critic would examine seventeenth-century views of Moors (as well as many other issues, of course, such as the position of women in society and their subservience to men). Historical critics are concerned less with the intrinsic literary value of works than with the characteristics that link them to a historical epoch or intellectual movement.

- To what extent do the action and the themes of "Young Goodman Brown" or of "A Rose for Emily" reflect the historical realities of life, including social attitudes, at the time and place in which they are set?

NEW HISTORICISM

New historicism is a more recent type of historical criticism (since the 1970s) that views literature as part of history but also views history itself as a construct rather than an objective truth, since historians' re-creation of the past can never be truly objective. Historians inevitably view the past with the bias of their own cultural and historical age. For new historicists, literary texts are part of cultural history, and history itself becomes a text as ambiguous as literary texts.

New historicism is related to cultural studies and tends to favor marginalized cultures. It is based on structuralist theories of language and analysis of cultural sign systems (see Structuralist Criticism, below). Being a network of sign systems, the whole of a given culture can be studied like a text, including such elements as religion, rites, clothing, food, or games. New historicism does not privilege literary texts above other kinds of "text" but deems them all equally worthy of study. Authors are seen not as autonomous creators but as transmitters of the codes prevalent in their culture, just as readers' responses to literature are governed by those same cultural codes. Thus literature, for new historicists, is inextricably bound up in history.

- How does our own historical context affect our reading of "Young Goodman Brown" or "A Rose for Emily"?

BIOGRAPHICAL CRITICISM

Biographies of authors have been popular since Samuel Johnson's *Lives of the Poets* (1779, 1781). As distinct from biographies (or autobiographies) per se, **biographical criticism** of a literary work assumes a relationship between the author's own world and the world of the work. It attempts to show for example how facts from the author's life are reflected in the events of his or her novel, or whether a poem contains allusions to the circumstances of the poet's family life. This approach can certainly illuminate aspects of a work, but only for authors whose biographies are known. It also runs the risk of attributing too much in the literary work to biographical data. There is a danger, too, of reducing the impact of the work by making too close a connection between a specific incident in the author's life and what has been transmuted in the literary text into a more general truth.

- Do you think Hawthorne's own biography played a part in his choice of setting for "Young Goodman Brown"?
- Was Faulkner's choice of a setting for "A Rose for Emily" influenced by his own biography?

- Is there a connection between William Wordsworth's "I wandered lonely as a cloud" and the poet's biographical experience?
- How far do you think the character and events in James Joyce's "Araby" reflect his own experience? Does the narrator express the author's own values?

FORMALIST (NEW) CRITICISM

As a reaction against the types of criticism that insisted on viewing works through the lens of a historical and cultural context, a new kind of criticism developed in the early twentieth century that paid attention more to the form of the work itself: **formalist criticism**, also called **new criticism** because it represented a new departure. *The New Criticism* (1941) is the title of a book by one of these critics, John Crowe Ransom. Beginning at the end of the 1920s and accompanying the rise of modernism, new criticism turned its back on historical and biographical context. The new critics concentrated their attention on the work itself and specifically on its literariness—the intrinsically literary qualities that make it a work of art rather than a reflection of historical tendencies or psychological development. They chose to view works in isolation and base their readings solely on the facts of the text. Close reading is associated with new criticism, which tends to be most effective for the study of poems or short extracts from longer texts.

- Show how the different elements of any short story—plot, characterization, point of view, setting, style, imagery, symbolism—reinforce its content and themes.
- For a poem, show how elements such as vocabulary, figurative language, sound, rhythm, and versification echo and support its meaning.

MARXIST CRITICISM

Karl Marx viewed human life in terms of economics, specifically the confrontation between the working classes and the forces of capitalism. Many literary works of the twentieth century reflect a concern with economic conditions and class struggle. **Marxist criticism** emphasizes the influence of economic forces in the determination of character and the development of plot, investigating for example how characters' experiences vary, in the course of a story or novel, as a result of their economic status, or how well the author conveys a sense of the various deprivations of the working class—in terms of education for example or living conditions.

- Show how the narrator's experience in Joyce's "Araby" depends to a large extent on his material circumstances.
- In what way, if any, does the narrator of "Araby" transcend the disadvantages of his background?
- What role does class difference play in "A Rose for Emily"?

STRUCTURALIST CRITICISM

Structuralist criticism, born in France, began to become popular in America in the 1960s. It shares with new criticism a focus on texts themselves, but tends to deal with narrative strategies and thus with longer works of fiction. Based on the notion that works of literature share similar structures and forms, it attempts to discover the underlying patterns and themes common to all narrative, such as: the journey of a hero (literal or metaphorical), his encounter with forces for good or evil, his testing—which may reveal his weakness or his strength—and his homecoming. Literary characters are viewed according to certain features or patterns: they are active or passive, they succeed or fail in the tests that life brings them, etc. Early structuralists studied a vast body of Russian folktales and identified a handful of basic common structures (or archetypes) of this sort.

Because structuralism deals with basic narrative patterns, it is applied not only to "great works" but also for example to folktales and fairy tales and all kinds of cultural sign systems. The French anthropologist Claude Lévi-Strauss claims that all elements of a given culture, such as religion and rites, tools, industry, clothing, and food, form sign systems that can be analyzed like language. He also examines myths in a way that reveals their common structures. His compatriot Roland Barthes analyzes the sign systems of multiple aspects of Western culture such as fashion, advertising, food, furniture, and cars.

- To what extent can "Young Goodman Brown" be seen as the journey of a hero who encounters forces of good and evil, is tested, and returns home? Is he an active or a passive hero? Does he emerge victorious from his test, or not? How well does he react to the test? How would you characterize his homecoming?
- In Faulkner's "A Rose for Emily," is Miss Emily active or passive? Is she tested in any way and if so what is the outcome?

ARCHETYPAL CRITICISM

Archetypal criticism shares with structuralism the aim of studying repeated patterns (archetypes) in literature. Certain literary figures can be seen as types that recur in different kinds of texts: the *femme fatale*, the innocent young maiden, the cruel stepmother, the rigid, tyrannical father, the steadfast friend, and so on. They are often placed in situations that also have an archetypal quality such as: a quest, a task or test, an initiation, loss of innocence, betrayal, repentance, sacrifice, renewal, or rebirth. Some critics suggest that such archetypes are the stuff of literature; others, such as Northrop Frye in his *Anatomy of Criticism* (1957) contend that they are a part of human life in general, incorporated into literature. This view is based on the work of the Swiss psychoanalyst Carl Jung (1875–1961) who believed that the archetypal patterns that govern human life and behavior are common to all countries and cultures and provide evidence for the notion of a universal human consciousness, the "collective unconscious."

- Is there an archetypal situation at the heart of Hawthorne's "Young Goodman Brown" and if so how would you describe it?
- Does Miss Emily in Faulkner's "A Rose for Emily" belong to any recurring literary type? (Consider her status as an unmarried woman in the society of her time, her dealings with the town officials, and the eventual outcome of the story.)
- Does Joyce's short story "Araby" enact an archetypical "loss of innocence" situation? How does the narrator see himself at the end compared to the beginning?

PSYCHOANALYTIC CRITICISM

Based on the writings of Sigmund Freud (1856-1939), **psychoanalytic criticism** attempts to establish the unconscious motives of characters in literary texts: Ernest Jones for example, in *Hamlet and Oedipus* (1949), claims that Hamlet suffers from an Oedipus complex. Psychoanalytic critics also bring their method to bear on authors, in order to explain how their own lives led them to choose certain subjects or situations or how their experience is reflected in the behavior of the characters. More recently, they have turned their attention to readers, attempting to explain how readers respond to literary texts. The critic Norman Holland, for example, suggests that readers have a subconscious reaction to certain elements of literary texts, making the text different for every reader.

- To what extent might Miss Emily's actions in Faulkner's "A Rose for Emily" be explained by her upbringing, her family history, and her relationship with her father?
- In Hawthorne's short story "Young Goodman Brown," what psychological failing in Goodman Brown's thinking or his personality leads to his downfall?
- Does "Araby" illustrate aspects of Joyce's own psychology?

DECONSTRUCTION

The French critic Jacques Derrida (1930-2004) is the main proponent of a type of criticism commonly known as **deconstruction**. Deconstruction concentrates on the relationship between language and meaning. Derrida looks at the ways meaning is constructed in texts (and understood by readers) and concludes that they are self-contradictory, since language itself is unreliable and unstable. Therefore, literary works contain no coherent meaning; they are ambiguous and indeterminate. Furthermore, he argues that a literary work forms a self-contained system independent of the real world; readers cannot retrieve meaning from texts because interpretations never point to the real world but only to more language. Language is inherently unstable and constantly evolving, thus allowing for many shades of meaning. Therefore, "All interpretation is misinterpretation"; there can be no accepted interpretation of a work but only a multiplicity of interpretations, all valid.

- What contradictions or opposing meanings do you detect in "Araby," "A Rose for Emily," or "Young Goodman Brown"?

FEMINIST AND GENDER CRITICISM

Feminist criticism, whose origins hark back to the works of Virginia Woolf and the seminal work by Simone de Beauvoir, *The Second Sex* (1949), was originally linked to the rise of the feminist movement in the 1960's. Feminist critics focus on the depiction of women in literature and often criticize the representation of women, in works written by men, as being dictated by a patriarchal view that considers women inherently inferior to men. Such critics also seek out works written by women in the past, and encourage the publication of contemporary women writers. They analyze women's writing from a female perspective and seek to recognize specifically feminine types of writing. How are literary works written by women different from those written by men? Are women different from men as readers, thanks to differences in their values and sensibility?

Recent feminist criticism has established a distinction between sex and gender (where sex represents the biological differences between male and female and gender represents the cultural differences), arguing that it is culture that determines "masculine" and "feminine" characteristics and behavior (so that women are seen for example as more passive, more subjective, less practical then men, and their roles in society and in the family are pre-determined). From consideration of female gender, feminist criticism has moved to other minority issues such as the literary representation of women of different ethnic and socioeconomic backgrounds.

Out of feminist criticism has arisen a broader movement known as **gender criticism**, which concerns itself with issues of heterosexuality and homosexuality in literature and seeks to eliminate homophobia. Also called queer theory, it considers questions such as whether lesbians and gays write (and read) differently from straight people.

- In Faulkner's "A Rose for Emily," how is Miss Emily treated by the town officials? How does the narrator of the story view her? The other townspeople? What is your own opinion of her? How do you think a feminist critic might react to this story? Or to Hawthorne's "Young Goodman Brown"?

- Consider from a feminist standpoint the reactions of Mrs. Mallard in Kate Chopin's "The Story of an Hour," or of the women in the play *Trifles* by Susan Glaspell (both works written by women), or of Nora in *A Doll House*. Do the women in these works accept their social roles?

- Is the content or the style of "The Story of an Hour" affected by the gender of the author?

READER-RESPONSE CRITICISM

As its name suggests, **reader-response criticism** emphasizes the importance of the reader's role in determining the meaning of a literary work. It is closely related to the philosophy known as phenomenology, which suggests that reality does not exist independently in the external world but depends on the individual's perception of it. According to reader-response theory, a literary work is not complete until it is read. An "informed reader" (one who is familiar with literary conventions) completes the creative process begun by the author by interpreting the work in the light of his or her own life-experience. By maintaining that the meaning of a work is produced by the reader as well as the author, reader-response criticism contrasts strongly with new criticism, which held that the text's meaning is wholly contained within the text.

Some reader-response critics, such as Stanley Fish, see readers not so much as individuals but as "interpretive communities." Since members of a given group reading at a given historical moment share many values and beliefs, they can come up with common interpretations.

- What experiences in your own life help you to interpret Hawthorne's "Young Goodman Brown"? How might your reactions differ from those of Hawthorne's contemporary audience?

- How do you react to Goodman Brown's acceptance of the suggestion that everyone is evil, as his "dream" in the forest seems to imply? Do you think he is right to suspect everyone around him of wrongdoing?

- Does your own life experience affect your reading of James Joyce's "Araby"?

Appendix 1

International Phonetic Alphabet

vowels		*consonants*	
IPA	**words**	**IPA**	**words**
ʌ	cup, luck	b	bad, lab
ɑː	arm, father	d	did, lady
æ	cat, black	f	find, if
ɛ	met, bed	g	give, flag
ə	away, cinema	h	how, hello
ɜːʳ	turn, learn	j	yes, yellow
ı	hit, sitting	k	cat, back
iː	see, heat	l	leg, little
p	hot, rock	m	man, lemon
ɔː	call, four	n	no, ten
u	put, could	ŋ	sing, finger
uː	blue, food	p	pet, map
aı	five, eye	r	red, try
au	now, out	s	sun, miss
ou	go, home	ʃ	she, crash
eəʳ	where, air	t	tea, getting
eı	say, eight	tʃ	check, church
ıəʳ	near, here	θ	think, both
ɔı	boy, join	ð	this, mother
uəʳ	pure, tourist	v	voice, five
		w	wet, window
		z	zoo, lazy
		ʒ	pleasure, vision
		dʒ	just, large

Appendix 2

Selected Poems

Many, but not all, of the following poems appear in part 1. They are given in alphabetical order according to the poet's surname.

Blake, William (1757–1827)

The Sick Rose

O rose, thou art sick.
The invisible worm
That flies in the night
In the howling storm

Has found out thy bed   5
Of crimson joy,
And his dark secret love
Does thy life destroy.

(1794)

The Tyger

Tyger! Tyger! burning bright
In the forests of the night,
What immortal hand or eye
Could frame thy fearful symmetry?

In what distant deeps or skies   5
Burnt the fire of thine eyes?
On what wings dare he aspire?
What the hand dare seize the fire?

And what shoulder, & what art,
Could twist the sinews of thy heart?   10
And when thy heart began to beat,
What dread hand & what dread feet?

What the hammer? what the chain?
In what furnace was thy brain?
What the anvil? what dread grasp   15
Dare its deadly terrors clasp?

When the stars threw down their spears
And water'd heaven with their tears,
Did he smile his work to see?
Did he who made the Lamb make thee?   20

Tyger! Tyger! burning bright
In the forests of the night,
What immortal hand or eye
Dare frame thy fearful symmetry?

                                                       (1790)

Browning, Robert *(1812–1889)*

Meeting at Night

The gray sea and the long black land;
And the yellow half-moon large and low;
And the startled little waves that leap
In fiery ringlets from their sleep,
As I gain the cove with pushing prow,   5
And quench its speed i' the slushy sand.

Then a mile of warm sea-scented beach;
Three fields to cross till a farm appears;
A tap at the pane, the quick sharp scratch
And blue spurt of a lighted match,   10
And a voice less loud, through its joys and fears,
Than the two hearts beating each to each!

                                                       (1845)

Byron, Lord George Gordon *(1788–1824)*

She Walks in Beauty

She walks in beauty, like the night
    Of cloudless climes and starry skies;
And all that's best of dark and bright
    Meet in her aspect and her eyes:
Thus mellowed to that tender light   5
    Which heaven to gaudy day denies.

One shade the more, one ray the less,
    Had half impaired the nameless grace
Which waves in every raven tress,
    Or softly lightens o'er her face;   10
Where thoughts serenely sweet express
    How pure, how dear their dwelling place.

And on that cheek, and o'er that brow,
    So soft, so calm, yet eloquent,
The smiles that win, the tints that glow,   15
    But tell of days in goodness spent,
A mind at peace with all below,
    A heart whose love is innocent!

                                                       (1815)

Coleridge, Samuel Taylor (1772–1834)

Kubla Khan

Or, a Vision in a Dream

In Xanadu did Kubla Khan
A stately pleasure-dome decree:
Where Alph, the sacred river, ran
Through caverns measureless to man
   Down to a sunless sea.   5

So twice five miles of fertile ground
With walls and towers were girdled round:
And here were gardens bright with sinuous rills
Where blossomed many an incense-bearing tree;
And here were forests ancient as the hills,   10
Enfolding sunny spots of greenery.

But oh! that deep romantic chasm which slanted
Down the green hill athwart a cedarn cover!
A savage place! as holy and enchanted
As e'er beneath a waning moon was haunted   15
By woman wailing for her demon-lover!
And from this chasm, with ceaseless turmoil seething,
As if this earth in fast thick pants were breathing,
A mighty fountain momently was forced,
Amid whose swift half-intermittent burst   20
Huge fragments vaulted like rebounding hail,
Or chaffy grain beneath the thresher's flail:
And 'mid these dancing rocks at once and ever
It flung up momently the sacred river,
Five miles meandering with a mazy motion   25
Through wood and dale the sacred river ran,
Then reached the caverns measureless to man,
And sank in tumult to a lifeless ocean:
And 'mid this tumult Kubla heard from far
Ancestral voices prophesying war!   30

   The shadow of the dome of pleasure
   Floated midway on the waves;
   Where was heard the mingled measure
   From the fountain and the caves.
It was a miracle of rare device,   35
A sunny pleasure dome with caves of ice!

   A damsel with a dulcimer
   In a vision once I saw:
   It was an Abyssinian maid,
   And on her dulcimer she played,   40
   Singing of Mount Abora.
   Could I revive within me
   Her symphony and song,
   To such a deep delight 'twould win me,

That with music loud and long,   45
I would build that dome in air,
That sunny dome! those caves of ice!
And all who heard should see them there,
And all should cry, Beware! Beware!
His flashing eyes, his floating hair!   50
Weave a circle round him thrice,
And close your eyes with holy dread,
For he on honey-dew hath fed,
And drunk the milk of Paradise.

(1798)

Dickinson, *Emily (1830–1886)*

Wild Nights—Wild Nights

Wild Nights—Wild Nights!
Were I with thee
Wild nights should be
Our luxury!

Futile—the Winds—   5
To a Heart in port—
Done with the Compass—
Done with the Chart!

Rowing in Eden—
Ah, the Sea!
Might I but moor—Tonight—   10
In thee!

(c. 1861)

Donne, *John (1572–1631)*

Death, be not proud

Death, be not proud, though some have callèd thee
Mighty and dreadful, for thou art not so;
For those whom thou think'st thou dost overthrow
Die not, poor Death, nor yet canst thou kill me.
From rest and sleep, which but thy pictures be,   5
Much pleasure; then from thee much more must flow,
And soonest our best men with thee do go,
Rest of their bones, and soul's delivery.
Thou art slave to fate, chance, kings, and desperate men,
And dost with poison, war, and sickness dwell,   10
And poppy or charms can make us sleep as well
And better than thy stroke; why swell'st thou then?
One short sleep past, we wake eternally
And death shall be no more; Death, thou shalt die.

(1633)

Dunbar, *Paul (1872–1906)*

We Wear the Mask

We wear the mask that grins and lies,
It hides our cheeks and shades our eyes, —
This debt we pay to human guile;
With torn and bleeding hearts we smile,
And mouth with myriad subtleties.   5

Why should the world be over-wise,
In counting all our tears and sighs?
Nay, let them only see us, while
    We wear the mask.

We smile, but, O great Christ, our cries   10
To thee from tortured souls arise.
We sing, but oh the clay is vile
Beneath our feet, and long the mile;
But let the world dream otherwise,
    We wear the mask!   15
                                                (1896)

Frost, *Robert (1874–1963)*

Acquainted with the Night

I have been one acquainted with the night.
I have walked out in rain—and back in rain.
I have outwalked the furthest city light.

I have looked down the saddest city lane.
I have passed by the watchman on his beat   5
And dropped my eyes, unwilling to explain.

I have stood still and stopped the sound of feet
When far away an interrupted cry
Came over houses from another street,

But not to call me back or say good-by;   10
And further still at an unearthly height
One luminary clock against the sky

Proclaimed the time was neither wrong nor right.
I have been one acquainted with the night.
                                                (1928)

Hayden, *Robert (1913–1980)*

Those Winter Sundays

Sundays too my father got up early
and put his clothes on in the blueblack cold,

then with cracked hands that ached
from labor in the weekday weather made
banked fires blaze. No one ever thanked him.   5

I'd wake and hear the cold splintering, breaking.
When the rooms were warm, he'd call,
and slowly I would rise and dress,
fearing the chronic angers of that house,

Speaking indifferently to him,   10
who had driven out the cold
and polished my good shoes as well.
What did I know, what did I know
of love's austere and lonely offices?

                                                                       (1966)

Heaney, *Seamus (b. 1939)*

Mid-Term Break

I sat all morning in the college sick-bay
Counting bells knelling classes to a close.
At two-o'clock our neighbours drove me home.

In the porch I met my father crying—
He had always taken funerals in his stride—   5
And Big Jim Evans saying it was a hard blow.

The baby cooed and laughed and rocked the pram
When I came in, and I was embarrassed
By old men standing up to shake my hand

And tell me they were "sorry for my trouble,"   10
Whispers informed strangers I was the eldest,
Away at school, as my mother held my hand

In hers and coughed out angry tearless sighs.
At ten o'clock the ambulance arrived
With the corpse, stanched and bandaged by the nurses.   15

Next morning I went up into the room. Snowdrops
And candles soothed the bedside; I saw him
For the first time in six weeks. Paler now,

Wearing a poppy bruise on his left temple,
He lay in the four foot box as in his cot.   20
No gaudy scars, the bumper knocked him clear.

A four foot box, a foot for every year.

                                                                       (1966)

Hughes, *Langston (1902–1967)*

Harlem (A Dream Deferred)

What happens to a dream deferred?
Does it dry up

Like a raisin in the sun?
Or fester like a sore—
And then run?   5
Does it stink like rotten meat?
Or crust and sugar over—
Like a syrupy sweet?

Maybe it just sags
Like a heavy load.   10

Or does it explode?

                                                                                    (1951)

Keats, *John (1795–1821)*

Ode on a Grecian Urn

1

Thou still unravished bride of quietness,
    Thou foster-child of silence and slow time,
Sylvan historian, who canst thus express
    A flowery tale more sweetly than our rhyme:
What leaf-fringed legend haunts about thy shape   5
    Of deities or mortals, or of both,
        In Tempe or the dales of Arcady?
What men or gods are these? What maidens loth?
    What mad pursuit? What struggle to escape?
        What pipes and timbrels? What wild ecstasy?   10

2

Heard melodies are sweet, but those unheard
    Are sweeter; therefore, ye soft pipes, play on;
Not to the sensual ear, but, more endear'd,
    Pipe to the spirit ditties of no tone:
Fair youth, beneath the trees, thou canst not leave   15
    Thy song, nor ever can those trees be bare;
        Bold lover, never, never canst thou kiss,
Though winning near the goal—yet, do not grieve;
    She cannot fade, though thou hast not thy bliss,
        For ever wilt thou love, and she be fair!   20

3

Ah, happy, happy boughs! that cannot shed
    Your leaves, not ever bid the spring adieu;
And, happy melodist, unwearied,
    For ever piping songs for ever new;
More happy love! more happy, happy love!   25
    For ever warm and still to be enjoy'd,
        For ever panting, and for ever young;
All breathing human passion far above,
    That leaves a heart high-sorrowful and cloyed,
        A burning forehead, and a parching tongue.   30

4

Who are these coming to the sacrifice?
    To what green altar, O mysterious priest,
Lead'st thou that heifer lowing at the skies,
    And all her silken flanks with garlands drest?
What little town by river or sea shore,   35
    Or mountain-built with peaceful citadel,
      Is emptied of its folk, this pious morn?
And, little town, thy streets for evermore
    Will silent be; and not a soul to tell
      Why thou art desolate, can e'er return.   40

5

O Attic shape! Fair attitude! with brede
    Of marble men and maidens overwrought,
With forest branches and the trodden weed;
    Thou, silent form, dost tease us out of thought
As doth eternity: Cold Pastoral!   45
    When old age shall this generation waste,
      Thou shalt remain, in midst of other woe
Than ours, a friend to man, to whom thou say'st,
    "Beauty is truth, truth beauty,"—that is all
      Ye know on earth, and all ye need to know.   50
                                   (1819, 1820)

Ode to a Nightingale

1

My heart aches, and a drowsy numbness pains
    My sense, as though of hemlock I had drunk,
Or emptied some dull opiate to the drains
    One minute past, and Lethe-wards had sunk:
'Tis not through envy of thy happy lot,   5
    But being too happy in thine happiness,—
      That thou, light-winged Dryad of the trees,
        In some melodious plot
    Of beechen green, and shadows numberless,
      Singest of summer in full-throated ease.   10

2

O, for a draught of vintage! that hath been
    Cooled a long age in the deep-delved earth,
Tasting of Flora and the country green,
    Dance, and Provencal song, and sunburnt mirth!
O for a beaker full of the warm South,   15
    Full of the true, the blushful Hippocrene,
      With beaded bubbles winking at the brim,
        And purple-stained mouth;

That I might drink, and leave the world unseen,
  And with thee fade away into the forest dim: 20

3

Fade far away, dissolve, and quite forget
  What thou among the leaves hast never known,
The weariness, the fever, and the fret
  Here, where men sit and hear each other groan;
Where palsy shakes a few, sad, last gray hairs,   25
  Where youth grows pale, and spectre-thin, and dies;
    Where but to think is to be full of sorrow
      And leaden-eyed despairs,
  Where Beauty cannot keep her lustrous eyes,
    Or new Love pine at them beyond to-morrow.   30

4

Away! away! for I will fly to thee,
  Not charioted by Bacchus and his pards,
But on the viewless wings of Poesy,
  Though the dull brain perplexes and retards:
Already with thee! tender is the night,   35
  And haply the Queen-Moon is on her throne,
    Clustered around by all her starry Fays;
      But here there is no light,
  Save what from heaven is with the breezes blown
    Through verdurous glooms and winding mossy ways.   40

5

I cannot see what flowers are at my feet,
  Nor what soft incense hangs upon the boughs,
But, in embalmed darkness, guess each sweet
  Wherewith the seasonable month endows
The grass, the thicket, and the fruit-tree wild;   45
  White hawthorn, and the pastoral eglantine;
    Fast fading violets cover'd up in leaves;
      And mid-May's eldest child,
  The coming musk-rose, full of dewy wine,
    The murmurous haunt of flies on summer eves.   50

6

Darkling I listen; and, for many a time
  I have been half in love with easeful Death,
Called him soft names in many a mused rhyme,
  To take into the air my quiet breath;
Now more than ever seems it rich to die,   55
  To cease upon the midnight with no pain,
    While thou art pouring forth thy soul abroad
      In such an ecstasy!
  Still wouldst thou sing, and I have ears in vain—
    To thy high requiem become a sod.   60

7

Thou wast not born for death, immortal Bird!
   No hungry generations tread thee down;
The voice I hear this passing night was heard
   In ancient days by emperor and clown:
Perhaps the self-same song that found a path   65
    Through the sad heart of Ruth, when, sick for home,
      She stood in tears amid the alien corn;
         The same that oft-times hath
    Charmed magic casements, opening on the foam
      Of perilous seas, in faery lands forlorn.   70

8

Forlorn! the very word is like a bell
   To toil me back from thee to my sole self!
Adieu! the fancy cannot cheat so well
   As she is famed to do, deceiving elf.
Adieu! adieu! thy plaintive anthem fades   75
    Past the near meadows, over the still stream,
      Up the hill-side; and now 'tis buried deep
         In the next valley-glades:
Was it a vision, or a waking dream?
    Fled is that music:—Do I wake or sleep?   80
                                      (1819)

To Autumn

1

Season of mists and mellow fruitfulness!
   Close bosom-friend of the maturing sun;
Conspiring with him how to load and bless
   With fruit the vines that round the thatch-eves run;
To bend with apples the mossed cottage-trees,   5
   And fill all fruit with ripeness to the core;
     To swell the gourd, and plump the hazel shells
With a sweet kernel; to set budding more,
   And still more, later flowers for the bees,
   Until they think warm days will never cease,   10
     For summer has o'er-brimmed their clammy cells.

2

Who hath not seen thee oft amid thy store?
   Sometimes whoever seeks abroad may find
Thee sitting careless on a granary floor,
   Thy hair soft-lifted by the winnowing wind;   15
Or on a half-reaped furrow sound asleep,
   Drowsed with the fume of poppies, while thy hook
     Spares the next swath and all its twinéd flowers:
And sometimes like a gleaner thou dost keep
   Steady thy laden head across a brook;   20

Or by a cider-press, with patient look,
    Thou watchest the last oozing hours by hours.

3

Where are the songs of Spring? Ay, where are they?
    Think not of them, thou hast thy music too—
While barréd clouds bloom the soft-dying day,   25
    And touch the stubble-plains with rosy hue;
Then in a wailful choir the small gnats mourn
    Among the river sallows, borne aloft
        Or sinking as the light wind lives or dies;
And full-grown lambs loud bleat from hilly bourn;   30
    Hedge-crickets sing; and now with treble soft
    The red-breast whistles from a garden-croft;
        And gathering swallows twitter in the skies.

        (1819)

Magee, John Gillespie (1922–1941)

High Flight

Oh! I have slipped the surly bonds of earth
    And danced the skies on laughter-silvered wings;
Sunward I've climbed, and joined the tumbling mirth
    Of sun-split clouds—and done a hundred things
You have not dreamed of—wheeled and soared and swung   5
    High in the sunlit silence. Hov'ring there
I've chased the shouting wind along, and flung
    My eager craft thro' footless halls of air.

Up, up, the long, delirious, burning blue
    I've topped the wind-swept heights with easy grace   10
Where never lark, nor even eagle flew—
    And while with silent, lifting mind I've trod
The high, untrespassed sanctity of space,
    Put out my hand and touched the face of God.

        (1945)

Marvell, Andrew (1621–1678)

To His Coy Mistress

    Had we but world enough, and time,
This coyness, lady, were no crime.
We would sit down and think which way
To walk, and pass our long love's day;
Thou by the Indian Ganges' side   5
Shouldst rubies find; I by the tide
Of Humber would complain. I would
Love you ten years before the Flood;
And you should, if you please, refuse
Till the conversion of the Jews.   10
My vegetable love should grow

Vaster than empires, and more slow.
An hundred years should go to praise
Thine eyes, and on thy forehead gaze;
Two hundred to adore each breast,   15
But thirty thousand to the rest;
An age at least to every part,
And the last age should show your heart.
For, lady, you deserve this state,
Nor would I love at lower rate.   20

    But at my back I always hear
Time's winged chariot hurrying near;
And yonder all before us lie
Deserts of vast eternity.
Thy beauty shall no more be found,   25
Nor, in thy marble vault, shall sound
My echoing song; then worms shall try
That long preserv'd virginity,
And your quaint honour turn to dust,
And into ashes all my lust.   30
The grave's a fine and private place,
But none I think do there embrace.

    Now therefore, while the youthful hue
Sits on thy skin like morning dew,
And while thy willing soul transpires   35
At every pore with instant fires,
Now let us sport us while we may;
And now, like am'rous birds of prey,
Rather at once our time devour,
Than languish in his slow-chapp'd power.   40
Let us roll all our strength, and all
Our sweetness, up into one ball;
And tear our pleasures with rough strife
Thorough the iron gates of life.
Thus, though we cannot make our sun   45
Stand still, yet we will make him run.

                                                  (1681)

McKay, Claude (1889–1948)

The White City

I will not toy with it nor bend an inch.
Deep in the secret chambers of my heart
I muse my life-long hate, and without flinch
I bear it nobly as I live my part.
My being would be a skeleton, a shell,   5
If this dark Passion that fills my every mood,
And makes my heaven in the white world's hell,
Did not forever feed me vital blood.
I see the mighty city through a mist—

The strident trains that speed the goaded mass,   10
The poles and spires and towers vapor-kissed,
The tides, the wharves, the dens I contemplate,
Are sweet like wanton loves because I hate.

(1922)

Nemerov, Howard (1920–1991)

The Vacuum

The house is so quiet now
The vacuum cleaner sulks in the corner closet,
Its bag limp as a stopped lung, its mouth
Grinning into the floor, maybe at my
Slovenly life, my dog-dead youth.   5

I've lived this way long enough,
But when my old woman died her soul
Went into that vacuum cleaner, and I can't bear
To see the bag swell like a belly, eating the dust
And the woolen mice, and begin to howl   10

Because there is old filth everywhere
She used to crawl, in the corner and under the stair.
I know now how life is cheap as dirt,
And still the hungry, angry heart
Hangs on and howls, biting at air.   15

(1955)

Pastan, Linda (b. 1932)

To a Daughter Leaving Home

When I taught you
at eight to ride
a bicycle, loping along
beside you
as you wobbled away   5
on two round wheels,
my own mouth rounding
in surprise when you pulled
ahead down the curved
path of the park,   10
I kept waiting
for the thud
of your crash as I
sprinted to catch up,
while you grew   15
smaller, more breakable
with distance,
pumping, pumping
for your life, screaming
with laughter,   20

the hair flapping
behind you like a
handkerchief waving
goodbye.

(1988)

Reed, *Henry (1914–1986)*

Naming of Parts

Today we have naming of parts. Yesterday,
We had daily cleaning. And tomorrow morning,
We shall have what to do after firing. But today,
Today we have naming of parts. Japonica
Glistens like coral in all of the neighboring gardens,   5
    And today we have naming of parts.

This is the lower sling swivel. And this
Is the upper sling swivel, whose use you will see,
When you are given your slings. And this is the piling swivel,
Which in your case you have not got. The branches   10
Hold in the gardens their silent, eloquent gestures,
    Which in our case we have not got.

This is the safety-catch, which is always released
With an easy flick of the thumb. And please do not let me
See anyone using his finger. You can do it quite easy   15
If you have any strength in your thumb. The blossoms
Are fragile and motionless, never letting anyone see
    Any of them using their finger.

And this you can see is the bolt. The purpose of this
Is to open the breech, as you see. We can slide it   20
Rapidly backwards and forwards: we call this
Easing the spring. And rapidly backwards and forwards
The early bees are assaulting and fumbling the flowers:
    They call it easing the Spring.

They call it easing the Spring: it is perfectly easy   25
If you have any strength in your thumb: like the bolt,
And the breech, and the cocking-piece, and the point of balance,
Which in our case we have not got; and the almond-blossom
Silent in all of the gardens and the bees going backwards and forwards,
    For today we have naming of parts.   30

(1946)

Rossetti, *Christina (1830–1894)*

Up-Hill

Does the road wind uphill all the way?
    Yes, to the very end.
Will the day's journey take the whole long day?
    From morn to night, my friend.

But is there for the night a resting-place?   5
    A roof for when the slow dark hours begin.
May not the darkness hide it from my face?
    You cannot miss that inn.

Shall I meet other wayfarers at night?
    Those who have gone before.   10
Then must I knock, or call when just in sight?
    They will not keep you standing at that door.

Shall I find comfort, travel-sore and weak?
    Of labor you shall find the sum.
Will there be beds for me and all who seek?   15
    Yea, beds for all who come.

(1861)

Shakespeare, William (1564–1616)

That time of year thou may'st in me behold
When yellow leaves, or none, or few, do hang
Upon those boughs which shake against the cold,
Bare ruined choirs where late the sweet birds sang.
In me thou see'st the twilight of such day   5
As after sunset fadeth in the west,
Which by-and-by black night doth take away,
Death's second self that seals up all in rest.
In me thou see'st the glowing of such fire
That on the ashes of his youth doth lie,   10
As the deathbed whereon it must expire,
Consumed with that which it was nourished by.
This thou perceiv'st, which makes thy love more strong,
To love that well which thou must leave ere long.

(1609)

Shelley, Percy Bysshe (1792–1822)

Ode to the West Wind

I

O wild West Wind, thou breath of Autumn's being
Thou from whose unseen presence the leaves dead
Are driven like ghosts from an enchanter fleeing,

Yellow, and black, and pale, and hectic red,
Pestilence-stricken multitudes! O thou   5
Who chariotest to their dark wintry bed

The wingèd seeds, where they lie cold and low,
Each like a corpse within its grave, until
Thine azure sister of the Spring shall blow

Her clarion o'er the dreaming earth, and fill   10
(Driving sweet buds like flocks to feed in air)
With living hues and odours plain and hill;

Wild Spirit, which art moving everywhere;
Destroyer and preserver; hear, O hear!

II

Thou on whose stream, 'mid the steep sky's commotion,   15
Loose clouds like earth's decaying leaves are shed,
Shook from the tangled boughs of heaven and ocean,

Angels of rain and lightning! there are spread
On the blue surface of thine airy surge,
Like the bright hair uplifted from the head   20

Of some fierce Mænad, even from the dim verge
Of the horizon to the zenith's height,
The locks of the approaching storm. Thou dirge

Of the dying year, to which this closing night
Will be the dome of a vast sepulchre   25
Vaulted with all thy congregated might

Of vapours, from whose solid atmosphere
Black rain, and fire, and hail, will burst: O hear!

III

Thou who didst waken from his summer dreams
The blue Mediterranean, where he lay,   30
Lull'd by the coil of his crystàlline streams,

Beside a pumice isle in Baiæ's bay,
And saw in sleep old palaces and towers
Quivering within the wave's intenser day,

All overgrown with azure moss, and flowers   35
So sweet, the sense faints picturing them! Thou
For whose path the Atlantic's level powers

Cleave themselves into chasms, while far below
The sea-blooms and the oozy woods which wear
The sapless foliage of the ocean, know   40

Thy voice, and suddenly grow gray with fear,
And tremble and despoil themselves: O hear!

IV

If I were a dead leaf thou mightest bear;
If I were a swift cloud to fly with thee;
A wave to pant beneath thy power, and share   45

The impulse of thy strength, only less free
Than thou, O uncontrollable! if even
I were as in my boyhood, and could be

The comrade of thy wanderings over heaven,
As then, when to outstrip thy skiey speed   50
Scarce seem'd a vision—I would ne'er have striven

As thus with thee in prayer in my sore need.
O! lift me as a wave, a leaf, a cloud!
I fall upon the thorns of life! I bleed!

A heavy weight of hours has chain'd and bow'd   55
One too like thee—tameless, and swift, and proud.

V

Make me thy lyre, even as the forest is:
What if my leaves are falling like its own?
The tumult of thy mighty harmonies

Will take from both a deep autumnal tone,   60
Sweet though in sadness. Be thou, Spirit fierce,
My spirit! Be thou me, impetuous one!

Drive my dead thoughts over the universe,
Like wither'd leaves, to quicken a new birth;
And, by the incantation of this verse,   65

Scatter, as from an unextinguish'd hearth
Ashes and sparks, my words among mankind!
Be through my lips to unawaken'd earth

The trumpet of a prophecy! O Wind,
If Winter comes, can Spring be far behind?   70
                                                                  (1820)

Tennyson, Lord Alfred (1809–1892)

The Eagle

He clasps the crag with crooked hands;
Close to the sun in lonely lands,
Ringed with the azure world, he stands.

The wrinkled sea beneath him crawls:
He watches from his mountain walls,   5
And like a thunderbolt he falls.
                                                                  (1851)

Ulysses

It little profits that an idle king,
By this still hearth, among these barren crags,
Match'd with an aged wife, I mete and dole
Unequal laws unto a savage race,
That hoard, and sleep, and feed, and know not me.   5
I cannot rest from travel; I will drink
Life to the lees. All times I have enjoy'd
Greatly, have suffer'd greatly, both with those
That loved me, and alone; on shore, and when
Thro' scudding drifts the rainy Hyades   10
Vext the dim sea. I am become a name;
For always roaming with a hungry heart

Much have I seen and known,— cities of men
And manners, climates, councils, governments,
Myself not least, but honor'd of them all, —
And drunk delight of battle with my peers,   15
Far on the ringing plains of windy Troy.
I am a part of all that I have met;
Yet all experience is an arch wherethro'
Gleams that untravell'd world whose margin fades   20
For ever and for ever when I move.
How dull it is to pause, to make an end,
To rust unburnish'd, not to shine in use!
As tho' to breathe were life! Life piled on life
Were all too little, and of one to me   25
Little remains; but every hour is saved
From that eternal silence, something more,
A bringer of new things; and vile it were
For some three suns to store and hoard myself,
And this gray spirit yearning in desire   30
To follow knowledge like a sinking star,
Beyond the utmost bound of human thought.

This is my son, mine own Telemachus,
To whom I leave the sceptre and the isle, —
Well-loved of me, discerning to fulfill   35
This labor, by slow prudence to make mild
A rugged people, and thro' soft degrees
Subdue them to the useful and the good.
Most blameless is he, centred in the sphere
Of common duties, decent not to fail   40
In offices of tenderness, and pay
Meet adoration to my household gods,
When I am gone. He works his work, I mine.

There lies the port; the vessel puffs her sail;
There gloom the dark, broad seas. My mariners,   45
Souls that have toil'd, and wrought, and thought with me, —
That ever with a frolic welcome took
The thunder and the sunshine, and opposed
Free hearts, free foreheads, —you and I are old;
Old age hath yet his honor and his toil.   50
Death closes all; but something ere the end,
Some work of noble note, may yet be done,
Not unbecoming men that strove with Gods.
The lights begin to twinkle from the rocks;
The long day wanes; the slow moon climbs; the deep   55
Moans round with many voices. Come, my friends.
'T is not too late to seek a newer world.
Push off, and sitting well in order smite
The sounding furrows; for my purpose holds
To sail beyond the sunset, and the baths   60
Of all the western stars, until I die.
It may be that the gulfs will wash us down;
It may be we shall touch the Happy Isles,

And see the great Achilles, whom we knew.
Tho' much is taken, much abides; and tho'   65
We are not now that strength which in old days
Moved earth and heaven, that which we are, we are, —
One equal temper of heroic hearts,
Made weak by time and fate, but strong in will
To strive, to seek, to find, and not to yield.   70

(1833)

Whitman, *Walt (1819–1892)*

A noiseless patient spider

A noiseless patient spider,
I mark'd where on a little promontory it stood isolated,
Mark'd how to explore the vacant vast surrounding,
It launch'd forth filament, filament, filament, out of itself,
Ever unreeling them, ever tirelessly speeding them.   5

And you O my soul where you stand,
Surrounded, detached, in measureless oceans of space,
Ceaselessly musing, venturing, throwing, seeking the spheres to connect them,
Till the bridge you will need be form'd, till the ductile anchor hold,
Till the gossamer thread you fling catch somewhere, O my soul.   10

(1881)

When I heard the learn'd astronomer

When I heard the learn'd astronomer,
When the proofs, the figures, were ranged in columns before me,
When I was shown the charts and diagrams, to add, divide, and measure them,
When I sitting heard the astronomer where he lectured with much
        applause in the lecture-room,
How soon unaccountable I became tired and sick,   5
Till rising and gliding out I wander'd off by myself,
In the mystical moist night-air, and from time to time,
Look'd up in perfect silence at the stars.

(1865)

Wordsworth, *William (1770–1850)*

Composed Upon Westminster Bridge

Earth has not anything to show more fair:
Dull would he be of soul who could pass by
A sight so touching in its majesty:
This City now doth like a garment wear
The beauty of the morning; silent, bare,   5
Ships, towers, domes, theatres, and temples lie
Open unto the fields, and to the sky;
All bright and glittering in the smokeless air.
Never did sun more beautifully steep
In his first splendor valley, rock, or hill;   10
Ne'er saw I, never felt, a calm so deep!

The river glideth at his own sweet will:
Dear God! the very houses seem asleep;
And all that mighty heart is lying still!

(1807)

It is a beauteous evening

It is a beauteous evening, calm and free,
The holy time is quiet as a Nun
Breathless with adoration; the broad sun
Is sinking down in its tranquillity;
The gentleness of heaven broods o'er the sea: 5
Listen! the mighty Being is awake,
And doth with his eternal motion make
A sound like thunder—everlastingly.
Dear Child! dear Girl! that walkest with me here,
If thou appear untouch'd by solemn thought,   10
Thy nature is not therefore less divine:
Thou liest in Abraham's bosom all the year,
And worshipp'st at the Temple's inner shrine,
God being with thee when we know it not.

(1807)

I wandered lonely as a cloud

I wandered lonely as a cloud
That floats on high o'er vales and hills,
When all at once I saw a crowd,
A host, of golden daffodils;
Beside the lake, beneath the trees,   5
Fluttering and dancing in the breeze.

Continuous as the stars that shine
And twinkle on the milky way,
They stretched in never-ending line
Along the margin of a bay: 10
Ten thousand saw I at a glance,
Tossing their heads in sprightly dance.

The waves beside them danced; but they
Outdid the sparkling waves in glee:
A poet could not but be gay,   15
In such a jocund company:
I gazed—and gazed—but little thought
What wealth the show to me had brought:

For oft, when on my couch I lie
In vacant or in pensive mood,   20
They flash upon that inward eye
Which is the bliss of solitude;
And then my heart with pleasure fills,
And dances with the daffodils.

(1807)

Appendix 3
Selected Short Stories

The following short stories appear in alphabetical order according to the author's surname:

Chekhov, Anton	"The Lady with the Dog"
Chopin, Kate	"The Storm"
	"The Story of an Hour"
Faulkner, Willliam	"A Rose for Emily"
Hawthorne, Nathaniel	"Young Goodman Brown"
Joyce, James	"Araby"
	"The Boarding House"
Maupassant, Guy de	"The Jewelry"
	"The Necklace"
Poe, Edgar Allan	"The Black Cat"
	"The Cask of Amontillado"
Tan, Amy	"A Pair of Tickets"
Updike, John	"A & P"

Chekhov, Anton (1860–1904)

The Lady with the Dog
(Translated by Constance Garnett)

I

It was said that a new person had appeared on the sea-front: a lady with a little dog. Dmitri Dmitritch Gurov, who had by then been a fortnight at Yalta, and so was fairly at home there, had begun to take an interest in new arrivals. Sitting in Verney's pavilion, he saw, walking on the sea-front, a fair-haired young lady of medium height, wearing a beret; a white Pomeranian dog was running behind her.

And afterwards he met her in the public gardens and in the square several times a day. She was walking alone, always wearing the same beret, and always with the same white dog; no one knew who she was, and every one called her simply "the lady with the dog."

"If she is here alone without a husband or friends, it wouldn't be amiss to make her acquaintance," Gurov reflected.

He was under forty, but he had a daughter already twelve years old, and two sons at school. He had been married young, when he was a student in his second year, and by now his wife seemed half as old again as he. She was a tall, erect woman with dark eyebrows, staid and dignified, and, as she said of herself, intellectual. She read a great deal, used phonetic spelling, called her husband, not Dmitri, but Dimitri, and he secretly considered her unintelligent, narrow, inelegant, was afraid of her, and did not like to be with her at home. He had begun being unfaithful to her long ago— had been unfaithful to her often, and, probably on that account, almost always spoke ill of women, and when they were talked about in his presence, used to call them "the lower race."

It seemed to him that he had been so schooled by bitter experience that he might call them   5
what he liked, and yet he could not get on for two days together without "the lower race." In the society of men he was bored and not himself, with them he was cold and uncommunicative; but when he was in the company of women he felt free, and knew what to say to them and how to behave; and he was at ease with them even when he was silent. In his appearance, in his character, in his whole nature, there was something attractive and elusive which allured women and dis-posed them in his favour; he knew that, and some force seemed to draw him, too, to them.

Experience often repeated, truly bitter experience, had taught him long ago that with decent people, especially Moscow people—always slow to move and irresolute—every intimacy, which at first so agreeably diversifies life and appears a light and charming adventure, inevitably grows into a regular problem of extreme intricacy, and in the long run the situation becomes unbearable. But at every fresh meeting with an interesting woman this experience seemed to slip out of his memory, and he was eager for life, and everything seemed simple and amusing.

One evening he was dining in the gardens, and the lady in the beret came up slowly to take the next table. Her expression, her gait, her dress, and the way she did her hair told him that she was a lady, that she was married, that she was in Yalta for the first time and alone, and that she was dull there. . . . The stories told of the immorality in such places as Yalta are to a great extent untrue; he despised them, and knew that such stories were for the most part made up by persons who would themselves have been glad to sin if they had been able; but when the lady sat down at the next table three paces from him, he remembered these tales of easy conquests, of trips to the mountains, and the tempting thought of a swift, fleeting love affair, a romance with an unknown woman, whose name he did not know, suddenly took possession of him.

He beckoned coaxingly to the Pomeranian, and when the dog came up to him he shook his finger at it. The Pomeranian growled: Gurov shook his finger at it again.

The lady looked at him and at once dropped her eyes.

"He doesn't bite," she said, and blushed.   10

"May I give him a bone?" he asked; and when she nodded he asked courteously, "Have you been long in Yalta?"

"Five days."

"And I have already dragged out a fortnight here."

There was a brief silence.

"Time goes fast, and yet it is so dull here!" she said, not looking at him.   15

"That's only the fashion to say it is dull here. A provincial will live in Belyov or Zhidra and not be dull, and when he comes here it's 'Oh, the dullness! Oh, the dust!' One would think he came from Grenada."

She laughed. Then both continued eating in silence, like strangers, but after dinner they walked side by side; and there sprang up between them the light jesting conversation of people who are free and satisfied, to whom it does not matter where they go or what they talk about. They walked and talked of the strange light on the sea: the water was of a soft warm lilac hue, and there was a golden streak from the moon upon it. They talked of how sultry it was after a hot day. Gurov told her that he came from Moscow, that he had taken his degree in Arts, but had a post in a bank; that he had trained as an opera-singer, but had given it up, that he owned two houses in Moscow. . . . And from her he learnt that she had grown up in Petersburg, but had lived in S—— since her marriage two years before, that she was staying another month in Yalta, and that her husband, who needed a holiday too, might perhaps come and fetch her. She was not sure whether her husband had a post in a Crown Department or under the Provincial Council—and was amused by her own ignorance. And Gurov learnt, too, that she was called Anna Sergeyevna.

Afterwards he thought about her in his room at the hotel—thought she would certainly meet him next day; it would be sure to happen. As he got into bed he thought how lately she had been a girl at school, doing lessons like his own daughter; he recalled the diffidence, the angularity, that was still manifest in her laugh and her manner of talking with a stranger. This must have been the first time in her life she had been alone in surroundings in which she was followed, looked at, and spoken to merely from a secret motive which she could hardly fail to guess. He recalled her slender, delicate neck, her lovely grey eyes.

"There's something pathetic about her, anyway," he thought, and fell asleep.

II

A week had passed since they had made acquaintance. It was a holiday. It was sultry indoors, 20 while in the street the wind whirled the dust round and round, and blew people's hats off. It was a thirsty day, and Gurov often went into the pavilion, and pressed Anna Sergeyevna to have syrup and water or an ice. One did not know what to do with oneself.

In the evening when the wind had dropped a little, they went out on the groyne to see the steamer come in. There were a great many people walking about the harbour; they had gathered to welcome some one, bringing bouquets. And two peculiarities of a well-dressed Yalta crowd were very conspicuous: the elderly ladies were dressed like young ones, and there were great numbers of generals.

Owing to the roughness of the sea, the steamer arrived late, after the sun had set, and it was a long time turning about before it reached the groyne. Anna Sergeyevna looked through her lorgnette at the steamer and the passengers as though looking for acquaintances, and when she turned to Gurov her eyes were shining. She talked a great deal and asked disconnected questions, forgetting next moment what she had asked; then she dropped her lorgnette in the crush.

The festive crowd began to disperse; it was too dark to see people's faces. The wind had completely dropped, but Gurov and Anna Sergeyevna still stood as though waiting to see some one else come from the steamer. Anna Sergeyevna was silent now, and sniffed the flowers without looking at Gurov.

"The weather is better this evening," he said. "Where shall we go now? Shall we drive somewhere?" She made no answer.   25

Then he looked at her intently, and all at once put his arm round her and kissed her on the lips, and breathed in the moisture and the fragrance of the flowers; and he immediately looked round him, anxiously wondering whether any one had seen them.

"Let us go to your hotel," he said softly.

And both walked quickly.

The room was close and smelt of the scent she had bought at the Japanese shop. Gurov looked at her and thought: "What different people one meets in the world!" From the past he preserved memories of careless, good-natured women, who loved cheerfully and were grateful to him for the happiness he gave them, however brief it might be; and of women like his wife who loved without any genuine feeling, with superfluous phrases, affectedly, hysterically, with an expression that suggested that it was not love nor passion, but something more significant; and of two or three others, very beautiful, cold women, on whose faces he had caught a glimpse of a rapacious expression—an obstinate desire to snatch from life more than it could give, and these were capricious, unreflecting, domineering, unintelligent women not in their first youth, and when Gurov grew cold to them their beauty excited his hatred, and the lace on their linen seemed to him like scales.

But in this case there was still the diffidence, the angularity of inexperienced youth, an awk- 30
ward feeling; and there was a sense of consternation as though some one had suddenly knocked at
the door. The attitude of Anna Sergeyevna—"the lady with the dog"—to what had happened was
somehow peculiar, very grave, as though it were her fall—so it seemed, and it was strange and
inappropriate. Her face dropped and faded, and on both sides of it her long hair hung down
mournfully; she mused in a dejected attitude like "the woman who was a sinner" in an old-fashioned
picture.

"It's wrong," she said. "You will be the first to despise me now."

There was a water-melon on the table. Gurov cut himself a slice and began eating it without
haste. There followed at least half an hour of silence.

Anna Sergeyevna was touching; there was about her the purity of a good, simple woman who
had seen little of life. The solitary candle burning on the table threw a faint light on her face, yet
it was clear that she was very unhappy.

"How could I despise you?" asked Gurov. "You don't know what you are saying."

"God forgive me," she said, and her eyes filled with tears. "It's awful."   35

"You seem to feel you need to be forgiven."

"Forgiven? No. I am a bad, low woman; I despise myself and don't attempt to justify myself.
It's not my husband but myself I have deceived. And not only just now; I have been deceiving
myself for a long time. My husband may be a good, honest man, but he is a flunkey! I don't know
what he does there, what his work is, but I know he is a flunkey! I was twenty when I was married
to him. I have been tormented by curiosity; I wanted something better. 'There must be a different sort of life,' I said to myself. I wanted to live! To live, to live! . . . I was fired by curiosity . . .
you don't understand it, but, I swear to God, I could not control myself; something happened to
me: I could not be restrained. I told my husband I was ill, and came here. . . . And here I have
been walking about as though I were dazed, like a mad creature; . . . and now I have become a
vulgar, contemptible woman whom any one may despise."

Gurov felt bored already, listening to her. He was irritated by the naïve tone, by this remorse,
so unexpected and inopportune; but for the tears in her eyes, he might have thought she was jesting or playing a part.

"I don't understand," he said softly. "What is it you want?"

She hid her face on his breast and pressed close to him.   40

"Believe me, believe me, I beseech you . . ." she said. "I love a pure, honest life, and sin is
loathsome to me. I don't know what I am doing. Simple people say: 'The Evil One has beguiled
me.' And I may say of myself now that the Evil One has beguiled me."

"Hush, hush! . . ." he muttered.

He looked at her fixed, scared eyes, kissed her, talked softly and affectionately, and by
degrees she was comforted, and her gaiety returned; they both began laughing.

Afterwards when they went out there was not a soul on the sea-front. The town with its
cypresses had quite a deathlike air, but the sea still broke noisily on the shore; a single barge was
rocking on the waves, and a lantern was blinking sleepily on it.

They found a cab and drove to Oreanda.   45

"I found out your surname in the hall just now: it was written on the board—Von Diderits," said
Gurov. "Is your husband a German?"

"No; I believe his grandfather was a German, but he is an Orthodox Russian himself."

At Oreanda they sat on a seat not far from the church, looked down at the sea, and were
silent. Yalta was hardly visible through the morning mist; white clouds stood motionless on the
mountain-tops. The leaves did not stir on the trees, grasshoppers chirruped, and the monotonous hollow sound of the sea rising up from below, spoke of the peace, of the eternal sleep
awaiting us. So it must have sounded when there was no Yalta, no Oreanda here; so it sounds
now, and it will sound as indifferently and monotonously when we are all no more. And in this
constancy, in this complete indifference to the life and death of each of us, there lies hid,

perhaps, a pledge of our eternal salvation, of the unceasing movement of life upon earth, of unceasing progress towards perfection. Sitting beside a young woman who in the dawn seemed so lovely, soothed and spellbound in these magical surroundings—the sea, mountains, clouds, the open sky—Gurov thought how in reality everything is beautiful in this world when one reflects: everything except what we think or do ourselves when we forget our human dignity and the higher aims of our existence.

A man walked up to them—probably a keeper—looked at them and walked away. And this detail seemed mysterious and beautiful, too. They saw a steamer come from Theodosia, with its lights out in the glow of dawn.

"There is dew on the grass," said Anna Sergeyevna, after a silence.   50

"Yes. It's time to go home."

They went back to the town.

Then they met every day at twelve o'clock on the sea-front, lunched and dined together, went for walks, admired the sea. She complained that she slept badly, that her heart throbbed violently; asked the same questions, troubled now by jealousy and now by the fear that he did not respect her sufficiently. And often in the square or gardens, when there was no one near them, he suddenly drew her to him and kissed her passionately. Complete idleness, these kisses in broad daylight while he looked round in dread of some one's seeing them, the heat, the smell of the sea, and the continual passing to and fro before him of idle, well-dressed, well-fed people, made a new man of him; he told Anna Sergeyevna how beautiful she was, how fascinating. He was impatiently passionate, he would not move a step away from her, while she was often pensive and continually urged him to confess that he did not respect her, did not love her in the least, and thought of her as nothing but a common woman. Rather late almost every evening they drove somewhere out of town, to Oreanda or to the waterfall; and the expedition was always a success, the scenery invariably impressed them as grand and beautiful.

They were expecting her husband to come, but a letter came from him, saying that there was something wrong with his eyes, and he entreated his wife to come home as quickly as possible. Anna Sergeyevna made haste to go.

"It's a good thing I am going away," she said to Gurov. "It's the finger of destiny!"   55

She went by coach and he went with her. They were driving the whole day. When she had got into a compartment of the express, and when the second bell had rung, she said:

"Let me look at you once more . . . look at you once again. That's right."

She did not shed tears, but was so sad that she seemed ill, and her face was quivering.

"I shall remember you . . . think of you," she said. "God be with you; be happy. Don't remember evil against me. We are parting forever—it must be so, for we ought never to have met. Well, God be with you."

The train moved off rapidly, its lights soon vanished from sight, and a minute later there was 60 no sound of it, as though everything had conspired together to end as quickly as possible that sweet delirium, that madness. Left alone on the platform, and gazing into the dark distance, Gurov listened to the chirrup of the grasshoppers and the hum of the telegraph wires, feeling as though he had only just waked up. And he thought, musing, that there had been another episode or adventure in his life, and it, too, was at an end, and nothing was left of it but a memory. . . . He was moved, sad, and conscious of a slight remorse. This young woman whom he would never meet again had not been happy with him; he was genuinely warm and affectionate with her, but yet in his manner, his tone, and his caresses there had been a shade of light irony, the coarse condescension of a happy man who was, besides, almost twice her age. All the time she had called him kind, exceptional, lofty; obviously he had seemed to her different from what he really was, so he had unintentionally deceived her. . . .

Here at the station was already a scent of autumn; it was a cold evening.

"It's time for me to go north," thought Gurov as he left the platform. "High time!"

III

At home in Moscow everything was in its winter routine; the stoves were heated, and in the morning it was still dark when the children were having breakfast and getting ready for school, and the nurse would light the lamp for a short time. The frosts had begun already. When the first snow has fallen, on the first day of sledge-driving it is pleasant to see the white earth, the white roofs, to draw soft, delicious breath, and the season brings back the days of one's youth. The old limes and birches, white with hoar-frost, have a good-natured expression; they are nearer to one's heart than cypresses and palms, and near them one doesn't want to be thinking of the sea and the mountains.

Gurov was Moscow born; he arrived in Moscow on a fine frosty day, and when he put on his fur coat and warm gloves, and walked along Petrovka, and when on Saturday evening he heard the ringing of the bells, his recent trip and the places he had seen lost all charm for him. Little by little he became absorbed in Moscow life, greedily read three newspapers a day, and declared he did not read the Moscow papers on principle! He already felt a longing to go to restaurants, clubs, dinner-parties, anniversary celebrations, and he felt flattered at entertaining distinguished lawyers and artists, and at playing cards with a professor at the doctors' club. He could already eat a whole plateful of salt fish and cabbage.

In another month, he fancied, the image of Anna Sergeyevna would be shrouded in a mist in his memory, and only from time to time would visit him in his dreams with a touching smile as others did. But more than a month passed, real winter had come, and everything was still clear in his memory as though he had parted with Anna Sergeyevna only the day before. And his memories glowed more and more vividly. When in the evening stillness he heard from his study the voices of his children, preparing their lessons, or when he listened to a song or the organ at the restaurant, or the storm howled in the chimney, suddenly everything would rise up in his memory: what had happened on the groyne, and the early morning with the mist on the mountains, and the steamer coming from Theodosia, and the kisses. He would pace a long time about his room, remembering it all and smiling; then his memories passed into dreams, and in his fancy the past was mingled with what was to come. Anna Sergeyevna did not visit him in dreams, but followed him about everywhere like a shadow and haunted him. When he shut his eyes he saw her as though she were living before him, and she seemed to him lovelier, younger, tenderer than she was; and he imagined himself finer than he had been in Yalta. In the evenings she peeped out at him from the bookcase, from the fireplace, from the corner—he heard her breathing, the caressing rustle of her dress. In the street he watched the women, looking for some one like her.

He was tormented by an intense desire to confide his memories to some one. But in his home it was impossible to talk of his love, and he had no one outside; he could not talk to his tenants nor to any one at the bank. And what had he to talk of? Had he been in love, then? Had there been anything beautiful, poetical, or edifying or simply interesting in his relations with Anna Sergeyevna? And there was nothing for him but to talk vaguely of love, of woman, and no one guessed what it meant; only his wife twitched her black eyebrows, and said: 65

"The part of a lady-killer does not suit you at all, Dimitri."

One evening, coming out of the doctors' club with an official with whom he had been playing cards, he could not resist saying:

"If only you knew what a fascinating woman I made the acquaintance of in Yalta!"

The official got into his sledge and was driving away, but turned suddenly and shouted:

"Dmitri Dmitritch!"

"What?" 70

"You were right this evening: the sturgeon was a bit too strong!"

These words, so ordinary, for some reason moved Gurov to indignation, and struck him as degrading and unclean. What savage manners, what people! What senseless nights, what uninteresting, uneventful days! The rage for card-playing, the gluttony, the drunkenness, the continual talk always about the same thing. Useless pursuits and conversations always about the same things absorb the better part of one's time, the better part of one's strength, and in the end there is left a life grovelling and curtailed, worthless and trivial, and there is no escaping or getting away from it—just as though one were in a madhouse or a prison.

Gurov did not sleep all night, and was filled with indignation. And he had a headache all next day. And the next night he slept badly; he sat up in bed, thinking, or paced up and down his room. He was sick of his children, sick of the bank; he had no desire to go anywhere or to talk of anything.

In the holidays in December he prepared for a journey, and told his wife he was going to 75 Petersburg to do something in the interests of a young friend—and he set off for S——. What for? He did not very well know himself. He wanted to see Anna Sergeyevna and to talk with her— to arrange a meeting, if possible.

He reached S——in the morning, and took the best room at the hotel, in which the floor was covered with grey army cloth, and on the table was an inkstand, grey with dust and adorned with a figure on horseback, with its hat in its hand and its head broken off. The hotel porter gave him the necessary information; Von Diderits lived in a house of his own in Old Gontcharny Street—it was not far from the hotel: he was rich and lived in good style, and had his own horses; every one in the town knew him. The porter pronounced the name "Dridirits."

Gurov went without haste to Old Gontcharny Street and found the house. Just opposite the house stretched a long grey fence adorned with nails.

"One would run away from a fence like that," thought Gurov, looking from the fence to the windows of the house and back again.

He considered: today was a holiday, and her husband would probably be at home. And in any case it would be tactless to go into the house and upset her. If he were to send her a note it might fall into her husband's hands, and then it might ruin everything. The best thing was to trust to chance. And he kept walking up and down the street by the fence, waiting for the chance. He saw a beggar go in at the gate and dogs fly at him; then an hour later he heard a piano, and the sounds were faint and indistinct. Probably it was Anna Sergeyevna playing. The front door suddenly opened, and an old woman came out, followed by the familiar white Pomeranian. Gurov was on the point of calling to the dog, but his heart began beating violently, and in his excitement he could not remember the dog's name.

He walked up and down, and loathed the grey fence more and more, and by now he thought 80 irritably that Anna Sergeyevna had forgotten him, and was perhaps already amusing herself with some one else, and that that was very natural in a young woman who had nothing to look at from morning till night but that confounded fence. He went back to his hotel room and sat for a long while on the sofa, not knowing what to do, then he had dinner and a long nap.

"How stupid and worrying it is!" he thought when he woke and looked at the dark windows: it was already evening. "Here I've had a good sleep for some reason. What shall I do in the night?"

He sat on the bed, which was covered by a cheap grey blanket, such as one sees in hospitals, and he taunted himself in his vexation:

"So much for the lady with the dog . . . so much for the adventure. . . . You're in a nice fix. . . ."

That morning at the station a poster in large letters had caught his eye. "The Geisha" was to be performed for the first time. He thought of this and went to the theatre.

"It's quite possible she may go to the first performance," he thought.   85

The theatre was full. As in all provincial theatres, there was a fog above the chandelier, the gallery was noisy and restless; in the front row the local dandies were standing up before the beginning of the performance, with their hands behind them; in the Governor's box the Governor's daughter, wearing a boa, was sitting in the front seat, while the Governor himself lurked modestly behind the curtain with only his hands visible; the orchestra was a long time tuning up; the stage curtain swayed. All the time the audience were coming in and taking their seats Gurov looked at them eagerly.

Anna Sergeyevna, too, came in. She sat down in the third row, and when Gurov looked at her his heart contracted, and he understood clearly that for him there was in the whole world no creature so near, so precious, and so important to him; she, this little woman, in no way remarkable, lost in a provincial crowd, with a vulgar lorgnette in her hand, filled his whole life now, was his sorrow and his joy, the one happiness that he now desired for himself, and to the sounds of the inferior orchestra, of the wretched provincial violins, he thought how lovely she was. He thought and dreamed.

A young man with small side-whiskers, tall and stooping, came in with Anna Sergeyevna and sat down beside her; he bent his head at every step and seemed to be continually bowing. Most likely this was the husband whom at Yalta, in a rush of bitter feeling, she had called a flunkey. And there really was in his long figure, his side-whiskers, and the small bald patch on his head, something of the flunkey's obsequiousness; his smile was sugary, and in his buttonhole there was some badge of distinction like the number on a waiter.

During the first intermission the husband went away to smoke; she remained alone in her stall. Gurov, who was sitting in the stalls, too, went up to her and said in a trembling voice, with a forced smile:

"Good-evening."   90

She glanced at him and turned pale, then glanced again with horror, unable to believe her eyes, and tightly gripped the fan and the lorgnette in her hands, evidently struggling with herself not to faint. Both were silent. She was sitting, he was standing, frightened by her confusion and not venturing to sit down beside her. The violins and the flute began tuning up. He felt suddenly frightened; it seemed as though all the people in the boxes were looking at them. She got up and went quickly to the door; he followed her, and both walked senselessly along passages, and up and down stairs, and figures in legal, scholastic, and civil service uniforms, all wearing badges, flitted before their eyes. They caught glimpses of ladies, of fur coats hanging on pegs; the draughts blew on them, bringing a smell of stale tobacco. And Gurov, whose heart was beating violently, thought:

"Oh, heavens! Why are these people here and this orchestra! . . ."

And at that instant he recalled how when he had seen Anna Sergeyevna off at the station he had thought that everything was over and they would never meet again. But how far they were still from the end!

On the narrow, gloomy staircase over which was written "To the Amphitheatre," she stopped.

"How you have frightened me!" she said, breathing hard, still pale and overwhelmed. "Oh,   95 how you have frightened me! I am half dead. Why have you come? Why?"

"But do understand, Anna, do understand . . ." he said hastily in a low voice. "I entreat you to understand. . . ."

She looked at him with dread, with entreaty, with love; she looked at him intently, to keep his features more distinctly in her memory.

"I am so unhappy," she went on, not heeding him. "I have thought of nothing but you all the time; I live only in the thought of you. And I wanted to forget, to forget you; but why, oh, why, have you come?"

On the landing above them two schoolboys were smoking and looking down, but that was nothing to Gurov; he drew Anna Sergeyevna to him, and began kissing her face, her cheeks, and her hands.

"What are you doing, what are you doing!" she cried in horror, pushing him away. "We are   100 mad. Go away to-day; go away at once. . . . I beseech you by all that is sacred, I implore you. . . . There are people coming this way!"

Some one was coming up the stairs.

"You must go away," Anna Sergeyevna went on in a whisper. "Do you hear, Dmitri Dmitritch? I will come and see you in Moscow. I have never been happy; I am miserable now, and I never, never shall be happy, never! Don't make me suffer still more! I swear I'll come to Moscow. But now let us part. My precious, good, dear one, we must part!"

She pressed his hand and began rapidly going downstairs, looking round at him, and from her eyes he could see that she really was unhappy. Gurov stood for a little while, listened, then, when all sound had died away, he found his coat and left the theatre.

IV

And Anna Sergeyevna began coming to see him in Moscow. Once in two or three months she left S——, telling her husband that she was going to consult a doctor about an internal complaint—and her husband believed her, and did not believe her. In Moscow she stayed at the Slaviansky Bazaar hotel, and at once sent a man in a red cap to Gurov. Gurov went to see her, and no one in Moscow knew of it.

Once he was going to see her in this way on a winter morning (the messenger had come the   105 evening before when he was out). With him walked his daughter, whom he wanted to take to school: it was on the way. Snow was falling in big wet flakes.

"It's three degrees above freezing-point, and yet it is snowing," said Gurov to his daughter. "The thaw is only on the surface of the earth; there is quite a different temperature at a greater height in the atmosphere."

"And why are there no thunderstorms in the winter, father?"

He explained that, too. He talked, thinking all the while that he was going to see her, and no living soul knew of it, and probably never would know. He had two lives: one, open, seen and known by all who cared to know, full of relative truth and of relative falsehood, exactly like the lives of his friends and acquaintances; and another life running its course in secret. And through some strange, perhaps accidental, conjunction of circumstances, everything that was essential, of interest and of value to him, everything in which he was sincere and did not deceive himself, everything that made the kernel of his life, was hidden from other people; and all that was false in him, the sheath in which he hid himself to conceal the truth—such, for instance, as his work in the bank, his discussions at the club, his "lower race," his presence with his wife at anniversary festivities—all that was open. And he judged of others by himself, not believing in what he saw, and always believing that every man had his real, most interesting life under the cover of secrecy and under the cover of night. All personal life rested on secrecy, and possibly it was partly on that account that civilised man was so nervously anxious that personal privacy should be respected.

After leaving his daughter at school, Gurov went on to the Slaviansky Bazaar. He took off his fur coat below, went upstairs, and softly knocked at the door. Anna Sergeyevna, wearing his favourite grey dress, exhausted by the journey and the suspense, had been expecting him since the evening before. She was pale; she looked at him, and did not smile, and he had hardly come in when she fell on his breast. Their kiss was slow and prolonged, as though they had not met for two years.

"Well, how are you getting on there?" he asked. "What news?"   110

"Wait; I'll tell you directly. . . . I can't talk."

She could not speak; she was crying. She turned away from him, and pressed her handkerchief to her eyes.

"Let her have her cry out. I'll sit down and wait," he thought, and he sat down in an arm-chair.

Then he rang and asked for tea to be brought him, and while he drank his tea she remained standing at the window with her back to him. She was crying from emotion, from the miserable consciousness that their life was so hard for them; they could only meet in secret, hiding themselves from people, like thieves! Was not their life shattered?

"Come, do stop!" he said.   115

It was clear to him that this love of theirs would not soon be over, that he could not see the end of it. Anna Sergeyevna grew more and more attached to him. She adored him, and it was unthinkable to say to her that it was bound to have an end some day; besides, she would not have believed it!

He went up to her and took her by the shoulders to say something affectionate and cheering, and at that moment he saw himself in the looking-glass.

His hair was already beginning to turn grey. And it seemed strange to him that he had grown so much older, so much plainer during the last few years. The shoulders on which his hands rested were warm and quivering. He felt compassion for this life, still so warm and lovely, but probably already not far from beginning to fade and wither like his own. Why did she love him so much? He always seemed to women different from what he was, and they loved in him not himself, but the man created by their imagination, whom they had been eagerly seeking all their lives; and afterwards, when they noticed their mistake, they loved him all the same. And not one of them had been happy with him. Time passed, he had made their acquaintance, got on with them, parted, but he had never once loved; it was anything you like, but not love.

And only now when his head was grey he had fallen properly, really in love—for the first time in his life.

Anna Sergeyevna and he loved each other like people very close and akin, like husband and   120
wife, like tender friends; it seemed to them that fate itself had meant them for one another, and they could not understand why he had a wife and she a husband; and it was as though they were a pair of birds of passage, caught and forced to live in different cages. They forgave each other for what they were ashamed of in their past, they forgave everything in the present, and felt that this love of theirs had changed them both.

In moments of depression in the past he had comforted himself with any arguments that came into his mind, but now he no longer cared for arguments; he felt profound compassion, he wanted to be sincere and tender. . . .

"Don't cry, my darling," he said. "You've had your cry; that's enough. . . . Let us talk now, let us think of some plan."

Then they spent a long while taking counsel together, talked of how to avoid the necessity for secrecy, for deception, for living in different towns and not seeing each other for long at a time. How could they be free from this intolerable bondage?

"How? How?" he asked, clutching his head. "How?"

And it seemed as though in a little while the solution would be found, and then a new and   125
splendid life would begin; and it was clear to both of them that they had still a long, long road before them, and that the most complicated and difficult part of it was only just beginning.

[1899]

Chopin, Kate *(1851–1904)*

The Storm

I

The leaves were so still that even Bibi thought it was going to rain. Bobinôt, who was accustomed to converse on terms of perfect equality with his little son, called the child's attention to certain somber clouds that were rolling with sinister intention from the west, accompanied by a sullen, threatening roar. They were at Friedheimer's store and decided to remain there till the storm had passed. They sat within the door on two empty kegs: Bibi was four years old and looked very wise.

"Mama'll be 'fraid, yes," he suggested with blinking eyes.

"She'll shut the house. Maybe she got Sylvie helpin' her this evenin'," Bobinôt responded reassuringly.

"No; she ent got Sylvie. Sylvie was helpin' her yistiday," piped Bibi.

Bobinôt arose and going across to the counter purchased a can of shrimps, of which Calixta   5
was very fond. Then he returned to his perch on the keg and sat stolidly holding the can of shrimps while the storm burst. It shook the wooden store and seemed to be ripping great furrows in the distant field. Bibi laid his little hand on his father's knee and was not afraid.

II

Calixta, at home, felt no uneasiness for their safety. She sat at a side window sewing furiously on a sewing machine. She was greatly occupied and did not notice the approaching storm. But she felt very warm and often stopped to mop her face on which the perspiration gathered in beads.

She unfastened her white sacque at the throat. It began to grow dark, and suddenly realizing the situation she got up hurriedly and went about closing windows and doors.

Out on the small front gallery she had hung Bobinôt's Sunday clothes to air and she hastened out to gather them before the rain fell. As she stepped outside, Alcée Laballière rode in at the gate. She had not seen him very often since her marriage, and never alone. She stood there with Bobinôt's coat in her hands, and the big rain drops began to fall. Alcée rode his horse under the shelter of a side projection where the chickens had huddled and there were plows and a harrow piled up in the corner.

"May I come and wait on your gallery till the storm is over, Calixta?" he asked.

"Come 'long in, M'sieur Alcée."

His voice and her own startled her as if from a trance, and she seized Bobinôt's vest. Alcée,   10
mounting to the porch, grabbed the trousers and snatched Bibi's braided jacket that was about to be carried away by a sudden gust of wind. He expressed an intention to remain outside, but it was soon apparent that he might as well have been out in the open: the water beat in upon the boards in driving sheets, and he went inside, closing the door after him. It was even necessary to put something beneath the door to keep the water out.

"My! What a rain! It's good two years sence it rain like that," exclaimed Calixta as she rolled up a piece of bagging and Alcée helped her to thrust it beneath the crack.

She was a little fuller of figure than five years before when she married, but she had lost nothing of her vivacity. Her blue eyes still retained their melting quality; and her yellow hair, dishevelled by the wind and rain, kinked more stubbornly than ever about her ears and temples.

The rain beat upon the low, shingled roof with a force and clatter that threatened to break an entrance and deluge them there. They were in the dining room—the sitting room—the general utility room. Adjoining was her bed room, with Bibi's couch along side her own. The door stood open, and the room with its white, monumental bed, its closed shutters, looked dim and mysterious.

Alcée flung himself into a rocker and Calixta nervously began to gather up from the floor the lengths of a cotton sheet which she had been sewing.

"If this keeps up, *Dieu sait* if the levees goin' to stan' it!" she exclaimed.   15

"What have you got to do with the levees?"

"I got enough to do! An' there's Bobinôt with Bibi out in that storm—if he only didn't left Friedheimer's!"

"Let us hope, Calixta, that Bobinôt's got sense enough to come in out of a cyclone."

She went and stood at the window with a greatly disturbed look on her face. She wiped the frame that was clouded with moisture. It was stiflingly hot. Alcée got up and joined her at the window, looking over her shoulder. The rain was coming down in sheets obscuring the view of far-off cabins and enveloping the distant wood in a gray mist. The playing of the lightning was incessant. A bolt struck a tall chinaberry tree at the edge of the field. It filled all visible space with a blinding glare and the crash seemed to invade the very boards they stood upon.

Calixta put her hands to her eyes, and with a cry, staggered backward. Alcée's arm encircled   20
her, and for an instant he drew her close and spasmodically to him.

"*Bonté!*" she cried, releasing herself from his encircling arm and retreating from the window, "the house'll go next! If I only knew w'ere Bibi was!" She would not compose herself; she would not be seated. Alcée clasped her shoulders and looked into her face. The contact of her warm, palpitating body when he had unthinkingly drawn her into his arms, had aroused all the old-time infatuation and desire for her flesh.

"Calixta," he said, "don't be frightened. Nothing can happen. The house is too low to be struck, with so many tall trees standing about. There! aren't you going to be quiet? say, aren't you?" He pushed her hair back from her face that was warm and steaming. Her lips were as red and moist as pomegranate seed. Her white neck and a glimpse of her full, firm bosom disturbed him powerfully. As she glanced up at him the fear in her liquid blue eyes had given place to a drowsy gleam that unconsciously betrayed a sensuous desire. He looked down into her eyes and there was nothing for him to do but to gather her lips in a kiss. It reminded him of Assumption.

"Do you remember—in Assumption, Calixta?" he asked in a low voice broken by passion. Oh! she remembered; for in Assumption he had kissed her and kissed and kissed her; until his senses would well nigh fail, and to save her he would resort to a desperate flight. If she was not an immaculate dove in those days, she was still inviolate; a passionate creature whose very defenselessness had made her defense, against which his honor forbade him to prevail. Now—well, now—her lips seemed in a manner free to be tasted, as well as her round, white throat and her whiter breasts.

They did not heed the crashing torrents, and the roar of the elements made her laugh as she lay in his arms. She was a revelation in that dim, mysterious chamber; as white as the couch she lay upon. Her firm, elastic flesh that was knowing for the first time its birthright, was like a creamy lily that the sun invites to contribute its breath and perfume to the undying life of the world.

The generous abundance of her passion, without guile or trickery, was like a white flame   25 which penetrated and found response in depths of his own sensuous nature that had never yet been reached.

When he touched her breasts they gave themselves up in quivering ecstasy, inviting his lips. Her mouth was a fountain of delight. And when he possessed her, they seemed to swoon together at the very borderland of life's mystery.

He stayed cushioned upon her, breathless, dazed, enervated, with his heart beating like a hammer upon her. With one hand she clasped his head, her lips lightly touching his forehead. The other hand stroked with a soothing rhythm his muscular shoulders.

The growl of the thunder was distant and passing away. The rain beat softly upon the shingles, inviting them to drowsiness and sleep. But they dared not yield.

The rain was over; and the sun was turning the glistening green world into a palace of gems. Calixta, on the gallery, watched Alcée ride away. He turned and smiled at her with a beaming face, and she lifted her pretty chin in the air and laughed aloud.

III

Bobinôt and Bibi, trudging home, stopped without at the cistern to make themselves presentable.   30

"My! Bibi, w'at will yo' mama say! You ought to be ashame'. You oughtn' put on those good pants. Look at 'em! An' that mud on yo' collar! How you got that mud on yo' collar, Bibi? I never saw such a boy!" Bibi was the picture of pathetic resignation. Bobinôt was the embodiment of serious solicitude as he strove to remove from his own person and his son's the signs of their tramp over heavy roads and through wet fields. He scraped the mud off Bibi's bare legs and feet with a stick and carefully removed all traces from his heavy brogans. Then, prepared for the worst—the meeting with an over-scrupulous housewife, they entered cautiously at the back door.

Calixta was preparing supper. She had set the table and was dripping coffee at the hearth. She sprang up as they came in.

"Oh, Bobinôt! You back! My! but I was uneasy. W'ere you been during the rain? An' Bibi? he ain't wet? he ain't hurt?" She had clasped Bibi and was kissing him effusively. Bobinôt's explanations and apologies which he had been composing all along the way, died on his lips as Calixta felt him to see if he were dry, and seemed to express nothing but satisfaction at their safe return.

"I brought you some shrimps, Calixta," offered Bobinôt, hauling the can from his ample side pocket and laying it on the table.

"Shrimps! Oh, Bobinôt! you too good fo' anything!" and she gave him a smacking kiss on the   35 cheek that resounded. "J'vous responds, we'll have a feas' to night! umph-umph!"

Bobinôt and Bibi began to relax and enjoy themselves, and when the three seated themselves at table they laughed much and so loud that anyone might have heard them as far away as Laballière's.

IV

Alcée Laballière wrote to his wife, Clarisse, that night. It was a loving letter, full of tender solicitude. He told her not to hurry back, but if she and the babies liked it at Biloxi, to stay a month
longer. He was getting on nicely; and though he missed them, he was willing to bear the separation a while longer—realizing that their health and pleasure were the first things to be considered.

V

As for Clarisse, she was charmed upon receiving her husband's letter. She and the babies were
doing well. The society was agreeable; many of her old friends and acquaintances were at the bay.
And the first free breath since her marriage seemed to restore the pleasant liberty of her maiden
days. Devoted as she was to her husband, their intimate conjugal life was something which she
was more than willing to forego for a while.

So the storm passed and everyone was happy.

[1898]

The Story of an Hour

Knowing that Mrs. Mallard was afflicted with a heart trouble, great care was taken to break to her
as gently as possible the news of her husband's death.

It was her sister Josephine who told her, in broken sentences: veiled hints that revealed in
half concealing. Her husband's friend Richards was there, too, near her. It was he who had been
in the newspaper office when intelligence of the railroad disaster was received, with Brently
Mallard's name leading the list of "killed." He had only taken the time to assure himself of its
truth by a second telegram, and had hastened to forestall any less careful, less tender friend in
bearing the sad message.

She did not hear the story as many women have heard the same, with a paralyzed inability to
accept its significance. She wept at once, with sudden, wild abandonment, in her sister's arms.
When the storm of grief had spent itself she went away to her room alone. She would have no
one follow her.

There stood, facing the open window, a comfortable, roomy armchair. Into this she sank,
pressed down by a physical exhaustion that haunted her body and seemed to reach into her soul.

She could see in the open square before her house the tops of trees that were all aquiver 5
with the new spring life. The delicious breath of rain was in the air. In the street below a peddler
was crying his wares. The notes of a distant song which some one was singing reached her faintly,
and countless sparrows were twittering in the eaves.

There were patches of blue sky showing here and there through the clouds that had met and
piled one above the other in the west facing her window.

She sat with her head thrown back upon the cushion of the chair, quite motionless, except
when a sob came up into her throat and shook her, as a child who has cried itself to sleep continues to sob in its dreams.

She was young, with a fair, calm face, whose lines bespoke repression and even a certain
strength. But now there was a dull stare in her eyes, whose gaze was fixed away off yonder on one
of those patches of blue sky. It was not a glance of reflection, but rather indicated a suspension of
intelligent thought.

There was something coming to her and she was waiting for it, fearfully. What was it? She did
not know; it was too subtle and elusive to name. But she felt it, creeping out of the sky, reaching
toward her through the sounds, the scents, the color that filled the air.

Now her bosom rose and fell tumultuously. She was beginning to recognize this thing that 10
was approaching to possess her, and she was striving to beat it back with her will—as powerless as
her two white slender hands would have been.

When she abandoned herself a little whispered word escaped her slightly parted lips. She said it over and over under her breath: "free, free, free!" The vacant stare and the look of terror that had followed it went from her eyes. They stayed keen and bright. Her pulses beat fast, and the coursing blood warmed and relaxed every inch of her body.

She did not stop to ask if it were or were not a monstrous joy that held her. A clear and exalted perception enabled her to dismiss the suggestion as trivial.

She knew that she would weep again when she saw the kind, tender hands folded in death; the face that had never looked save with love upon her, fixed and gray and dead. But she saw beyond that bitter moment a long procession of years to come that would belong to her absolutely. And she opened and spread her arms out to them in welcome.

There would be no one to live for during those coming years; she would live for herself. There would be no powerful will bending hers in that blind persistence with which men and women believe they have a right to impose a private will upon a fellow-creature. A kind intention or a cruel intention made the act seem no less a crime as she looked upon it in that brief moment of illumination.

And yet she had loved him—sometimes. Often she had not. What did it matter! What could 15 love, the unsolved mystery, count for in face of this possession of self-assertion which she suddenly recognized as the strongest impulse of her being!

"Free! Body and soul free!" she kept whispering.

Josephine was kneeling before the closed door with her lips to the keyhole, imploring for admission. "Louise, open the door! I beg; open the door—you will make yourself ill. What are you doing, Louise? For heaven's sake open the door."

"Go away. I am not making myself ill." No; she was drinking in a very elixir of life through that open window.

Her fancy was running riot along those days ahead of her. Spring days, and summer days, and all sorts of days that would be her own. She breathed a quick prayer that life might be long. It was only yesterday she had thought with a shudder that life might be long.

She arose at length and opened the door to her sister's importunities. There was a feverish 20 triumph in her eyes, and she carried herself unwittingly like a goddess of Victory. She clasped her sister's waist, and together they descended the stairs. Richards stood waiting for them at the bottom.

Some one was opening the front door with a latchkey. It was Brently Mallard who entered, a little travel-stained, composedly carrying his grip-sack and umbrella. He had been far from the scene of the accident, and did not even know there had been one. He stood amazed at Josephine's piercing cry: at Richards' quick motion to screen him from the view of his wife.

But Richards was too late.

When the doctors came they said she had died of heart disease—of joy that kills.

[1894]

Faulkner, Willliam (1897–1962)

A Rose for Emily

I

When Miss Emily Grierson died, our whole town went to her funeral: the men through a sort of respectful affection for a fallen monument, the women mostly out of curiosity to see the inside of her house, which no one save an old manservant—a combined gardener and cook—had seen in at least ten years.

It was a big, squarish frame house that had once been white, decorated with cupolas and spires and scrolled balconies in the heavily lightsome style of the seventies, set on what had once been our most select street. But garages and cotton gins had encroached and obliterated even the august names of that neighborhood; only Miss Emily's house was left, lifting its stubborn and coquettish decay above the cotton wagons and the gasoline pumps—an eyesore among eyesores. And now Miss Emily had gone to join the representatives of those august names where they lay in the cedar-bemused cemetery among the ranked and anonymous graves of Union and Confederate soldiers who fell at the battle of Jefferson.

Alive, Miss Emily had been a tradition, a duty, and a care; a sort of hereditary obligation upon the town, dating from that day in 1894 when Colonel Sartoris, the mayor—he who fathered the edict that no Negro woman should appear on the streets without an apron—remitted her taxes, the dispensation dating from the death of her father on into perpetuity. Not that Miss Emily would have accepted charity. Colonel Sartoris invented an involved tale to the effect that Miss Emily's father had loaned money to the town, which the town, as a matter of business, preferred this way of repaying. Only a man of Colonel Sartoris' generation and thought could have invented it, and only a woman could have believed it.

When the next generation, with its more modern ideas, became mayors and aldermen, this arrangement created some little dissatisfaction. On the first of the year they mailed her a tax notice. February came, and there was no reply. They wrote her a formal letter, asking her to call at the sheriff's office at her convenience. A week later the mayor wrote her himself, offering to call or to send his car for her, and received in reply a note on paper of an archaic shape, in a thin, flowing calligraphy in faded ink, to the effect that she no longer went out at all. The tax notice was also enclosed, without comment.

They called a special meeting of the Board of Aldermen. A deputation waited upon her, 5 knocked at the door through which no visitor had passed since she ceased giving china-painting lessons eight or ten years earlier. They were admitted by the old Negro into a dim hall from which a stairway mounted into still more shadow. It smelled of dust and disuse—a close, dank smell. The Negro led them into the parlor. It was furnished in heavy, leather-covered furniture. When the Negro opened the blinds of one window, they could see that the leather was cracked; and when they sat down, a faint dust rose sluggishly about their thighs, spinning with slow motes in the single sunray. On a tarnished gilt easel before the fireplace stood a crayon portrait of Miss Emily's father.

They rose when she entered—a small, fat woman in black, with a thin gold chain descending to her waist and vanishing into her belt, leaning on an ebony cane with a tarnished gold head. Her skeleton was small and spare; perhaps that was why what would have been merely plumpness in another was obesity in her. She looked bloated, like a body long submerged in motionless water, and of that pallid hue. Her eyes, lost in the fatty ridges of her face, looked like two small pieces of coal pressed into a lump of dough as they moved from one face to another while the visitors stated their errand.

She did not ask them to sit. She just stood in the door and listened quietly until the spokesman came to a stumbling halt. Then they could hear the invisible watch ticking at the end of the gold chain.

Her voice was dry and cold. "I have no taxes in Jefferson. Colonel Sartoris explained it to me. Perhaps one of you can gain access to the city records and satisfy yourselves."

"But we have. We are the city authorities, Miss Emily. Didn't you get a notice from the sheriff, signed by him?"

"I received a paper, yes," Miss Emily said. "Perhaps he considers himself the sheriff . . . I have 10 no taxes in Jefferson."

"But there is nothing on the books to show that, you see. We must go by the—"

"See Colonel Sartoris. I have no taxes in Jefferson."

"But, Miss Emily—"

"See Colonel Sartoris." (Colonel Sartoris had been dead almost ten years.) "I have no taxes in Jefferson. Tobe!" The Negro appeared. "Show these gentle-men out."

II

So she vanquished them, horse and foot, just as she had vanquished their fathers thirty years 15
before about the smell. That was two years after her father's death and a short time after her
sweetheart—the one we believed would marry her—had deserted her. After her father's death
she went out very little; after her sweetheart went away, people hardly saw her at all. A few of the
ladies had the temerity to call, but were not received, and the only sign of life about the place was
the Negro man—a young man then—going in and out with a market basket.

"Just as if a man—any man—could keep a kitchen properly," the ladies said; so they were not
surprised when the smell developed. It was another link between the gross, teeming world and
the high and mighty Griersons.

A neighbor, a woman, complained to the mayor, Judge Stevens, eighty years old.

"But what will you have me do about it, madam?" he said.

"Why, send her word to stop it," the woman said. "Isn't there a law?"

"I'm sure that won't be necessary," Judge Stevens said. "It's probably just a snake or a rat that 20
nigger of hers killed in the yard. I'll speak to him about it."

The next day he received two more complaints, one from a man who came in diffident depreca-
tion. "We really must do something about it, Judge. I'd be the last one in the world to bother Miss
Emily, but we've got to do something." That night the Board of Aldermen met—three graybeards and
one younger man, a member of the rising generation.

"It's simple enough," he said. "Send her word to have her place cleaned up. Give her a certain time to do it in; and if she don't . . ."

"Dammit, sir," Judge Stevens said, "will you accuse a lady to her face of smelling bad?"

So the next night, after midnight, four men crossed Miss Emily's lawn and slunk about
the house like burglars, sniffing along the base of the brickwork and at the cellar openings
while one of them performed a regular sowing motion with his hand out of a sack slung from
his shoulder. They broke open the cellar door and sprinkled lime there, and in all the out-
buildings. As they recrossed the lawn, a window that had been dark was lighted and Miss Emily
sat in it, the light behind her, and her upright torso motionless as that of an idol. They crept
quietly across the lawn and into the shadow of the locusts that lined the street. After a week or
two the smell went away.

That was when people had begun to feel really sorry for her. People in our town, remember- 25
ing how old lady Wyatt, her great-aunt, had gone completely crazy at last, believed that the
Griersons held themselves a little too high for what they really were. None of the young men were
quite good enough for Miss Emily and such. We had long thought of them as a tableau, Miss
Emily a slender figure in white in the background, her father a spraddled silhouette in the fore-
ground, his back to her and clutching a horsewhip, the two of them framed by the back-flung
front door. So when she got to be thirty and was still single, we were not pleased exactly, but vindicated; even with insanity in the family she wouldn't have turned down all of her chances if they
had really materialized.

When her father died, it got about that the house was all that was left to her; and in a way, people were glad. At last they could pity Miss Emily. Being left alone, and a pauper, she had become
humanized. Now she too would know the old thrill and the old despair of a penny more or less.

The day after his death all the ladies prepared to call at the house and offer condolence and
aid, as is our custom. Miss Emily met them at the door, dressed as usual and with no trace of grief
on her face. She told them that her father was not dead. She did that for three days, with the min-
isters calling on her, and the doctors, trying to persuade her to let them dispose of the body. Just
as they were about to resort to law and force, she broke down, and they buried her father quickly.

We did not say she was crazy then. We believed she had to do that. We remembered all the
young men her father had driven away, and we knew that with nothing left, she would have to
cling to that which had robbed her, as people will.

III

She was sick for a long time. When we saw her again, her hair was cut short, making her look like a girl, with a vague resemblance to those angels in colored church windows—sort of tragic and serene.

The town had just let the contracts for paving the sidewalks, and in the summer after her 30 father's death they began the work. The construction company came with niggers and mules and machinery, and a foreman named Homer Barron, a Yankee—a big, dark, ready man, with a big voice and eyes lighter than his face. The little boys would follow in groups to hear him cuss the niggers, and the niggers singing in time to the rise and fall of picks. Pretty soon he knew everybody in town. Whenever you heard a lot of laughing anywhere about the square, Homer Barron would be in the center of the group. Presently we began to see him and Miss Emily on Sunday afternoons driving in the yellow-wheeled buggy and the matched team of bays from the livery stable.

At first we were glad that Miss Emily would have an interest, because the ladies all said, "Of course a Grierson would not think seriously of a Northerner, a day laborer." But there were still others, older people, who said that even grief could not cause a real lady to forget *noblesse oblige*—without calling it *noblesse oblige*. They just said, "Poor Emily. Her kinsfolk should come to her." She had some kin in Alabama; but years ago her father had fallen out with them over the estate of old lady Wyatt, the crazy woman, and there was no communication between the two families. They had not even been represented at the funeral.

And as soon as the old people said, "Poor Emily," the whispering began. "Do you suppose it's really so?" they said to one another. "Of course it is. What else could . . ." This behind their hands; rustling of craned silk and satin behind jalousies closed upon the sun of Sunday afternoon as the thin, swift clop-clop-clop of the matched team passed: "Poor Emily."

She carried her head high enough—even when we believed that she was fallen. It was as if she demanded more than ever the recognition of her dignity as the last Grierson, as if it had wanted that touch of earthiness to reaffirm her imperviousness. Like when she bought the rat poison, the arsenic. That was over a year after they had begun to say "Poor Emily," and while the two female cousins were visiting her.

"I want some poison," she said to the druggist. She was over thirty then, still a slight woman, though thinner than usual, with cold, haughty black eyes in a face the flesh of which was strained across the temples and about the eyesockets as you imagine a lighthouse-keeper's face ought to look. "I want some poison," she said.

"Yes, Miss Emily. What kind? For rats and such? I'd recom—"   35

"I want the best you have. I don't care what kind."

The druggist named several. "They'll kill anything up to an elephant. But what you want is—"

"Arsenic," Miss Emily said. "Is that a good one?"

"Is . . . arsenic? Yes, ma'am. But what you want—"

"I want arsenic."   40

The druggist looked down at her. She looked back at him, erect, her face like a strained flag. "Why, of course," the druggist said. "If that's what you want. But the law requires you to tell what you are going to use it for."

Miss Emily just stared at him, her head tilted back in order to look him eye for eye, until he looked away and went and got the arsenic and wrapped it up. The Negro delivery boy brought her the package; the druggist didn't come back. When she opened the package at home there was written on the box, under the skull and bones: "For rats."

IV

So the next day we all said, "She will kill herself"; and we said it would be the best thing. When she had first begun to be seen with Homer Barron, we had said, "She will marry him." Then we said, "She will persuade him yet," because Homer himself had remarked—he liked men, and it was known that he drank with the younger men in the Elks' Club—that he was not a marrying man. Later we said, "Poor Emily" behind the jalousies as they passed on Sunday afternoon in the glittering buggy. Miss Emily with her head high and Homer Barron with his hat cocked and a cigar in his teeth, reins and whip in a yellow glove.

Then some of the ladies began to say that it was a disgrace to the town and a bad example to the young people. The men did not want to interfere, but at last the ladies forced the Baptist minister—Miss Emily's people were Episcopal—to call upon her. He would never divulge what happened during that interview, but he refused to go back again. The next Sunday they again drove about the streets, and the following day the minister's wife wrote to Miss Emily's relations in Alabama.

So she had blood-kin under her roof again and we sat back to watch developments. At first 45 nothing happened. Then we were sure that they were to be married. We learned that Miss Emily had been to the jeweler's and ordered a man's toilet set in silver, with the letters H. B. on each piece. Two days later we learned that she had bought a complete outfit of men's clothing, including a nightshirt, and we said, "They are married." We were really glad. We were glad because the two female cousins were even more Grierson than Miss Emily had ever been.

So we were not surprised when Homer Barron—the streets had been finished some time since—was gone. We were a little disappointed that there was not a public blowing-off, but we believed that he had gone on to prepare for Miss Emily's coming, or to give her a chance to get rid of the cousins. (By that time it was a cabal, and we were all Miss Emily's allies to help circumvent the cousins.) Sure enough, after another week they departed. And, as we had expected all along, within three days Homer Barron was back in town. A neighbor saw the Negro man admit him at the kitchen door at dusk one evening.

And that was the last we saw of Homer Barron. And of Miss Emily for some time. The Negro man went in and out with the market basket, but the front door remained closed. Now and then we would see her at a window for a moment, as the men did that night when they sprinkled the lime, but for almost six months she did not appear on the streets. Then we knew that this was to be expected too; as if that quality of her father which had thwarted her woman's life so many times had been too virulent and too furious to die.

When we next saw Miss Emily, she had grown fat and her hair was turning gray. During the next few years it grew grayer and grayer until it attained an even pepper-and-salt iron-gray, when it ceased turning. Up to the day of her death at seventy-four it was still that vigorous iron-gray, like the hair of an active man.

From that time on her front door remained closed, save for a period of six or seven years, when she was about forty, during which she gave lessons in china-painting. She fitted up a studio in one of the downstairs rooms, where the daughters and granddaughters of Colonel Sartoris' contemporaries were sent to her with the same regularity and in the same spirit that they were sent to church on Sundays with a twenty-five-cent piece for the collection plate. Meanwhile her taxes had been remitted.

Then the newer generation became the backbone and the spirit of the town, and the painting 50 pupils grew up and fell away and did not send their children to her with boxes of color and tedious brushes and pictures cut from the ladies' magazines. The front door closed upon the last one and remained closed for good. When the town got free postal delivery, Miss Emily alone refused to let them fasten the metal numbers above her door and attach a mailbox to it. She would not listen to them.

Daily, monthly, yearly we watched the Negro grow grayer and more stooped, going in and out with the market basket. Each December we sent her a tax notice, which would be returned by the post office a week later, unclaimed. Now and then we would see her in one of the downstairs windows—she had evidently shut up the top floor of the house—like the carven torso of an idol in a niche, looking or not looking at us, we could never tell which. Thus she passed from generation to generation—dear, inescapable, impervious, tranquil, and perverse.

And so she died. Fell ill in the house filled with dust and shadows, with only a doddering Negro man to wait on her. We did not even know she was sick; we had long since given up trying to get any information from the Negro. He talked to no one, probably not even to her, for his voice had grown harsh and rusty, as if from disuse.

She died in one of the downstairs rooms, in a heavy walnut bed with a curtain, her gray head propped on a pillow yellow and moldy with age and lack of sunlight.

V

The Negro met the first of the ladies at the front door and let them in, with their hushed, sibilant voices and their quick, curious glances, and then he disappeared. He walked right through the house and out the back and was not seen again.

The two female cousins came at once. They held the funeral on the second day, with the town coming to look at Miss Emily beneath a mass of bought flowers, with the crayon face of her father musing profoundly above the bier and the ladies sibilant and macabre; and the very old men—some in their brushed Confederate uniforms—on the porch and the lawn, talking of Miss Emily as if she had been a contemporary of theirs, believing that they had danced with her and courted her perhaps, confusing time with its mathematical progression, as the old do, to whom all the past is not a diminishing road but, instead, a huge meadow which no winter ever quite touches, divided from them now by the narrow bottle-neck of the most recent decade of years.

Already we knew that there was one room in that region above stairs which no one had seen in forty years, and which would have to be forced. They waited until Miss Emily was decently in the ground before they opened it.

The violence of breaking down the door seemed to fill this room with pervading dust. A thin, acrid pall as of the tomb seemed to lie everywhere upon this room decked and furnished as for a bridal: upon the valance curtains of faded rose color, upon the rose-shaded lights, upon the dressing table, upon the delicate array of crystal and the man's toilet things backed with tarnished silver, silver so tarnished that the monogram was obscured. Among them lay a collar and tie, as if they had just been removed, which, lifted, left upon the surface a pale crescent in the dust. Upon a chair hung the suit, carefully folded; beneath it the two mute shoes and the discarded socks.

The man himself lay in the bed.

For a long while we just stood there, looking down at the profound and fleshless grin. The body had apparently once lain in the attitude of an embrace, but now the long sleep that outlasts love, that conquers even the grimace of love, had cuckolded him. What was left of him, rotted beneath what was left of the night-shirt, had become inextricable from the bed in which he lay; and upon him and upon the pillow beside him lay that even coating of the patient and biding dust.

Then we noticed that in the second pillow was the indentation of a head. One of us lifted something from it, and leaning forward, that faint and invisible dust dry and acrid in the nostrils, we saw a long strand of iron-gray hair.

[1931]

Hawthorne, *Nathaniel (1804–1864)*

Young Goodman Brown

Young Goodman Brown came forth at sunset, into the street of Salem village, but put his head back, after crossing the threshold, to exchange a parting kiss with his young wife. And Faith, as the wife was aptly named, thrust her own pretty head into the street, letting the wind play with the pink ribbons of her cap, while she called to Goodman Brown.

"Dearest heart," whispered she, softly and rather sadly, when her lips were close to his ear, "prithee, put off your journey until sunrise, and sleep in your own bed tonight. A lone woman is troubled with such dreams and such thoughts, that she's afeared of herself, sometimes. Pray, tarry with me this night, dear husband, of all nights in the year!"

"My love and my Faith," replied young Goodman Brown, "of all nights in the year, this one night must I tarry away from thee. My journey, as thou callest it, forth and back again, must needs be done 'twixt now and sunrise. What, my sweet, pretty wife, dost thou doubt me already, and we but three months married!"

"Then God bless you!" said Faith with the pink ribbons, "and may you find all well, when you come back."

"Amen!" cried Goodman Brown. "Say thy prayers, dear Faith, and go to bed at dusk, and no 5 harm will come to thee."

So they parted; and the young man pursued his way, until, being about to turn the corner by the meeting-house, he looked back and saw the head of Faith still peeping after him, with a melancholy air, in spite of her pink ribbons.

"Poor little Faith!" thought he, for his heart smote him. "What a wretch am I, to leave her on such an errand! She talks of dreams, too. Methought, as she spoke, there was trouble in her face, as if a dream had warned her what work is to be done tonight. But no, no! 't would kill her to think it. Well; she's a blessed angel on earth; and after this one night, I'll cling to her skirts and follow her to Heaven."

With this excellent resolve for the future, Goodman Brown felt himself justified in making more haste on his present evil purpose. He had taken a dreary road, darkened by all the gloomiest trees of the forest, which barely stood aside to let the narrow path creep through, and closed immediately behind. It was all as lonely as could be; and there is this peculiarity in such a solitude, that the traveller knows not who may be concealed by the innumerable trunks and the thick boughs overhead; so that, with lonely footsteps, he may yet be passing through an unseen multitude.

"There may be a devilish Indian behind every tree," said Goodman Brown to himself; and he glanced fearfully behind him, as he added, "What if the devil himself should be at my very elbow!"

His head being turned back, he passed a crook of the road, and looking forward again, 10 beheld the figure of a man, in grave and decent attire, seated at the foot of an old tree. He arose at Goodman Brown's approach, and walked onward, side by side with him.

"You are late, Goodman Brown," said he. "The clock of the Old South was striking, as I came through Boston; and that is full fifteen minutes agone."

"Faith kept me back awhile," replied the young man, with a tremor in his voice, caused by the sudden appearance of his companion, though not wholly unexpected.

It was now deep dusk in the forest, and deepest in that part of it where these two were journeying. As nearly as could be discerned, the second traveller was about fifty years old, apparently in the same rank of life as Goodman Brown, and bearing a considerable resemblance to him, though perhaps more in expression than features. Still, they might have been taken for father and son. And yet, though the elder person was as simply clad as the younger, and as simple in manner too, he had an indescribable air of one who knew the world, and would not have felt abashed at the governor's dinner-table, or in King William's court, were it possible that his affairs should call him thither. But the only thing about him that could be fixed upon as remarkable, was his staff, which bore the likeness of a great black snake, so curiously wrought, that it might almost be seen to twist and wriggle itself like a living serpent. This, of course, must have been an ocular deception, assisted by the uncertain light.

"Come, Goodman Brown!" cried his fellow-traveller, "this is a dull pace for the beginning of a journey. Take my staff, if you are so soon weary."

"Friend," said the other, exchanging his slow pace for a full stop, "having kept covenant by 15 meeting thee here, it is my purpose now to return whence I came. I have scruples, touching the matter thou wot'st of.

"Sayest thou so?" replied he of the serpent, smiling apart. "Let us walk on, nevertheless, reasoning as we go, and if I convince thee not, thou shalt turn back. We are but a little way in the forest, yet."

"Too far, too far!" exclaimed the goodman, unconsciously resuming his walk. "My father never went into the woods on such an errand, nor his father before him. We have been a race of honest men and good Christians, since the days of the martyrs. And shall I be the first of the name of Brown that ever took this path and kept—"

"Such company, thou wouldst say," observed the elder person, interrupting his pause. "Well said, Goodman Brown! I have been as well acquainted with your family as ever a one among the Puritans; and that's no trifle to say. I helped your grandfather, the constable, when he lashed the Quaker woman so smartly through the streets of Salem. And it was I that brought your father a pitch-pine knot, kindled at my own hearth, to set fire to an Indian village, in King Philip's war. They were my good friends, both; and many a pleasant walk have we had along this path, and returned merrily after midnight. I would fain be friends with you, for their sake."

"If it be as thou sayest," replied Goodman Brown, "I marvel they never spoke of these matters. Or, verily, I marvel not, seeing that the least rumor of the sort would have driven them from New England. We are a people of prayer, and good works to boot, and abide no such wickedness."

"Wickedness or not," said the traveller with twisted staff, "I have a very general acquaintance   20 here in New England. The deacons of many a church have drunk the communion wine with me; the selectmen, of divers towns, make me their chairman; and a majority of the Great and General Court are firm supporters of my interest. The governor and I, too—but these are state secrets."

"Can this be so!" cried Goodman Brown, with a stare of amazement at his undisturbed companion. "Howbeit, I have nothing to do with the governor and council; they have their own ways, and are no rule for a simple husbandman like me. But, were I to go on with thee, how should I meet the eye of that good old man, our minister, at Salem village? Oh, his voice would make me tremble, both Sabbath-day and lecture-day!"

Thus far, the elder traveller had listened with due gravity, but now burst into a fit of irrepressible mirth, shaking himself so violently, that his snakelike staff actually seemed to wriggle in sympathy.

"Ha! ha! ha!" shouted he, again and again; then composing himself, "Well, go on, Goodman Brown, go on; but, prithee, don't kill me with laughing!"

"Well, then, to end the matter at once," said Goodman Brown, considerably nettled, "there is my wife, Faith. It would break her dear little heart; and I'd rather break my own!"

"Nay, if that be the case," answered the other, "e'en go thy ways, Goodman Brown. I would not,   25 for twenty old women like the one hobbling before us, that Faith should come to any harm."

As he spoke, he pointed his staff at a female figure on the path, in whom Goodman Brown recognized a very pious and exemplary dame, who had taught him his catechism in youth, and was still his moral and spiritual adviser, jointly with the minister and Deacon Gookin.

"A marvel, truly, that Goody Cloyse should be so far in the wilderness, at nightfall!" said he. "But, with your leave, friend, I shall take a cut through the woods, until we have left this Christian woman behind. Being a stranger to you, she might ask whom I was consorting with, and whither I was going."

"Be it so," said his fellow-traveller. "Betake you to the woods, and let me keep the path."

Accordingly, the young man turned aside, but took care to watch his companion, who advanced softly along the road, until he had come within a staff's length of the old dame. She, meanwhile, was making the best of her way, with singular speed for so aged a woman, and mumbling some indistinct words, a prayer, doubtless, as she went. The traveller put forth his staff, and touched her withered neck with what seemed the serpent's tail.

"The devil!" screamed the pious old lady.   30

"Then Goody Cloyse knows her old friend?" observed the traveller, confronting her, and leaning on his writhing stick.

"Ah, forsooth, and is it your worship, indeed?" cried the good dame. "Yea, truly is it, and in the very image of my old gossip, Goodman Brown, the grandfather of the silly fellow that now is. But, would your worship believe it? My broomstick hath strangely disappeared, stolen, as I suspect, by that unhanged witch, Goody Cory, and that, too, when I was all anointed with the juice of smallage and cinquefoil and wolf's-bane—"

"Mingled with fine wheat and the fat of a new-born babe," said the shape of old Goodman Brown.

"Ah, your worship knows the recipe," cried the old lady, cackling aloud. "So, as I was saying, being all ready for the meeting, and no horse to ride on, I made up my mind to foot it; for they tell me there is a nice young man to be taken into communion tonight. But now your good worship will lend me your arm, and we shall be there in a twinkling."

"That can hardly be," answered her friend. "I will not spare you my arm, Goody Cloyse, but 35
here is my staff, if you will."

So saying, he threw it down at her feet, where, perhaps, it assumed life, being one of the rods
which its owner had formerly lent to the Egyptian Magi. Of this fact, however, Goodman Brown
could not take cognizance. He had cast up his eyes in astonishment, and looking down again,
beheld neither Goody Cloyse nor the serpentine staff, but his fellow-traveller alone, who waited
for him as calmly as if nothing had happened.

"That old woman taught me my catechism!" said the young man; and there was a world of
meaning in this simple comment.

They continued to walk onward, while the elder traveller exhorted his companion to make
good speed and persevere in the path, discoursing so aptly, that his arguments seemed rather to
spring up in the bosom of his auditor, than to be suggested by himself. As they went he plucked a
branch of maple, to serve for a walking-stick, and began to strip it of the twigs and little boughs,
which were wet with evening dew. The moment his fingers touched them, they became strangely
withered and dried up, as with a week's sunshine. Thus the pair proceeded, at a good free pace,
until suddenly, in a gloomy hollow of the road, Goodman Brown sat himself down on the stump of
a tree, and refused to go any farther.

"Friend," said he, stubbornly, "my mind is made up. Not another step will I budge on this
errand. What if a wretched old woman do choose to go to the devil, when I thought she was going
to Heaven! Is that any reason why I should quit my dear Faith, and go after her?"

"You will think better of this by and by," said his acquaintance, composedly. "Sit here and rest 40
yourself a while; and when you feel like moving again, there is my staff to help you along."

Without more words, he threw his companion the maple stick, and was as speedily out of
sight as if he had vanished into the deepening gloom. The young man sat a few moments by the
roadside, applauding himself greatly, and thinking with how clear a conscience he should meet
the minister, in his morning walk, nor shrink from the eye of good old Deacon Gookin. And what
calm sleep would be his, that very night, which was to have been spent so wickedly, but purely and
sweetly now, in the arms of Faith! Amidst these pleasant and praiseworthy meditations, Goodman
Brown heard the tramp of horses along the road, and deemed it advisable to conceal himself
within the verge of the forest, conscious of the guilty purpose that had brought him thither,
though now so happily turned from it.

On came the hoof-tramps and the voices of the riders, two grave old voices, conversing
soberly as they drew near. These mingled sounds appeared to pass along the road, within a few
yards of the young man's hiding-place; but owing, doubtless, to the depth of the gloom, at that
particular spot, neither the travellers nor their steeds were visible. Though their figures brushed
the small boughs by the wayside, it could not be seen that they intercepted, even for a moment,
the faint gleam from the strip of bright sky, athwart which they must have passed. Goodman Brown
alternately crouched and stood on tiptoe, pulling aside the branches, and thrusting forth his head
as far as he durst, without discerning so much as a shadow. It vexed him the more, because he
could have sworn, were such a thing possible, that he recognized the voices of the minister and
Deacon Gookin, jogging along quietly, as they were wont to do, when bound to some ordination
or ecclesiastical council. While yet within hearing, one of the riders stopped to pluck a switch.

"Of the two, reverend Sir," said the voice like the deacon's, "I had rather miss an ordination
dinner than to-night's meeting. They tell me that some of our community are to be here from
Falmouth and beyond, and others from Connecticut and Rhode Island; besides several of the
Indian powwows, who, after their fashion, know almost as much deviltry as the best of us.
Moreover, there is a goodly young woman to be taken into communion."

"Mighty well, Deacon Gookin!" replied the solemn old tones of the minister. "Spur up, or we
shall be late. Nothing can be done, you know, until I get on the ground."

The hoofs clattered again, and the voices, talking so strangely in the empty air, passed on 45
through the forest, where no church had ever been gathered, nor solitary Christian prayed.

Whither, then, could these holy men be journeying, so deep into the heathen wilderness? Young Goodman Brown caught hold of a tree, for support, being ready to sink down on the ground, faint and over-burthened with the heavy sickness of his heart. He looked up to the sky, doubting whether there really was a Heaven above him. Yet, there was the blue arch, and the stars brightening in it.

"With Heaven above, and Faith below, I will yet stand firm against the devil!" cried Goodman Brown.

While he still gazed upward, into the deep arch of the firmament, and had lifted his hands to pray, a cloud, though no wind was stirring, hurried across the zenith, and hid the brightening stars. The blue sky was still visible, except directly overhead, where this black mass of cloud was sweeping swiftly northward. Aloft in the air, as if from the depths of the cloud, came a confused and doubtful sound of voices. Once, the listener fancied that he could distinguish the accents of town's people of his own, men and women, both pious and ungodly, many of whom he had met at the communion-table, and had seen others rioting at the tavern. The next moment, so indistinct were the sounds, he doubted whether he had heard aught but the murmur of the old forest, whispering without a wind. Then came a stronger swell of those familiar tones, heard daily in the sunshine, at Salem village, but never, until now, from a cloud at night. There was one voice, of a young woman, uttering lamentations, yet with an uncertain sorrow, and entreating for some favor, which, perhaps, it would grieve her to obtain. And all the unseen multitude, both saints and sinners, seemed to encourage her onward.

"Faith!" shouted Goodman Brown, in a voice of agony and desperation; and the echoes of the forest mocked him, crying—"Faith! Faith!" as if bewildered wretches were seeking her, all through the wilderness.

The cry of grief, rage, and terror was yet piercing the night, when the unhappy husband held his breath for a response. There was a scream, drowned immediately in a louder murmur of voices fading into far-off laughter, as the dark cloud swept away, leaving the clear and silent sky above Goodman Brown. But something fluttered lightly down through the air, and caught on the branch of a tree. The young man seized it and beheld a pink ribbon.

"My Faith is gone!" cried he, after one stupefied moment. "There is no good on earth, and   50 sin is but a name. Come, devil! for to thee is this world given."

And maddened with despair, so that he laughed loud and long, did Goodman Brown grasp his staff and set forth again, at such a rate, that he seemed to fly along the forest path, rather than to walk or run. The road grew wilder and drearier, and more faintly traced, and vanished at length, leaving him in the heart of the dark wilderness, still rushing onward, with the instinct that guides mortal man to evil. The whole forest was peopled with frightful sounds; the creaking of the trees, the howling of wild beasts, and the yell of Indians; while, sometimes, the wind tolled like a distant church bell, and sometimes gave a broad roar around the traveller, as if all Nature were laughing him to scorn. But he was himself the chief horror of the scene, and shrank not from its other horrors.

"Ha! ha! ha!" roared Goodman Brown, when the wind laughed at him. "Let us hear which will laugh loudest! Think not to frighten me with your deviltry! Come witch, come wizard, come Indian powwow, come devil himself! and here comes Goodman Brown. You may as well fear him as he fear you!"

In truth, all through the haunted forest, there could be nothing more frightful than the figure of Goodman Brown. On he flew, among the black pines, brandishing his staff with frenzied gestures, now giving vent to an inspiration of horrid blasphemy, and now shouting forth such laughter, as set all the echoes of the forest laughing like demons around him. The fiend in his own shape is less hideous than when he rages in the breast of man. Thus sped the demoniac on his course, until, quivering among the trees, he saw a red light before him, as when the felled trunks and branches of a clearing have been set on fire, and throw up their lurid blaze against the sky, at the hour of midnight. He paused, in a lull of the tempest that had driven him onward, and heard the swell of what seemed a hymn, rolling solemnly from a distance, with the weight of many voices. He knew the tune. It was a familiar one in the choir of the village meeting-house. The verse died heavily away, and was lengthened by a chorus, not of human voices, but of all the sounds of the benighted wilderness, pealing in awful harmony together. Goodman Brown cried out; and his cry was lost to his own ear, by its unison with the cry of the desert.

In the interval of silence, he stole forward, until the light glared full upon his eyes. At one extremity of an open space, hemmed in by the dark wall of the forest, arose a rock, bearing some rude, natural resemblance either to an altar or a pulpit, and surrounded by four blazing pines, their tops aflame, their stems untouched, like candles at an evening meeting. The mass of foliage, that had overgrown the summit of the rock, was all on fire, blazing high into the night, and fitfully illuminating the whole field. Each pendent twig and leafy festoon was in a blaze. As the red light arose and fell, a numerous congregation alternately shone forth, then disappeared in shadow, and again grew, as it were, out of the darkness, peopling the heart of the solitary woods at once.

"A grave and dark-clad company!" quoth Goodman Brown.   55

In truth, they were such. Among them, quivering to-and-fro, between gloom and splendor, appeared faces that would be seen, next day, at the council-board of the province, and others which, Sabbath after Sabbath, looked devoutly heavenward, and benignantly over the crowded pews, from the holiest pulpits in the land. Some affirm that the lady of the governor was there. At least, there were high dames well known to her, and wives of honored husbands, and widows a great multitude, and ancient maidens, all of excellent repute, and fair young girls, who trembled lest their mothers should espy them. Either the sudden gleams of light, flashing over the obscure field, bedazzled Goodman Brown, or he recognized a score of the church members of Salem village, famous for their especial sanctity. Good old Deacon Gookin had arrived, and waited at the skirts of that venerable saint, his reverend pastor. But, irreverently consorting with these grave, reputable, and pious people, these elders of the church, these chaste dames and dewy virgins, there were men of dissolute lives and women of spotted fame, wretches given over to all mean and filthy vice, and suspected even of horrid crimes. It was strange to see, that the good shrank not from the wicked, nor were the sinners abashed by the saints. Scattered, also, among their pale-faced enemies, were the Indian priests, or powwows, who had often scared their native forest with more hideous incantations than any known to English witchcraft.

"But, where is Faith?" thought Goodman Brown; and, as hope came into his heart, he trembled.

Another verse of the hymn arose, a slow and mournful strain, such as the pious love, but joined to words which expressed all that our nature can conceive of sin, and darkly hinted at far more. Unfathomable to mere mortals is the lore of fiends. Verse after verse was sung, and still the chorus of the desert swelled between, like the deepest tone of a mighty organ. And, with the final peal of that dreadful anthem, there came a sound, as if the roaring wind, the rushing streams, the howling beasts, and every other voice of the unconverted wilderness were mingling and according with the voice of guilty man, in homage to the prince of all. The four blazing pines threw up a loftier flame, and obscurely discovered shapes and visages of horror on the smoke-wreaths, above the impious assembly. At the same moment, the fire on the rock shot redly forth, and formed a glowing arch above its base, where now appeared a figure. With reverence be it spoken, the apparition bore no slight similitude, both in garb and manner, to some grave divine of the New England churches.

"Bring forth the converts!" cried a voice, that echoed through the field and rolled into the forest.

At the word, Goodman Brown stepped forth from the shadow of the trees, and approached 60 the congregation, with whom he felt a loathful brotherhood, by the sympathy of all that was wicked in his heart. He could have well-nigh sworn, that the shape of his own dead father beckoned him to advance, looking downward from a smoke-wreath, while a woman, with dim features of despair, threw out her hand to warn him back. Was it his mother? But he had no power to retreat one step, nor to resist, even in thought, when the minister and good old Deacon Gookin seized his arms, and led him to the blazing rock. Thither came also the slender form of a veiled female, led between Goody Cloyse, that pious teacher of the catechism, and Martha Carrier, who had received the devil's promise to be queen of hell. A rampant hag was she! And there stood the proselytes, beneath the canopy of fire.

"Welcome, my children," said the dark figure, "to the communion of your race! Ye have found, thus young, your nature and your destiny. My children, look behind you!"

They turned; and flashing forth, as it were, in a sheet of flame, the fiend-worshippers were seen; the smile of welcome gleamed darkly on every visage.

"There," resumed the sable form, "are all whom ye have reverenced from youth. Ye deemed them holier than yourselves, and shrank from your own sin, contrasting it with their lives of right-eousness and prayerful aspirations heavenward. Yet, here are they all, in my worshipping assembly! This night it shall be granted you to know their secret deeds; how hoary-bearded elders of the church have whispered wanton words to the young maids of their households; how many a woman, eager for widow's weeds, has given her husband a drink at bedtime, and let him sleep his last sleep in her bosom; how beardless youths have made haste to inherit their father's wealth; and how fair damsels—blush not, sweet ones!—have dug little graves in the garden, and bidden me, the sole guest, to an infant's funeral. By the sympathy of your human hearts for sin, ye shall scent out all the places—whether in church, bed-chamber, street, field, or forest—where crime has been committed, and shall exult to behold the whole earth one stain of guilt, one mighty blood-spot. Far more than this! It shall be yours to penetrate, in every bosom, the deep mystery of sin, the fountain of all wicked arts, and which inexhaustibly supplies more evil impulses than human power—than my power, at its utmost!—can make manifest in deeds. And now, my children, look upon each other."

They did so; and, by the blaze of the hell-kindled torches, the wretched man beheld his Faith, and the wife her husband, trembling before that unhallowed altar.

"Lo! there ye stand, my children," said the figure, in a deep and solemn tone, almost sad, with   65 its despairing awfulness, as if his once angelic nature could yet mourn for our miserable race. "Depending upon one another's hearts, ye had still hoped that virtue were not all a dream! Now are ye undeceived!—Evil is the nature of mankind. Evil must be your only happiness. Welcome, again, my children, to the communion of your race!"

"Welcome!" repeated the fiend-worshippers, in one cry of despair and triumph.

And there they stood, the only pair, as it seemed, who were yet hesitating on the verge of wickedness, in this dark world. A basin was hollowed, naturally, in the rock. Did it contain water, reddened by the lurid light? or was it blood? or, perchance, a liquid flame? Herein did the Shape of Evil dip his hand, and prepare to lay the mark of baptism upon their foreheads, that they might be partakers of the mystery of sin, more conscious of the secret guilt of others, both in deed and thought, than they could now be of their own. The husband cast one look at his pale wife, and Faith at him. What polluted wretches would the next glance show them to each other, shuddering alike at what they disclosed and what they saw!

"Faith! Faith!" cried the husband. "Look up to Heaven, and resist the Wicked One!"

Whether Faith obeyed, he knew not. Hardly had he spoken, when he found himself amid calm night and solitude, listening to a roar of the wind, which died heavily away through the forest. He staggered against the rock, and felt it chill and damp, while a hanging twig, that had been all on fire, besprinkled his cheek with the coldest dew.

The next morning, young Goodman Brown came slowly into the street of Salem village star-   70 ing around him like a bewildered man. The good old minister was taking a walk along the grave-yard, to get an appetite for breakfast and meditate his sermon, and bestowed a blessing, as he passed, on Goodman Brown. He shrank from the venerable saint, as if to avoid an anathema. Old Deacon Gookin was at domestic worship, and the holy words of his prayer were heard through the open window. "What God doth the wizard pray to?" quoth Goodman Brown. Goody Cloyse, that excellent old Christian, stood in the early sunshine, at her own lattice, catechising a little girl, who had brought her a pint of morning's milk. Goodman Brown snatched away the child, as from the grasp of the fiend himself. Turning the corner by the meetinghouse, he spied the head of Faith, with the pink ribbons, gazing anxiously forth, and bursting into such joy at the sight of him that she skipt along the street, and almost kissed her husband before the whole village. But Goodman Brown looked sternly and sadly into her face, and passed on without a greeting.

Had Goodman Brown fallen asleep in the forest, and only dreamed a wild dream of a witch-meeting?

Be it so, if you will. But, alas! it was a dream of evil omen for young Goodman Brown. A stern, a sad, a darkly meditative, a distrustful, if not a desperate man did he become, from the night of that fearful dream. On the Sabbath day, when the congregation were singing a holy psalm, he could not listen, because an anthem of sin rushed loudly upon his ear, and drowned all the blessed strain. When the minister spoke from the pulpit, with power and fervid eloquence, and with his hand on the open Bible, of the sacred truths of our religion, and of saint-like lives and triumphant deaths, and of future bliss or misery unutterable, then did Goodman Brown turn pale, dreading lest the roof should thunder down upon the gray blasphemer and his hearers. Often, awaking suddenly at midnight, he shrank from the bosom of Faith, and at morning or eventide, when the family knelt down in prayer, he scowled, and muttered to himself, and gazed sternly at his wife, and turned away. And when he had lived long, and was borne to his grave, a hoary corpse, followed by Faith, an aged woman, and children and grandchildren, a goodly procession, besides neighbors not a few, they carved no hopeful verse upon his tombstone; for his dying hour was gloom.

[1835]

Joyce, James (1882–1941)

Araby

North Richmond Street, being blind, was a quiet street except at the hour when the Christian Brothers' School set the boys free. An uninhabited house of two storeys stood at the blind end, detached from its neighbours in a square ground. The other houses of the street, conscious of decent lives within them, gazed at one another with brown imperturbable faces.

The former tenant of our house, a priest, had died in the back drawing room. Air, musty from having long been enclosed, hung in all the rooms, and the waste room behind the kitchen was littered with old useless papers. Among these I found a few paper-covered books, the pages of which were curled and damp: *The Abbott*, by Walter Scott, *The Devout Communicant* and *The Memoirs of Vidocq*. I liked the last best because its leaves were yellow. The wild garden behind the house contained a central apple-tree and a few straggling bushes under one of which I found the late tenant's rusty bicycle-pump. He had been a very charitable priest; in his will he had left all his money to institutions and the furniture of his house to his sister.

When the short days of winter came dusk fell before we had well eaten our dinners. When we met in the street the houses had grown sombre. The space of sky above us was the colour of ever-changing violet and towards it the lamps of the street lifted their feeble lanterns. The cold air stung us and we played till our bodies glowed. Our shouts echoed in the silent street. The career of our play brought us through the dark muddy lanes behind the houses where we ran the gauntlet of the rough tribes from the cottages, to the back doors of the dark dripping gardens where odours arose from the ashpits, to the dark odorous stables where a coachman smoothed and combed the horse or shook music from the buckled harness. When we returned to the street light from the kitchen windows had filled the areas. If my uncle was seen turning the corner we hid in the shadow until we had seen him safely housed. Or if Mangan's sister came out on the doorstep to call her brother in to his tea we watched her from our shadow peer up and down the street. We waited to see whether she would remain or go in and, if she remained, we left our shadow and walked up to Mangan's steps resignedly. She was waiting for us, her figure defined by the light from the half-opened door. Her brother always teased her before he obeyed and I stood by the railings looking at her. Her dress swung as she moved her body and the soft rope of her hair tossed from side to side.

Every morning I lay on the floor in the front parlor watching her door. The blind was pulled down within an inch of the sash so that I could not be seen. When she came out on the doorstep my heart leaped. I ran to the hall, seized my books and followed her. I kept her brown figure always in my eye and, when we came near the point at which our ways diverged, I quickened my pace and passed her. This happened morning after morning. I had never spoken to her, except for a few casual words, and yet her name was like a summons to all my foolish blood.

Her image accompanied me even in places the most hostile to romance. On Saturday 5 evenings when my aunt went marketing I had to go to carry some of the parcels. We walked through the flaring street, jostled by drunken men and bargaining women, amid the curses of labourers, the shrill litanies of shop-boys who stood on guard by the barrels of pigs' cheeks, the nasal chanting of street singers, who sang a *come-all-you* about O'Donovan Rossa, or a ballad about the troubles in our native land. These noises converged in a single sensation of life for me: I imagined that I bore my chalice safely through the throng of foes. Her name sprang to my lips at moments in strange prayers and praises which I myself did not understand. My eyes were often full of tears (I could not tell why) and at times a flood from my heart seemed to pour itself out into my bosom. I thought little of the future. I did not know whether I would ever speak to her or not or, if I spoke to her, how I could tell her of my confused adoration. But my body was like a harp and her words and gestures were like fingers running upon the wires.

One evening I went into the back drawing-room in which the priest had died. It was a dark rainy evening and there was no sound in the house. Through one of the broken panes I heard the rain impinge upon the earth, the fine incessant needles of water playing in the sodden beds. Some distant lamp or lighted window gleamed below me. I was thankful that I could see so little. All my senses seemed to desire to veil themselves and, feeling that I was about to slip from them, I pressed the palms of my hands together until they trembled, murmuring: *O love! O love!* many times.

At last she spoke to me. When she addressed the first words to me I was so confused that I did not know what to answer. She asked me was I going to *Araby*. I forget whether I answered yes or no. It would be a splendid bazaar, she said; she would love to go.

—And why can't you? I asked.

While she spoke she turned a silver bracelet round and round her wrist. She could not go, she said, because there would be a retreat that week in her convent. Her brother and two other boys were fighting for their caps and I was alone at the railings. She held one of the spikes, bowing her head towards me. The light from the lamp opposite our door caught the white curve of her neck, lit up her hair that rested there and, falling, lit up the hand upon the railing. It fell over one side of her dress and caught the white border of a petticoat, just visible as she stood at ease.

—It's well for you, she said.   10

—If I go, I said, I will bring you something.

What innumerable follies laid waste my waking and sleeping thoughts after that evening! I wished to annihilate the tedious intervening days. I chafed against the work of school. At night in my bedroom and by day in the classroom her image came between me and the page I strove to read. The syllables of the word *Araby* were called to me through the silence in which my soul luxuriated and cast an Eastern enchantment over me. I asked for leave to go to the bazaar on Saturday night. My aunt was surprised and hoped it was not some Freemason affair. I answered few questions in class. I watched my master's face pass from amiability to sternness; he hoped I was not beginning to idle. I could not call my wandering thoughts together. I had hardly any patience with the serious work of life which, now that it stood between me and my desire, seemed to me child's play, ugly monotonous child's play.

On Saturday morning I reminded my uncle that I wished to go to the bazaar in the evening. He was fussing at the hall-stand, looking for the hatbrush, and answered me curtly:

—Yes, boy, I know.

As he was in the hall I could not go into the front parlour and lie at the window. I left the 15 house in bad humour and walked slowly towards the school. The air was pitilessly raw and already my heart misgave me.

When I came home to dinner my uncle had not yet been home. Still, it was early. I sat staring at the clock for some time and, when its ticking began to irritate me, I left the room. I mounted the staircase and gained the upper part of the house. The high cold empty gloomy rooms liberated me and I went from room to room singing. From the front window I saw my companions playing below in the street. Their cries reached me weakened and indistinct and, leaning my forehead against the cool glass, I looked over at the dark house where she lived. I may have stood there for an hour, seeing nothing but the brown-clad figure cast by my imagination, touched discreetly by the lamplight at the curved neck, at the hand upon the railing and at the border below the dress.

When I came downstairs again I found Mrs. Mercer sitting at the fire. She was an old garrulous woman, a pawnbroker's widow, who collected used stamps for some pious purpose. I had to endure the gossip of the tea-table. The meal was prolonged beyond an hour and still my uncle did not come. Mrs. Mercer stood up to go: she was sorry she couldn't wait any longer, but it was after eight o'clock and she did not like to be out late, as the night air was bad for her. When she had gone I began to walk up and down the room, clenching my fists. My aunt said:

—I'm afraid you may put off your bazaar for this night of Our Lord.

At nine o'clock I heard my uncle's latchkey in the halldoor. I heard him talking to himself and heard the hall-stand rocking when it had received the weight of his overcoat. I could interpret these signs. When he was midway through his dinner I asked him to give me the money to go to the bazaar. He had forgotten.

—The people are in bed and after their first sleep now, he said.   20

I did not smile. My aunt said to him energetically:

—Can't you give him the money and let him go? You've kept him late enough as it is.

My uncle said he was very sorry he had forgotten. He said he believed in the old saying: *All work and no play makes Jack a dull boy.* He asked me where I was going and, when I had told him a second time he asked me did I know *The Arab's Farewell to his Steed.* When I left the kitchen he was about to recite the opening lines of the piece to my aunt.

I held a florin tightly in my hand as I strode down Buckingham Street towards the station. The sight of the streets thronged with buyers and glaring with gas recalled to me the purpose of my journey. I took my seat in a third-class carriage of a deserted train. After an intolerable delay the train moved out of the station slowly. It crept onward among ruinous houses and over the twinkling river. At Westland Row Station a crowd of people pressed to the carriage doors; but the porters moved them back, saying that it was a special train for the bazaar. I remained alone in the bare carriage. In a few minutes the train drew up beside an improvised wooden platform. I passed out on to the road and saw by the lighted dial of a clock that it was ten minutes to ten. In front of me was a large building which displayed the magical name.

I could not find any sixpenny entrance and, fearing that the bazaar would be closed, I passed   25
in quickly through a turnstile, handing a shilling to a weary-looking man. I found myself in a big hall girdled at half its height by a gallery. Nearly all the stalls were closed and the greater part of the hall was in darkness. I recognized a silence like that which pervades a church after a service. I walked into the centre of the bazaar timidly. A few people were gathered about the stalls which were still open. Before a curtain, over which the words *Café Chantant* were written in coloured lamps, two men were counting money on a salver. I listened to the fall of the coins.

Remembering with difficulty why I had come I went over to one of the stalls and examined porcelain vases and flowered tea-sets. At the door of the stall a young lady was talking and laughing with two young gentlemen. I remarked their English accents and listened vaguely to their conversation.

—O, I never said such a thing!

—O, but you did!

—O, but I didn't!

—Didn't she say that?   30

—Yes I heard her.

—O, there's a . . . fib!

Observing me the young lady came over and asked me did I wish to buy anything. The tone in her voice was not encouraging; she seemed to have spoken to me out of a sense of duty.

I looked humbly at the great jars that stood like eastern guards at either side of the dark entrance to the stall and murmured:

—No, thank you.

The young lady changed the position of one of the vases and went back to the two young 35 men. They began to talk of the same subject. Once or twice the young lady glanced at me over her shoulder.

I lingered before her stall, though I knew my stay was useless, to make my interest in her wares seem the more real. Then I turned away slowly and walked down the middle of the bazaar. I allowed the two pennies to fall against the sixpence in my pocket. I heard a voice call from one end of the gallery that the light was out. The upper part of the hall was now completely dark.

Gazing up into the darkness I saw myself as a creature driven and derided by vanity; and my eyes burned with anguish and anger.

[1914]

The Boarding House

Mrs. Mooney was a butcher's daughter. She was a woman who was quite able to keep things to herself: a determined woman. She had married her father's foreman and opened a butcher's shop near Spring Gardens. But as soon as his father-in-law was dead Mr. Mooney began to go to the devil. He drank, plundered the till, ran headlong into debt. It was no use making him take the pledge: he was sure to break out again a few days after. By fighting his wife in the presence of customers and by buying bad meat he ruined his business. One night he went for his wife with the cleaver and she had to sleep in a neighbour's house.

After that they lived apart. She went to the priest and got a separation from him with care of the children. She would give him neither money nor food nor house-room; and so he was obliged to enlist himself as a sheriff's man. He was a shabby stooped little drunkard with a white face and a white moustache and white eyebrows, pencilled above his little eyes, which were pink-veined and raw; and all day long he sat in the bailiff's room, waiting to be put on a job. Mrs. Mooney, who had taken what remained of her money out of the butcher business and set up a boarding house in Hardwicke Street, was a big imposing woman. Her house had a floating population made up of tourists from Liverpool and the Isle of Man and, occasionally, *artistes* from the music halls. Its resident population was made up of clerks from the city. She governed the house cunningly and firmly, knew when to give credit, when to be stern and when to let things pass. All the resident young men spoke of her as *The Madam*.

Mrs. Mooney's young men paid fifteen shillings a week for board and lodgings (beer or stout at dinner excluded). They shared in common tastes and occupations and for this reason they were very chummy with one another. They discussed with one another the chances of favourites and outsiders. Jack Mooney, the Madam's son, who was clerk to a commission agent in Fleet Street, had the reputation of being a hard case. He was fond of using soldiers' obscenities: usually he came home in the small hours. When he met his friends he had always a good one to tell them and he was always sure to be on to a good thing—that is to say, a likely horse or a likely *artiste*. He was also handy with the mits and sang comic songs. On Sunday nights there would often be a reunion in Mrs. Mooney's front drawing-room. The music-hall *artistes* would oblige; and Sheridan played waltzes and polkas and vamped accompaniments. Polly Mooney, the Madam's daughter, would also sing. She sang:

> *I'm a . . . naughty girl.*
> *You needn't sham:*
> *You know I am.*

Polly was a slim girl of nineteen; she had light soft hair and a small full mouth. Her eyes, which were grey with a shade of green through them, had a habit of glancing upwards when she spoke with anyone, which made her look like a little perverse madonna. Mrs. Mooney had first sent her daughter to be a typist in a corn-factor's office but, as a disreputable sheriff's man used to come every other day to the office, asking to be allowed to say a word to his daughter, she had taken her daughter home again and set her to do housework. As Polly was very lively the intention was to give her the run of the young men. Besides, young men like to feel that there is a young woman not very far away. Polly, of course, flirted with the young men but Mrs. Mooney, who was a shrewd judge, knew that the young men were only passing the time away: none of them meant business. Things went on so for a long time and Mrs. Mooney began to think of sending Polly back to typewriting when she noticed that something was going on between Polly and one of the young men. She watched the pair and kept her own counsel.

Polly knew that she was being watched, but still her mother's persistent silence could not be   5 misunderstood. There had been no open complicity between mother and daughter, no open understanding but, though people in the house began to talk of the affair, still Mrs. Mooney did not intervene. Polly began to grow a little strange in her manner and the young man was evidently perturbed. At last, when she judged it to be the right moment, Mrs. Mooney intervened. She dealt with moral problems as a cleaver deals with meat: and in this case she had made up her mind.

It was a bright Sunday morning of early summer, promising heat, but with a fresh breeze blowing. All the windows of the boarding house were open and the lace curtains ballooned gently towards the street beneath the raised sashes. The belfry of George's Church sent out constant peals and worshippers, singly or in groups, traversed the little circus before the church, revealing their purpose by their self-contained demeanour no less than by the little volumes in their gloved hands. Breakfast was over in the boarding house and the table of the breakfast room was covered with plates on which lay yellow streaks of eggs with morsels of bacon-fat and bacon-rind. Mrs. Mooney sat in the straw armchair and watched the servant Mary remove the breakfast things. She made Mary collect the crusts and pieces of broken bread to help to make Tuesday's bread-pudding. When the table was cleared, the broken bread collected, the sugar and butter safe under lock and key, she began to reconstruct the interview which she had had the night before with Polly. Things were as she had suspected: she had been frank in her questions and Polly had been frank in her answers. Both had been somewhat awkward, of course. She had been made awkward by her not wishing to receive the news in too cavalier a fashion or to seem to have connived and Polly had been made awkward not merely because allusions of that kind always made her awkward but also because she did not wish it to be thought that in her wise innocence she had divined the intention behind her mother's tolerance.

Mrs. Mooney glanced instinctively at the little gilt clock on the mantelpiece as soon as she had become aware through her revery that the bells of George's Church had stopped ringing. It was seventeen minutes past eleven: she would have lots of time to have the matter out with Mr. Doran and then catch short twelve at Marlborough Street. She was sure she would win. To begin with she had all the weight of social opinion on her side: she was an outraged mother. She had allowed him to live beneath her roof, assuming that he was a man of honour, and he had simply abused her hospitality. He was thirty-four or thirty-five years of age, so that youth could not be pleaded as his excuse; nor could ignorance be his excuse since he was a man who had seen something of the world. He had simply taken advantage of Polly's youth and inexperience: that was evident. The question was: What reparation would he make?

There must be reparation made in such case. It is all very well for the man: he can go his ways as if nothing had happened, having had his moment of pleasure, but the girl has to bear the brunt. Some mothers would be content to patch up such an affair for a sum of money; she had known cases of it. But she would not do so. For her only one reparation could make up for the loss of her daughter's honour: marriage.

She counted all her cards again before sending Mary up to Mr. Doran's room to say that she wished to speak with him. She felt sure she would win. He was a serious young man, not rakish or loud-voiced like the others. If it had been Mr. Sheridan or Mr. Meade or Bantam Lyons her task would have been much harder. She did not think he would face publicity. All the lodgers in the house knew something of the affair; details had been invented by some. Besides, he had been employed for thirteen years in a great Catholic winemerchant's office and publicity would mean for him, perhaps, the loss of his job. Whereas if he agreed all might be well. She knew he had a good screw for one thing and she suspected he had a bit of stuff put by.

Nearly the half-hour! She stood up and surveyed herself in the pierglass. The decisive 10
expression of her great florid face satisfied her and she thought of some mothers she knew who could not get their daughters off their hands.

Mr. Doran was very anxious indeed this Sunday morning. He had made two attempts to shave but his hand had been so unsteady that he had been obliged to desist. Three days' reddish beard fringed his jaws and every two or three minutes a mist gathered on his glasses so that he had to take them off and polish them with his pocket-handkerchief. The recollection of his confession of the night before was a cause of acute pain to him; the priest had drawn out every ridiculous detail of the affair and in the end had so magnified his sin that he was almost thankful at being afforded a loophole of reparation. The harm was done. What could he do now but marry her or run away? He could not brazen it out. The affair would be sure to be talked of and his employer would be certain to hear of it. Dublin is such a small city: everyone knows everyone else's business. He felt his heart leap warmly in his throat as he heard in his excited imagination old Mr. Leonard calling out in his rasping voice: "Send Mr. Doran here, please."

All his long years of service gone for nothing! All his industry and diligence thrown away! As a young man he had sown his wild oats, of course; he had boasted of his free-thinking and denied the existence of God to his companions in public-houses. But that was all passed and done with . . . nearly. He still bought a copy of *Reynolds's Newspaper* every week but he attended to his religious duties and for nine-tenths of the year lived a regular life. He had money enough to settle down on; it was not that. But the family would look down on her. First of all there was her disreputable father and then her mother's boarding house was beginning to get a certain fame. He had a notion that he was being had. He could imagine his friends talking of the affair and laughing. She *was* a little vulgar; some times she said "I seen" and "If I had've known." But what would grammar matter if he really loved her? He could not make up his mind whether to like her or despise her for what she had done. Of course he had done it too. His instinct urged him to remain free, not to marry. Once you are married you are done for, it said.

While he was sitting helplessly on the side of the bed in shirt and trousers she tapped lightly at his door and entered. She told him all, that she had made a clean breast of it to her mother and that her mother would speak with him that morning. She cried and threw her arms round his neck, saying:

"Oh Bob! Bob! What am I to do? What am I to do at all?"

She would put an end to herself, she said. 15

He comforted her feebly, telling her not to cry, that it would be all right, never fear. He felt against his shirt the agitation of her bosom.

It was not altogether his fault that it had happened. He remembered well, with the curious patient memory of the celibate, the first casual caresses her dress, her breath, her fingers had given him. Then late one night as he was undressing for bed she had tapped at his door, timidly. She wanted to relight her candle at his for hers had been blown out by a gust. It was her bath night. She wore a loose open combing-jacket of printed flannel. Her white instep shone in the opening of her furry slippers and the blood glowed warmly behind her perfumed skin. From her hands and wrists too as she lit and steadied her candle a faint perfume arose.

On nights when he came in very late it was she who warmed up his dinner. He scarcely knew what he was eating feeling her beside him alone, at night, in the sleeping house. And her thoughtfulness! If the night was anyway cold or wet or windy there was sure to be a little tumbler of punch ready for him. Perhaps they could be happy together. . . .

They used to go upstairs together on tiptoe, each with a candle, and on the third landing exchange reluctant good-nights. They used to kiss. He remembered well her eyes, the touch of her hand and his delirium. . . .

But delirium passes. He echoed her phrase, applying it to himself: "*What am I to do?*" The 20
instinct of the celibate warned him to hold back. But the sin was there; even his sense of honour
told him that reparation must be made for such a sin.

While he was sitting with her on the side of the bed Mary came to the door and said that the
missus wanted to see him in the parlour. He stood up to put on his coat and waistcoat, more helpless than ever. When he was dressed he went over to her to comfort her. It would be all right,
never fear. He left her crying on the bed and moaning softly: "*O my God!*"

Going down the stairs his glasses became so dimmed with moisture that he had to take them
off and polish them. He longed to ascend through the roof and fly away to another country
where he would never hear again of his trouble, and yet a force pushed him downstairs step by
step. The implacable faces of his employer and of the Madam stared upon his discomfiture. On
the last flight of stairs he passed Jack Mooney who was coming up from the pantry nursing two
bottles of *Bass*. They saluted coldly; and the lover's eyes rested for a second or two on a thick bull-
dog face and a pair of thick short arms. When he reached the foot of the staircase he glanced up
and saw Jack regarding him from the door of the return-room.

Suddenly he remembered the night when one of the music-hall *artistes*, a little blond Londoner,
had made a rather free allusion to Polly. The reunion had been almost broken up on account of
Jack's violence. Everyone tried to quiet him. The music-hall *artiste*, a little paler than usual, kept smiling and saying that there was no harm meant: but Jack kept shouting at him that if any fellow tried
that sort of a game on with his sister he'd bloody well put his teeth down his throat, so he would.

Polly sat for a little time on the side of the bed, crying. Then she dried her eyes and went
over to the looking-glass. She dipped the end of the towel in the water-jug and refreshed her eyes
with the cool water. She looked at herself in profile and readjusted a hairpin above her ear. Then
she went back to the bed again and sat at the foot. She regarded the pillows for a long time and
the sight of them awakened in her mind secret, amiable memories. She rested the nape of her
neck against the cool iron bed-rail and fell into a reverie. There was no longer any perturbation
visible on her face.

She waited on patiently, almost cheerfully, without alarm, her memories gradually giving place 25
to hopes and visions of the future. Her hopes and visions were so intricate that she no longer saw
the white pillows on which her gaze was fixed or remembered that she was waiting for anything.

At last she heard her mother calling. She started to her feet and ran to the banisters.

"Polly! Polly!"

"Yes, mamma?"

"Come down, dear. Mr. Doran wants to speak to you." Then she remembered what she had
been waiting for.

[1914]

Maupassant, Guy de (1850–1893)

The Jewelry
(Translated by Lafcadio Hearn)

Having met the girl one evening, at the house of the office-superintendent, M. Lantin became
enveloped in love as in a net.

She was the daughter of a country-tutor, who had been dead for several years. Afterward she
had come to Paris with her mother, who made regular visits to several bourgeois families of the
neighborhood, in hopes of being able to get her daughter married. They were poor and respectable,
quiet and gentle. The young girl seemed to be the very ideal of that pure good woman to whom
every young man dreams of entrusting his future. Her modest beauty had a charm of angelic shy-
ness; and the slight smile that always dwelt about her lips seemed a reflection of her heart.

Everybody sang her praises; all who knew her kept saying: "The man who gets her will be lucky. No one could find a nicer girl than that."

M. Lantin, who was then chief clerk in the office of the Minister of the Interior, with a salary of 3,500 francs a year, demanded her hand, and married her.

He was unutterably happy with her. She ruled his home with an economy so adroit that they 5 really seemed to live in luxury. It would be impossible to conceive of any attentions, tendernesses, playful caresses which she did not lavish upon her husband; and such was the charm of her person that, six years after he married her, he loved her even more than he did the first day.

There were only two points upon which he ever found fault with her—her love of the theater, and her passion for false jewelry.

Her lady-friends (she was acquainted with the wives of several small office holders) were always bringing her tickets for the theaters; whenever there was a performance that made a sensation, she always had her *loge* secured, even for first performances; and she would drag her husband with her to all these entertainments, which used to tire him horribly after his day's work. So at last he begged her to go to the theater with some lady-acquaintances who would consent to see her home afterward. She refused for quite a while—thinking it would not look very well to go out thus unaccompanied by her husband. But finally she yielded, just to please him; and he felt infinitely grateful to her therefor.

Now this passion for the theater at last evoked in her the desire of dress. It was true that her toilette remained simple, always in good taste, but modest; and her sweet grace, her irresistible grace, ever smiling and shy, seemed to take fresh charm from the simplicity of her robes. But she got into the habit of suspending in her pretty ears two big cut pebbles, fashioned in imitation of diamonds; and she wore necklaces of false pearls, bracelets of false gold, and haircombs studded with paste-imitations of precious stones.

Her husband, who felt shocked by this love of tinsel and show, would often say—"My dear, when one has not the means to afford real jewelry, one should appear adorned with one's natural beauty and grace only—and these gifts are the rarest of jewels."

But she would smile sweetly and answer: "What does it matter? I like those things—that is my 10 little whim. I know you are right; but one can't make oneself over again. I've always loved jewelry so much!"

And then she would roll the pearls of the necklaces between her fingers, and make the facets of the cut crystals flash in the light, repeating: "Now look at them—see how well the work is done. You would swear it was real jewelry."

He would then smile in his turn, and declare to her: "You have the tastes of a regular Gypsy."

Sometimes, in the evening, when they were having a chat by the fire, she would rise and fetch the morocco box in which she kept her "stock" (as M. Lantin called it)—would put it on the tea-table, and begin to examine the false jewelry with passionate delight, as if she experienced some secret and mysterious sensations of pleasure in their contemplation; and she would insist on putting one of the necklaces round her husband's neck, and laugh till she couldn't laugh any more, crying out: "Oh! how funny you look!" Then she would rush into his arms, and kiss him furiously.

One winter's night, after she had been to the Opera, she came home chilled through, and trembling. Next day she had a bad cough. Eight days after that, she died of pneumonia.

Lantin was very nearly following her into the tomb. His despair was so frightful that in one 15 single month his hair turned white. He wept from morning till night, feeling his heart torn by inexpressible suffering—ever haunted by the memory of her, by the smile, by the voice, by all the charm of the dead woman.

Time did not assuage his grief. Often during office hours his fellow-clerks went off to a corner to chat about this or that topic of the day—his cheeks might have been seen to swell up all of a sudden, his nose wrinkle, his eyes fill with water—he would pull a frightful face, and begin to sob.

He had kept his dead companion's room just in the order she had left it, and he used to lock himself up in it every evening to think about her—all the furniture, and even all her dresses, remained in the same place they had been on the last day of her life.

But life became hard for him. His salary, which, in his wife's hands, had amply sufficed for all household needs, now proved scarcely sufficient to supply his own few wants. And he asked himself in astonishment how she had managed always to furnish him with excellent wines and with delicate eating which he could not now afford at all with his scanty means.

He got a little into debt, like men obliged to live by their wits. At last one morning that he happened to find himself without a cent in his pocket, and a whole week to wait before he could draw his monthly salary, he thought of selling something; and almost immediately it occurred to him to sell his wife's "stock"—for he had always borne a secret grudge against the flash-jewelry that used to annoy him so much in former days. The mere sight of it, day after day, somewhat spoiled the sad pleasure of thinking of his darling.

He tried a long time to make a choice among the heap of trinkets she had left behind her—for   20 up to the very last day of her life she had kept obstinately buying them, bringing home some new thing almost every night—and finally he resolved to take the big pearl necklace which she used to like the best of all, and which he thought ought certainly to be worth six or eight francs, as it was really very nicely mounted for an imitation necklace.

He put it in his pocket, and walked toward the office, following the boulevards, and looking for some jewelry-store on the way, where he could enter with confidence.

Finally he saw a place and went in; feeling a little ashamed of thus exposing his misery, and of trying to sell such a trifling object.

"Sir," he said to the jeweler, "please tell me what this is worth."

The jeweler took the necklace, examined it, weighed it, took up a magnifying glass, called his clerk, talked to him in whispers, put down the necklace on the counter, and drew back a little bit to judge of its effect at a distance.

M. Lantin, feeling very much embarrassed by all these ceremonies, opened his mouth and   25 began to declare—"Oh! I know it can't be worth much" . . . when the jeweler interrupted him saying:

"Well, sir, that is worth between twelve and fifteen thousand francs; but I cannot buy it unless you can let me know exactly how you came by it."

The widower's eyes opened enormously, and he stood gaping—unable to understand. Then after a while he stammered out: "You said? . . . Are you sure?" The jeweler, misconstruing the cause of this astonishment, replied in a dry tone—"Go elsewhere if you like, and see if you can get any more for it. The very most I would give for it is fifteen thousand. Come back and see me again, if you can't do better."

M. Lantin, feeling perfectly idiotic, took his necklace and departed; obeying a confused desire to find himself alone and to get a chance to think.

But the moment he found himself in the street again, he began to laugh, and he muttered to himself: "The fool!—oh! what a fool; If I had only taken him at his word. Well, well!—a jeweler who can't tell paste from real jewelry!"

And he entered another jewelry-store, at the corner of the Rue de la Paix. The moment the   30 jeweler set eyes on the necklace, he examined—"Hello! I know that necklace well—it was sold here!"

M. Lantin, very nervous, asked:

"What's it worth?"

"Sir, I sold it for twenty-five thousand francs. I am willing to buy it back again for eighteen thousand—if you can prove to me satisfactorily, according to legal presciptions, how you came into possession of it"—This time, M. Lantin was simply paralyzed with astonishment. He said: "Well . . . but please look at it again, sir. I always thought until now that it was . . . was false."

The jeweler said:

"Will you give me your name, sir?"   35

"Certainly. My name is Lantin; I am employed at the office of the Minister of the Interior. I live at No. 16, Rue des Martyrs."

The merchant opened the register, looked, and said: "Yes; this necklace was sent to the address of Madame Lantin, 16 Rue des Martyrs, on July 20th, 1876."

And the two men looked into each other's eyes—the clerk wild with surprise; the jeweler suspecting he had a thief before him.

The jeweler resumed:

"Will you be kind enough to leave this article here for twenty-four hours only—I'll give you a   40 receipt."

M. Lantin stuttered: "Yes-ah! certainly." And he went out folding up the receipt, which he put in his pocket.

Then he crossed the street, went the wrong way, found out his mistake, returned by way of the Tuileries, crossed the Seine, found out he had taken the wrong road again, and went back to the Champs-Élysées without being able to get one clear idea into his head. He tried to reason, to understand. His wife could never have bought so valuable an object as that. Certainly not. But then, it must have been a present! . . . A present from whom? What for?

He stopped and stood stock-still in the middle of the avenue.

A horrible suspicion swept across his mind. . . . She? . . . But then all those other pieces of jewelry must have been presents also! . . . Then it seemed to him that the ground was heaving under his feet; that a tree, right in front of him, was falling toward him; he thrust out his arms instinctively, and fell senseless.

He recovered his consciousness again in a drug-store to which some bystanders had carried   45 him. He had them lead him home, and he locked himself into his room.

Until nightfall he cried without stopping, biting his handkerchief to keep himself from screaming out. Then, completely worn out with grief and fatigue, he went to bed, and slept a leaden sleep.

A ray of sunshine awakened him, and he rose and dressed himself slowly to go to the office. It was hard to have to work after such a shock. Then he reflected that he might be able to excuse himself to the superintendent, and he wrote to him. Then he remembered he would have to go back to the jeweler's; and shame made his face purple. He remained thinking a long time. Still he could not leave the necklace there; he put on his coat and went out.

It was a fine day; the sky extended all blue over the city, and seemed to make it smile. Strollers were walking aimlessly about, with their hands in their pockets.

Lantin thought as he watched them passing: "How lucky the men are who have fortunes! With money a man can even shake off grief—you can go where you please—travel—amuse yourself! Oh! if I were only rich!"

He suddenly discovered he was hungry—not having eaten anything since the evening before.   50 But his pockets were empty; and he remembered the necklace. Eighteen thousand francs! Eighteen thousand francs!—that was a sum—that was!

He made his way to the Rue de la Paix and began to walk backward and forward on the sidewalk in front of the store. Eighteen thousand francs! Twenty times he started to go in; but shame always kept him back.

Still he was hungry—very hungry—and had not a cent. He made one brusque resolve, and crossed the street almost at a run, so as not to let himself have time to think over the matter; and he rushed into the jeweler's.

As soon as he saw him, the merchant hurried forward, and offered him a chair with smiling politeness. Even the clerks came forward to stare at Lantin, with gaiety in their eyes and smiles about their lips.

The jeweler said: "Sir, I made inquiries; and if you are still so disposed, I am ready to pay you down the price I offered you."

The clerk stammered: "Why, yes—sir, certainly."   55

The jeweler took from a drawer eighteen big bills, counted them, and held them out to Lantin, who signed a little receipt, and thrust the money feverishly into his pocket.

Then, as he was on the point of leaving, he turned to the ever-smiling merchant, and said, lowering his eyes: "I have some—I have some other jewelry, which came to me in the same—from the same inheritance. Would you purchase them also from me?"

The merchant bowed, and answered: "Why, certainly, sir—certainly. . . ." One of the clerks rushed out to laugh at his ease; another kept blowing his nose as hard as he could.

Lantin, impassive, flushed and serious, said: "I will bring them to you."

And he hired a cab to get the jewelry.   60

When he returned to the store, an hour later, he had not yet breakfasted. They examined the jewelry—piece by piece—putting a value on each. Nearly all had been purchased from that very house.

Lantin, now, disputed estimates made, got angry, insisted on seeing the books, and talked louder and louder the higher the estimates grew.

The big diamond earrings were worth 20,000 francs; the bracelets, 35,000; the brooches, rings and medallions, 16,000; a set of emeralds and sapphires, 14,000; solitaire, suspended to a gold neckchain, 40,000; the total value being estimated at 196,000 francs.

The merchant observed with mischievous good nature: "The person who owned these must have put all her savings into jewelry."

Lantin answered with gravity: "Perhaps that is as good a way of saving money as any other."   65 And he went off, after having agreed with the merchant that an expert should make a counter-estimate for him the next day.

When he found himself in the street again, he looked at the Column Vendôme with the desire to climb it, as if it were a May pole. He felt jolly enough to play leapfrog over the Emperor's head—up there in the blue sky.

He breakfasted at Voisin's restaurant, and ordered wine at 20 francs a bottle.

Then he hired a cab and drove out to the Bois. He looked at the carriages passing with a sort of contempt, and a wild desire to yell out to the passers-by: "I am rich, too—I am! I have 200,000 francs!"

The recollection of the office suddenly came back to him. He drove there, walked right into the superintendent's private room, and said: "Sir, I come to give you my resignation. I have just come into a fortune of *three* hundred thousand francs." Then he shook hands all round with his fellow-clerks; and told them all about his plans for a new career. Then he went .to dinner at the Café Anglais.

Finding himself seated at the same table with a man who seemed to him quite genteel, he   70 could not resist the itching desire to tell him, with a certain air of coquetry, that he had just inherited a fortune of *four* hundred thousand francs.

For the first time in his life he went to the theater without feeling bored by the performance; and he passed the night in revelry and debauch.

Six months after he married again. His second wife was the most upright of spouses, but had a terrible temper. She made his life very miserable.

[1883]

The Necklace
(Translated by Edgar V. Roberts)

She was one of those pretty and charming women, born, as if by an error of destiny, into a family of clerks and copyists. She had no dowry, no prospects, no way of getting known, courted, loved, married by a rich and distinguished man. She finally settled for a marriage with a minor clerk in the Ministry of Education.

Without the money to dress well, she had to wear everyday clothes, and she was as unhappy as if she had really gone down in the world, for women have neither rank nor race. In place of high birth or important family connections, they can rely only on their beauty, their grace, and their charm. Their inborn finesse, their elegant taste, their engaging personalities, which are their only power, make working-class women the equals of the grandest ladies.

She suffered constantly, feeling herself destined for all delicacies and luxuries. She suffered because of her grim apartment with its drab walls, threadbare furniture, ugly curtains. All such things, which most other women in her situation would not even have noticed, tortured her and filled her with despair. The sight of the young country girl who did her simple housework awakened in her only a sense of desolation and lost hopes. She daydreamed of large, silent anterooms, decorated with oriental tapestries and lighted by high bronze floor lamps, with two elegant valets in short culottes dozing in large armchairs under the effects of forced-air heaters. She imagined large drawing rooms draped in the most expensive silks, with fine end tables on which were placed knickknacks of inestimable value. She dreamed of the perfume of dainty private rooms, which were designed only for intimate tête-à-têtes with the closest friends, who because of their achievements and fame would make her the envy of all other women.

When she sat down to dinner at her round little table covered with a cloth that had not been washed for three days, in front of her husband who opened the kettle while declaring ecstatically, "Ah, good old beef stew! I don't know anything better," she dreamed of expensive banquets with shining place settings, and wall hangings portraying ancient heroes and exotic birds in an enchanted forest. She imagined a gourmet-prepared main course carried on the most exquisite trays and served on the most beautiful dishes, with whispered gallantries that she would hear with a sphinxlike smile as she dined on the pink meat of a trout or the delicate wing of a quail.

She had no decent dresses, no jewels, nothing. And she loved nothing but these; she believed   5
herself born only for these. She burned with the desire to please, to be envied, to be attractive and sought after.

She had a rich friend, a comrade from convent days, whom she did not want to see anymore because she suffered so much when she returned home. She would weep for the entire day afterward with sorrow, regret, despair, and misery.

Well, one evening, her husband came home glowing and carrying a large envelope.

"Here," he said, "this is something for you."

She quickly tore open the envelope and took out a card engraved with these words:

> The Chancellor of Eduction and Mrs. George Ramponneau request that Mr. and Mrs. Loisel do them the honor of coming to dinner at the Ministry of Education on the evening of January 8.

Instead of being delighted, as her husband had hoped, she threw the invitation spitefully on   10
the table, muttering:

"What do you expect me to do with this?"

"But Sweetie, I thought you'd be glad. You never get to go out, and this is a special occasion! I had a lot of trouble getting the invitation. The demand is high and not many clerks get invited. Everyone important will be there."

She looked at him angrily and stated impatiently:

"What do you expect me to wear to go there?"

He had not thought of that. He stammered: 15

"But your theater dress. That seems nice to me . . ."

He stopped, amazed and bewildered, as his wife began to cry. Large tears fell slowly from the corners of her eyes to her mouth. He said falteringly:

"What's wrong? What's the matter?"

But with a strong effort she had recovered, and she answered calmly as she wiped her damp cheeks:

"Nothing, except that I have nothing to wear and therefore can't go to the party. Give your   20
invitation to someone else at the office whose wife will have nicer clothes than mine."

Distressed, he responded:

"Well, all right, Mathilde. How much would a new dress cost, something you could use at other times, but not anything fancy?"

She thought for a few moments, adding things up and thinking also of an amount that she could ask without getting an immediate refusal and a frightened outcry from the frugal clerk.

Finally she responded tentatively:

"I don't know exactly, but it seems to me that I could get by on four hundred francs."   25

He blanched slightly at this, because he had set aside just that amount to buy a shotgun for Sunday lark-hunts the next summer with a few friends in the Plain of Nanterre.

However, he said:

"All right, you've got four hundred francs, but make it a pretty dress."

As the day of the party drew near, Mrs. Loisel seemed sad, uneasy, anxious, even though her gown was already. One evening her husband said to her:

"What's the matter? You've been acting funny for several days."   30

She answered:

"It's awful, but I don't have any jewels to wear, not a single gem, nothing to dress up my outfit. I'll look like a beggar. I'd almost rather not go to the party."

He responded:

"You can wear a corsage of cut flowers. This year it's all the rage. For only ten francs you can get two or three gorgeous roses."

She was not convinced.   35

"No . . . there's nothing more humiliating than looking shabby in the company of rich women."

But her husband exclaimed:

"God, but you're silly! Go to your friend Mrs. Forestier, and ask her to lend you some jewelry. You know her well enough to do that."

She uttered a cry of joy:

"That's right. I hadn't thought of that."   40

The next day she went to her friend's house and described her problem.

Mrs. Forestier went to her mirrored wardrobe, took out a large jewel box, opened it, and said to Mrs. Loisel:

"Choose, my dear."

She saw bracelets, then a pearl necklace, then a Venetian cross of finely worked gold and gems. She tried on the jewelry in front of a mirror, and hesitated, unable to make up her mind about each one. She kept asking:

"Do you have anything else?"   45

"Certainly. Look to your heart's content. I don't know what you'd like best."

Suddenly she found a superb diamond necklace in a black satin box, and her heart throbbed with desire for it. Her hands shook as she picked it up. She fastened it around her neck, watched it gleam at her throat, and looked at herself ecstatically.

Then she asked, haltingly and anxiously:

"Could you lend me this, nothing but this?"

"Why yes, certainly."   50

She jumped up, hugged her friend joyfully, then hurried away with her treasure.

The day of the party came. Mrs. Loisel was a success. She was prettier than anyone else, stylish, graceful, smiling and wild with joy. All the men saw her, asked her name, sought to be introduced. All the important administrators stood in line to waltz with her. The Chancellor himself eyed her.

She danced joyfully, passionately, intoxicated with pleasure, thinking of nothing but the moment, in the triumph of her beauty, in the glory of her success, on Cloud Nine with happiness made up of all the admiration, of all the aroused desire, of this victory so complete and so sweet to the heart of any woman.

She did not leave until four o'clock in the morning. Her husband, since midnight, had been sleeping in a little empty room with three other men whose wives had also been enjoying themselves.

He threw, over her shoulders, the shawl that he had brought for the trip home—a modest   55 everyday wrap, the poverty of which contrasted sharply with the elegance of her evening gown. She felt it and hurried away to avoid being noticed by the other women who luxuriated in rich furs.

Loisel tried to hold her back:

"Wait a minute. You'll catch cold outdoors. I'll call a cab."

But she paid no attention and hurried down the stairs. When they reached the street they found no carriages. They began to look for one, shouting at cabmen passing by at a distance.

They walked toward the Seine, desperate, shivering. Finally, on a quay, they found one of those old night-going buggies that are seen in Paris only after dark, as if they were ashamed of their wretched appearance in daylight.

It took them to their door, on the Street of Martyrs, and they sadly climbed the stairs to their 60 flat. For her, it was finished. As for him, he could think only that he had to begin work at the Ministry of Education at ten o'clock.

She took the shawl off her shoulders, in front of the mirror, to see herself once more in her glory. But suddenly she cried out. The necklace was no longer around her neck!

Her husband, already half undressed, asked:

"What's wrong?"

She turned toward him frantically:

"I . . . I . . . I no longer have Mrs. Forestier's necklace."   65

He stood up, bewildered:

"What! . . . How! . . . It's not possible!"

And they looked in the folds of the gown, in the folds of the shawl, in the pockets, everywhere. They found nothing.

He asked:

"You're sure you still had it when you left the party?"   70

"Yes. I checked it in the vestibule of the Ministry."

"But if you'd lost it in the street, we would've heard it fall. It must be in the cab."

"Yes, probably. Did you notice the number?"

"No. Did you see it?"

"No."   75

Overwhelmed, they looked at each other. Finally, Loisel got dressed again:

"I'm going out to retrace all our steps," he said, "to see if I can find the necklace that way."

And he went out. She stayed in her evening dress, without the energy to get ready for bed, stretched out in a chair, drained of strength and thought.

Her husband came back at about seven o'clock. He had found nothing.

He went to Police Headquarters and to the newspapers to announce a reward. He went to 80 the small cab companies, and finally he followed up even the slightest hopeful lead.

She waited the entire day, in the same enervated state, in the face of this frightful disaster.

Loisel came back in the evening, his face pale and haggard. He had found nothing.

"You'll have to write to your friend," he said, "that you broke a clasp on her necklace and that you're having it fixed. That'll give us time to look around."

She wrote as he dictated.

By the end of the week they had lost all hope.   85

And Loisel, looking five years older, declared:

"We'll have to see about replacing the jewels."

The next day they took the case that had contained the necklace and went to the jeweler whose name was inside. He looked at his books:

"I wasn't the one, Madam, who sold the necklace. I only made the case."

Then they went from jeweler to jeweler, searching for a necklace like the other one, racking 90 their memories, both of them sick with worry and anguish.

In a shop in the Palais-Royal, they found a necklace of diamonds that seemed to them exactly like the one they were looking for. It was priced at forty thousand francs. They could buy it for thirty-six thousand.

They got the jeweler to promise not to sell it for three days. And they made an agreement that he would buy it back for thirty-four thousand francs if the original were recovered before the end of February.

Loisel had saved eighteen thousand francs that his father had left him. He would have to borrow the rest.

He borrowed, asking a thousand francs from one, five hundred from another, five louis here, three louis there. He wrote promissory notes, undertook ruinous obligations, did business with finance companies and the whole tribe of loan sharks. He compromised himself for the remainder of his days, risked his signature without knowing whether he would be able to honor it; and, terrified by anguish over the future, by the black misery that was about to descend on him, by the prospect of all kinds of physical deprivations and moral tortures, he went to get the new necklace, and put down thirty-six thousand francs on the jeweler's counter.

Mrs. Loisel took the necklace back to Mrs. Forestier, who said with an offended tone: 95
"You should have brought it back sooner; I might have needed it."

She did not open the case, as her friend feared she might. If she had noticed the substitution, what would she have thought? What would she have said? Would she not have taken her for a thief?

Mrs. Loisel soon discovered the horrible life of the needy. She did her share, however, completely, heroically. That horrifying debt had to be paid. She would pay. They dismissed the maid; they changed their address; they rented an attic flat.

She learned to do the heavy housework, dirty kitchen jobs. She washed the dishes, wearing away her manicured fingernails on greasy pots and encrusted baking dishes. She handwashed dirty linen, shirts, and dish towels that she hung out on the line to dry. Each morning, she took the garbage down to the street, and she carried up water, stopping at each floor to catch her breath. And, dressed in cheap housedresses, she went to the fruit dealer, the grocer, the butchers, with her basket under her arms, haggling, insulting, defending her measly cash penny by penny.

They had to make installment payments every month, and, to buy more time, to refinance loans.   100

The husband worked evenings to make fair copies of tradesmen's accounts, and late into the night he made copies at five cents a page.

And this life lasted ten years.

At the end of ten years, they had paid back everything—everything—including the extra charges imposed by loan sharks and the accumulation of compound interest.

Mrs. Loisel looked old now. She had become the strong, hard, and rude woman of poor households. Her hair unkempt, with uneven skirts and rough, red hands, she spoke loudly, washed floors with large buckets of water. But sometimes, when her husband was at work, she sat down near the window, and she dreamed of that evening so long ago, of that party, where she had been so beautiful and so admired.

What would life have been like if she had not lost that necklace? Who knows? Who knows?   105
Life is so peculiar, so uncertain. How little a thing it takes to destroy you or to save you!

Well, one Sunday, when she had gone for a stroll along the Champs-Elysées to relax from the cares of the week, she suddenly noticed a woman walking with a child. It was Mrs. Forestier, still youthful, still beautiful, still attractive.

Mrs. Loisel felt moved. Would she speak to her? Yes, certainly. And now that she had paid, she could tell all. Why not?

She walked closer.

"Hello, Jeanne."

The other gave no sign of recognition and was astonished to be addressed so familiarly by   110
this working-class woman. She stammered:

"But . . . Madam! . . . I don't know. . . . You must have made a mistake."

"No. I'm Mathilde Loisel."

Her friend cried out:

"Oh! . . . My poor Mathilde, you've changed so much."

"Yes. I've had some tough times since I saw you last; in fact hardships . . . and all because of 115
you! . . ."

"Of me . . . how so?"

"You remember the diamond necklace that you lent me to go to the party at the Ministry of
Education?"

"Yes. What then?"

"Well, I lost it."
                                                                                    120
"How, since you gave it back to me?"

"I returned another exactly like it. And for ten years we've been paying for it. You understand this wasn't easy for us, who have nothing. . . . Finally it's over, and I'm damn glad."

Mrs. Forestier stopped her.

"You say that you bought a diamond necklace to replace mine?"

"Yes, you didn't notice it, eh? It was exactly like yours."

And she smiled with proud and childish joy.

Mrs. Forestier, deeply moved, took both her hands.
                                                                                    125
"Oh, my poor Mathilde! But mine was only costume jewelry. At most, it was worth only five
hundred francs! . . .

[1884]

Poe, *Edgar Allan (1809–1849)*

The Black Cat

For the most wild, yet most homely narrative which I am about to pen, I neither expect nor solicit
belief. Mad indeed would I be to expect it, in a case where my very senses reject their own evidence.
Yet, mad am I not—and very surely do I not dream. But to-morrow I die, and to-day I would unburden my soul. My immediate purpose is to place before the world, plainly, succinctly, and without
comment, a series of mere household events. In their consequences, these events have terrified—
have tortured—have destroyed me. Yet I will not attempt to expound them. To me, they have presented little but Horror—to many they will seem less terrible than *barroques*. Hereafter, perhaps, some
intellect may be found which will reduce my phantasm to the common-place—some intellect more
calm, more logical, and far less excitable than my own, which will perceive, in the circumstances I
detail with awe, nothing more than an ordinary succession of very natural causes and effects.

From my infancy I was noted for the docility and humanity of my disposition. My tenderness of
heart was even so conspicuous as to make me the jest of my companions. I was especially fond of
animals, and was indulged by my parents with a great variety of pets. With these I spent most of my
time, and never was so happy as when feeding and caressing them. This peculiarity of character
grew with my growth, and in my manhood, I derived from it one of my principal sources of pleasure. To those who have cherished an affection for a faithful and sagacious dog, I need hardly be at
the trouble of explaining the nature or the intensity of the gratification thus derivable. There is
something in the unselfish and self-sacrificing love of a brute, which goes directly to the heart of
him who has had frequent occasion to test the paltry friendship and gossamer fidelity of mere *Man*.

I married early, and was happy to find in my wife a disposition not uncongenial with my own.
Observing my partiality for domestic pets, she lost no opportunity of procuring those of the most
agreeable kind. We had birds, gold-fish, a fine dog, rabbits, a small monkey, and *a cat*.

This latter was a remarkably large and beautiful animal, entirely black, and sagacious to an
astonishing degree. In speaking of his intelligence, my wife, who at heart was not a little tinctured
with superstition, made frequent allusion to the ancient popular notion, which regarded all black
cats as witches in disguise. Not that she was ever *serious* upon this point—and I mention the matter at all for no better reason than that it happens, just now, to be remembered.

Pluto—this was the cat's name—was my favorite pet and playmate. I alone fed him, and he 5 attended me wherever I went about the house. It was even with difficulty that I could prevent him from following me through the streets.

Our friendship lasted, in this manner, for several years, during which my general temperament and character—through the instrumentality of the Fiend Intemperance—had (I blush to confess it) experienced a radical alteration for the worse. I grew, day by day, more moody, more irritable, more regardless of the feelings of others. I suffered myself to use intemperate language to my wife. At length, I even offered her personal violence. My pets, of course, were made to feel the change in my disposition. I not only neglected, but ill-used them. For Pluto, however, I still retained sufficient regard to restrain me from maltreating him, as I made no scruple of maltreating the rabbits, the monkey, or even the dog, when by accident, or through affection, they came in my way. But my disease grew upon me—for what disease is like Alcohol!—and at length even Pluto, who was now becoming old, and consequently somewhat peevish—even Pluto began to experience the effects of my ill temper.

One night, returning home, much intoxicated, from one of my haunts about town, I fancied that the cat avoided my presence. I seized him; when, in his fright at my violence, he inflicted a slight wound upon my hand with his teeth. The fury of a demon instantly possessed me. I knew myself no longer. My original soul seemed, at once, to take its flight from my body and a more than fiendish malevolence, gin-nurtured, thrilled every fibre of my frame. I took from my waistcoat-pocket a pen-knife, opened it, grasped the poor beast by the throat, and deliberately cut one of its eyes from the socket! I blush, I burn, I shudder, while I pen the damnable atrocity.

When reason returned with the morning—when I had slept off the fumes of the night's debauch—I experienced a sentiment half of horror, half of remorse, for the crime of which I had been guilty; but it was, at best, a feeble and equivocal feeling, and the soul remained untouched. I again plunged into excess, and soon drowned in wine all memory of the deed.

In the meantime the cat slowly recovered. The socket of the lost eye presented, it is true, a frightful appearance, but he no longer appeared to suffer any pain. He went about the house as usual, but, as might be expected, fled in extreme terror at my approach. I had so much of my old heart left, as to be at first grieved by this evident dislike on the part of a creature which had once so loved me. But this feeling soon gave place to irritation. And then came, as if to my final and irrevocable overthrow, the spirit of PERVERSENESS. Of this spirit philosophy takes no account. Yet I am not more sure that my soul lives, than I am that perverseness is one of the primitive impulses of the human heart—one of the indivisible primary faculties, or sentiments, which give direction to the character of Man. Who has not, a hundred times, found himself committing a vile or a silly action, for no other reason than because he knows he should not? Have we not a perpetual inclination, in the teeth of our best judgment, to violate that which is *Law*, merely because we understand it to be such? This spirit of perverseness, I say, came to my final overthrow. It was this unfathomable longing of the soul *to vex itself*—to offer violence to its own nature—to do wrong for the wrong's sake only—that urged me to continue and finally to consummate the injury I had inflicted upon the unoffending brute. One morning, in cool blood, I slipped a noose about its neck and hung it to the limb of a tree;—hung it with the tears streaming from my eyes, and with the bitterest remorse at my heart;—hung it *because* I knew that it had loved me, and *because* I felt it had given me no reason of offence;—hung it *because* I knew that in so doing I was committing a sin—a deadly sin that would so jeopardize my immortal soul as to place it—if such a thing were possible—even beyond the reach of the infinite mercy of the Most Merciful and Most Terrible God.

On the night of the day on which this cruel deed was done, I was aroused from sleep by the 10 cry of fire. The curtains of my bed were in flames. The whole house was blazing. It was with great difficulty that my wife, a servant, and myself, made our escape from the conflagration. The destruction was complete. My entire worldly wealth was swallowed up, and I resigned myself thenceforward to despair.

I am above the weakness of seeking to establish a sequence of cause and effect, between the disaster and the atrocity. But I am detailing a chain of facts—and wish not to leave even a possible link imperfect. On the day succeeding the fire, I visited the ruins. The walls, with one exception, had fallen in. This exception was found in a compartment wall, not very thick, which stood about the middle of the house, and against which had rested the head of my bed. The plastering had here, in great measure, resisted the action of the fire—a fact which I attributed to its having been recently spread. About this wall a dense crowd were collected, and many persons seemed to be examining a particular portion of it with very minute and eager attention. The words "strange!" "singular!" and other similar expressions, excited my curiosity. I approached and saw, as if graven in *bas relief* upon the white surface, the figure of a gigantic *cat*. The impression was given with an accuracy truly marvellous. There was a rope about the animal's neck.

When I first beheld this apparition—for I could scarcely regard it as less—my wonder and my terror were extreme. But at length reflection came to my aid. The cat, I remembered, had been hung in a garden adjacent to the house. Upon the alarm of fire, this garden had been immediately filled by the crowd—by some one of whom the animal must have been cut from the tree and thrown, through an open window, into my chamber. This had probably been done with the view of arousing me from sleep. The falling of other walls had compressed the victim of my cruelty into the substance of the freshly-spread plaster; the lime of which, with the flames, and the *ammonia* from the carcass, had then accomplished the portraiture as I saw it.

Although I thus readily accounted to my reason, if not altogether to my conscience, for the startling fact just detailed, it did not the less fail to make a deep impression upon my fancy. For months I could not rid myself of the phantasm of the cat; and, during this period, there came back into my spirit a half-sentiment that seemed, but was not, remorse. I went so far as to regret the loss of the animal, and to look about me, among the vile haunts which I now habitually frequented, for another pet of the same species, and of somewhat similar appearance, with which to supply its place.

One night as I sat, half stupefied, in a den of more than infamy, my attention was suddenly drawn to some black object, reposing upon the head of one of the immense hogsheads of Gin, or of Rum, which constituted the chief furniture of the apartment. I had been looking steadily at the top of this hogshead for some minutes, and what now caused me surprise was the fact that I had not sooner perceived the object thereupon. I approached it, and touched it with my hand. It was a black cat—a very large one—fully as large as Pluto, and closely resembling him in every respect but one. Pluto had not a white hair upon any portion of his body; but this cat had a large, although indefinite splotch of white, covering nearly the whole region of the breast.

Upon my touching him, he immediately arose, purred loudly, rubbed against my hand, and appeared delighted with my notice. This, then, was the very creature of which I was in search. I at once offered to purchase it of the landlord; but this person made no claim to it—knew nothing of it—had never seen it before.   15

I continued my caresses, and, when I prepared to go home, the animal evinced a disposition to accompany me. I permitted it to do so; occasionally stooping and patting it as I proceeded. When it reached the house it domesticated itself at once, and became immediately a great favorite with my wife.

For my own part, I soon found a dislike to it arising within me. This was just the reverse of what I had anticipated; but—I know not how or why it was—its evident fondness for myself rather disgusted and annoyed. By slow degrees, these feelings of disgust and annoyance rose into the bitterness of hatred. I avoided the creature; a certain sense of shame, and the remembrance of my former deed of cruelty, preventing me from physically abusing it. I did not, for some weeks, strike, or otherwise violently ill use it; but gradually—very gradually—I came to look upon it with unutterable loathing, and to flee silently from its odious presence, as from the breath of a pestilence.

What added, no doubt, to my hatred of the beast, was the discovery, on the morning after I brought it home, that, like Pluto, it also had been deprived of one of its eyes. This circumstance, however, only endeared it to my wife, who, as I have already said, possessed, in a high degree, that humanity of feeling which had once been my distinguishing trait, and the source of many of my simplest and purest pleasures.

With my aversion to this cat, however, its partiality for myself seemed to increase. It followed my footsteps with a pertinacity which it would be difficult to make the reader comprehend. Whenever I sat, it would crouch beneath my chair, or spring upon my knees, covering me with its loathsome caresses. If I arose to walk it would get between my feet and thus nearly throw me down, or, fastening its long and sharp claws in my dress, clamber, in this manner, to my breast. At such times, although I longed to destroy it with a blow, I was yet withheld from so doing, partly by a memory of my former crime, but chiefly—let me confess it at once—by absolute dread of the beast.

This dread was not exactly a dread of physical evil—and yet I should be at a loss how otherwise to   20 define it. I am almost ashamed to own—yes, even in this felon's cell, I am almost ashamed to own— that the terror and horror with which the animal inspired me, had been heightened by one of the merest chimaeras it would be possible to conceive. My wife had called my attention, more than once, to the character of the mark of white hair, of which I have spoken, and which constituted the sole visible difference between the strange beast and the one I had destroyed. The reader will remember that this mark, although large, had been originally very indefinite; but, by slow degrees—degrees nearly imperceptible, and which for a long time my Reason struggled to reject as fanciful—it had, at length, assumed a rigorous distinctness of outline. It was now the representation of an object that I shudder to name—and for this, above all, I loathed, and dreaded, and would have rid myself of the monster *had I dared*—it was now, I say, the image of a hideous—of a ghastly thing—of the GALLOWS!—oh, mournful and terrible engine of Horror and of Crime—of Agony and of Death!

And now was I indeed wretched beyond the wretchedness of mere Humanity. And *a brute beast*—whose fellow I had contemptuously destroyed—*a brute beast* to work out for *me*—for me a man, fashioned in the image of the High God—so much of insufferable woe! Alas! neither by day nor by night knew I the blessing of Rest any more! During the former the creature left me no moment alone; and, in the latter, I started, hourly, from dreams of unutterable fear, to find the hot breath of *the thing* upon my face, and its vast weight—an incarnate Night-Mare that I had no power to shake off—incumbent eternally upon my *heart!*

Beneath the pressure of torments such as these, the feeble remnant of the good within me succumbed. Evil thoughts became my sole intimates—the darkest and most evil of thoughts. The moodiness of my usual temper increased to hatred of all things and of all mankind; while, from the sudden, frequent, and ungovernable outbursts of a fury to which I now blindly abandoned myself, my uncomplaining wife, alas! was the most usual and the most patient of sufferers.

One day she accompanied me, upon some household errand, into the cellar of the old building which our poverty compelled us to inhabit. The cat followed me down the steep stairs, and, nearly throwing me headlong, exasperated me to madness. Uplifting an axe, and forgetting, in my wrath, the childish dread which had hitherto stayed my hand, I aimed a blow at the animal which, of course, would have proved instantly fatal had it descended as I wished. But this blow was arrested by the hand of my wife. Goaded, by the interference, into a rage more than demoniacal, I withdrew my arm from her grasp and buried the axe in her brain. She fell dead upon the spot, without a groan.

This hideous murder accomplished, I set myself forthwith, and with entire deliberation, to the task of concealing the body. I knew that I could not remove it from the house, either by day or by night, without the risk of being observed by the neighbors. Many projects entered my mind. At one period I thought of cutting the corpse into minute fragments, and destroying them by fire. At another, I resolved to dig a grave for it in the floor of the cellar. Again, I deliberated about casting it in the well in the yard—about packing it in a box, as if merchandize, with the usual arrangements, and so getting a porter to take it from the house. Finally I hit upon what I considered a far better expedient than either of these. I determined to wall it up in the cellar—as the monks of the middle ages are recorded to have walled up their victims.

For a purpose such as this the cellar was well adapted. Its walls were loosely constructed,   25 and had lately been plastered throughout with a rough plaster, which the dampness of the atmosphere had prevented from hardening. Moreover, in one of the walls was a projection, caused by a false chimney, or fireplace, that had been filled up, and made to resemble the red of the cellar. I made no doubt that I could readily displace the bricks at this point, insert the corpse, and wall the whole up as before, so that no eye could detect any thing suspicious. And in this calculation I was not deceived. By means of a crow-bar I easily dislodged the bricks, and, having carefully deposited the body against the inner wall, I propped it in that position, while, with little trouble, I re-laid the whole structure as it originally stood. Having procured mortar, sand, and hair, with every possible precaution, I prepared a plaster which could not be distinguished from the old, and with this I very carefully went over the new brickwork. When I had finished, I felt satisfied that all was right. The wall did not present the slightest appearance of having been disturbed. The rubbish on the floor was picked up with the minutest care. I looked around triumphantly, and said to myself—"Here at least, then, my labor has not been in vain."

My next step was to look for the beast which had been the cause of so much wretchedness; for I had, at length, firmly resolved to put it to death. Had I been able to meet with it, at the moment, there could have been no doubt of its fate; but it appeared that the crafty animal had been alarmed at the violence of my previous anger, and forebore to present itself in my present mood. It is impossible to describe, or to imagine, the deep, the blissful sense of relief which the absence of the detested creature occasioned in my bosom. It did not make its appearance during the night—and thus for one night at least, since its introduction into the house, I soundly and tranquilly slept; aye, slept even with the burden of murder upon my soul!

The second and the third day passed, and still my tormentor came not. Once again I breathed as a freeman. The monster, in terror, had fled the premises forever! I should behold it no more! My happiness was supreme! The guilt of my dark deed disturbed me but little. Some few inquiries had been made, but these had been readily answered. Even a search had been instituted—but of course nothing was to be discovered. I looked upon my future felicity as secured.

Upon the fourth day of the assassination, a party of the police came, very unexpectedly, into the house, and proceeded again to make rigorous investigation of the premises. Secure, however, in the inscrutability of my place of concealment, I felt no embarrassment whatever. The officers bade me accompany them in their search. They left no nook or corner unexplored. At length, for the third or fourth time, they descended into the cellar. I quivered not in a muscle. My heart beat calmly as that of one who slumbers in innocence. I walked the cellar from end to end. I folded my arms upon my bosom, and roamed easily to and fro. The police were thoroughly satisfied and prepared to depart. The glee at my heart was too strong to be restrained. I burned to say if but one word, by way of triumph, and to render doubly sure their assurance of my guiltlessness.

"Gentlemen," I said at last, as the party ascended the steps, "I delight to have allayed your suspicions. I wish you all health, and a little more courtesy. By the bye, gentlemen, this—this is a very well constructed house." [In the rabid desire to say something easily, I scarcely knew what I uttered at all.]—"I may say an *excellently* well constructed house. These walls—are you going, gentlemen?—these walls are solidly put together;" and here, through the mere frenzy of bravado, I rapped heavily, with a cane which I held in my hand, upon that very portion of the brick-work behind which stood the corpse of the wife of my bosom.

But may God shield and deliver me from the fangs of the Arch-Fiend! No sooner had the 30 reverberation of my blows sunk into silence, than I was answered by a voice from within the tomb!—by a cry, at first muffled and broken, like the sobbing of a child, and then quickly swelling into one long, loud, and continuous scream, utterly anomalous and inhuman—a howl—a wailing shriek, half of horror and half of triumph, such as might have arisen only out of hell, conjointly from the throats of the damned in their agony and of the demons that exult in the damnation.

Of my own thoughts it is folly to speak. Swooning, I staggered to the opposite wall. For one instant the party upon the stairs remained motionless, through extremity of terror and of awe. In the next, a dozen stout arms were toiling at the wall. It fell bodily. The corpse, already greatly decayed and clotted with gore, stood erect before the eyes of the spectators. Upon its head, with red extended mouth and solitary eye of fire, sat the hideous beast whose craft had seduced me into murder, and whose informing voice had consigned me to the hangman. I had walled the monster up within the tomb!

[1843]

The Cask of Amontillado

The thousand injuries of Fortunato I had borne as I best could; but when he ventured upon insult, I vowed revenge. You, who so well know the nature of my soul, will not suppose, however, that I gave utterance to a threat. *At length* I would be avenged; this was a point definitively settled—but the very definitiveness with which it was resolved, precluded the idea of risk. I must not only punish, but punish with impunity. A wrong is unredressed when retribution overtakes its redresser. It is equally unredressed when the avenger fails to make himself felt as such to him who has done the wrong.

It must be understood, that neither by word nor deed had I given Fortunato cause to doubt my good will. I continued, as was my wont, to smile in his face, and he did not perceive that my smile *now* was at the thought of his immolation.

He had a weak point—this Fortunato—although in other regards he was a man to be respected and even feared. He prided himself on his connoisseurship in wine. Few Italians have the true virtuoso spirit. For the most part their enthusiasm is adopted to suit the time and opportunity—to practice imposture upon the British and Austrian *millionaires*. In painting and gemmary, Fortunato, like his countrymen, was a quack—but in the matter of old wines he was sincere. In this respect I did not differ from him materially: I was skilful in the Italian vintages myself, and bought largely whenever I could.

It was about dusk, one evening during the supreme madness of the carnival season, that I encountered my friend. He accosted me with excessive warmth, for he had been drinking much. The man wore motley. He had on a tight-fitting parti-striped dress, and his head was surmounted by the conical cap and bells. I was so pleased to see him, that I thought I should never have done wringing his hand.

I said to him—"My dear Fortunato, you are luckily met. How remarkably well you are look- 5
ing to-day! But I have received a pipe of what passes for Amontillado, and I have my doubts."

"How?" said he. "Amontillado? A pipe? Impossible! And in the middle of the carnival!"

"I have my doubts," I replied; "and I was silly enough to pay the full Amontillado price without consulting you in the matter. You were not to be found, and I was fearful of losing a bargain."

"Amontillado!"

"I have my doubts."

"Amontillado!"   10

"And I must satisfy them."

"Amontillado!"

"As you are engaged, I am on my way to Luchesi. If any one has a critical turn, it is he. He will tell me—"

"Luchesi cannot tell Amontillado from Sherry."

"And yet some fools will have it that his taste is a match for your own."   15

"Come, let us go."

"Whither?"

"To your vaults."

"My friend, no; I will not impose upon your good nature. I perceive you have an engagement. Luchesi—"

"I have no engagement;—come."   20

"My friend, no. It is not the engagement, but the severe cold with which I perceive you are afflicted. The vaults are insufferably damp. They are encrusted with nitre."

"Let us go, nevertheless. The cold is merely nothing. Amontillado! You have been imposed upon. And as for Luchesi, he cannot distinguish Sherry from Amontillado."

Thus speaking, Fortunato possessed himself of my arm. Putting on a mask of black silk, and drawing a *roquelaire* closely about my person, I suffered him to hurry me to my palazzo.

There were no attendants at home; they had absconded to make merry in honor of the time. I had told them that I should not return until the morning, and had given them explicit orders not to stir from the house. These orders were sufficient, I well knew, to insure their immediate disappearance, one and all, as soon as my back was turned.

I took from their sconces two flambeaux, and giving one to Fortunato, bowed him through several suites of rooms to the archway that led into the vaults. I passed down a long and winding staircase, requesting him to be cautious as he followed. We came at length to the foot of the descent, and stood together on the damp ground of the catacombs of the Montresors.

The gait of my friend was unsteady, and the bells upon his cap jingled as he strode.

"The pipe," said he.

"It is farther on," said I; "but observe the white web-work which gleams from these cavern walls."

He turned towards me, and looked into my eyes with two filmy orbs that distilled the rheum of intoxication.

"Nitre?" he asked, at length.

"Nitre," I replied. "How long have you had that cough?"

"Ugh! ugh! ugh!—ugh! ugh! ugh!—ugh! ugh! ugh!—ugh! ugh! ugh!—ugh! ugh! ugh!"

My poor friend found it impossible to reply for many minutes.

"It is nothing," he said, at last.

"Come," I said, with decision, "we will go back; your health is precious. You are rich, respected, admired, beloved; you are happy, as once I was. You are a man to be missed. For me it is no matter. We will go back; you will be ill, and I cannot be responsible. Besides, there is Luchesi—"

"Enough," he said; "the cough is a mere nothing; it will not kill me. I shall not die of a cough."

"True—true," I replied; "and, indeed, I had no intention of alarming you unnecessarily—but you should use all proper caution. A draught of this Medoc will defend us from the damps."

Here I knocked off the neck of a bottle which I drew from a long row of its fellows that lay upon the mould.

"Drink," I said, presenting him the wine.

He raised it to his lips with a leer. He paused and nodded to me familiarly, while his bells jingled.

"I drink," he said, "to the buried that repose around us."

"And I to your long life."

He again took my arm, and we proceeded.

"These vaults," he said, "are extensive."

"The Montresors," I replied, "were a great and numerous family."

"I forget your arms."

"A huge human foot d'or, in a field azure; the foot crushes a serpent rampant whose fangs are imbedded in the heel."

"And the motto?"

"Nemo me impune lacessit."

"Good!" he said.

The wine sparkled in his eyes and the bells jingled. My own fancy grew warm with the Medoc. We had passed through walls of piled bones, with casks and puncheons intermingling, into the inmost recesses of the catacombs. I paused again, and this time I made bold to seize Fortunato by an arm above the elbow.

"The nitre!" I said: "see, it increases. It hangs like moss upon the vaults. We are below the river's bed. The drops of moisture trickle among the bones. Come, we will go back ere it is too late. Your cough—"

"It is nothing," he said; "let us go on. But first, another draught of the Medoc."

I broke and reached him a flagon of De Grave. He emptied it at a breath. His eyes flashed with a fierce light. He laughed and threw the bottle upwards with a gesticulation I did not understand.

I looked at him in surprise. He repeated the movement—a grotesque one.

"You do not comprehend?" he said.

"Not I," I replied.

"Then you are not of the brotherhood."

"How?"

"You are not of the masons."

"Yes, yes," I said, "yes, yes." 60

"You? Impossible! A mason?"

"A mason," I replied.

"A sign," he said.

"It is this," I answered, producing a trowel from beneath the folds of my *roquelaire*. 65

"You jest," he exclaimed, recoiling a few paces. "But let us proceed to the Amontillado."

"Be it so," I said, replacing the tool beneath the cloak, and again offering him my arm. He leaned upon it heavily. We continued our route in search of the Amontillado. We passed through a range of low arches, descended, passed on, and descending again, arrived at a deep crypt, in which the foulness of the air caused our flambeaux rather to glow than flame.

At the most remote end of the crypt there appeared another less spacious. Its walls had been lined with human remains, piled to the vault overhead, in the fashion of the great catacombs of Paris. Three sides of this interior crypt were still ornamented in this manner. From the fourth the bones had been thrown down, and lay promiscuously upon the earth, forming at one point a mound of some size. Within the wall thus exposed by the displacing of the bones, we perceived a still interior recess, in depth about four feet, in width three, in height six or seven. It seemed to have been constructed for no especial use in itself, but formed merely the interval between two of the colossal supports of the roof of the catacombs, and was backed by one of their circumscribing walls of solid granite.

It was in vain that Fortunato, uplifting his dull torch, endeavored to pry into the depths of the recess. Its termination the feeble light did not enable us to see.

"Proceed," I said; "herein is the Amontillado. As for Luchesi—" 70

"He is an ignoramus," interrupted my friend, as he stepped unsteadily forward, while I followed immediately at his heels. In an instant he had reached the extremity of the niche, and finding his progress arrested by the rock, stood stupidly bewildered. A moment more and I had fettered him to the granite. In its surface were two iron staples, distant from each other about two feet, horizontally. From one of these depended a short chain, from the other a padlock. Throwing the links about his waist, it was but the work of a few seconds to secure it. He was too much astounded to resist. Withdrawing the key I stepped back from the recess.

"Pass your hand," I said, "over the wall; you cannot help feeling the nitre. Indeed it is *very damp. Once more let me implore* you to return. No? Then I must positively leave you. But I must first render you all the little attentions in my power."

"The Amontillado!" ejaculated my friend, not yet recovered from his astonishment.

"True," I replied; "the Amontillado."

As I said these words I busied myself among the pile of bones of which I have before spoken. 75 Throwing them aside, I soon uncovered a quantity of building stone and mortar. With these materials and with the aid of my trowel, I began vigorously to wall up the entrance of the niche.

I had scarcely laid the first tier of my masonry when I discovered that the intoxication of Fortunato had in a great measure worn off. The earliest indication I had of this was a low moaning cry from the depth of the recess. It was *not* the cry of a drunken man. There was then a long and obstinate silence. I laid the second tier, and the third, and the fourth; and then I heard the furious vibrations of the chain. The noise lasted for several minutes, during which, that I might hearken to it with the more satisfaction, I ceased my labors and sat down upon the bones. When at last the clanking subsided, I resumed the trowel, and finished without interruption the fifth, the sixth, and the seventh tier. The wall was now nearly upon a level with my breast. I again paused, and holding the flambeaux over the mason-work, threw a few feeble rays upon the figure within.

A succession of loud and shrill screams, bursting suddenly from the throat of the chained form, seemed to thrust me violently back. For a brief moment I hesitated—I trembled. Unsheathing my rapier, I began to grope with it about the recess: but the thought of an instant reassured me. I placed my hand upon the solid fabric of the catacombs, and felt satisfied. I reapproached the wall. I replied to the yells of him who clamored. I re-echoed—I aided—I surpassed them in volume and in strength. I did this, and the clamorer grew still.

It was now midnight, and my task was drawing to a close. I had completed the eighth, the ninth, and the tenth tier. I had finished a portion of the last and the eleventh; there remained but a single stone to be fitted and plastered in. I struggled with its weight; I placed it partially in its destined position. But now there came from out the niche a low laugh that erected the hairs upon my head. It was succeeded by a sad voice, which I had difficulty in recognizing as that of the noble Fortunato. The voice said—

"Ha! ha! ha!—he! he!—a very good joke indeed—an excellent jest. We will have many a rich laugh about it at the palazzo—he! he! he!—over our wine—he! he! he!"

"The Amontillado!" I said.   80

"He! he! he!—he! he! he!—yes, the Amontillado. But is it not getting late? Will not they be awaiting us at the palazzo, the Lady Fortunato and the rest? Let us be gone."

"Yes," I said, "let us be gone."

"For the love of God, Montresor!"

"Yes," I said, "for the love of God!"

But to these words I hearkened in vain for a reply. I grew impatient. I called aloud—   85

"Fortunato!"

No answer. I called again—

"Fortunato!"

No answer still. I thrust a torch through the remaining aperture and let it fall within. There came forth in return only a jingling of the bells. My heart grew sick—on account of the dampness of the catacombs. I hastened to make an end of my labor. I forced the last stone into its position; I plastered it up. Against the new masonry I re-erected the old rampart of bones. For the half of a century no mortal has disturbed them. *In pace requiescat!*

[1846]

Tan, Amy (1952–)

A Pair of Tickets

The minute our train leaves the Hong Kong border and enters Shenzhen, China, I feel different. I can feel the skin on my forehead tingling, my blood rushing through a new course, my bones aching with a familiar old pain. And I think, My mother was right. I am becoming Chinese.

"Cannot be helped," my mother said when I was fifteen and had vigorously denied that I had any Chinese whatsoever below my skin. I was a sophomore at Galileo High in San Francisco, and all my Caucasian friends agreed: I was about as Chinese as they were. But my mother had studied at a famous nursing school in Shanghai, and she said she knew all about genetics. So there was no doubt in her mind, whether I agreed or not: Once you are born Chinese, you cannot help but feel and think Chinese.

"Someday you will see," said my mother. "It is in your blood, waiting to be let go."

And when she said this, I saw myself transforming like a werewolf, a mutant tag of DNA suddenly triggered, replicating itself insidiously into a *syndrome*, a cluster of telltale Chinese behaviors, all those things my mother did to embarrass me—haggling with store owners, pecking her mouth with a toothpick in public, being color-blind to the fact that lemon yellow and pale pink are not good combinations for winter clothes.

But today I realize I've never really known what it means to be Chinese. I am thirty-six years   5 old. My mother is dead and I am on a train, carrying with me her dreams of coming home. I am going to China.

We are first going to Guangzhou, my seventy-two-year-old father, Canning Woo, and I, where we will visit his aunt, whom he has not seen since he was ten years old. And I don't know whether it's the prospect of seeing his aunt or if it's because he's back in China, but now he looks like he's a young boy, so innocent and happy I want to button his sweater and pat his head. We are sitting across from each other, separated by a little table with two cold cups of tea. For the first time I can ever remember, my father has tears in his eyes, and all he is seeing out the train window is a sectioned field of yellow, green, and brown, a narrow canal flanking the tracks, low rising hills, and three people in blue jackets riding an ox-driven cart on this early October morning. And I can't help myself. I also have misty eyes, as if I had seen this a long, long time ago, and had almost forgotten.

In less than three hours, we will be in Guangzhou, which my guidebook tells me is how one properly refers to Canton these days. It seems all the cities I have heard of, except Shanghai, have changed their spellings. I think they are saying China has changed in other ways as well. Chungking is Chongqing. And Kweilin is Guilin. I have looked these names up, because after we see my father's aunt in Guangzhou, we will catch a plane to Shanghai, where I will meet my two half-sisters for the first time.

They are my mother's twin daughters from her first marriage, little babies she was forced to abandon on a road as she was fleeing Kweilin for Chungking in 1944. That was all my mother had told me about these daughters, so they had remained babies in my mind, all these years, sitting on the side of a road, listening to bombs whistling in the distance while sucking their patient red thumbs.

And it was only this year that someone found them and wrote with this joyful news. A letter came from Shanghai, addressed to my mother. When I first heard about this, that they were alive, I imagined my identical sisters transforming from little babies into six-year-old girls. In my mind, they were seated next to each other at a table, taking turns with the fountain pen. One would write a neat row of characters: *Dearest Mama. We are alive.* She would brush back her wispy bangs and hand the other sister the pen, and she would write: *Come get us. Please hurry.*

Of course they could not know that my mother had died three months before, suddenly, 10 when a blood vessel in her brain burst. One minute she was talking to my father, complaining about the tenants upstairs, scheming how to evict them under the pretense that relatives from China were moving in. The next minute she was holding her head, her eyes squeezed shut, groping for the sofa, and then crumpling softly to the floor with fluttering hands.

So my father had been the first one to open the letter, a long letter it turned out. And they did call her Mama. They said they always revered her as their true mother. They kept a framed picture of her. They told her about their life, from the time my mother last saw them on the road leaving Kweilin to when they were finally found.

And the letter had broken my father's heart so much—these daughters calling my mother from another life he never knew—that he gave the letter to my mother's old friend Auntie Lindo and asked her to write back and tell my sisters, in the gentlest way possible, that my mother was dead.

But instead Auntie Lindo took the letter to the Joy Luck Club and discussed with Auntie Ying and Auntie An-mei what should be done, because they had known for many years about my mother's search for her twin daughters, her endless hope. Auntie Lindo and the others cried over this double tragedy, of losing my mother three months before, and now again. And so they couldn't help but think of some miracle, some possible way of reviving her from the dead, so my mother could fulfill her dream.

So this is what they wrote to my sisters in Shanghai: "Dearest Daughters, I too have never forgotten you in my memory or in my heart. I never gave up hope that we would see each other again in a joyous reunion. I am only sorry it has been too long. I want to tell you everything about my life since I last saw you. I want to tell you this when our family comes to see you in China. . . ." They signed it with my mother's name.

It wasn't until all this had been done that they first told me about my sisters, the letter they 15 received, the one they wrote back.

"They'll think she's coming, then," I murmured. And I had imagined my sisters now being ten or eleven, jumping up and down, holding hands, their pigtails bouncing, excited that their mother—*their* mother—was coming, whereas my mother was dead.

"How can you say she is not coming in a letter?" said Auntie Lindo. "She is their mother. She is your mother. You must be the one to tell them. All these years, they have been dreaming of her." And I thought she was right.

But then I started dreaming, too, of my mother and my sisters and how it would be if I arrived in Shanghai. All these years, while they waited to be found, I had lived with my mother and then had lost her. I imagined seeing my sisters at the airport. They would be standing on their tip-toes, looking anxiously, scanning from one dark head to another as we got off the plane. And I would recognize them instantly, their faces with the identical worried look.

"*Jyejye, Jyejye.* Sister, Sister. We are here," I saw myself saying in my poor version of Chinese.

"Where is Mama?" they would say, and look around, still smiling, two flushed and eager 20
faces. "Is she hiding?" And this would have been like my mother, to stand behind just a bit, to tease a little and make people's patience pull a little on their hearts. I would shake my head and tell my sisters she was not hiding.

"Oh, that must be Mama, no?" one of my sisters would whisper excitedly, pointing to another small woman completely engulfed in a tower of presents. And that, too, would have been like my mother, to bring mountains of gifts, food, and toys for children—all bought on sale—shunning thanks, saying the gifts were nothing, and later turning the labels over to show my sisters, "Calvin Klein, 100% wool."

I imagined myself starting to say, "Sisters, I am sorry, I have come alone . . ." and before I could tell them—they could see it in my face—they were wailing, pulling their hair, their lips twisted in pain, as they ran away from me. And then I saw myself getting back on the plane and coming home.

After I had dreamed this scene many times—watching their despair turn from horror into anger—I begged Auntie Lindo to write another letter. And at first she refused.

"How can I say she is dead? I cannot write this," said Auntie Lindo with a stubborn look.

"But it's cruel to have them believe she's coming on the plane," I said. "When they see it's 25
just me, they'll hate me."

"Hate you? Cannot be." She was scowling. "You are their own sister, their only family."

"You don't understand," I protested.

"What I don't understand?" she said.

And I whispered, "They'll think I'm responsible, that she died because I didn't appreciate her."

And Auntie Lindo looked satisfied and sad at the same time, as if this were true and I had 30
finally realized it. She sat down for an hour, and when she stood up she handed me a two-page letter. She had tears in her eyes. I realized that the very thing I had feared, she had done. So even if she had written the news of my mother's death in English, I wouldn't have had the heart to read it.

"Thank you," I whispered.

The landscape has become gray, filled with low flat cement buildings, old fac-tories, and then tracks and more tracks filled with trains like ours passing by in the opposite direction. I see platforms crowded with people wearing drab Western clothes, with spots of bright colors: little children wearing pink and yellow, red and peach. And there are soldiers in olive green and red, and old ladies in gray tops and pants that stop mid-calf. We are in Guangzhou.

Before the train even comes to a stop, people are bringing down their belongings from above their seats. For a moment there is a dangerous shower of heavy suitcases laden with gifts to relatives, half-broken boxes wrapped in miles of string to keep the contents from spilling out, plastic bags filled with yarn and vegetables and packages of dried mushrooms, and camera cases. And then we are caught in a stream of people rushing, shoving, pushing us along, until we find ourselves in one of a dozen lines waiting to go through customs. I feel as if I were getting on the number 30 Stockton bus in San Francisco. I am in China, I remind myself. And somehow the crowds don't bother me. It feels right. I start pushing too.

I take out the declaration forms and my passport. "Woo," it says at the top, and below that, "June May," who was born in "California, U.S.A.," in 1951. I wonder if the customs people will question whether I'm the same person in the passport photo. In this picture, my chin-length hair is swept back and artfully styled. I am wearing false eyelashes, eye shadow, and lip liner. My cheeks are hollowed out by bronze blusher. But I had not expected the heat in October. And now my hair hangs limp with the humidity. I wear no makeup; in Hong Kong my mascara had melted into dark circles and everything else had felt like layers of grease. So today my face is plain, unadorned except for a thin mist of shiny sweat on my forehead and nose.

Even without makeup, I could never pass for true Chinese. I stand five-foot-six, and my head   35 pokes above the crowd so that I am eye level only with other tourists. My mother once told me my height came from my grandfather, who was a northerner, and may have even had some Mongol blood. "This is what your grandmother once told me," explained my mother. "But now it is too late to ask her. They are all dead, your grandparents, your uncles, and their wives and children, all killed in the war, when a bomb fell on our house. So many generations in one instant."

She had said this so matter-of-factly that I thought she had long since gotten over any grief she had. And then I wondered how she knew they were all dead.

"Maybe they left the house before the bomb fell," I suggested.

"No," said my mother. "Our whole family is gone. It is just you and I."

"But how do you know? Some of them could have escaped."

"Cannot be," said my mother, this time almost angrily. And then her frown was washed over   40 by a puzzled blank look, and she began to talk as if she were trying to remember where she had misplaced something. "I went back to that house. I kept looking up to where the house used to be. And it wasn't a house, just the sky. And below, underneath my feet, were four stories of burnt bricks and wood, all the life of our house. Then off to the side I saw things blown into the yard, nothing valuable. There was a bed someone used to sleep in, really just a metal frame twisted up at one corner. And a book, I don't know what kind, because every page had turned black. And I saw a teacup which was unbroken but filled with ashes. And then I found my doll, with her hands and legs broken, her hair burned off. . . . When I was a little girl, I had cried for that doll, seeing it all alone in the store window, and my mother had bought it for me. It was an American doll with yellow hair. It could turn its legs and arms. The eyes moved up and down. And when I married and left my family home, I gave the doll to my youngest niece, because she was like me. She cried if that doll was not with her always. Do you see? If she was in the house with that doll, her parents were there, and so everybody was there, waiting together, because that's how our family was."

The woman in the customs booth stares at my documents, then glances at me briefly, and with two quick movements stamps everything and sternly nods me along. And soon my father and I find ourselves in a large area filled with thousands of people and suitcases. I feel lost and my father looks helpless.

"Excuse me," I say to a man who looks like an American. "Can you tell me where I can get a taxi?" He mumbles something that sounds Swedish or Dutch.

"Syau Yen! Syau Yen!" I hear a piercing voice shout from behind me. An old woman in a yellow knit beret is holding up a pink plastic bag filled with wrapped trinkets. I guess she is trying to sell us something. But my father is staring down at this tiny sparrow of a woman, squinting into her eyes. And then his eyes widen, his face opens up and he smiles like a pleased little boy.

"Aiyi! Aiyi!"—Auntie Auntie!—he says softly.

"Syau Yen!" coos my great-aunt. I think it's funny she has just called my father "Little Wild   45 Goose." It must be his baby milk name, the name used to discourage ghosts from stealing children.

They clasp each other's hands—they do not hug—and hold on like this, taking turns saying, "Look at you! You are so old. Look how old you've become!" They are both crying openly, laughing at the same time, and I bite my lip, trying not to cry. I'm afraid to feel their joy. Because I am thinking how different our arrival in Shanghai will be tomorrow, how awkward it will feel.

Now Aiyi beams and points to a Polaroid picture of my father. My father had wisely sent pictures when he wrote and said we were coming. See how smart she was, she seems to intone as she compares the picture to my father. In the letter, my father had said we would call her from the hotel once we arrived, so this is a surprise, that they've come to meet us. I wonder if my sisters will be at the airport.

It is only then that I remember the camera. I had meant to take a picture of my father and his aunt the moment they met. It's not too late.

"Here, stand together over here," I say, holding up the Polaroid. The camera flashes and I hand them the snapshot. Aiyi and my father still stand close together, each of them holding a corner of the picture, watching as their images begin to form. They are almost reverentially quiet. Aiyi is only five years older than my father, which makes her around seventy-seven. But she looks ancient, shrunken, a mummified relic. Her thin hair is pure white, her teeth are brown with decay. So much for stories of Chinese women looking young forever, I think to myself.

Now Aiyi is crooning to me: "*Jandale.*" So big already. She looks up at me, at my full height, 50 and then peers into her pink plastic bag—her gifts to us, I have figured out—as if she is wondering what she will give to me, now that I am so old and big. And then she grabs my elbow with her sharp pincerlike grasp and turns me around. A man and woman in their fifties are shaking hands with my father, everybody smiling and saying, "Ah! Ah!" They are Aiyi's oldest son and his wife, and standing next to them are four other people, around my age, and a little girl who's around ten. The introductions go by so fast, all I know is that one of them is Aiyi's grandson, with his wife, and the other is her granddaughter, with her husband. And the little girl is Lili, Aiyi's great-granddaughter.

Aiyi and my father speak the Mandarin dialect from their childhood, but the rest of the family speaks only the Cantonese of their village. I understand only Mandarin but can't speak it that well. So Aiyi and my father gossip unrestrained in Mandarin, exchanging news about people from their old village. And they stop only occasionally to talk to the rest of us, sometimes in Cantonese, sometimes in English.

"Oh, it is as I suspected," says my father, turning to me. "He died last summer." And I already understood this. I just don't know who this person, Li Gong, is. I feel as if I were in the United Nations and the translators had run amok.

"Hello," I say to the little girl. "My name is Jing-mei." But the little girl squirms to look away, causing her parents to laugh with embarrassment. I try to think of Cantonese words I can say to her, stuff I learned from friends in Chinatown, but all I can think of are swear words, terms for bodily functions, and short phrases like "tastes good," "tastes like garbage," and "she's really ugly." And then I have another plan: I hold up the Polaroid camera, beckoning Lili with my finger. She immediately jumps forward, places one hand on her hip in the manner of a fashion model, juts out her chest, and flashes me a toothy smile. As soon as I take the picture she is standing next to me, jumping and giggling every few seconds as she watches herself appear on the greenish film.

By the time we hail taxis for the ride to the hotel, Lili is holding tight onto my hand, pulling me along.

In the taxi, Aiyi talks nonstop, so I have no chance to ask her about the different sights we 55 are passing by.

"You wrote and said you would come only for one day," says Aiyi to my father in an agitated tone. "One day! How can you see your family in one day! Toishan is many hours' drive from Guangzhou. And this idea to call us when you arrive. This is nonsense. We have no telephone."

My heart races a little. I wonder if Auntie Lindo told my sisters we would call from the hotel in Shanghai?

Aiyi continues to scold my father. "I was so beside myself, ask my son, almost turned heaven and earth upside down trying to think of a way! So we decided the best was for us to take the bus from Toishan and come into Guangzhou—meet you right from the start."

And now I am holding my breath as the taxi driver dodges between trucks and buses, honking his horn constantly. We seem to be on some sort of long freeway overpass, like a bridge above the city. I can see row after row of apartments, each floor cluttered with laundry hanging out to dry on the balcony. We pass a public bus, with people jammed in so tight their faces are nearly wedged against the window. Then I see the skyline of what must be downtown Guangzhou. From a distance, it looks like a major American city, with high rises and construction going on everywhere. As we slow down in the more congested part of the city, I see scores of little shops, dark inside, lined with counters and shelves. And then there is a building, its front laced with scaffolding made of bamboo poles held together with plastic strips. Men and women are standing on narrow platforms, scraping the sides, working without safety straps or helmets. Oh, would OSHA have a field day here, I think.

Aiyi's shrill voice rises up again: "So it is a shame you can't see our village, our house. My 60 sons have been quite successful, selling our vegetables in the free market. We had enough these last few years to build a big house, three stories, all of new brick, big enough for our whole family and then some. And every year, the money is even better. You Americans aren't the only ones who know how to get rich!"

The taxi stops and I assume we've arrived, but then I peer out at what looks like a grander version of the Hyatt Regency. "This is communist China?" I wonder out loud. And then I shake my head toward my father. "This must be the wrong hotel." I quickly pull out our itinerary, travel tickets, and reservations. I had explicitly instructed my travel agent to choose something inexpensive, in the thirty-to-forty-dollar range. I'm sure of this. And there it says on our itinerary: Garden Hotel, Huanshi Dong Lu. Well, our travel agent had better be prepared to eat the extra, that's all I have to say.

The hotel is magnificent. A bellboy complete with uniform and sharp-creased cap jumps forward and begins to carry our bags into the lobby. Inside, the hotel looks like an orgy of shopping arcades and restaurants all encased in granite and glass. And rather than be impressed, I am worried about the expense, as well as the appearance it must give Aiyi, that we rich Americans cannot be without our luxuries even for one night.

But when I step up to the reservation desk, ready to haggle over this booking mistake, it is confirmed. Our rooms are prepaid, thirty-four dollars each. I feel sheepish, and Aiyi and the others seem delighted by our temporary surroundings. Lili is looking wide-eyed at an arcade filled with video games.

Our whole family crowds into one elevator, and the bellboy waves, saying he will meet us on the eighteenth floor. As soon as the elevator door shuts, everybody becomes very quiet, and when the door finally opens again, everybody talks at once in what sounds like relieved voices. I have the feeling Aiyi and the others have never been on such a long elevator ride.

Our rooms are next to each other and are identical. The rugs, drapes, bedspreads are all in 65 shades of taupe. There's a color television with remote-control panels built into the lamp table between the two twin beds. The bathroom has marble walls and floors. I find a built-in wet bar with a small refrigerator stocked with Heineken beer, Coke Classic, and Seven-Up, mini-bottles of Johnnie Walker Red, Bacardi rum, and Smirnoff vodka, and packets of M & M's, honey-roasted cashews, and Cadbury chocolate bars. And again I say out loud, "This is communist China?"

My father comes into my room. "They decided we should just stay here and visit," he says, shrugging his shoulders. "They say, Less trouble that way. More time to talk."

"What about dinner?" I ask. I have been envisioning my first real Chinese feast for many days already, a big banquet with one of those soups steaming out of a carved winter melon, chicken wrapped in clay, Peking duck, the works.

My father walks over and picks up a room service book next to a *Travel & Leisure* magazine. He flips through the pages quickly and then points to the menu. "This is what they want," says my father.

So it's decided. We are going to dine tonight in our rooms, with our family, sharing hamburgers, french fries, and apple pie à la mode.

Aiyi and her family are browsing the shops while we clean up. After a hot ride on the train, 70 I'm eager for a shower and cooler clothes.

The hotel has provided little packets of shampoo which, upon opening, I discover is the consistency and color of hoisin sauce. This is more like it, I think. This is China. And I rub some in my damp hair.

Standing in the shower, I realize this is the first time I've been by myself in what seems like days. But instead of feeling relieved, I feel forlorn. I think about what my mother said, about activating my genes and becoming Chinese. And I wonder what she meant.

Right after my mother died, I asked myself a lot of things, things that couldn't be answered, to force myself to grieve more. It seemed as if I wanted to sustain my grief, to assure myself that I had cared deeply enough.

But now I ask the questions mostly because I want to know the answers. What was that pork stuff she used to make that had the texture of sawdust? What were the names of the uncles who died in Shanghai? What had she dreamt all these years about her other daughters? All the times when she got mad at me, was she really thinking about them? Did she wish I were they? Did she regret that I wasn't?

At one o'clock in the morning, I awake to tapping sounds on the window. I must have dozed off and now I feel my body uncramping itself. I'm sitting on the floor, leaning against one of the twin beds. Lili is lying next to me. The others are asleep, too, sprawled out on the beds and floor. Aiyi is seated at a little table, looking very sleepy. And my father is staring out the window, tapping his fingers on the glass. The last time I listened my father was telling Aiyi about his life since he last saw her. How he had gone to Yenching University, later got a post with a newspaper in Chungking, met my mother there, a young widow. How they later fled together to Shanghai to try to find my mother's family house, but there was nothing there. And then they traveled eventually to Canton and then to Hong Kong, then Haiphong and finally to San Francisco. . . .

"Suyuan didn't tell me she was trying all these years to find her daughters," he is now saying in a quiet voice. "Naturally, I did not discuss her daughters with her. I thought she was ashamed she had left them behind."

"Where did she leave them?" asks Aiyi. "How were they found?"

I am wide awake now. Although I have heard parts of this story from my mother's friends.

"It happened when the Japanese took over Kweilin," says my father.

"Japanese in Kweilin?" says Aiyi. "That was never the case. Couldn't be. The Japanese never came to Kweilin."

"Yes, that is what the newspapers reported. I know this because I was working for the news bureau at the time. The Kuomintang often told us what we could say and could not say. But we knew the Japanese had come into Kwangsi Province. We had sources who told us how they had captured the Wuchang-Canton railway. How they were coming overland, making very fast progress, marching toward the provincial capital."

Aiyi looks astonished. "If people did not know this, how could Suyuan know the Japanese were coming?"

"An officer of the Kuomintang secretly warned her," explains my father. "Suyuan's husband also was an officer and everybody knew that officers and their families would be the first to be killed. So she gathered a few possessions and, in the middle of the night, she picked up her daughters and fled on foot. The babies were not even one year old."

"How could she give up those babies!" sighs Aiyi. "Twin girls. We have never had such luck in our family." And then she yawns again.

"What were they named?" she asks. I listen carefully. I had been planning on using just the familiar "Sister" to address them both. But now I want to know how to pronounce their names.

"They have their father's surname, Wang," says my father. "And their given names are Chwun Yu and Chwun Hwa."

"What do the names mean?" I ask.

"Ah." My father draws imaginary characters on the window. "One means 'Spring Rain,' the other 'Spring Flower,'" he explains in English, "because they born in the spring, and of course rain come before flower, same order these girls are born. Your mother like a poet, don't you think?"

I nod my head. I see Aiyi nod her head forward, too. But it falls forward and stays there. She is breathing deeply, noisily. She is asleep.

"And what does Ma's name mean?" I whisper.   90

"'Suyuan,'" he says, writing more invisible characters on the glass. "The way she write it in Chinese, it mean 'Long-Cherished Wish.' Quite a fancy name, not so ordinary like flower name. See this first character, it mean something like 'Forever Never Forgotten.' But there is another way to write 'Suyuan.' Sound exactly the same, but the meaning is opposite." His finger creates the brushstrokes of another character. "The first part look the same: 'Never Forgotten.' But the last part add to first part make the whole word mean 'Long-Held Grudge.' Your mother get angry with me, I tell her her name should be Grudge."

My father is looking at me, moist-eyed. "See, I pretty clever, too, hah?"

I nod, wishing I could find some way to comfort him. "And what about my name," I ask, "what does 'Jing-mei' mean?"

"Your name also special," he says. I wonder if any name in Chinese is not something special. " 'Jing' like excellent *jing*. Not just good, it's something pure, essential, the best quality. *Jing* is good leftover stuff when you take impurities out of something like gold, or rice, or salt. So what is left—just pure essence. And 'Mei,' this is common *mei*, as in *meimei*, 'younger sister.'"

I think about this. My mother's long-cherished wish. Me, the younger sister who was supposed   95
to be the essence of the others. I feed myself with the old grief, wondering how disappointed my mother must have been. Tiny Aiyi stirs suddenly, her head rolls and then falls back, her mouth opens as if to answer my question. She grunts in her sleep, tucking her body more closely into the chair.

"So why did she abandon those babies on the road?" I need to know, because now I feel abandoned too.

"Long time I wondered this myself," says my father. "But then I read that letter from her daughters in Shanghai now, and I talk to Auntie Lindo, all the others. And then I knew. No shame in what she done. None."

"What happened?"

"Your mother running away—" begins my father.

"No, tell me in Chinese," I interrupt. "Really, I can understand."   100

He begins to talk, still standing at the window, looking into the night.

After fleeing Kweilin, your mother walked for several days trying to find a main road. Her thought was to catch a ride on a truck or wagon, to catch enough rides until she reached Chungking, where her husband was stationed.

She had sewn money and jewelry into the lining of her dress, enough, she thought, to barter rides all the way. If I am lucky, she thought, I will not have to trade the heavy gold bracelet and jade ring. These were things from her mother, your grandmother.

By the third day, she had traded nothing. The roads were filled with people, everybody running and begging for rides from passing trucks. The trucks rushed by, afraid to stop. So your mother found no rides, only the start of dysentery pains in her stomach.

Her shoulders ached from the two babies swinging from scarf slings. Blisters grew on her   105
palms from holding two leather suitcases. And then the blisters burst and began to bleed. After a while, she left the suitcases behind, keeping only the food and a few clothes. And later she also dropped the bags of wheat flour and rice and kept walking like this for many miles, singing songs to her little girls, until she was delirious with pain and fever.

Finally, there was not one more step left in her body. She didn't have the strength to carry those babies any farther. She slumped to the ground. She knew she would die of her sickness, or perhaps from thirst, from starvation, or from the Japanese, who she was sure were marching right behind her.

She took the babies out of the slings and sat them on the side of the road, then lay down next to them. You babies are so good, she said, so quiet. They smiled back, reaching their chubby hands for her, wanting to be picked up again. And then she knew she could not bear to watch her babies die with her.

She saw a family with three young children in a cart going by. "Take my babies, I beg you," she cried to them. But they stared back with empty eyes and never stopped.

She saw another person pass and called out again. This time a man turned around, and he had such a terrible expression—your mother said it looked like death itself—she shivered and looked away.

When the road grew quiet, she tore open the lining of her dress, and stuffed jewelry under 110 the shirt of one baby and money under the other. She reached into her pocket and drew out the photos of her family, the picture of her father and mother, the picture of herself and her husband on their wedding day. And she wrote on the back of each the names of the babies and this same message: "Please care for these babies with the money and valuables provided. When it is safe to come, if you bring them to Shanghai, 9 Weichang Lu, the Li family will be glad to give you a generous reward. Li Suyuan and Wang Fuchi."

And then she touched each baby's cheek and told her not to cry. She would go down the road to find them some food and would be back. And without looking back, she walked down the road, stumbling and crying, thinking only of this one last hope, that her daughters would be found by a kindhearted person who would care for them. She would not allow herself to imagine anything else.

She did not remember how far she walked, which direction she went, when she fainted, or how she was found. When she awoke, she was in the back of a bouncing truck with several other sick people, all moaning. And she began to scream, thinking she was now on a journey to Buddhist hell. But the face of an American missionary lady bent over her and smiled, talking to her in a soothing language she did not understand. And yet she could somehow understand. She had been saved for no good reason, and it was now too late to go back and save her babies.

When she arrived in Chungking, she learned her husband had died two weeks before. She told me later she laughed when the officers told her this news, she was so delirious with madness and disease. To come so far, to lose so much and to find nothing.

I met her in a hospital. She was lying on a cot, hardly able to move, her dysentery had drained her so thin. I had come in for my foot, my missing toe, which was cut off by a piece of falling rubble. She was talking to herself, mumbling.

"Look at these clothes," she said, and I saw she had on a rather unusual dress for wartime. It 115 was silk satin, quite dirty, but there was no doubt it was a beautiful dress.

"Look at this face," she said, and I saw her dusty face and hollow cheeks, her eyes shining back. "Do you see my foolish hope?"

"I thought I had lost everything, except these two things," she murmured. "And I wondered which I would lose next. Clothes or hope? Hope or clothes?"

"But now, see here, look what is happening," she said, laughing, as if all her prayers had been answered. And she was pulling hair out of her head as easily as one lifts new wheat from wet soil.

It was an old peasant woman who found them. "How could I resist?" the peasant woman later told your sisters when they were older. They were still sitting obediently near where your mother had left them, looking like little fairy queens waiting for their sedan to arrive.

The woman, Mei Ching, and her husband, Mei Han, lived in a stone cave. There were thou- 120 sands of hidden caves like that in and around Kweilin so secret that the people remained hidden even after the war ended. The Meis would come out of their cave every few days and forage for food supplies left on the road, and sometimes they would see something that they both agreed was a tragedy to leave behind. So one day they took back to their cave a delicately painted set of rice bowls, another day a little footstool with a velvet cushion and two new wedding blankets. And once, it was your sisters.

They were pious people, Muslims, who believed the twin babies were a sign of double luck, and they were sure of this when, later in the evening, they discovered how valuable the babies were. She and her husband had never seen rings and bracelets like those. And while they admired the pictures, knowing the babies came from a good family, neither of them could read or write. It was not until many months later that Mei Ching found someone who could read the writing on the back. By then, she loved these baby girls like her own.

In 1952 Mei Han, the husband, died. The twins were already eight years old, and Mei Ching now decided it was time to find your sisters' true family.

She showed the girls the picture of their mother and told them they had been born into a great family and she would take them back to see their true mother and grandparents. Mei Ching told them about the reward, but she swore she would refuse it. She loved these girls so much, she only wanted them to have what they were entitled to—a better life, a fine house, educated ways. Maybe the family would let her stay on as the girls' amah. Yes, she was certain they would insist.

Of course, when she found the place at 9 Weichang Lu, in the old French Concession, it was something completely different. It was the site of a factory building, recently constructed, and none of the workers knew what had become of the family whose house had burned down on that spot.

Mei Ching could not have known, of course, that your mother and I, her new husband, had already returned to that same place in 1945 in hopes of finding both her family and her daughters. 125

Your mother and I stayed in China until 1947. We went to many different cities—back to Kweilin, to Changsha, as far south as Kunming. She was always looking out of one corner of her eye for twin babies, then little girls. Later we went to Hong Kong, and when we finally left in 1949 for the United States, I think she was even looking for them on the boat. But when we arrived, she no longer talked about them. I thought, At last, they have died in her heart.

When letters could be openly exchanged between China and the United States, she wrote immediately to old friends in Shanghai and Kweilin. I did not know she did this. Auntie Lindo told me. But of course, by then, all the street names had changed. Some people had died, others had moved away. So it took many years to find a contact. And when she did find an old school-mate's address and wrote asking her to look for her daughters, her friend wrote back and said this was impossible, like looking for a needle on the bottom of the ocean. How did she know her daughters were in Shanghai and not somewhere else in China? The friend, of course, did not ask, How do you know your daughters are still alive?

So her schoolmate did not look. Finding babies lost during the war was a matter of foolish imagination, and she had no time for that.

But every year, your mother wrote to different people. And this last year, I think she got a big idea in her head, to go to China and find them herself. I remember she told me, "Canning, we should go, before it is too late, before we are too old." And I told her we were already too old, it was already too late.

I just thought she wanted to be a tourist! I didn't know she wanted to go and look for her 130 daughters. So when I said it was too late, that must have put a terrible thought in her head that her daughters might be dead. And I think this possibility grew bigger and bigger in her head, until it killed her.

Maybe it was your mother's dead spirit who guided her Shanghai schoolmate to find her daughters. Because after your mother died, the schoolmate saw your sisters, by chance, while shopping for shoes at the Number One Department Store on Nanjing Dong Road. She said it was like a dream, seeing these two women who looked so much alike, moving down the stairs together. There was something about their facial expressions that reminded the schoolmate of your mother.

She quickly walked over to them and called their names, which of course, they did not rec-ognize at first, because Mei Ching had changed their names. But your mother's friend was so sure, she persisted. "Are you not Wang Chwun Yu and Wang Chwun Hwa?" she asked them. And then these double-image women became very excited, because they remembered the names writ-ten on the back of an old photo, a photo of a young man and woman they still honored, as their much-loved first parents, who had died and become spirit ghosts still roaming the earth looking for them.

At the airport, I am exhausted. I could not sleep last night. Aiyi had followed me into my room at three in the morning, and she instantly fell asleep on one of the twin beds, snoring with the might of a lumberjack. I lay awake thinking about my mother's story, realizing how much I have never known about her, grieving that my sisters and I had both lost her.

And now at the airport, after shaking hands with everybody, waving good-bye, I think about all the different ways we leave people in this world. Cheerily waving good-bye to some at airports, knowing we'll never see each other again. Leaving others on the side of the road, hoping that we will. Finding my mother in my father's story and saying good-bye before I have a chance to know her better.

Aiyi smiles at me as we wait for our gate to be called. She is so old. I put one arm around 135
her and one around Lili. They are the same size, it seems. And then it's time. As we wave good-bye one more time and enter the waiting area, I get the sense I am going from one funeral to another. In my hand I'm clutching a pair of tickets to Shanghai. In two hours we'll be there.

The plane takes off. I close my eyes. How can I describe to them in my broken Chinese about our mother's life? Where should I begin?

"Wake up, we're here," says my father. And I awake with my heart pounding in my throat. I look out the window and we're already on the runway. It's gray outside.

And now I'm walking down the steps of the plane, onto the tarmac and toward the building. If only, I think, if only my mother had lived long enough to be the one walking toward them. I am so nervous I cannot even feel my feet. I am just moving somehow.

Somebody shouts, "She's arrived!" And then I see her. Her short hair. Her small body. And that same look on her face. She has the back of her hand pressed hard against her mouth. She is crying as though she had gone through a terrible ordeal and were happy it is over.

And I know it's not my mother, yet it is the same look she had when I was five and had disap- 140
peared all afternoon, for such a long time, that she was convinced I was dead. And when I mirac-ulously appeared, sleepy-eyed, crawling from underneath my bed, she wept and laughed, biting the back of her hand to make sure it was true.

And now I see her again, two of her, waving, and in one hand there is a photo, the Polaroid I sent them. As soon as I get beyond the gate, we run toward each other, all three of us embracing, all hesitations and expectations forgotten.

"Mama, Mama," we all murmur, as if she is among us.

My sisters look at me, proudly. *"Meimei jandale,"* says one sister proudly to the other. "Little Sister has grown up." I look at their faces again and I see no trace of my mother in them. Yet they still look familiar. And now I also see what part of me is Chinese. It is so obvious. It is my family. It is in our blood. After all these years, it can finally be let go.

My sisters and I stand, arms around each other, laughing and wiping the tears from each other's eyes. The flash of the Polaroid goes off and my father hands me the snapshot. My sisters and I watch quietly together, eager to see what develops.

The gray-green surface changes to the bright colors of our three images, sharpening and deep- 145
ening all at once. And although we don't speak, I know we all see it: Together we look like our mother. Her same eyes, her same mouth, open in surprise to see, at last, her long-cherished wish.

[1989]

Updike, John (1932–2009)

A & P

In walks these three girls in nothing but bathing suits. I'm in the third checkout slot, with my back to the door, so I don't see them until they're over by the bread. The one that caught my eye first was the one in the plaid green two-piece. She was a chunky kid, with a good tan and a sweet broad soft-looking can with those two crescents of white just under it, where the sun never seems to hit, at the top of the backs of her legs. I stood there with my hand on a box of HiHo crackers trying to remember if I rang it up or not. I ring it up again and the customer starts giving me hell. She's one of these cash-register-watchers, a witch about fifty with rouge on her cheekbones and no eyebrows, and I know it made her day to trip me up. She'd been watching cash registers for fifty years and probably never seen a mistake before.

By the time I got her feathers smoothed and her goodies into a bag—she gives me a little snort in passing, if she'd been born at the right time they would have burned her over in Salem— by the time I get her on her way the girls had circled around the bread and were coming back, without a pushcart, back my way along the counters, in the aisle between the checkouts and the Special bins. They didn't even have shoes on. There was this chunky one, with the two-piece—it was bright green and the seams on the bra were still sharp and her belly was still pretty pale so I guessed she just got it (the suit)—there was this one, with one of those chubby berry-faces, the lips all bunched together under her nose, this one, and a tall one, with black hair that hadn't quite frizzed right, and one of these sunburns right across under the eyes, and a chin that was too long—you know, the kind of girl other girls think is very "striking" and "attractive" but never quite makes it, as they very well know, which is why they like her so much—and then the third one, that wasn't quite so tall. She was the queen. She kind of led them, the other two peeking around and making their shoulders round. She didn't look around, not this queen, she just walked straight on slowly, on these long white prima-donna legs. She came down a little hard on her heels, as if she didn't walk in her bare feet that much, putting down her heels and then let-ting the weight move along to her toes as if she was testing the floor with every step, putting a lit-tle deliberate extra action into it. You never know for sure how girls' minds work (do you really think it's a mind in there or just a little buzz like a bee in a glass jar?) but you got the idea she had talked the other two into coming in here with her, and now she was showing them how to do it, walk slow and hold yourself straight.

She had on a kind of dirty-pink—beige, maybe, I don't know—bathing suit with a little nub-ble all over it and, what got me, the straps were down. They were off her shoulders looped loose around the cool tops of her arms, and I guess as a result the suit had slipped a little on her, so all around the top of the cloth there was this shining rim. If it hadn't been there you wouldn't have known there could have been anything whiter than those shoulders. With the straps pushed off, there was nothing between the top of the suit and the top of her head except just *her*, this clean bare plane of the top of her chest down from the shoulder bones like a dented sheet of metal tilted in the light. I mean, it was more than pretty.

She had sort of oaky hair that the sun and salt had bleached, done up in a bun that was unraveling, and a kind of prim face. Walking into the A & P with your straps down, I suppose it's the only kind of face you *can* have. She held her head so high her neck, coming up out of those white shoulders, looked kind of stretched, but I didn't mind. The longer her neck was, the more of her there was.

She must have felt in the corner of her eye me and over my shoulder Stokesie in the second   5 slot watching, but she didn't tip. Not this queen. She kept her eyes moving across the racks, and stopped, and turned so slow it made my stomach rub the inside of my apron, and buzzed to the other two, who kind of huddled against her for relief, and then they all three of them went up the cat-and-dog-food-breakfast-cereal-macaroni-rice-raisins-seasonings-spreads-spaghetti soft-drinks-crackers-and-cookies aisle. From the third slot I look straight up this aisle to the meat counter, and I watched them all the way. The fat one with the tan sort of fumbled with the cookies, but on sec-ond thought she put the package back. The sheep pushing their carts down the aisle—the girls were walking against the usual traffic (not that we have one-way signs or anything)—were pretty hilarious. You could see them, when Queenie's white shoulders dawned on them, kind of jerk, or hop, or hiccup, but their eyes snapped back to their own baskets and on they pushed. I bet you could set off dynamite in an A & P and the people would by and large keep reaching and check-ing oatmeal off their lists and muttering "Let me see, there was a third thing, began with A, asparagus, no ah, yes, applesauce!" or whatever it is they do mutter. But there was no doubt, this jiggled them. A few houseslaves in pin curlers even looked around after pushing their carts past to make sure what they had seen was correct.

You know, it's one thing to have a girl in a bathing suit down on the beach, where what with the glare nobody can look at each other much anyway, and another thing in the cool of the A & P, under the fluorescent lights, against all those stacked packages, with her feet paddling along naked over our checkerboard green-and-cream rubber-tile floor.

"Oh Daddy," Stokesie said beside me. "I feel so faint."

"Darling," I said. "Hold me tight." Stokesie's married, with two babies chalked up on his fuselage already, but as far as I can tell that's the only difference. He's twenty-two, and I was nineteen this April.

"Is it done?" he asks, the responsible married man finding his voice. I forgot to say he thinks he's going to be manager some sunny day, maybe in 1990 when it's called the Great Alexandrov and Petrooshki Tea Company or something.

What he meant was, our town is five miles from the beach, with a big summer colony out on   10
the Point, but we're right in the middle of town, and the women generally put on a shirt or shorts or something before they get out of the car into the street. And anyway these are usually women with six children and varicose veins mapping their legs and nobody, including them could care less. As I say, we're right in the middle of town, and if you stand at our front doors you can see two banks and the Congregational church and the newspaper store and three real-estate offices and about twenty-seven old freeloaders tearing up Central Street because the sewer broke again. It's not as if we're on the Cape, we're north of Boston and there's people in this town haven't seen the ocean for twenty years.

The girls had reached the meat counter and were asking McMahon something. He pointed, they pointed, and they shuffled out of sight behind a pyramid of Diet Delight peaches. All that was left for us to see was old McMahon patting his mouth and looking after them sizing up their joints. Poor kids, I began to feel sorry for them, they couldn't help it.

Now here comes the sad part of the story, at least my family says it's sad, but I don't think it's so sad myself. The store's pretty empty, it being Thursday afternoon, so there was nothing much to do except lean on the register and wait for the girls to show up again. The whole store was like a pinball machine and I didn't know which tunnel they'd come out of. After a while they come around out of the far aisle, around the light bulbs, records at discount of the Caribbean Six or Tony Martin Sings or some such gunk you wonder they waste the wax on, sixpacks of candy bars, and plastic toys done up in cellophane that fall apart when a kid looks at them anyway. Around they come, Queenie still leading the way, and holding a little gray jar in her hand. Slots Three through Seven are unmanned and I could see her wondering between Stokes and me, but Stokesie with his usual luck draws an old party in baggy gray pants who stumbles up with four giant cans of pineapple juice (what do these bums *do* with all that pineapple juice? I've often asked myself) so the girls come to me. Queenie puts down the jar and I take it into my fingers icy cold. Kingfish Fancy Herring Snacks in Pure Sour Cream: 49¢. Now her hands are empty, not a ring or a bracelet, bare as God made them, and I wonder where the money's coming from. Still with that prim look she lifts a folded dollar bill out of the hollow at the center of her nubbed pink top. The jar went heavy in my hand. Really, I thought that was so cute.

Then everybody's luck begins to run out. Lengel comes in from haggling with a truck full of cabbages on the lot and is about to scuttle into that door marked MANAGER behind which he hides all day when the girls touch his eye. Lengel's pretty dreary, teaches Sunday school and the rest, but he doesn't miss that much. He comes over and says, "Girls, this isn't the beach."

Queenie blushes, though maybe it's just a brush of sunburn I was noticing for the first time, now that she was so close. "My mother asked me to pick up a jar of herring snacks." Her voice kind of startled me, the way voices do when you see the people first, coming out so flat and dumb yet kind of tony, too, the way it ticked over "pick up" and "snacks." All of a sudden I slid right down her voice into her living room. Her father and the other men were standing around in ice-cream coats and bow ties and the women were in sandals picking up herring snacks on toothpicks off a big glass plate and they were all holding drinks the color of water with olives and sprigs of mint in them. When my parents have somebody over they get lemonade and if it's a real racy affair Schlitz in tall glasses with "They'll Do It Every Time" cartoons stenciled on.

"That's all right," Lengel said. "But this isn't the beach." His repeating this struck me as funny, 15 as if it had just occurred to him, and he had been thinking all these years the A & P was a great big dune and he was the head lifeguard. He didn't like my smiling—as I say he doesn't miss much—but he concentrates on giving the girls that sad Sunday-school-superintendent stare.

Queenie's blush is no sunburn now, and the plump one in plaid, that I liked better from the back—a really sweet can—pipes up, "We weren't doing any shopping. We just came in for the one thing."

"That makes no difference," Lengel tells her, and I could see from the way his eyes went that he hadn't noticed she was wearing a two-piece before. "We want you decently dressed when you come in here."

"We *are* decent," Queenie says suddenly, her lower lip pushing, getting sore now that she remembers her place, a place from which the crowd that runs the A & P must look pretty crummy. Fancy Herring Snacks flashed in her very blue eyes.

"Girls, I don't want to argue with you. After this come in here with your shoulders covered. It's our policy." He turns his back. That's policy for you. Policy is what the kingpins want. What the others want is juvenile delinquency.

All this while, the customers had been showing up with their carts but, you know, sheep, seeing 20 a scene, they had all bunched up on Stokesie, who shook open a paper bag as gently as peeling a peach, not wanting to miss a word. I could feel in the silence everybody getting nervous, most of all Lengel, who asks me, "Sammy, have you rung up their purchase?"

I thought and said "No" but it wasn't about that I was thinking. I go through the punches, 4, 9, GROC, TOT—it's more complicated than you think, and after you do it often enough, it begins to make a little song, that you hear words to, in my case "Hello (*bing*) there, you (*gung*) hap-py pee-pul (*splat*)!"—the *splat* being the drawer flying out. I uncrease the bill, tenderly as you may imagine, it just having come from between the two smoothest scoops of vanilla I had ever known were there, and pass a half and a penny into her narrow pink palm, and nestle the herrings in a bag and twist its neck and hand it over, all the time thinking.

The girls, and who'd blame them, are in a hurry to get out, so I say "I quit" to Lengel quick enough for them to hear, hoping they'll stop and watch me, their unsuspected hero. They keep right on going, into the electric eye; the door flies open and they flicker across the lot to their car, Queenie and Plaid and Big Tall Goony-Goony (not that as raw material she was so bad), leaving me with Lengel and a kink in his eyebrow.

"Did you say something, Sammy?"

"I said I quit."

"I thought you did."   25

"You didn't have to embarrass them."

"It was they who were embarrassing us."

I started to say something that came out "Fiddle-de-doo." It's a saying of my grand-mother's, and I know she would have been pleased.

"I don't think you know what you're saying," Lengel said.

"I know you don't," I said. "But I do." I pull the bow at the back of my apron and start shrug- 30 ging it off my shoulders. A couple customers that had been heading for my slot begin to knock against each other, like scared pigs in a chute.

Lengel sighs and begins to look very patient and old and gray. He's been a friend of my parents for years. "Sammy, you don't want to do this to your Mom and Dad," he tells me. It's true, I don't. But it seems to me that once you begin a gesture it's fatal not to go through with it. I fold the apron, "Sammy" stitched in red on the pocket, and put it on the counter, and drop the bow tie on top of it. The bow tie is theirs, if you've ever wondered. "You'll feel this for the rest of your life," Lengel says, and I know that's true, too, but remembering how he made that pretty girl blush makes me so scrunchy inside I punch the No Sale tab and the machine whirs "pee-pul" and the drawer splats out. One advantage to this scene taking place in summer, I can follow this up with a clean exit, there's no fumbling around getting your coat and galoshes, I just saunter into the electric eye in my white shirt that my mother ironed the night before, and the door heaves itself open, and outside the sunshine is skating around on the asphalt.

I look around for my girls, but they're gone, of course. There wasn't anybody but some young married screaming with her children about some candy they didn't get by the door of a powder-blue Falcon station wagon. Looking back in the big windows, over the bags of peat moss and aluminum lawn furniture stacked on the pavement, I could see Lengel in my place in the slot, checking the sheep through. His face was dark gray and his back stiff, as if he'd just had an injection of iron, and my stomach kind of fell as I felt how hard the world was going to be to me hereafter.

[1961]

Appendix 4

Selected Drama

Glaspell, Susan (1876–1948)

Trifles

CAST OF CHARACTERS

George Henderson, *county attorney*
Henry Peters, *sheriff*
Lewis Hale, a *neighboring farmer*
Mrs. Peters
Mrs. Hale

SCENE: *The kitchen in the now abandoned farmhouse of* JOHN WRIGHT, *a gloomy kitchen, and left without having been put in order—unwashed pans under the sink, a loaf of bread outside the bread-box, a dish-towel on the table—other signs of incompleted work. At the rear the outer door opens and the* SHERIFF *comes in followed by the* COUNTY ATTORNEY *and* HALE. *The* SHERIFF *and* HALE *are men in middle life, the* COUNTY ATTORNEY *is a young man; all are much bundled up and go at once to the stove. They are followed by the two women—the* SHERIFF'*s wife first; she is a slight wiry woman, a thin nervous face.* MRS. HALE *is larger and would ordinarily be called more comfortable looking, but she is disturbed now and looks fearfully about as she enters. The women have come in slowly, and stand close together near the door.*

COUNTY ATTORNEY: [*Rubbing his hands.*] This feels good. Come up to the fire, ladies.
MRS. PETERS: [*After taking a step forward.*] I'm not—cold.
SHERIFF: [*Unbuttoning his overcoat and stepping away from the stove as if to mark the beginning of official business.*] Now, Mr. Hale, before we move things about, you explain to Mr. Henderson just what you saw when you came here yesterday morning.
COUNTY ATTORNEY: By the way, has anything been moved? Are things just as you left them yesterday?   5
SHERIFF: [*Looking about.*] It's just the same. When it dropped below zero last night I thought I'd better send Frank out this morning to make a fire for us—no use getting pneumonia with a big case on, but I told him not to touch anything except the stove—and you know Frank.
COUNTY ATTORNEY: Somebody should have been left here yesterday.
SHERIFF: Oh—yesterday. When I had to send Frank to Morris Center for that man who went crazy—I want you to know I had my hands full yesterday. I knew you could get back from Omaha by today and as long as I went over everything here myself—
COUNTY ATTORNEY: Well, Mr. Hale, tell just what happened when you came here yesterday morning.
HALE: Harry and I had started to town with a load of potatoes. We came along the road from   10
my place and as I got here I said, "I'm going to see if I can't get John Wright to go in with me on a party telephone." I spoke to Wright about it once before and he put me off, saying folks talked too much anyway, and all he asked was peace and quiet—I guess you know

about how much he talked himself; but I thought maybe if I went to the house and talked
about it before his wife, though I said to Harry that I didn't know as what his wife wanted
made much difference to John—

COUNTY ATTORNEY: Let's talk about that later, Mr. Hale. I do want to talk about that, but tell
now just what happened when you got to the house.

HALE: I didn't hear or see anything; I knocked at the door, and still it was all quiet inside. I
knew they must be up, it was past eight o'clock. So I knocked again, and I thought I heard
somebody say, "Come in." I wasn't sure, I'm not sure yet, but I opened. the door—this
door [*Indicating the door by which the two women are still standing.*] *and there in that rocker—*
[*Pointing to it.*] sat Mrs. Wright.

[*They all look at the rocker.*]

COUNTY ATTORNEY: What—was she doing?

HALE: She was rockin' back and forth. She had her apron in her hand and was kind of— 15
pleating it.

COUNTY ATTORNEY: And how did she—look?

HALE: Well, she looked queer.

COUNTY ATTORNEY: How do you mean—queer?

HALE: Well, as if she didn't know what she was going to do next. And kind of done up.

COUNTY ATTORNEY: How did she seem to feel about your coming? 20

HALE: Why, I don't think she minded—one way or other. She didn't pay much attention. I said,
"How do, Mrs. Wright, it's cold, ain't it?" And she said, "Is it?"—and went on kind of pleating at her apron. Well, I was surprised; she didn't ask me to come up to the stove, or to set
down, but just sat there, not even looking at me, so I said, "I want to see John." And then
she—laughed. I guess you would call it a laugh. I thought of Harry and the team outside, so
I said a little sharp: "Can't I see John?" "No," she says, kind o' dull like. "Ain't he home?"
says I. "Yes," says she, "he's home." "Then why can't I see him?" I asked her, out of patience.
"'Cause he's dead," says she. "*Dead?*" says I. She just nodded her head, not getting a bit
excited, but rockin' back and forth. "Why—where is he?" says I, not knowing what to say.
She just pointed upstairs—like that. [*Himself pointing to the room above.*] I got up, with the
idea of going up there. I walked from there to here—then I says, "Why, what did he die of?"
"He died of a rope round his neck," says she, and just went on pleatin' at her apron. Well, I
went out and called Harry. I thought I might—need help. We went upstairs and there he
was lyin'—

COUNTY ATTORNEY: I think I'd rather have you go into that upstairs, where you can point it all
out. Just go on now with the rest of the story.

HALE: Well, my first thought was to get that rope off. It looked . . . [*Stops, his face twitches.*] . . .
but Harry, he went up to him, and he said, "No, he's dead all right, and we'd better not
touch anything." So we went back downstairs. She was still sitting that same way. "Has anybody been notified?" I asked. "No," says she, unconcerned. "Who did this, Mrs. Wright?"
said Harry. He said it businesslike—and she stopped pleatin' of her apron. "I don't know,"
she says. "You don't *know?*" says Harry. "No," says she. "Weren't you sleepin' in the bed with
him?" says Harry. "Yes," says she, "but I was on the inside." "Somebody slipped a rope round
his neck and strangled him and you didn't wake up?" says Harry. "I didn't wake up," she
said after him. We must 'a looked as if we didn't see how that could be, for after a minute
she said, "I sleep sound." Harry was going to ask her more questions but I said maybe we
ought to let her tell her story first to the coroner, or the sheriff, so Harry went fast as he
could to Rivers' place, where there's a telephone.

COUNTY ATTORNEY: And what did Mrs. Wright do when she knew that you had gone for the coroner?

HALE: She moved from that chair to this one over here [*Pointing to a small chair in the corner.*] 25
and just sat there with her hands held together and looking down. I got a feeling that I

ought to make some conversation, so I said I had come in to see if John wanted to put in a telephone, and at that she started to laugh, and then she stopped and looked at me— scared. [*The* COUNTY ATTORNEY, *who has had his notebook out, makes a note.*] I dunno, maybe it wasn't scared. I wouldn't like to say it was. Soon Harry got back, and then Dr. Lloyd came, and you, Mr. Peters, and so I guess that's all I know that you don't.

COUNTY ATTORNEY: [*Looking around.*] I guess we'll go upstairs first—and then out to the barn and around there. [*To the* SHERIFF.] You're convinced that there was nothing important here—nothing that would point to any motive.

SHERIFF: Nothing here but kitchen things.

[*THE* COUNTY ATTORNEY, *after again looking around the kitchen, opens the door of a cupboard closet. He gets up on a chair and looks on a shelf. Pulls his hand away, sticky.*]

COUNTY ATTORNEY: Here's a nice mess.

[*The women draw nearer.*]   30

MRS. PETERS: [*To the other woman.*] Oh, her fruit; it did freeze. [*To the* LAWYER.] She worried about that when it turned so cold. She said the fire'd go out and her jars would break.

SHERIFF: Well, can you beat the women! Held for murder and worryin' about her preserves.

COUNTY ATTORNEY: I guess before we're through she may have something more serious than preserves to worry about.

HALE: Well, women are used to worrying over trifles.

[*The two women move a little closer together.*]   35

COUNTY ATTORNEY: [*With the gallantry of a young politician.*] And yet, for all their worries, what would we do without the ladies? [*The women do not unbend. He goes to the sink, takes a dipperful of water from the pail and pouring it into a basin, washes his hands. Starts to wipe them on the roller towel, turns it for a cleaner place.*] Dirty towels! [*Kicks his foot against the pans under the sink.*] Not much of a housekeeper, would you say, ladies?

MRS HALE: [*Stiffly.*] There's a great deal of work to be done on a farm.

COUNTY ATTORNEY: To be sure. And yet [*With a little bow to her.*] I know there are some Dickson county farmhouses which do not have such roller towels.

[*He gives it a pull to expose its full length again.*]

MRS HALE: Those towels get dirty awful quick. Men's hands aren't always as clean as they might be.   40

COUNTY ATTORNEY: Ah, loyal to your sex, I see. But you and Mrs. Wright were neighbors. I suppose you were friends, too.

MRS HALE: [*Shaking her head.*] I've not seen much of her of late years. I've not been in this house—it's more than a year.

COUNTY ATTORNEY: And why was that? You didn't like her?

MRS HALE: I liked her all well enough. Farmers' wives have their hands full, Mr. Henderson. And then—

COUNTY ATTORNEY: Yes—?   45

MRS HALE: [*Looking about.*] It never seemed a very cheerful place.

COUNTY ATTORNEY: No—it's not cheerful. I shouldn't say she had the homemaking instinct.

MRS HALE: Well. I don't know as Wright had, either.

COUNTY ATTORNEY: You mean that they didn't get on very well?

MRS HALE: No, I don't mean anything. But I don't think a place'd be any cheerfuller for   50 John Wright's being in it.

COUNTY ATTORNEY: I'd like to talk more of that a little later. I want to get the lay of things upstairs now.

[*He goes to the left, where three steps lead to a stair door.*]

SHERIFF: I suppose anything Mrs. Peters does'll be all right. She was to take in some clothes for her, you know, and a few little things. We left in such a hurry yesterday.

COUNTY ATTORNEY: Yes, but I would like to see what you take, Mrs. Peters, and keep an eye out for anything that might be of use to us.

MRS. PETERS: Yes, Mr. Henderson.   55

[*The women listen to the men's steps on the stairs, then look about the kitchen.*]

MRS HALE: I'd hate to have men coming into my kitchen, snooping around and criticising.

[*She arranges the pans under the sink which the Lawyer had shoved out of place.*]

MRS. PETERS: Of course it's no more than their duty.

MRS HALE: Duty's all right, but I guess that deputy sheriff that came out to make the fire might   60
have got a little of this on. [*Gives the roller towel a pull.*] Wish I'd thought of that sooner. Seems mean to talk about her for not having things slicked up when she had to come away in such a hurry.

MRS. PETERS: [*Who had gone to a small table in the left rear corner of the room, and lifted one end of a towel that covers a pan.*] She had bread set.

[*Stands still.*]

MRS. HALE: [*Eyes fixed on a loaf of bread beside the breadbox, which is on a low shelf at the other side of the room. Moves slowly toward it.*] She was going to put this in there. [*Picks up loaf, then abruptly drops it. In a manner of returning to familiar things.*] It's a shame about her fruit. I wonder if it's all gone. [*Gets up on the chair and looks.*] I think there's some here that's all right, Mrs. Peters. Yes—here; [*Holding it toward the window.*] this is cherries, too. [*Looking again.*] I declare I believe that's the only one. [*Gets down, bottle in her hand. Goes to the sink and wipes it off on the outside.*] She'll feel awful bad after all her hard work in the hot weather. I remember the afternoon I put up my cherries last summer.

[*She puts the bottle on the big kitchen table, center of the room. With a sigh, is about to sit down in the rocking-chair. Before she is seated realizes what chair it is; with a slow look at it, steps back. The chair which she has touched rocks back and forth.*]

MRS. PETERS: Well, I must get those things from the front room closet. [*She goes to the door at the   65
right, but after looking into the other room, steps back.*] You coming with me, Mrs. Hale? You could help me carry them.

[*They go in the other room; reappear, MRS. PETERS carrying a dress and skirt, MRS. HALE following with a pair of shoes.*]

MRS. PETERS: My, it's cold in there.

[*She puts the clothes on the big table and hurries to the stove.*]

MRS. HALE: [*Examining the skirt.*] Wright was close. I think maybe that's why she kept so much to herself. She didn't even belong to the Ladies Aid. I suppose she felt she couldn't do her part, and then you don't enjoy things when you feel shabby. She used to wear pretty clothes and be lively, when she was Minnie Foster, one of the town girls singing in the choir. But that—oh, that was thirty years ago. This all you was to take in?

MRS. PETERS: She said she wanted an apron. Funny thing to want, for there isn't much to get you   70
dirty in jail, goodness knows. But I suppose just to make her feel more natural. She said they was in the top drawer in this cupboard. Yes, here. And then her little shawl that always hung behind the door. [*Opens stair door and looks.*] Yes, here it is.

[*Quickly shuts door leading upstairs.*]

MRS. HALE: [*Abruptly moving toward her.*] Mrs. Peters?

MRS. PETERS: Yes, Mrs. Hale?

MRS. HALE: Do you think she did it?

MRS. PETERS: [*In a frightened voice.*] Oh, I don't know.   75

MRS. HALE: Well, I don't think she did. Asking for an apron and her little shawl. Worrying
about her fruit.

MRS. PETERS: [*Starts to speak, glances up, where footsteps are heard in the room above. In a low voice.*]
Mr. Peters says it looks bad for her. Mr. Henderson is awful sarcastic in a speech and he'll
make fun of her sayin' she didn't wake up.

MRS. HALE: Well, I guess John Wright didn't wake when they was slipping that rope under his neck.

MRS. PETERS: No, it's strange. It must have been done awful crafty and still. They say it was such
a—funny way to kill a man, rigging it all up like that.

MRS. HALE: That's just what Mr. Hale said. There was a gun in the house. He says that's what he   80
can't understand.

MRS. PETERS: Mr. Henderson said coming out that what was needed for the case was a motive;
something to show anger, or—sudden feeling.

MRS. HALE: [*Who is standing by the table.*] Well, I don't see any signs of anger around here. [*She
puts her hand on the dish towel which lies on the table, stands looking down at table, one half of which
is clean, the other half messy.*] It's wiped to here. [*Makes a move as if to finish work, then turns and
looks at loaf of bread outside the breadbox. Drops towel. In that voice of coming back to familiar
things.*] Wonder how they are finding things upstairs. I hope she had it a little more redd-up
up there. You know, it seems kind of *sneaking*. Locking her up in town and then coming out
here and trying to get her own house to turn against her!

MRS. PETERS: But Mrs. Hale, the law is the law.

MRS. HALE: I s'pose 'tis. [*Unbuttoning her coat.*] Better loosen up your things.

MRS. PETERS: You won't feel them when you go out.   85

[*Mrs. Peters takes off her fur tippet, goes to hang it on hook at back of room, stands looking at the under
part of the small corner table.*]

MRS. PETERS: She was piecing a quilt.

[*She brings the large sewing basket and they look at the bright pieces.*]

MRS. HALE: It's log cabin pattern. Pretty, isn't it? I wonder if she was goin' to quilt it or just knot it?

[*Footsteps have been heard coming down the stairs. The* SHERIFF *enters followed by* HALE *and the* COUNTY   90
ATTORNEY.]

SHERIFF: They wonder if she was going to quilt it or just knot it!

[*The men laugh; the women look abashed.*]

COUNTY ATTORNEY: [*Rubbing his hands over the stove.*] Frank's fire didn't do much up there, did
it? Well, let's go out to the barn and get that cleared up.

[*The men go outside.*]

MRS. HALE: [*Resentfully.*] I don't know as there's anything so strange, our takin' up our time with   95
little things while we're waiting for them to get the evidence. [*She sits down at the big table
smoothing out a block with decision.*] I don't see as it's anything to laugh about.

MRS. PETERS: [*Apologetically.*] Of course they've got awful important things on their minds.

[*Pulls up a chair and joins* MRS. HALE *at the table.*]

MRS. HALE: [*Examining another block.*] Mrs. Peters, look at this one. Here, this is the one she was working on, and look at the sewing! All the rest of it has been so nice and even. And look at this! It's all over the place! Why, it looks as if she didn't know what she was about!

[*After she has said this they look at each other, then start to glance back at the door. After an instant MRS. HALE has pulled at a knot and ripped the sewing.*]

MRS. PETERS: Oh, what are you doing, Mrs. Hale?   100

MRS. HALE: [*Mildly.*] Just pulling out a stitch or two that's not sewed very good. [*Threading a needle.*] Bad sewing always made me fidgety.

MRS. PETERS: [*Nervously.*] I don't think we ought to touch things.

MRS. HALE: I'll just finish up this end. [*Suddenly stopping and leaning forward.*] Mrs. Peters?

MRS. PETERS: Yes, Mrs. Hale?

MRS. HALE: What do you suppose she was so nervous about?   105

MRS. PETERS: Oh—I don't know. I don't know as she was nervous. I sometimes sew awful queer when I'm just tired. [*MRS. HALE starts to say something, looks at MRS. PETERS, then goes on sewing.*] Well I must get these things wrapped up. They may be through sooner than we think. [*Putting apron and other things together.*] I wonder where I can find a piece of paper, and string.

MRS. HALE: In that cupboard, maybe.

MRS. PETERS: [*Looking in cupboard.*] Why, here's a bird-cage. [*Holds it up.*] Did she have a bird, Mrs. Hale?

MRS. HALE: Why, I don't know whether she did or not—I've not been here for so long. There was a man around last year selling canaries cheap, but I don't know as she took one; maybe she did. She used to sing real pretty herself.

MRS. PETERS: [*Glancing around.*] Seems funny to think of a bird here. But she must have had   110
one, or why would she have a cage? I wonder what happened to it?

MRS. HALE: I s'pose maybe the cat got it.

MRS. PETERS: No, she didn't have a cat. She's got that feeling some people have about cats—being afraid of them. My cat got in her room and she was real upset and asked me to take it out.

MRS. HALE: My sister Bessie was like that. Queer, ain't it?

MRS. PETERS: [*Examining the cage.*] Why, look at this door. It's broke. One hinge is pulled apart.

MRS. HALE: [*Looking too.*] Looks as if someone must have been rough with it.   115

MRS. PETERS: Why, yes.

[*She brings the cage forward and puts it on the table.*]

MRS. HALE: I wish if they're going to find any evidence they'd be about it. I don't like this place.

MRS. PETERS: But I'm awful glad you came with me, Mrs. Hale. It would be lonesome for me sitting here alone.

MRS. HALE: It would, wouldn't it? [*Dropping her sewing.*] But I tell you what I do wish,   120
Mrs. Peters. I wish I had come over sometimes when she was here. I—[*Looking around the room.*]—wish I had.

MRS. PETERS: But of course you were awful busy, Mrs. Hale—your house and your children.

MRS. HALE: I could've come. I stayed away because it weren't cheerful—and that's why I ought to have come. I—I've never liked this place. Maybe because it's down in a hollow and you don't see the road. I dunno what it is, but it's a lonesome place and always was. I wish I had come over to see Minnie Foster sometimes. I can see now—

[*Shakes her head.*]

MRS. PETERS: Well, you mustn't reproach yourself, Mrs. Hale. Somehow we just don't see how it is with other folks until—something comes up.

MRS. HALE: Not having children makes less work—but it makes a quiet house, and Wright out   125
to work all day, and no company when he did come in. Did you know John Wright, Mrs. Peters?

MRS. PETERS: Not to know him; I've seen him in town. They say he was a good man.

MRS. HALE: Yes—good; he didn't drink, and kept his word as well as most, I guess, and paid his debts. But he was a hard man, Mrs. Peters. Just to pass the time of day with him—[*Shivers.*] Like a raw wind that gets to the bone. [*Pauses, her eye falling on the cage.*] I should think she would 'a wanted a bird. But what do you suppose went with it?

MRS. PETERS: I don't know, unless it got sick and died.

[*She reaches over and swings the broken door, swings it again, both women watch it.*]

MRS. HALE: You weren't raised round here, were you? [*MRS. PETERS shakes her head.*] You didn't   130
know—her?

MRS. PETERS: Not till they brought her yesterday.

MRS. HALE: She—come to think of it, she was kind of like a bird herself—real sweet and pretty, but kind of timid and—fluttery. How—she—did—change. [*Silence; then as if struck by a happy thought and relieved to get back to everyday things.*] Tell you what, Mrs. Peters, why don't you take the quilt in with you? It might take up her mind.

MRS. PETERS: Why, I think that's a real nice idea, Mrs. Hale. There couldn't possibly be any objection to it, could there? Now, just what would I take? I wonder if her patches are in here—and her things.

[*They look in the sewing basket.*]

MRS. HALE: Here's some red. I expect this has got sewing things in it. [*Brings out a fancy box.*]   135
What a pretty box. Looks like something somebody would give you. Maybe her scissors are in here. [*Opens box. Suddenly puts her hand to her nose.*] Why— [*MRS. PETERS bends nearer, then turns her face away.*] There's something wrapped up in this piece of silk.

MRS. PETERS: Why, this isn't her scissors.

MRS. HALE: [*Lifting the silk.*] Oh, Mrs. Peters—it's—

[*Mrs. Peters bends closer.*]

MRS. PETERS: It's the bird.

MRS. HALE: [*Jumping up.*] But, Mrs. Peters—look at it! Its neck! Look at its neck! It's all—other   140
side *to.*

MRS. PETERS: Somebody—wrung—its—neck.

[*Their eyes meet. A look of growing comprehension, of horror. Steps are heard outside. MRS. HALE slips box under quilt pieces, and sinks into her chair. Enter SHERIFF and COUNTY ATTORNEY. MRS. PETERS rises.*]

COUNTY ATTORNEY: [*As one turning from serious things to little pleasantries.*] Well, ladies, have you decided whether she was going to quilt it or knot it?

MRS. PETERS: We think she was going to—knot it.

COUNTY ATTORNEY: Well, that's interesting, I'm sure. [*Seeing the bird-cage.*] Has the bird flown?   145

MRS. HALE: [*Putting more quilt pieces over the box.*] We think the—cat got it.

COUNTY ATTORNEY: [*Preoccupied.*] Is there a cat?

[*MRS. HALE glances in a quick covert way at MRS. PETERS.*]

MRS. PETERS: Well, not *now.* They're superstitious, you know. They leave.

COUNTY ATTORNEY: [*To* SHERIFF PETERS, *continuing an interrupted conversation.*] No sign at all of   150
anyone having come from the outside. Their own rope. Now let's go up again and go over it
piece by piece. [*They start upstairs.*] It would have to have been someone who knew just
the—

[MRS. PETERS *sits down. The two women sit there not looking at one another, but as if peering into some-*
thing and at the same time holding back. When they talk now it is in the manner of feeling their way over
strange ground, as if afraid of what they are saying, but as if they cannot help saying it.]

MRS. HALE: She liked the bird. She was going to bury it in that pretty box.
MRS. PETERS: [*In a whisper.*] When I was a girl—my kitten—there was a boy took a hatchet, and
before my eyes—and before I could get there—[*Covers her face an instant.*] If they hadn't
held me back I would have—[*Catches herself, looks upstairs where steps are heard, falters*
weakly.]—hurt him.
MRS. HALE: [*With a slow look around her.*] I wonder how it would seem never to have had any
children around. [*Pause.*] No, Wright wouldn't like the bird—a thing that sang. She used to
sing. He killed that, too.
MRS. PETERS: [*Moving uneasily.*] We don't know who killed the bird.   155
MRS. HALE: I knew John Wright.
MRS. PETERS: It was an awful thing was done in this house that night, Mrs. Hale. Killing a man
while he slept, slipping a rope around his neck that choked the life out of him.
MRS. HALE: His neck. Choked the life out of him.

[*Her hand goes out and rests on the bird-cage.*]

MRS. PETERS: [*With rising voice.*] We don't know who killed him. We don't know.   160
MRS. HALE: [*Her own feeling not interrupted.*] If there'd been years and years of nothing, then a
bird to sing to you, it would be awful—still, after the bird was still.
MRS. PETERS: [*Something within her speaking.*] I know what stillness is. When we homesteaded in
Dakota, and my first baby died—after he was two years old, and me with no other then—
MRS. HALE: [*Moving.*] How soon do you suppose they'll be through, looking for the evidence?
MRS. PETERS: I know what stillness is. [*Pulling herself back.*] The law has got to punish crime,
Mrs. Hale.
MRS. HALE: [*Not as if answering that.*] I *wish* you'd seen Minnie Foster when she wore a white   165
dress with blue ribbons and stood up there in the choir and sang. [*A look around the room.*]
Oh, I wish I'd come over here once in a while! That was a crime! That was a crime! Who's
going to punish that?
MRS. PETERS: [*Looking upstairs.*] We mustn't—take on.
MRS. HALE: I might have known she needed help! I know how things can be—for women. I tell
you, it's queer, Mrs. Peters. We live close together and we live far apart. We all go through
the same things—it's all just a different kind of the same thing. [*Brushes her eyes, noticing the*
bottle of fruit, reaches out for it.] If I was you I wouldn't tell her her fruit was gone. Tell her it
ain't. Tell her it's all right. Take this in to prove it to her. She—she may never know whether
it was broke or not.
MRS. PETERS: [*Takes the bottle, looks about for something to wrap it in; takes petticoat from the clothes*
brought from the other room, very nervously begins winding this around the bottle. In a false voice.]
My, it's a good thing the men couldn't hear us. Wouldn't they just laugh! Getting all stirred
up over a little thing like a—dead canary. As if that could have anything to do with—with—
wouldn't they *laugh*!

[*The men are heard coming down stairs.*]

MRS. HALE: [*Under her breath.*] Maybe they would—maybe they wouldn't.   170

COUNTY ATTORNEY: No, Peters, it's all perfectly clear except a reason for doing it. But you know juries when it comes to women. If there was some definite thing. Something to show— something to make a story about—a thing that would connect up with this strange way of doing it—

[*The women's eyes meet for an instant. Enter HALE from outer door.*]

HALE: Well, I've got the team around. Pretty cold out there.

COUNTY ATTORNEY: I'm going to stay here a while by myself. [*To the SHERIFF.*] You can send Frank out for me, can't you? I want to go over everything. I'm not satisfied that we can't do better.

SHERIFF: Do you want to see what Mrs. Peters is going to take in?   175

[*The COUNTY ATTORNEY goes to the table, picks up the apron, laughs.*]

COUNTY ATTORNEY: Oh, I guess they're not very dangerous things the ladies have picked out. [*Moves a few things about, disturbing the quilt pieces which cover the box. Steps back.*] No, Mrs. Peters doesn't need supervising. For that matter, a sheriff's wife is married to the law. Ever think of it that way, Mrs. Peters?

MRS. PETERS: Not—just that way.

SHERIFF: [*Chuckling.*] Married to the law. [*Moves toward the other room.*] I just want you to come in here a minute, George. We ought to take a look at these windows.

COUNTY ATTORNEY: [*Scoffingly.*] Oh, windows!   180

SHERIFF: We'll be right out, Mr. Hale.

[*HALE goes outside. The SHERIFF follows the COUNTY ATTORNEY into the other room. Then MRS. HALE rises, hands tight together, looking intensely at MRS. PETERS, whose eyes make a slow turn, finally meeting MRS. HALE's. A moment MRS. HALE holds her, then her own eyes point the way to where the box is concealed. Suddenly MRS. PETERS throws back quilt pieces and tries to put the box in the bag she is wearing. It is too big. She opens box, starts to take bird out, cannot touch it, goes to pieces, stands there helpless. Sound of a knob turning in the other room. MRS. HALE snatches the box and puts it in the pocket of her big coat. Enter COUNTY ATTORNEY and SHERIFF.*]

COUNTY ATTORNEY: [*Facetiously.*] Well, Henry, at least we found out that she was not going to quilt it. She was going to—what is it you call it, ladies?

MRS. HALE: [*Her hand against her pocket.*] We call it—knot it, Mr. Henderson.

CURTAIN
[1916]

Appendix 5

Glossary of Literary Terms

Words appearing in bold within definitions can be found listed in this glossary.

absurd   See **Theater of the Absurd**.

affective   Relating to emotion.

allegory   A type of poem or narrative that presents a sequence of related concrete items clearly symbolizing abstract ideas, in order to convey a moral or religious message. In Christina Rossetti's poem "Uphill," the road that winds uphill probably represents life's progress, "the whole long day"—a lifespan, "night"—death, and the "inn" with its "beds"—the graveyard. John Bunyan's *Pilgrim's Progress* is another example of an allegorical work.

alliteration   Repetition of identical sounds, especially at the beginning of words, e.g., "Season of *m*ists and *m*ellow fruitfulness." Strictly speaking, repetition of consonant sounds is termed *consonance* and repetition of vowel sounds, *assonance*.

allusion   An indirect reference to a well-known event, character, or story that has some connection to the context of the work containing the allusion.

anapest   A **foot** of three syllables, the first two unstressed and the third stressed; e.g., "as I wálk."

antagonist   A character who opposes the main character (**protagonist**) in a play or a work of prose fiction.

antithesis   A rhetorical device that juxtaposes two opposing ideas, using a similar syntactic construction for each.

apostrophe   Address to an absent person or to a thing as if expecting an answer, like Shelley's command to the wind, "O hear!" in his "Ode to the West Wind."

approximate rhyme   Rhymes sharing similar, but not identical, consonant or vowel sounds, or rhymes whose final consonants *or* vowels are the same, but not both as in a normal, full rhyme. Also called "slant rhyme." Examples: *thumb/gun, face/Greece*.

archetype   A **motif** or image so universal in world literature that it seems to go back to the beginnings of literary expression and resonates profoundly in the collective unconscious of readers.

archetypal criticism   A type of criticism that interprets literature with reference to archetypal elements.

aside   In drama, a brief address by a character either to himself/herself or directly to the audience, supposedly not overheard by other characters on stage.

assonance   Repetition of similar vowel sounds.

atmosphere   The emotional effect or mood created in a work.

ballad   A popular narrative poem originally composed to be sung, written in alternating **iambic tetrameters** (lines 1 + 3) and **trimeters** (lines 2 + 4), often in stanzas of four lines (quatrains) with a rhyme scheme *abcb*.

biographical criticism   A type of literary criticism that stresses the links between the author's own life and his/her works.

blank verse   Verse that has **meter** (iambic pentameter) but no **rhyme**.

caesura   A pause within a line of verse.

canon   A body of literary works that are highly regarded within a given culture and that are consistently studied in schools and universities.

catharsis   A term used by Aristotle to designate the audience's reaction of pity and terror to the events affecting characters in a tragedy.

characterization   The process by which an author creates fictional characters, whether through depiction of their words and actions, through the **narrator**'s description and commentary, or through other characters' perceptions of them.

climax   The point at which the dramatic tension inherent in the plot of a novel or play comes to a head, leading to the plot's resolution.

comparison-contrast   A way of discussing two works or two authors by examining their similarities and differences.

conceit   A type of elaborate and very original extended **metaphor**.

conflict   Most plots involve some kind of conflict, whether between characters, between a character and his society or environment, or internal conflict within one character.

connotation   Meaning suggested by a word or associated with it rather than the main meaning it directly conveys (see **denotation**).

cosmic irony   See **irony**.

couplet   Two consecutive lines of verse, usually of identical **meter**, that share a **rhyme**.

critical theory   Interpretative stances or viewpoints that form a basis for different kinds of literary criticism such as Marxist, feminist, psychoanalytic, or structuralist theory.

dactyl   A **foot** of three syllables with stress on the first syllable but not the other two, as in the word *átmosphere* or the phrase *"Yés," she said.*

deconstruction   A theory that views language and literary texts as inherently contradictory and ambiguous and denies the possibility of a definitive interpretation.

denotation   The literal meaning of a word as found in a dictionary without the associations (**connotations**) it may have in the context of a given culture or society.

dénouement   The resolution (or "unknotting") of the tensions of the **plot** in a drama or novel.

deus ex machina   In drama, an artificial device such as the sudden arrival of a long-lost relative or of a god ("*deus*") that helps to resolve characters' problems or conflicts and conclude the play.

dialogue   Spoken conversation of characters. In a play this represents the whole text (apart from stage directions).

didactic   A term describing a work, especially an essay but also certain poems and other literary texts, that aims to teach or convey a moral lesson.

dimeter   In verse, a line of two metrical **feet**.

drama   One of the three major genres of literature; or, an individual play.

dramatic irony   Occurs when an audience at a play knows more about a given character's situation than he or she does; for example, if another character is hidden in a closet, eavesdropping, unbeknownst to one or more of the characters on the stage.

dramatic monologue   A poem representing the speech of a character engaged in a dramatic situation who is identified by name, profession, or social status and therefore clearly differentiated from the poet (unlike a **lyric** poem where the "I" is more vague). Examples are Browning's "My Last Duchess," Tennyson's "Ulysses," and T.S. Eliot's "Love Song of J. Alfred Prufrock."

elegy   A fairly long poem on a serious subject such as death or loss.

elision   Omission of words or sounds.

end rhyme   Identical vowel and consonant sounds at the ends of two lines of poetry.

end-stopped line   A line of poetry that is more or less self-contained syntactically (as opposed to an **enjambed** line where the sense runs on into the next line). An end-stopped line usually ends with some kind of punctuation.

enjambment   A line of verse whose meaning and syntax flow on without pause into the next line is called an enjambed or run-on line. Enjambment is this process.

epic   A long narrative poem dealing with the exploits of heroes and composed in a lofty style.

epigram   A short, witty, often **satirical** poem.

epigraph   A brief quotation in verse or prose placed at the beginning of a work and relevant to it.

epistolary   Written in the form of a letter, whether in prose or verse. An epistolary novel is composed of letters to and from various fictional characters.

explication   A detailed, line-by-line analysis of a text; a close reading.

exposition   The introductory section of a novel or a drama in which characters and their situation are presented before the action gets underway. Some works begin *in medias res*, i.e., without exposition.

eye-rhyme   **Rhyme** whose sounds are not identical though the letters look the same on the page, e.g., *low/prow* in Browning's "Meeting at Night."

farce   An element of comedy that involves physical action such as characters falling down, pushing, throwing objects, etc. Also, a whole work based on such slapstick humor.

feminine rhyme   A **rhyme** of two or more syllables where the stress falls on a syllable other than the last one (e.g., *binding/winding*).

feminist criticism   A method of analyzing literature that focuses on the depiction of women (and often criticizes male authors for an overly patriarchal treatment of female figures). Feminist criticism has also been responsible for the revision of the literary **canon** in order to include previously overlooked or under-represented female authors.

figurative language, figures of speech   Words and expressions whose meaning is not to be taken literally but as a more imaginative and forceful way of expressing a thought or emotion. **Metaphors**, **similes**, and **symbols** are among the most common figures of speech.

first person narrator   See **point of view**.

fixed form poetry   Poems whose form follows certain pre-set patterns concerning number of lines, **stanza** formation, **meter**, and **rhyme scheme**. The **sonnet** and the **villanelle** are examples of fixed forms.

flashback   A return from the narrative "present" to an earlier episode in a character's life.

flat character   An unchanging character, always displaying the same character trait (e.g., explosive temper, jealousy)—as opposed to a fully rounded or "**round" character**.

foot   In metrical poetry, the basic rhythmic unit. A foot consists of two or three syllables, and feet are differentiated by the placement of stresses; e.g., an **iambic** foot has two syllables, the first unstressed and the second stressed.

foreshadowing   In narrative, a hint or suggestion of an event that will happen later in the story.

form   A poem's form concerns its division into stanzas or other sections, its line length and meter, rhythmic effects, rhyme, alliteration or other sound effects. Form is sometimes opposed to content, though in fact it is usually an expression of content.

formalist criticism   A type of literary criticism that began in Russia in the early twentieth century and was perpetuated through **new criticism** in the United States. Formalist critics stress the importance of form and of the specifically literary aspects of works rather than concentrating on content.

frame   An element of narrative that presents an initial setting and characters in order to introduce another story and also to conclude it (the initial setting reappears at the end). The main focus of attention is the inner story, the one within the "frame."

free verse   From the French *vers libre*, poetry whose form is "free," i.e., not structured by rules of **meter**, **rhyme**, or **stanza** length. Free verse has lines of different lengths and is often unrhymed or has irregular rhymes.

gender criticism   Studies the representation of gender in literature and views gender as a social and cultural construct. Gender criticism distinguishes between male and female ways of writing (and reading).

genre   Type of literary work; literature is usually divided into three main genres: poetry, prose fiction, and drama. Some kinds of nonfiction may be considered a fourth genre.

heptameter   A line of poetry with seven **feet**.

hero, heroine   The main character (not necessarily heroic) of a narrative or dramatic work (cf. **protagonist**).

heroic couplet   Two rhyming lines of **iambic pentameter**; the second line is usually **end-stopped**.

hexameter   A line of poetry with six **feet**.

historical criticism   A type of literary criticism that emphasizes the importance of historical context for works of literature.

hubris   Excessive pride—a flaw of personality (**tragic flaw**) in some tragic heroes.

hyperbole   A figure of speech that depends on exaggeration to emphasize an idea.

iamb, iambic   A **foot** of two syllables, the first unstressed, the second stressed, as in the word *allów*.

image, imagery   An image evokes a sensory perception, whether a mental picture, in a visual image, a sound (auditory image), a smell (olfactory image), a taste (gustatory), or the sense of touch (tactile). **Imagery** refers to the combination of individual images in a work.

in medias res   A Latin phrase meaning "in the middle of things" used to describe a work that begins without an **exposition**.

interior monologue   Narrative discourse seeking to reproduce the uninterrupted flow of thoughts, ideas, and sensations entering a character's mind that is generally termed the **stream of consciousness**.

internal rhyme   Rhyming words within one line of poetry.

irony   A situation or speech that suggests a contrast or contradiction. Verbal irony implies a contrast between what is said and what is meant. Cosmic or situational irony involves a discrepancy between a character's plans or dreams and their outcome (suggesting that human beings are the puppets of fate). See also **dramatic irony**.

Italian sonnet   See **sonnet**.

limited omniscience   The **point of view** of a third-person narrator who reveals the thoughts and feelings of only one character (or two) rather than of all the main characters in a work.

litotes   See **understatement.**

lyric   A short poem, originally sung and generally (but not necessarily) in the first person, that presents a speaker's thoughts or emotions or describes a scene.

magical realism   A term referring to fiction that presents a mixture of realistic and supernatural elements.

Marxist criticism   Based on the theories of Karl Marx, Marxist criticism interprets literature largely in terms of economic forces and class struggle.

masculine rhyme   **Rhymes** of words with one syllable or of longer words whose stress is on the final syllable, e.g., *short/port, arráyed/survéyed.*

melodrama   A type of drama full of extraordinary happenings and dangerous encounters but ending happily. The characters are often **stereotypes**.

metaphor   A figure of speech where one thing is referred to as another without using any word indicating a comparison (such as "like" or "resembles"). An extended metaphor is one that forms the basis of a whole work, usually a poem.

meter   The rhythmic pattern of a poem, dependent on the recurrence of groups of stressed and unstressed syllables (**feet**) within a line.

metonymy   A figure of speech that, instead of naming a thing directly, refers to it by naming something closely associated with it, as the phrase "crowned heads" can signify kings and queens.

mimesis   The idea that the action of a play should imitate life.

monologue   A long, uninterrupted speech by a fictional character, usually in a play.

monometer   A line of poetry with only one metrical **foot**.

montage   A cinematographic term referring to the editing process that assembles selected "takes" of scenes to create a film; applied to literature, it refers to the narrative technique of "cutting" from one scene to another.

mood   See **atmosphere**.

motif   A recurring element, such as an **image** or **theme**, in a work or works.

myth, mythology   A myth is a story handed down through generations that illustrates some aspect of human nature or features of a certain culture, or provides an explanation for various natural phenomena. A body of such stories is termed a **mythology** (e.g., Greek mythology).

narrative voice   See **point of view**.

narrator   The speaker telling the story or commenting on his/her own experience in a literary work. The narrator does not usually equate to the author of the work. The narrator's viewpoint can greatly influence the reader's reaction to the text.

new criticism   A type of literary criticism that considers the text a self-sufficient whole and interprets it through analysis of its form and structure rather than by referring to historical and biographical influences or critical theories.

new historicism   Literary criticism that views literature as part of history but also views history itself as a construct rather than an objective truth, since historians' re-creation of the past can never be truly objective.

novel   A long work of prose fiction.

novella   A work of fiction that is longer than a short story but shorter than a novel.

ode   A fairly long poem in stanza form, often celebrating a person, thing or event.

omniscient narrator   A third-person narrator who can "see inside" the characters and describe their thoughts and feelings. See **point of view**.

onomatopoeia   The use of words that sound like what they mean (e.g., *buzz, tick-tock*).

oxymoron   A figure of speech that strikingly juxtaposes two apparently contradictory phrases or words (often an adjective and a noun) that nevertheless make sense together, e.g., Romeo's exclamation "O loving hate!" in Act 1, scene 1, of *Romeo and Juliet*.

parable   A short allegorical story illustrating a moral or religious lesson.

paradox   A statement that apparently contradicts itself but which actually has a profound meaning that is emphasized by this figure of speech, e.g., "More haste less speed."

paraphrase   A restatement of a text in different words.

parody   A literary work that imitates the **theme**, characters, or **style** of another work, usually for humorous effect.

pentameter   A poetic line of five **feet**.

persona   From the Latin word for *mask*; the narrator of a prose work or a poem. Use of this term makes it possible to distinguish between the speaker of a text and its author.

personification   A figure of speech that attributes human qualities to non-human entities, such as natural phenomena.

Petrarchan sonnet   See **sonnet**.

plot   In a work of fiction, the arrangement by the author of fictional or historical events into a story or some kind of satisfying whole.

point of view   In fictional works, the standpoint of the narrator is termed point of view (or **narrative voice**). A first-person narrator plays a role in the story and speaks of himself or herself as "I." A narrator who tells a story in the third person may be objective, omniscient (knowing and telling the thoughts and feelings of all the characters), or have limited omniscience (omniscience limited to one, or occasionally two, of the characters).

poststructuralism   In the realm of literary criticism, poststructuralism, like deconstruction, emphasizes the ambiguities involved in analyzing literary expression using language, which is inherently flawed and can never accurately translate experience.

prose fiction   One of the three major genres of literature; fictional narratives such as **novels** and **short stories**.

prose poem   A poem written in prose, i.e., without any kind of verse line, not even **free verse**, but with other attributes of poetry such as use of **figurative language**, rhythmic and auditory devices, and **structure**.

prosody   The elements of **versification**: **meter**, **rhyme**, **stanza**-form.

protagonist   The main character in a **drama** or a work of **prose fiction**.

psychoanalytic criticism   A type of criticism that uses principles of psychoanalytic theory—such as the ideas of Sigmund Freud, Carl Jung, and Jacques Lacan—in its interpretation of literary works. It focuses on the psyche both of fictional characters and of authors.

pyrrhic foot   A metrical **foot** containing two unstressed syllables.

quatrain   A four-lined **stanza** or a group of four lines within a longer unit (e.g., a **sonnet**).

reader-response criticism   A type of literary criticism that suggests a work's meaning is incomplete before the work is read and that readers supplement the author's creation of meaning.

realism   A type of literature that presents everyday characters in everyday situations and settings. A nineteenth-century literary movement that aims to portray everyday life in fiction.

rhetorical device   An expression used in some non-literal way or in a way that emphasizes its meaning. See **figures of speech**.

rhetorical question   A question to which no answer is sought.

rhyme   Repetition of identical (or very closely related) sounds, usually in final syllables at the end of lines of poetry. See also **approximate rhyme**, **eye rhyme**, **internal rhyme**, **masculine**, and **feminine rhyme**.

rhyme scheme   The pattern of a poem's rhymes. It can be indicated by using letters, e.g., *abba*.

rhythm   The pattern of stressed and unstressed sounds governed by a poem's **meter**; also, the sense of movement conveyed by the use of long or short words or lines, by **enjambment** and by use of (or absence of) punctuation.

romance   A type of narrative featuring love relationships and extraordinary adventures, beginning with medieval courtly romances concerning knights and other heroes, composed in verse, and continuing with prose narratives notably in sixteenth- and seventeenth-century Spanish and French literature.

romanticism   Early nineteenth century literary movement characterized by the self-expression of the individual, love for nature, and a tendency to value emotion over reason (in reaction to the rational philosophies of the eighteenth century Age of Enlightenment).

round character   A many sided, complex character, as opposed to a **flat**, unchanging one.

run-on line   See **enjambment**.

satire   Literature that ridicules human behavior, especially human vices, in a humorous way.

scanning, scansion   The process of determining a poem's **meter** by counting and grouping its stressed and unstressed syllables.

semantic   Relating to the sense or meaning of a work.

sestet   A **stanza** of six lines, or a group of six lines in a longer poem, especially the last six lines of a Petrarchan sonnet (see **sonnet**).

setting   The time and place in which the events of a literary work occur.

Shakespearean sonnet   See **sonnet**.

short story   A compact work of **prose fiction** often just a few pages long.

simile   A **figure of speech** involving an explicit comparison (using words such as *like, as, seems*).

situational irony   See **irony**.

soliloquy   A speech in which a character alone on the stage expresses his/her thoughts aloud.

sonnet   A poem of fourteen lines, usually in **iambic pentameter**. The Petrarchan (or Italian) sonnet divides its fourteen lines into a group of eight lines (octave) followed by a group of six (sestet). The octave is subdivided into two groups of four lines (quatrains), with the **rhyme scheme** *abbaabba*; the rhyme scheme of the **sestet** varies. The Shakespearean (or English) sonnet consists of three **quatrains** followed by a **couplet**, usually with a rhyme scheme *ababcdcdefefgg*.

spondee   A metrical **foot** containing two stressed syllables.

stage directions   The only part of the text of a play that is not dialogue spoken by the characters. Instructions (printed in italics) from a playwright to the stage manager and actors of a play indicating details of setting, actors' gestures or tone of voice, etc.

stanza   A group of lines forming a repeated unit in a poem, usually with a recurring pattern of **rhymes** and **meter**.

stereotype, stock character   A character who seems more like a type than an individual, displaying only one or two basic characteristics, who does not develop and whose personality is not explored in depth.

stream of consciousness   The uninterrupted flow of thoughts, associations, and impressions that pass through the mind. Writers of **prose fiction** often present it in the form of **interior monologue**.

stress   The accentuation of a syllable. All English words of more than one syllable have stress on at least one syllable. In metrical poetry, the arrangement of stressed and unstressed syllables forms a rhythmic pattern.

structuralism   Based on the notion that works of literature share similar structures and forms, Structuralist critics attempt to discover the underlying patterns and themes common to all narrative. They also maintain that all elements of a given culture, such as religion, industry, clothing, and food, form sign systems that can be analyzed like language.

structure   The internal organization of a literary work; the elements that form it into a coherent whole.

style   The way a work is written, the choice of vocabulary (e.g., colloquial or formal), length of sentences, use or avoidance of **figurative language**, **imagery**, etc.

subplot   A secondary **plot**, dependent on the main plot and related to it but not essential to it.

suspension of disbelief   The convention whereby, in the theater, the audience accepts ("believes") the fictional world of a play as if it were real, for the duration of the performance.

symbol   A concrete image representing an abstract idea, as a key may represent freedom or the possibility of opening metaphorical doors.

synecdoche   A figure of speech that refers to a thing or a person in terms of one of its parts, as a sail may represent a whole boat.

tenor   In figures of speech such as **metaphors** and **symbols**, the tenor is the meaning conveyed by the image or concrete element (the **vehicle**).

tercet   A group of three lines of verse; also known as a **triplet**.

terza rima   A three-line stanza form in which the second line of the first stanza rhymes with the first and third lines of the second stanza and so on throughout the poem (*aba bcb cdc*, etc.).

tetrameter   A line of verse with four **feet**.

Theater of the Absurd   A type of theater or drama popular in the 1950s and 1960s that seems "absurd" in some ways on the surface but embodies deeper meaning, often emphasizing the pointlessness of life, the impossibility of real human communication and the contradictions inherent in human personality.

theme   The central idea behind a literary work; it can usually be summarized in a sentence or two.

thesis   The argument that a writer is seeking to prove.

thesis sentence   An introductory sentence that briefly announces the point a writer wishes to discuss or argue.

third person narrator   See **point of view**.

tone   The attitude of the narrator to the events narrated or to characters, conveyed by his or her language. (The tone may be for instance sympathetic, amused, hostile, ironic, detached, or indifferent.)

topic sentence   A sentence that introduces the subject of a given paragraph.

tragedy   A play that depicts the downfall and often the death of a hero.

tragic flaw   A character fault or weakness in the hero of a tragedy that leads to his or her downfall.

tragicomedy   A type of "bittersweet" play that contains elements of both tragedy and comedy.

trimeter   A line of verse consisting of three feet.

triplet   See **tercet**.

trochee, trochaic   A metrical **foot** of two syllables, the first stressed, the second unstressed, as in the word *séntence*.

trope   A **figure of speech** signifying something other than the literal meaning of the words used.

understatement   Used for rhetorical effect (often, paradoxically, to emphasize an idea) by negating a positive statement, e.g., "He could not be called outgoing" meaning "He was very quiet/shy."

unreliable narrator   A narrator who cannot be relied on to report events or judge characters accurately because he or she is either naïve (e.g., a child) or has a vested interest in distorting the truth.

vehicle   The image or other element in a **figure of speech** that serves to convey the meaning (**tenor**).

verbal irony   See **irony**.

verisimilitude   Likelihood of being real or true.

versification   The organization of **meter**, **stanza** form, and **rhyme scheme** in poems.

vers libre   See **free verse**.

villanelle   A **fixed form** poem of nineteen lines, five **tercets** followed by a final **quatrain**. It is a difficult form based on just two **rhymes** and requiring the repetition of certain lines according to a fixed pattern. Dylan Thomas's "Do not go gentle into that good night" is a good example of a villanelle.

Credits

Index of Terms, Authors, and Titles

Italicized numerals in the index indicate pages where a term is defined or discussed in greatest detail, or where a work is the subject of a close reading or essay.